"*Revolutionary Care* invites people of the world to unite for a more caring society. Hamington's radical as well as nuanced rereading of care ethics breathes new life into feminist philosophy ontologically, epistemologically, and politically as a transformative grand theory for every being."
**Yayo Okano**, *Professor, Graduate School of Global Studies, Doshisha University, Japan*

"Care ethics' initial feminist motivation was to draw upon common experiences and practices of care and show their potential for a world of peace, responsibility, equality, and epistemic justice. This book elaborates the philosophical arguments for care, while also offering powerful practical programs of moral behavior that caring persons could identify with: feminism, socialism, (post)humanism, and veganism. Hamington's book thereby takes the revolutionary potential of care to the next level."
**Prof. Dr. Inge van Nistelrooij**, *Associate Professor, University of Humanistic Studies, the Netherlands*

"In this groundbreaking new book, Maurice Hamington, already recognized as an original and important thinker on the ethics of care, goes beyond the acknowledged values of care and reflects on the radicality of care—radical in the sense that it takes us back to the roots or the core of ethics and politics, to what matters. Care is often not seen as a radical concept in terms of political activism, probably because of the association of care with women's work. However, *Revolutionary Care* sheds new light on the very power of care, showing how a genuine commitment to care requires resistance to dominant neoliberal values, and an actual non-violent revolution."

**Sandra Laugier**, *Professor of Philosophy, Université Paris 1 Panthéon-Sorbonne*

"This work argues for care's transformative potential given its relational ontology and epistemology of general and concrete knowing, which connect the human and posthuman through reflexive dependencies. It reflects beyond the cliched dualisms of care's absence versus abundance to focus on the phenomenology of embodied caring practices through their vicissitudes. Hamington pioneers care's ability to heal conflicts through insights drawn from everyday sensitive and attentive actions, often unsteady and requiring immense patience with their complex fallibilisms. This stands in contrast to the cut and dry abstract intellectualism of ideal theories and rational deliberations. It is a must read as its nuanced articulations of the normativity of caring practices have a global relevance."

**Kanchana Mahadevan**, *Professor of Philosophy, University of Mumbai*

# REVOLUTIONARY CARE

Written by one of the world's most respected care scholars, *Revolutionary Care* provides original theoretical insights and novel applications to offer a comprehensive approach to care as personal, political, and revolutionary. The text has nine chapters divided into two major sections. Section 1, "Thinking About Better Care," offers four theoretical chapters that reinforce the primacy of care as a moral ideal worthy of widespread commitment across ideological and cultural differences. Unlike other moral approaches, care is framed as a process morality and provides a general trajectory that can only determine the best course of action in the moment/context of need. Section 2, "Invitations and Provocations: Imagining Transformative Possibilities," employs four case studies on toxic masculinity, socialism and care economy, humanism and posthumanism, pacifism, and veganism to demonstrate the radical and revolutionary nature of care. Exploring the thinking and writing of many disciplines, including authors of color, queer scholars, and indigenous thinkers, this book is an exciting and cutting-edge contribution to care ethics scholarship as well as a useful teaching resource.

**Maurice Hamington** is Professor of Philosophy and Affiliate Faculty in Women, Gender, and Sexuality Studies at Portland State University. As a care ethicist, he is interested in both the theory and application of care. Among other positions, Hamington is a Steering Committee Member for the International Care Ethics Research Consortium (CERC), Utrecht, the Netherlands. He is also a member of the Advisory Board for Care Aesthetics: Research Exploration (CARE), a multi-year research project funded by the Arts and Humanities Research Council in the United Kingdom. As the author, or editor, of 16 books and over 25 articles in refereed journals, Hamington has given invited presentations on care ethics across the globe. See mhamington.com for more information on his scholarship.

# REVOLUTIONARY CARE

Commitment and Ethos

Maurice Hamington

NEW YORK AND LONDON

Designed cover image: Group of activists with holding hands protesting in the city. Rebellions doing demonstration on the street holding hands. Release information: Signed model release on file with Shutterstock, Inc.

Photo Contributor: Jacob Lund

First published 2024
by Routledge
605 Third Avenue, New York, NY 10158

and by Routledge
4 Park Square, Milton Park, Abingdon, Oxon, OX14 4RN

*Routledge is an imprint of the Taylor & Francis Group, an informa business*

© 2024 Maurice Hamington.

The right of Maurice Hamington to be identified as author of this work has been asserted in accordance with sections 77 and 78 of the Copyright, Designs and Patents Act 1988.

All rights reserved. No part of this book may be reprinted or reproduced or utilised in any form or by any electronic, mechanical, or other means, now known or hereafter invented, including photocopying and recording, or in any information storage or retrieval system, without permission in writing from the publishers.

*Trademark notice*: Product or corporate names may be trademarks or registered trademarks, and are used only for identification and explanation without intent to infringe.

ISBN: 9781032437293 (hbk)
ISBN: 9781032437316 (pbk)
ISBN: 9781003368625 (ebk)

DOI: 10.4324/9781003368625

Typeset in Times New Roman
by Deanta Global Publishing Services, Chennai, India

For Stephanie

# CONTENTS

| | |
|---|---|
| *Acknowledgments* | *xi* |
| Inquiry *By Lisa DeVuono* | *xiii* |
| Introduction: Is Care a Radical Idea? | 1 |

**SECTION 1**
**Thinking about Better Care** 23

| | |
|---|---|
| 1 Good Care | 25 |
| 2 Care and Normativity | 45 |
| 3 A Categorical Commitment to Care | 66 |
| 4 A Care Ethos | 87 |

**SECTION 2**
**Invitations and Provocations: Imagining Transformative Possibilities** 111

| | |
|---|---|
| 5 Feminism and Resisting Toxic Masculinity | 113 |
| 6 Socialism and Creating a Care Economy | 132 |

**x** Contents

7  Humanism and Balancing the Primacy of Care with
   Religious Authority                                              157

8  Veganism and Post-Human Care                                     178

   Conclusion: *Disponibilité*, Moral Progress, and Revolution      200

*Closing Quote*                                                     *223*
*Bibliography*                                                      *224*
*Index*                                                             *250*

# ACKNOWLEDGMENTS

There are compelling reasons to find fault with higher education today. Nevertheless, for many scholars, an extraordinary commitment to seeking knowledge flourishes. I have been fortunate to encounter many intelligent and generous people who have helped me in my academic journey and have no real financial incentive to assist me. In particular, I repeatedly find that care theorists practice what they theorize about, making for a delightful community of warm scholars who are easy to work with and learn from. This book is a product of numerous tremendous academic relationships. At the risk of being played off the stage by the orchestra, I acknowledge various people who made *Revolutionary Care: Commitment and Ethos* possible.

First, I must thank my writing companion of many years, the polymath Michael Flower, who read and commented on every chapter. We have been meeting together regularly for years. Having someone read through your work is a fantastic gift of time and effort. I was fortunate to have many scholars help me in this fashion, including Daniel Engster, University of Houston; Maggie FitzGerald, University of Saskatchewan; Seisuke Hayakawa, University of Tokyo; and James McMaster, University of Wisconsin, Madison.

This project also benefited from a month-long series of graduate seminars at the University of Paris 8 as part of a Fulbright specialist visit I made in October of 2022, where I presented and received feedback on the Introduction and Chapters 1, 4, and 5. Caroline Ibos and Christine Leroy organized the seminars that included graduate students and French scholars of care: Justine Madiot, Taciana Brito, Flora Malverde Léonore Brassard, Éric Fassin, Tatia Dvali, Bénédicte Gattère, Adèle Sueur, Anne-Cécile Caseau, Jan Kasnik, and

**xii** Acknowledgments

Patricia Paperman. A Faculty Research Grant from Portland State University facilitated my stay in Paris.

In January of 2023, I benefited from a presentation at the University of Manchester sponsored by James Thompson and the Care Aesthetics Research Exploration Project, where I discussed the notion of care as a process morality. Finally, in May of 2023, the Introduction and Chapter 9 were a focal point for a day-long discussion with philosophy faculty from the University of Oregon, including Steven Brence, Mark Johnson, Erin McKenna, Scott Pratt, and Peg Brand Weiser, and graduate students Asher Caplan, Massimo Cisternino, Amanda Dubrule, Audrey Fayad, Matthew Tuten, Rugile Kasperiunaite, and Julie Williams-Reyes.

I thank my home institution, Portland State University, for granting me my first sabbatical in 20 years (the time gap was primarily because of a long tenure in administration) during the 2021–2022 academic year. Throughout that sabbatical, I made a series of presentations testing ideas in various chapters and receiving excellent feedback. Specifically, I want to thank Ruth E. Groenhout and Shannon Sullivan at the University of North Carolina Charlotte; Dan Engster and the Elizabeth D. Rockwell Center on Ethics and Leadership at the University of Houston; Julinna Oxley and the Jackson Family Center on Ethics and Values, Coastal Carolina University; and Christine Garlough, and the Ethics of Care Initiative, University of Wisconsin, Madison. It was intellectually generative to have so many stimulating discussions about care.

I also acknowledge many conversations with brilliant scholars who thoughtfully challenged my ideas, including Joan Tronto, Sophie Bourgault, Estelle Ferrarese, and Gregory Fernando Papagiannakis.

A special thanks to Benjamin Kenofer for helping me with the index and catching several errors.

I am particularly grateful to Natalija Mortensen, Senior Editor at Routledge for her enthusiasm for this project, as well as Charlotte Christie, Editorial Assistant for her production management.

I thank the librarians and staff at Portland State University and the Bibliotheque Sainte Genevieve of Sorbonne University. I also appreciate the many podcasters who exposed me to new research, including David Guignion's Theory and Philosophy and Robert Talisse's New Books in Philosophy. Finally, I apologize to all who assisted me that I have overlooked in these acknowledgments.

My acknowledgments would not be complete without thanking the center of my care world, Stephanie Delgatto Hamington, my longtime partner and the love of my life.

# *INQUIRY*

*By Lisa DeVuono*

Start with your own question.
It doesn't have to be profound.
It just has to have a wondering

so you have no idea where it might lead.

Not only no idea but no worry
About how far from your own clutching
It might take you

a question that doesn't have one answer
rather opens the possibility for even more

not ones that have been living under that tired story
buried on the back of your heart.

Start with a question that doesn't make you feel like
*this is the only one you'll ever have*

but one that can hold you like a hammock
or a cradle or an old painted rowboat
in which you might
let yourself drift
far enough away

from the shore of familiar.

*[used by permission]*

# INTRODUCTION

## Is Care a Radical Idea?

### Prologue: Radical Transformation Through Care

Born in 1989 in West Palm Beach, Florida, Derek Black was the heir apparent to the white nationalist movement in the United States (Saslow, 2018). His godfather is David Duke, former Grand Wizard of the Knights of the Ku Klux Klan. His father, Don Black, popularized the term "White Nationalism" and created the racist website, Stormfront.org. Heidi Beirich of the Southern Poverty Law Center describes Stormfront as the "murder capital of the internet" because of the number of racially motivated murders committed by members (2014: 1–7). It is the most popular white extremist website, with 300,000 registered members (Southern Poverty Law Center, 2021). At 10, Derek Black devoloped a website for white nationalist children. In his early teens, Black hosted a white nationalist radio program with his father. Despite his youth, he was an articulate and popular speaker at white nationalist meetings. Black was also charismatic and quite comfortable defending his views in debates, having often confronted reasoned arguments for white supremacism's flaws. As Eli Saslow, who documented Derek Black's personal transformation in *Rising Out of Hatred: The Awakening of A Former White Nationalist,* describes,

> On the air, he repeatedly theorized about "the criminal nature of blacks" and the "inferior natural intelligence of blacks and Hispanics." He said President Obama was "anti-white culture," "a radical black activist," and "inherently un-American." There was nothing micro about Derek's aggressions.
>
> *(2018: 29)*

DOI: 10.4324/9781003368625-1

**2** Introduction

Black's original posture of exclusion makes a fascinating case for care theorists to contemplate, given his evolution into an open-minded and compassionate individual. His biography also challenges those who view themselves as caring. Specifically, can we care for someone with Black's moral and political outlook?

In 2010, still steeped in white nationalism, Black began attending New College of Florida in Sarasota. Black maintained a low profile in college and surreptitiously hosted a radio show. He would run off campus to emcee regular broadcasts. However, eventually, his identity came to light in the college community. Some students angrily confronted him, but Black was an experienced and well-equipped apologist for white supremacy and rebuffed pointed arguments and accusations.

A few classmates took a different approach. Several students, including Allison Gornik and Jewish students Matthew Stevenson and Moshe Ash, befriended Black despite their reservations regarding his extreme positions. They endeavored to understand him better and perhaps start a dialogue with him as friends. After much time spent together, including difficult but respectful listening and responding, Black gradually began to have a change of heart and mind. His friends did not moralize. They started an ongoing discussion in an environment of mutual care. At one point, Stevenson explicitly told Gornik that the relationship was transformative enough, and he did not want to push too hard on directly challenging Black's beliefs (Saslow, 2018: 126). However, the presence of accepting Jewish friends who welcomed him—an idea anathema to many white nationalist beliefs—was sufficient for Black to question his views regarding cultural superiority (Dickson, 2013b). Fast-forwarding through numerous shared meals and discussions, Black publicly renounced his white nationalism, drawing the ire of his former organizations and his family. Since then, Black has pursued an academic career, becoming a frequent television commentator who speaks out against white nationalism.

One can interpret Black's transformation in various ways. Like most human journeys, the causation was complex and included many variables. Nevertheless, at least in one interview, Saslow credits the accepting academic environment for the change:

> Derek understands the value of civil discourse in his life, but he's only open to conversations that challenge his beliefs because of the civil resistance that isolates him on campus. And those conversations were informed by what they were learning in their classrooms. Alison [Gornik] almost weaponizes her "Stigma and Prejudice" syllabus.
>
> *(Flannery, 2018)*

There is no question that the academic context for Black's epiphany mattered, but rational deliberation does not provide the whole story. The process of Derek Black's transformation was, in part, care work—time-consuming and responsive—rather than an adjudication of an ethical quandary—solving a moral dilemma. Black indicates as much in his "coming out" letter to the *New York Times*:

> Several years ago, I began attending a liberal college where my presence prompted huge controversy. Through many talks with devoted and diverse people there—people who chose to invite me into their dorms and conversations rather than ostracize me—I began to realize the damage I had done.
>
> *(Black, 2016)*

A caring connection created the personal and intellectual space for Black's conversion away from deep-seated racism. One of Black's first friendships at New College was with Rose (Saslow only uses her first name), a Jewish student. Of course, Black's public rhetoric included strong anti-Semitism. However, Black now faced a reality that contradicted his white nationalist views. As Saslow describes, "It was easy to be certain and firm when the enemy remained impersonal, and the issue was purely abstract, but now the issue was Rose" (Saslow, 2018: 36). Although his experience with Rose opened the door for self-reflection, it was not easy to shed beliefs that he had grown up with; he understandably felt comfortable with his family and the white nationalist community that loved and nurtured him.

Black experienced further relational provocation from friends who cared about him at college. Stevenson's efforts were intentional in befriending Black. Stevenson was a practicing Jew and a political conservative. His marginalization on the New College campus made him recognize that ostracizing Black might make him defensive and ossify his positions, so he pointedly chose an approach of "nonjudgmental inclusion." Stevenson kept inviting Black to Saturday Shabbat meals. However, more than that, he listened to Black's radio shows and recognized how Black could deflect and repel any argument against white nationalism. Thus, Stevenson engaged him but within a friendship. They spent quality time together. According to Saslow, "Instead of trying to build a case, Matthew began working to build a relationship in which Derek might be able to learn what the enemy was actually like. 'Matthew said,' The goal was just to make Jews more human for him" (Ibid: 81).

Stevenson and Black experienced the relationship as authentic caring—both responded to the other and were changed by the relationship.[1] In 2017, journalist Caitlin Dickson wrote an exposé for the political tabloid *Daily Beast* titled "Derek Black, the Reluctant Racist, and His Exit from White Nationalism" (Dickson, 2013a). Subsequently, Black corresponded with Dickson and told her he thought the article was "pretty fair." Dickson published his letter, which indicated that the only thing he wanted to clarify was that those who publicly disagreed with him did not convince him to change his mind. Rather,

> The people who were important in the process of changing my mind were those who were my friends regardless, but who let me know when we talked about it that they thought my beliefs were wrong for specific reasons and took the time to provide evidence and civil arguments. I didn't always agree with their ideas, but I listened and they listened to me.
>
> *(Black quoted in Dickson, 2013a)*

Care is a contextually driven moral approach, and the care Black received resulted in a moral epiphany that was personal and yet entailed political significance. Black publicly lamented his role, however small, in the rise of extremist views that manifested in the US election in 2016. Moreover, Black's transformation engenders an enduring hope for the country: "I've moved from extreme views and this country can too" (Black, 2016: 6). Although he does not use the word "care," Black recognizes that many people in the United States would need a change of heart; better legal protections for marginalized individuals are not nearly enough. He claims, "No checks and balances can redeem what we've unleashed" (Ibid).

The Derek Black story points to one of care's radical potential benefits: bridging deep human divisions. In his analysis of operant social epistemology, C. Thi Nguyen distinguishes between epistemic bubbles and echo chambers. Epistemic bubbles are the sources of information we create for ourselves through a mix of choices regarding trusted voices of knowledge and external limitations, such as news algorithms that select what is presented to us (2020: 143–45). Nguyen indicates that although providing an incomplete picture of the world, new information outside the bubble relatively quickly disrupts epistemic bubbles. However, epistemic echo chambers are more problematic. He defines them as

> An epistemic community which creates a significant disparity in trust between members and non-members. This disparity is created by excluding non-members through epistemic discrediting, while simultaneously amplifying members' epistemic credentials. Finally, echo chambers are such that general agreement with some core set of beliefs is a prerequisite for membership, where those core beliefs include beliefs that support that disparity in trust.
>
> *(Ibid: 146)*

An echo chamber actively seeks to divide and control human beliefs by employing techniques akin to cult organizations; therefore, escaping the epistemic position is exceedingly tricky (Ibid: 147). For Nguyen, exiting the echo chamber requires nothing short of a "social epistemic reboot"(Ibid: 157)—a relearning of knowledge in the company of others. Echo chambers prevent such reboots by discrediting outside sources. Nguyen argues that Black was raised in an echo chamber of extremist white nationalism. As a result, Black was intellectually prepared to resist outside sources of knowledge. Only by "forming a trusting relationship with an outsider" was such a moral and epistemic epiphany possible (Ibid: 158). This is an indicator of care's revolutionary potential.

Philosopher Tracy Llanera expands Nguyen's brief consideration of the caring relationship needed for a social epistemic reboot. Llanera describes Black's transformation as nothing short of apostasy. Black did not just expand his universe of ideas. He had an "existential flip," resulting in a rare "condemnation of the hate group ideology and disassociation from the group" (2019: 15). For Llanera, the tipping point for Black's transformation was Stevenson and others' relationships with Black. His new friends at New College provided information, which was a factor. However, Black's inquiry occurred within a care ethos, and that spirit allowed his moral imagination to expand his sphere of empathy. In this manner, the process morality of care challenges today's echo chambers: "Belonging to a hate group that promotes group-love restricts the ability to care for outsiders, even removing the need to develop it" (Ibid: 22). Black's transformation is perhaps not common, but it symbolizes hope for the possibility of further caring across divisions.

Human divisions are enormous and cannot be trivialized; however, at its best, care theory can help bridge differences to find workable understanding between peoples and perhaps point the way to social amelioration in a cosmopolitan world.[2] Black's story suggests the complexity and fluidity of care. Care is not a panacea for an easy fix to human challenges. Furthermore, care theory does not offer a simple formula for overcoming division. The human experience is much too complex for reductive methods. The above account of Black's transformation does not indicate that a similar approach will work in all, or even most comparable circumstances. However, the fact that it can happen is inspiring.

Care emerges when we seek understanding, connection, and responsive moral practices. Care is how humanity has always sustained itself and flourished, and it always will be. Is care a radical idea in the sense of being extreme or fantastical? No. However, it is radical in terms of returning us to our roots. The origins of the word "radical" were centered on returning to the roots or fundamentals. Accordingly, "radical reform" means changing the roots of a system. Care is fundamental to humanity. To value care is radical in that it returns us to our core humanity.

Often we forget how powerful and essential care is to our existence. Care may not be a radical idea by the standards of a masculinist understanding of violent change. However, care can lead us to some radical conclusions. Perhaps even revolutionary ones.

## Valorizing Care

People simply matter, and that is reason enough to care.

—Deva Woodly (2022: 92)

Can we agree on the value of care in our lives? I hope so. Every fruitful deliberation needs a baseline agreement—a common ground. Many intractable social divisions have their basis in failure to find a common foundation for discussion. This book develops an argument about care that begins with the premise that *everybody needs care.* Although we may disagree on the requisite forms of care or the nature of optimal care practices, I propose that a universal assent to the value of care in our lives should exist. All identities in the population— political, religious, cultural, and social—need care. Given their helpless state, humans clearly require care when they are born, and most will need it at various crisis moments in their lives. However, even at our best, we need to experience care. No matter one's convictions or their complex intersection of subject positions, care is essential to survival and flourishing. The type of care needed differs by context, but the necessity for care never disappears. Progressives and liberals need care. City dwellers and rural community members need care. A privileged person happily living their finest life needs care, and an oppressed person in a deep destructive depression needs care.

The need for care is dynamic and reciprocal. The character and intensity of care changes based on circumstance, but, like air, the requirement is always present. When overwhelmed by life's demands, we might sometimes imagine not being burdened by relational connections and their emotional strain. However, the reality is that we all need to care for others and be cared for. Care is a human (and nonhuman) condition; the fact of our embodiment ensures this condition.

For the arc of the argument in this book, care is viewed as a significant, if not *the most* significant, moral value and moral good that everyone can commit to. I suggest that a commitment to care is foundational for morality. One can commit to care and still utilize consequentialism or rules to help reflect on complex moral dilemmas. Still, one error of Western philosophy is to sometimes think that such systems constitute the whole of morality. Care is much more than a rational ethical framework. As Asha Bhandary describes, "Care is the spine of culture. How care is provided, to whom, and by whom, is the primary structuring concern in every social form" (2022: 816). Care is the engine of morality and the ultimate test of the ethical. Of course, such claims require unpacking. This book explores what it means to have a commitment to care. Most of us know what a commitment to care is because friendship and family ideally represent such a commitment. Ethics challenges us to reflect on the nature of that care and extend the commitment to less-familiar others. This book explores some of the radical implications of a commitment to care. It is easy to claim that one is caring or committed to care. In the following pages, we look at what is entailed in enriching such dedication to deliver good care and some of the revolutionary repercussions of committing to care.

Introduction **7**

## Essential Care Terms

Ensuring a shared understanding of terms in an argument is always good practice to mitigate misunderstanding. This shared understanding is crucial in this project because "care" and "radical" are used ubiquitously. So, I explicate five essential terms for this project: care, care ethics, effective care, commitment, and radical. These terms are fleshed out throughout the book, but I offer these working definitions for now.

**Care**, despite its abundant use, is a complex term to define because of the nuances of how this ubiquitous term is employed. I differentiate the everyday subjective use of "care" from the moral ideal of care. Generally speaking, people intend care to be a positive term for helping and tending to those in need. As indicated earlier, when the moral ideal of care is actualized, care is an existential imperative for the sustenance of humanity and our world. However, people do not have a common standard for using the word. Are the actions of parents, healthcare professionals, or teachers caring by virtue of their position in a relationship? Given their foibles and biases, human beings sometimes invoke care as motivation for their actions and often with great sincerity, but the actions are not experienced as such. Recognizing that "caring" actions often fall short of being positive experiences, this book primarily addresses care as a moral ideal rather than a subjective sense.

Care theory can be described as addressing a moral ideal, care, within the confines of a non-ideal theory. Care theory is nonideal because a society of perfect widespread caring is not a reasonable objective. Furthermore, there is no monolithic form of care. Each context requires something different in care. However, care, in its various forms, is the constant—thus, care is a non-ideal theory wrapped around a moral ideal. Like much feminist theory, care is grounded in human experience, and so the caring society sought is one that raises the profile and valorization of care without conforming to a standard of perfection. In other words, care theory is about getting better and more inclusive in our ability and practices to tend to others and ourselves—a process morality.

Accordingly, a particular subset of care can be described as the moral ideal of care entailed in what is called care ethics. Such practices respectfully contribute to the well-being of others in a manner that maintains their dignity. The most widely reprinted definition of care within the context of feminist care theory was created by Berenice Fischer and Joan Tronto, the latter being a leading voice of a political ethic of care. Their definition reflects the moral ideal of care:

> On the most general level, we suggest that caring be viewed as *a species activity that includes everything that we do to maintain, continue, and repair our "world" so that we can live in it as well as possible.*
>
> *(1990: 40)*

**8** Introduction

Embedded in this definition is the blurring of two critical ethical considerations that motivate the moral ideal of care. One consideration is that care is most often need directed ("repair our world"). This meeting of needs can be a responsive consequence of emergent challenges, and at other times it can anticipate needs through proactive actions. The second concept woven into the Fischer and Tronto definition is care as pursuing the good. The definition does not address how care adjudicates right and wrong. Instead, the moral ideal of care seeks to make the world a better place.

Furthermore, care clouds the means/ends distinction, as sometimes the good of care is found in the process of caring. In this respect, care theory can be viewed as a process morality, discussed further in Chapter 2. For example, when someone truly listens to someone else to ascertain how to best respond to their needs, even before any action is taken to meet those needs, the one listened to often feels cared for because they have been heard. This claim regarding the indeterminacy of means and ends is reminiscent of Deweyan pragmatism. In his observations, John Dewey had elements of postmodern analysis regarding the continuity between epistemology and ethics, knowledge and physical action, and means and ends. As he described, "Means and ends are two sides of the same reality" (1983 [1922]: 28). Given Dewey's concern for process, relationship, embodiment, and experience, I am confident that were Dewey alive today, he would find resonance with care theory.

Even in this very brief delineation, one can see some of the complexity of care. Typical uses of the word care are not mutually exclusive to the moral ideal of care, but we pursue what makes actions caring in the latter sense. Caring behavior falls on a continuum that includes detrimental, ineffective, superficial, and life-affirming practices. Thus, for this book, we move away from considering care in the abstract and focus on practices that aim toward the care ideal. I refer to these practices and processes of betterment and improvement as good care.

**Care ethics** is a systematic reflection on care practices. The attachment of the term "ethics" to care implies a normative understanding of what moral actions we should and should not undertake. In 1995, I offered a definition of an ethic of care that I updated a bit in 2019. However, I failed to add the word "ethic" to the term, which reflects my struggles with describing the approach as an ethic:

> Care describes an approach to personal and social morality that shifts ethical considerations to context, relationships, and affective knowledge in a manner that can only be fully understood if its embodied [and performative] dimension is recognized. Care is committed to the flourishing and growth of individuals; yet acknowledges our interconnectedness and interdependence.
>
> *(Hamington and Rosenow, 2019: 3)*

This definition emphasizes care's relational, embodied, and experiential aspects.

**Care Theory** is a term that I prefer over "care ethics" to mark the notion that care engages in different work than most traditional normative systems of morality. This extra-normative approach to ethics is not to say that there is no significant normative component to care theory, as demonstrated by the discussion of radical implications of care in Section 2 of this book. Nevertheless, care is more than an adjudicative ethic. In addition to its normative dimensions, care hinges on the relational ontology (i.e., a fundamental way of being) of humans, as well as an epistemology (i.e., coming to knowledge) of particular others in addition to its moral dimensions. So I employ the term care ethics because that is the convention, but I mean it within a more comprehensive understanding of care theory. My use of "care theory" shares Mercer E. Gary's expansive approach articulated as a "pluralist feminist theory of care" (2022).

Care theory is quintessentially nonideal. For those not steeped in contemporary social and political theory, this claim might appear odd given that care is the ideal aspired to. Charles Mills offered one of the definitive delineations and assessments of ideal versus non-ideal theory. Glossing over some nuances, ideal theory remains at the level of abstraction and generalization, excluding reality and particularization. Mills argues that ideal theory can become an ideology because it can ignore the complexity and power differentials of real-life experience in service of the imagined ideal (2005: 172). Non-ideal theory squarely faces the foibles of human existence, recognizing that systems fail, people sometimes have ill will and make mistakes. However, ideals are not absent from non-ideal theory. As Mills describes, "I would suggest that a nonideal approach is also superior to an ideal approach in being better able to realize the ideals, by virtue of realistically recognizing the obstacles to their acceptance and implementation" (Ibid: 181). For Mills, non-ideal theory's ideals are particularly true for moral theory. Philosopher Anca Gheaus extends Mills's analysis by arguing that some theorists are so caught up in traditional ideal theories of distributive justice that there is a false implicit assumption that political practices and institutions can solve care deficits. Gheaus contends that although such social changes can facilitate care, the quality depends on individuals. Egalitarian theories of justice endeavor to overcome the moral luck of poor care through distributive transformation. Gheaus suggests that individual recognition of the excellent fortune of care in their lives should create a self-realized moral responsibility to recreate that care in those not so lucky (2009: 117).

**Good care** or effective care is an evaluative term that reflects the quality of care practices. Given the complexity of human experience, the quality of care falls on a continuum rather than simple binaries of care/no care or good care/bad care. The assessment of care quality must include and respect the perspective of the one cared for when possible. I view effective care as entailing humble inquiry, inclusive connection, and responsive action. Each of these aspects works in conjunction with the other two. Knowledge, both generalized and

**10** Introduction

particular to the context, is an important starting place for care. Connection, or attuned empathy, provides the impetus for sustained engagement with the one cared for. Ultimately, care is a practice and not merely a disposition, so action is the ultimate manifestation of care. Habits of inquiry, connection, and action sustain the labor of good care. One challenge in defining effective care is framing it as either a philosophical/theoretical idea or, conversely, too clinical or procedural. This analysis reflects on the overlooked practices of care. Effective care is understood and captured in the habits of caregivers' bodies/minds/hearts, even though, in practice, it does not usually require such scrutiny. However, if we are to valorize good care, careful thought must be applied. Paradoxically, good care represents the moral ideal at the center of the non-ideal theory of care. The claims in this brief description of good care are fleshed out in Chapter 1.

**Commitment** is a dedication to something or some purpose. Commitment is another common term used to reflect a moral direction with a vague end. As employed in this project, a commitment does not imply moral absolutes (such as rules), nor does it demand specific practices. A commitment to care is to carry a moral value or good that requires an individual to navigate various and often uncertain contexts. I am employing the term commitment in the sense of a trajectory that lacks a specific plan or activities. However, a commitment is abiding because it suggests a degree of ongoing loyalty and dedication. A commitment to care, explored in Chapter 3, is an enduring desire to care effectively and improve at caring. If good care entails inquiry, connection, and action, a commitment to care translates into a steadfast willingness to learn, empathize, and act. These are the processes of this process morality. On the one hand, a commitment to care is abstract, an open-ended dedication to a way of being in the world. This approach seems at odds with feminist care theorizing because the latter emphasizes concrete experience. However, the abstract commitment to care is always quickly concretized in the drawing from and seeking experiences. I commit to care not to valorize a virtue, but because of the tangible good it will do in the world and/or for myself.

**Radical** labels are often used to marginalize groups of people and thus rhetorically discount them as, for example, "radical feminists" or "radical Islamists." When Kathie Sarachild penned a description of the nascent feminist consciousness-raising movement in 1968, she reclaimed and embraced the word "radical." Sarachild noted the Latin root of the term "radical" as originating in the root; thus, as radicals, feminists endeavored to get to the root of society's misogyny (1978: 144). In one sense, care is radical because valuing it inverts the prevailing hierarchy of social regard. However, in another sense, valuing care is also a path that leads to the roots of the human condition. Indeed, the term "radical" describes a position outside standard social and moral norms, and I am employing it as a modifier indicative of the implications of a commitment to care. Radicality is relative and driven by context. For example, same-sex marriage is considered a radical idea in some contexts and morally acceptable in others. Care is generally not considered a radical concept regarding bold, political actions such as overthrowing a government in a revolution. However, it is profound care that leads to those events.

Quite the opposite, many find care to be a mundane topic. It has been historically overlooked in moral theory, perhaps primarily due to sexism and the association of care with women's labor. However, the new light on care has raised the specter of its radical nature compared to dominant neoliberal values that eschew care. The radicality invoked in this book is about the implications of committing to an ethic of care. Accordingly, Madeline Bunting finds a contrarian streak in those committed to caring, "Care requires a resistance to a dominant cultural preoccupation with the self—its image, desires and their fulfilment. Carers find themselves rebels in a culture which no longer promotes or values their labours" (2020: 36). Section 2 of this book suggests that a real commitment to care has radical implications.

**Revolution** is another fairly common word that I employ in a particular manner in this book. Typically associated with historical events of bloodshed and violent overthrow of regimes, the type of revolution addressed here is a methodical social and political transformation not led by generals or ministers but potentially everyone—a populist revolution of caring. In 1967, Martin Luther King was a year from his tragic assassination. His public rhetoric had become increasingly radical in opposing the Vietnam War and advocating for more socialistic practices. In a famous speech, "Beyond Vietnam: A Time to Break Silence," King invokes and reappropriates the term "revolution." He initially decries the US military and its covert roles in political revolutions and laments that the United States would no longer be associated with democratic revolutions for freedom. King then applies the term in a nonviolent context:

> I am convinced that if we are to get on the right side of the world revolution, we as a nation must undergo a radical revolution of values. We must rapidly begin the shift from a "thing-oriented" society to a "person-oriented" society. When machines and computers, profit motives and property rights are considered more important than people, the giant triplets of racism, materialism, and militarism are incapable of being conquered.
>
> *(1967)*

King would repeat this theme elsewhere in his writing (2010: 196).

In arguing for an inclusive feminist revolution driven by education transformation, bell hooks leverages King's notion of a radical revolution of ideas. hooks ties the notion of progress to peaceful intellectual revolutions that confront denying and maintaining false narratives around identity. This book similarly adopts an understanding of revolution not as a hypermasculinist

**12** Introduction

violent disruption of structures (although disrupting uncaring systems of oppression can result from care) but as an internal transformation that leads to relational and institutional change. The approach here is consistent with German feminist philosopher Eva von Redecker's concept of processional revolution (2021). Care, a process morality, entails a revolution of heart and mind that we can all participate in through everyday interactions that aggregate and congeal into a social renovation. I return to the subject of a care revolution and von Redecker's analysis at the conclusion of this book. James and Grace Lee Boggs describe that a revolution is not "a single tactical event or episode" but a social transformation motivated by a vision of an evolved humanity (2008: 15).

Later, I suggest some ideas that might be viewed as morally radical in some circles, but for now, I simply argue that such notions should not be considered radical if one earnestly commits to care. In some ways, care is a conundrum in that it at once constitutes a familiar and common term, yet care can provoke people to great moral efforts. Care can be revolutionary. Despite living in an age of unprecedented technological surveillance, the next social revolution "will not be televised" (Heron, 1971).[3] A care revolution will not likely come from a discernible leader or source. It will be co-created by individuals acting in their relationships and interactions while simultaneously engaging in communal efforts to institute caring practices and structures. A revolution of mind, heart, and hand is within our grasp if we imagine the world differently—not as a utopia or fantasy but as leveraging what we know about the power of effective care.

### Methodological Notes

A few notes about the methodological approach taken in this book: this is a work of philosophy, broadly understood, and it makes an argument about the nature and implications of care morality. I qualify the philosophy in this book with the term "broadly understood" because I employ natural language as much as possible, and technical terms are explained. In addition, personal stories, human interest anecdotes, and poetry are integrated into the text, along with heavy reliance on other fields in the humanities and the social sciences. Therefore, some in the field might not label this book "philosophy" in the strict analytic sense of the term. However, I am a philosopher by training and take an expansive approach to the discipline. In that regard, I delineate a few methodological approaches below, including the feminist, non-binary, and tension-filled character of the care exploration undertaken in this book.

This book endeavors to be feminist in nature. What I mean by "feminist" is that the lens of analysis is attentive to identity and oppression as well as the power and politics of subject positions. Gender matters. Race matters. Sexuality matters. Care ethics was born out of women's experiences and feminist analysis, and although the theory is being applied widely, its origins and initial trajectory should not be forgotten. Chapter 5 addresses feminism as a radical implication of a commitment to care. Still, that spotlight should not diminish the fundamental feminist character of the argument in the entire book. You may have warranted skepticism regarding a privileged white cis-gendered male writing a book from a feminist perspective. I aspire to a feminist approach in my life and my vocational claim of "feminist care ethicist." However, I also recognize that patriarchy is endemic to our society, and I fail more often than I am aware. I welcome and accept critiques of my inadequacies as a feminist voice.

Care ethics is steeped in human experience in all its complexity and contradictions. Both rationality and emotion are at play when it comes to care. Accordingly, tidy categories are seldom in the offing. In particular, binary thinking does not reflect the operations of care. Care exists within the human world of continuums or degrees rather than static bounded understandings. The dichotomies of care/not care or good care/bad care are only helpful as hypotheticals or thought experiments. Still, the reality of care is that it operates in the liminal space between these categories. Thus, just as we have come to recognize that human gender identity is non-binary, so too the concept of care and its characteristics are non-binary (Malatino, 2019: 131). Even when I provide pretty good care through inquiry, connection, and action, there is always the potential to offer better care or that I make a few bad choices among my good decisions. As a dynamic notion, care is not always adequately contained within the boundaries of words we are comfortable with. Liminality and proportionality frame the thinking about care throughout this book.

Given the emphasis on non-binary thinking as a means to argue for the intellectual space between categories, does that mean that care thinking is subjective? The answer is appropriately yes and no. Subjectivity is the bane of traditional moral theory, which emphasizes rational impartiality. Introducing nonrational criteria for morality opens up the possibility of bias contaminating any ethical approach. There is a related concern regarding relativism, given that nonrationality will give rise to partiality, such as emotional attachments. Care ethics has been subject to such criticism. However, as feminist theorists and others have pointed out, even the most highly rational approach is open to the bias of the theorist espousing it. Kant, who has so significantly influenced contemporary moral thinking, was a product of the particularities of his context. His worldview was shaped by patriarchy and the values of his time. Accordingly, his notion of autonomy is grounded in an individualistic understanding of identity. As Robert Johnson and Adam Cureton describe, for Kant, "our status as free rational agents" is the basis of human dignity and worth and "the source of the authority behind the very moral laws that bind us" (2022). Such an approach has been criticized for lacking the relationality essential to human ontology and autonomy. For example, Marcia Brown finds Kant advancing a masculinist autonomy that valorizes detachment of affect with other persons (1997). By contrast, care ethics has an element of subjectivity in that no

**14** Introduction

unified or universalizable subject or agent exists. There are just human beings with a moral commitment to care.

Another critical methodological approach related to the previous point is that the path to care theory is comfortable holding tensions. For example, caring for an enemy or someone who has done great harm may seem contradictory. However, caring is not the same as moral vindication. I have been asked whether I could care for someone with political positions quite different from mine, and I immediately said yes. Caring for someone—learning, connecting, and acting—is not an assent to or exoneration of their morality. Like the Derek Black case at the beginning of this Introduction, such caring for opposed others represents hope for a better, more caring world. Caring for enemies or repugnant others is not easy and must be engaged in with a concern for self-care, but it can be done. Caring about disliked others is one of the many tensions or contradictions that care theory, as a comprehensive way of being and not just an ideal moral theory, cannot ignore. Another tension arises from whether care is an "end," a goal to strive for, or a "means," a process that brings you to the good. I suggest that the answer is affirmative to both. Care is a personal and social good that allows individuals and society to sustain and flourish. However, care is a process or practice that creates other goods, such as life, happiness, and security. For example, Klaartje Klaver and Andries Baart claim that attentiveness which care theorists widely accept as a crucial element of care is "not only the first step in care but a good in itself" (2011: 689). Means and ends are not always distinct when it comes to care. As the following suggests, the tensions held under the umbrella of an ethics of care make it challenging to define.

A care ethic is—and is more. A care ethic:

- Entails empathy, but empathy is not enough.
- Includes rationality but requires more than calculation.
- Engages emotion but is more than a feeling.
- Involves a disposition, but is more than temperament.
- Is responsive but sometimes requires proactivity.
- Needs action, but also humble reflexivity.

This book also assumes the potency of social composition (sometimes called "social construction") in our world. Many staunch ideas about how the world works—our truths—derive from the social rather than a fixed sense of the natural. In other words, we have helped to compose or curate our world through narrative, story, and imagination (or the lack of imagination). This claim is not intended to be deterministic or comprehensive. The hopeful nature of social composition is that it can be undone. For example, consider the barrier to care that exclusive norms of heterosexual marriage represent. The dominant mores regarding heterosexual marriage prevent many people from signifying their love and commitment to their partners in socially

Introduction **15**

permissible ways. Exclusive heterosexual marriage is a social composition fostered by human narratives, primarily religious, that is being undone the world over, albeit slowly. However, the perspective in this project is not one of social composition as fatalistic. Many truths are not derived from the social. For instance, although embodiment and the earth's ecology are heaped with social meaning, their existence and operations are not questioned. Section 2 focuses on care implications for the transformation of established social truths. Such change requires inquiry, empathetic imagination, and acting responsively.

## The Journey Ahead

This book is divided into two sections. Each section chapter begins with a vignette that explores how care manifests in human experience. Section 1, "Thinking About Better Care," includes four chapters exploring aspects of care that can lead to a care revolution. Chapter one, Good Care, endeavors to enrich the understanding of care ethics by addressing its performative, posthuman, and holistic aspects as personal and political. This chapter delves into the nature of care ethics with a twist. There exists extensive literature delineating the nature of care ethics. I only offer a brief foray into definitional concerns and, instead, focus on the character of good or effective care. The distinction is significant in moving away from binary understandings of care as present or absent and toward a more liminal notion of care manifested in gradations. Continuums of care match the relationality of reality and resist complacency, given that one may continually improve care and do better. The non-binary approach also matches the process nature of care theory.

Chapter 2 addresses the nature of normativity in care ethics. The argument is that although care ethics has substantial normative implications, it also entails significant extra-normative considerations. The chapter explores balancing *a priori* and a *posteriori morality*. Accordingly, care is framed as having an "emergent normativity" driven by the value of care but sensitive to the context of needs. This seemingly oxymoronic tension reflects care as a non-ideal theory centered on a moral ideal.

Chapter 3 argues for a commitment to care as something we should widely assent to despite all that fractures society. "Commitment" is the ethical term of choice here because it suggests personal agency rather than externally imposed moral restrictions. Care is offered as a categorical moral commitment. Reframing Kant's categorical imperative, a categorical commitment to care is presented as the foundational moral position of embodied beings—one that should be easily chosen given human capacities and needs.[4] Committing to care (in the manner of humble inquiry, inclusive connection, and responsive action) exceeds the ethical potential of rules, duties, or consequences, which can and have been undermined by game playing.

**16** Introduction

Chapter 4 introduces the notion of a care ethos as a co-created spirit of care that can fuel both personal and social moral commitment. In this context, ethos is a term that describes an indefinite moral commitment, a co-created moral identity, and an integration of emotional, visceral, and rational commitments. Therefore, an ethos of care is akin to a spirit or disposition of care. The concept of an ethos of care is vital because moral and social change cannot be wrought simply by changing policies and laws—they also require a change of spirit to fund a care revolution fully. Laws and policies can advance us to a more caring society, but progress is inconsistent and fragile until there is a greater caring spirit or ethos.

In Section 2 of this book, "Invitations and Provocations: Imagining Transformative Possibilities," I offer concrete normative considerations based on extending the arguments of the first section. These chapters explore the radical implications of care. I describe the topics discussed as provocations because they are not mainstream frameworks and have been marginalized in various ways and degrees. However, these chapters are also invitations for consideration in light of a care commitment. Granting that a care ethic and care ethos are vital moral approaches for humanity, one must commit to learning, inclusion, and action for good or effective care to be realized. What personal and political practices must I consider to fulfill a caring identity? All moral approaches ask us to aspire to ethical ideals, whether maximizing good or following challenging rules of what is right. Ethical theorists are often reluctant to offer specific courses of action because of the potential for criticisms of bias and subjectivity. This reluctance is particularly true for care theorists who tend to focus on the practices of caring relationships rather than specific programs of moral behavior. However, here we will offer provocations that, if one embraces a caring worldview, imply at least leaving open the possibility of endorsing the social frameworks. Specifically, I argue that a caring individual should consider identifying with feminism, socialism, humanism (and posthumanism), and veganism.

None of the provocation/invitation chapters is intended to be an exhaustive examination of its topic area. Instead, a particular aspect is drawn out to show how these radical and marginalized social positions can participate in a care revolution. Chapter 5's discussion of feminism addresses resisting toxic masculinity. Many forms of masculinity overtly value non-caring, thus representing a barrier to building a caring society. Chapter 6 focuses on socialism, not in a technical, economic sense but in advocating for values that create a caring society. Accordingly, changing our economic imagination and rethinking taxation, infrastructure spending, labor unions, and debt relationships are addressed. Chapter 7 on humanism explores the primacy of care considerations over abstract religious, moral authority. The discussion includes an acknowledgment of posthumanism and a reframing of agnosticism. Moreover, care theory is agnostic about religion except when its precepts damage human relationships and need. Chapter 8, perhaps this section's most "radical" subject, suggests that veganism reflects a posthuman commitment to care. This provocation of care mingles care for ourselves with nonhuman animals and the environment. The four provocations are intended to demonstrate that committing to care is more radical than it might appear at first, given the warm and fuzzy associations we often have with the notion of care. A revolution resulting in a social transformation toward greater caring will necessarily challenge existing social norms, and Section 2 explores some possible changes.

The conclusion reminds us that care theory is an open-ended process morality, a good thing given that life's invitations and provocations for change will be many—far beyond what was offered in Section 2. A few additional examples are suggested in this final chapter: pacifism, environmentalism, and anti-racism. The conclusion addresses the sense of disponibilité or openness accompanying a commitment to care and permeates a caring ethos. In addition, discussions of care as vital for moral progress, as a social movement, and finally, as a rich processual revolution are offered. Rather than surrendering the terms "revolution" and "radical" to extreme masculinist understandings that entail physical violence and relational disruption, I employ a contemporary feminist rethinking of revolution in light of the interrelationship of personal and social practices that can change the paradigms and institutions of modernity. Finally, there is a significant temporal framework of care. A caring revolution is not characterized by a moment in time or an event but rather by a gradual transformation that envelops society resulting in a change of behavioral norms. Derek Black's transformation is likely more dramatic than most, but a single action or activity did not result in a sudden epiphany; it was a slow and steady process.

## Crisis or Abundance: A False Dichotomy

I indicated above that care theory is comfortable with contradictions, and the contemporary context is replete with tensions. One seeming contradiction is regarding the state of care in the world. It has become common to indicate that we are living through a care crisis, and there is much to support those claims. A simple search of the phrase "crisis of care" on my university's library database returned over 65 entries between 2017 and the writing of this manuscript. As early as 2007, then-presidential candidate and Senator Barack Obama described an "empathy deficit" (2007). Influential feminist philosopher, Nancy Fraser, describes the contemporary crisis narrative:

> The 'crisis of care' is currently a major topic of public debate. Often linked to ideas of 'time poverty', 'family-work balance', and 'social depletion', it refers to the pressures from several directions that are currently squeezing a key set of social capacities: those available for birthing and raising children, caring for friends and family members, maintaining households and broader communities, and sustaining connections more generally. Historically, these processes

**18** Introduction

of 'social reproduction' have been cast as women's work, although men have always done some of it too. Comprising both affective and material labour, and often performed without pay, it is indispensable to society. Without it there could be no culture, no economy, no political organization. No society that systematically undermines social reproduction can endure for long. Today, however, a new form of capitalist society is doing just that. The result is a major crisis, not simply of care, but of social reproduction in this broader sense.

*(2016: 99)*

Fraser makes a particularly dire indictment of capitalism in that its disruption of care threatens society's ability to reproduce itself functionally. The hidden contradiction of capitalism is that it requires care to exist, yet its systems undermine and threaten society's ability to care.

Fraser has many companions claiming that we are in a moment of crisis. Consider two books with "crisis of care" in the title: *The Crisis of Care: What Caused It and How Can We End It?* by sociologist Emma Dowling (2021) and *Labours of Love: The Crisis of Care* by Madeleine Bunting (2020). Both books emerged from the United Kingdom and focus on care work. Dowling is wary of crying "crisis" in an age of so many crises: "To speak of crisis—any kind of crisis—is to join a litany of crisis lamentations that crowd the public sphere and make us numb to its urgency" (2021: 6). Like Fraser, Dowling is concerned with social reproduction and how market forces oppress care. Dowling is ambivalent about invoking the term "crisis" for many reasons, including the implication that it romanticizes a time before the crisis that was better. However, no amount of Normal Rockwell nostalgia or warm and fuzzy feelings about growing up in a caring family can adequately point to when care was abundant in society for all. As Dowling states, "If we look back in time, we see that the status quo of care has never been up to standard. The current care crisis, then, does not demand a return to a better past, but rather a struggle for a better future" (Ibid: 8).

With literary aplomb, Bunting weaves interviews, research, and personal anecdotes into a narrative about the present-day care crisis. After discussions with care workers and care scholars, Bunting finds a comprehensive crisis:

The care crisis is one of culture, politics and ethics in the face of dramatic social change. A deep-seated historical prejudice against the value and importance of care is colliding with twenty-first-century lives. The crisis has two dimensions: care is either unavailable and gaps are opening up, or its quality is deeply compromised.

*(2020: 10)*

However, like Fraser and Dowling, Bunting is not fatalistic about the present crisis. Bunting's interviews reveal pain, sorrow, and frustration but also joy and fulfillment in the work of care. These authors offer hope for improved care systems, albeit through an uneasy road forward.

The pervasive carelessness in the world prompted an interdisciplinary group of scholars in London to start a reading group in 2017 called The Care Collective.[5] One of the outcomes of their work was the concise, *The Care Manifesto: The Politics of Interdependence* (2020). The authors point to a lack of care and an active undermining of care work, further revealed through the worldwide Covid-19 pandemic. In particular, the Care Collective is concerned that society has become comfortable and even honors the idea of not caring.[6] They describe this as "the banality of carelessness" (Ibid: 18). Nevertheless, the Care Collective tempers its indictment of society with a positive message of hope, hence the manifesto. They offer a "vision of a world that takes the idea of care as its organizing principle seriously, an idea that has been repudiated and disavowed for too long" (Ibid: 19). None of these authors deem the crisis of care hopeless, nor do I.

So, what type of crisis is this? Humans have an extraordinary potential to care even under the most oppressive circumstances. We have demonstrated it in the past; we are demonstrating it now and will demonstrate it in the future. Referring to the present age as one with a care crisis reveals the limits of our language and categorical thinking. In a world of about 8 billion people, there is a terrible care crisis for many people suffering horribly. The crisis is tragic because so much violence and precarity are avoidable—we have the means to make the world much less precarious (Hamington and Flower, 2021). However, simultaneous with this crisis is an abundance of care. There are ample experiences of outstanding care on both personal and systemic levels—family members and friends care for one another daily. Social work systems, education, and health services unremarkably and regularly provide excellent care. Humans have a tremendous capacity to care; most people exercise those skills regularly. Both stories are true: one of crisis and one of abundance. This seeming contradiction is one of the complexities of the contemporary human condition: a care crisis and a care abundance are not mutually exclusive. There is much work to do to widen the circle of care so that more people, animals, and environments experience quality care, but the starting point for moral progress toward a more caring world is not bankrupt. However, we must imagine morality and our role in it differently. I suggest that we need to make an ethical commitment to care with all its associated commitments and radical implications. Then, we can participate in the care revolution.

## The "I Am Here" Imperative

We have lived with liberal approaches to solving strife for some time. Passing a caring law, expanding individual rights, or electing caring officials are positive steps. A more caring future entails all of these measures. However, they are insufficient for our enormous tasks and wicked problems. Environmental

**20** Introduction

degradation, identity-based oppression, rampant violence, and poverty seem intractable, and perhaps they are. We will only make inroads with new solutions that engage hearts, minds, and actions as individuals and a collective society. A paradigm shift that bends toward care is something that we can all participate in.

Why is a personal and institutional commitment to care necessary? First, care is the hope of the world. It is the foundation of all morality, and it is not a mere abstract ethical system imposed upon humanity but a morality that emerges from our embodied and social existence. As Carol Gilligan describes: "We are, by nature, responsive, relational beings, born with a voice and into relationship, hard-wired for empathy and cooperation, and that our capacity for mutual understanding was—and may well be—key to our survival as a species" (2011: 3). Care entails motivation and emotion, and all that is bound up with being human. Care takes courage and sacrifice, but it can also be beautiful, inspiring, and meaningful. If we wish to "repair our world," we need to care about one another, our ecosystems, our fellow beings, and ourselves. The standard of loving everyone is too high and unattainable, but care's flexible and liminal nature makes it an accessible moral practice.

This book is not about an unachievable fantasy. Nor will a pervasive commitment to care end challenges and strife in the world. However, there is tangible evidence that we can make the world a better place—less precarious, more secure (broadly understood), and more comfortable—with the advent of some significant, but not impossible, changes in our disposition and behavior. If you wish for an exercise in moral imagination, envision an existence where when challenges befall you, you are confident that someone has your back, whether they be friends, your community, your government, or your employer. It is a caring vision that does not negate the struggle of human existence but instead enacts a fuller realization of our relational being. As Nel Noddings described, "The response of the carer to cared-for in either [the private or public] domain is a reassuring, 'I am here'" (2002a: 301). The knowledge, feeling, and actions of being better cared for can significantly influence the quality of our lives. This book endeavors to chart a possible path to a caring future.

## Notes

1 There have been scholars who have heard me describe Black's transformation and have objected that Stevenson had an agenda and, therefore, questioned whether this relationship can be described as authentic care. I have three responses, and they are pertinent to the methodology of this book. First, as discussed later in this introduction, care theory must break out of the modernist mold and claim the reality of its non-binary status. The care/not-care dichotomy does not reflect the human condition. Although it is popular to declare, "I just don't care," such expressions do not capture the complexity of the claim. Caring exists on a continuum rather than as an on/off switch. Black and Stevenson's relationship was as complex as many other

relationships. Second, although care is an ideal, as Nel Noddings describes, care theory is a non-ideal theory. A purity test for care sacrifices the good for an abstract notion of perfection. I argue that care theory is postmodern in some respects because it cannot be constrained by categorical thinking. Even though many acts approximate it, there is no such thing as pure altruistic care. Finally, caregivers often have an agenda in the provision of assistance. That agenda can be positive or negative but it does not *ipso facto* nullify the value of that care. Stevenson's mixed motives do not negate the caring in the relationship. I thank Carlo Leget for helping me hone these ideas.

2 Some might raise the objection that care appears to be a slave morality which demands a great deal of effort on the part of some to care for hateful individuals that have disengaged from caring. Certainly, care can be abused. This subject is addressed in Chapter 1, but a couple of points can be offered at this juncture. First, caring about someone is not condoning their actions. Understanding the environment that shaped the young Derek Black is not equivalent to approving of it, but it does humanize his trajectory. Second, a moral norm of care has accordion-like qualities in that it is driven by context and the depth of care has a number of factors including self-care. We might consider the years of relationship-building on the part of Black's New College friends ethically supererogatory or beyond what we could ethically expect anyone to do. On the other hand, the care continuum acts like an accordion in that it can be expansive. Any interaction with another person can be superficial or it can lead to a deeper connection.

3 Poet, writer, and singer Scott-Heron (1949–2011) was a foundational figure in modern rap. This song has become an anthem for social change and the lyrics point to the dichotomy between neoliberal commercialistic values and the needs of people in the streets. To read more about Scott-Heron's nonviolent response to tragedy and unrest see, Baram (2014).

4 In her work applying care ethics to animal morality, Josephine Donovan similarly references Kant: "most feminist animal care theorists have … proposed that care and compassion is a practice that can and should be applied—universally—a categorical imperative, if you will—to all animals (human and non)" (2006: 310).

5 The Care Collective consists of Andreas Chatzidakis, Professor in the School of Business and Management, Royal Holloway; Jamie Hakim, Lecturer in Media Studies in the School of Art, Media, and American Studies, University of East Anglia; Jo Littler, Professor in the Department of Sociology and Director of the Gender and Sexualities Research Centre at City; Catherine Rottenberg, Associate Professor in the Department of American and Canadian Studies, University of Nottingham; and Lynne Segal, Anniversary Professor at Birkbeck, University of London.

6 A popular meme in the 2010s and 2020s relates to the notion of "Not Giving A Fuck"—a declaration of uncaring consistent with a notion of the banality of care. Self-help author Mark Manson endeavors to retrieve the notion by interpreting "Not Giving A Fuck" as a matter of priorities: one should not care about that which is unimportant and place care more significance on that which is important such as "friends, family, purpose" (2016: 16). However, it is not clear that everyone understands the meme in a proportional manner. The Care Collective references the banality of carelessness in the image of US First Lady Ivanka Trump wearing a jacket with the words, "I Just Don't Care. Do U?" in big letters while visiting a refugee camp where children had been separated from their families. This visual and performative display reveals the level of social acceptance for uncaring themes.

# SECTION 1

# Thinking about Better Care

Beginning in the 1980s, feminist theorists named the previously unnamed concept of care ethics in Western scholarship. Rather than a definitional journey regarding an ethic of care, the chapters in this section explore elements of revolutionary care. By revolutionary care, I mean personal, social, and political transformations not through a Scrooge-like epiphany that changes someone from uncaring to caring overnight but rather a steady shift of values, disposition, and practices that deepen and extend care. Perfect care is unobtainable, yet, we can all improve our care awareness, methods, and actions. As embodied beings, care is vital in our lives and should command greater attention and reflection. These chapters reflect on propositional ideas regarding care—what good care is, norms of care, the need for personal and social commitment to care, and a spirit of care for how we get better at caring that are more specifically concretized in Section 2.

DOI: 10.4324/9781003368625-2

# 1

# GOOD CARE

## Prologue: The Human Capacity to Care Well

> Due to a terrorist attack in the United States, we will be landing in Gander.
> —Captain of Air France Flight 004 due to land
> at Newark Liberty International at 11:00 am on
> September 11, 2001. (Tuerff, 2018: 13)

September 11, 2001, has left such an indelible impression on the minds and imaginations of people worldwide, especially in the United States, that decades later, invoking the simple two-number moniker "9/11" still elicits a common understanding of the event referred to. Like many catastrophic occurrences, the tragic happenings of that day created unexpected needs and vulnerabilities that simultaneously afforded people an opportunity to respond with extraordinary care. One example of collective care among many in response to the tragedy was in Gander, Canada.

On that fateful day, events occurred quickly. First, a hijacked plane struck the North Tower of the World Trade Center at 8:46 am; at 9:03 am, a second plane hit the South Tower. Shortly after that, at 9:37 am, a plane struck the Pentagon, and the fourth and final plane crashed into a field outside of southeastern Pittsburgh. Finally, at 9:42 am Eastern Daylight Time, the Federal Aviation Administration ordered a complete clearing of US airspace for the first time in a century of US flights (Defede, 2021). Officials took this unprecedented action as they scrambled to understand the events and assess further potential threats. American domestic flights landed at US airports, but 400 inbound international flights were turned away.[1] Some planes could reverse course, but most had traveled too far already.

DOI: 10.4324/9781003368625-3

**26** Thinking about Better Care

Fortunately, Canadians welcomed 250 US-bound international flights on their soil, and planes landed across the country (Ibid: 6). Thirty-eight planes with nearly 6,600 passengers aboard landed at the Gander airport.

A small city of about 10,000 residents, Gander is located in Newfoundland, an island situated northeast of Maine. Once a strategic military airport and later a refueling location, the Gander airport had long runaways and plenty of space to hold the planes. However, developments in plane technology allowed for longer flights without refueling which helped diminish Gander's role in international travel and thus reduced the number of visitors. Furthermore, the local area suffered from high unemployment because of the sagging fishing and timber industries. Yet, despite the economic hardships, the community had not lost its moral capacity for care and compassion (Ibid: 4).

The time in Gander is 90 minutes ahead of the US Eastern Standard Time. Canadian officials immediately responded to allow planes to land in Gander and have them sit on the tarmac until further instructions. The first plane arrived at 11:00 am local time. Even before that plane touched down, city leaders made plans to handle the influx of unexpected visitors. The people and businesses of Gander immediately mobilized to welcome and assist their unanticipated guests. Lacking anything close to a hotel capacity that could accommodate such an upswell of people, local schools became makeshift shelters. School bus drivers, who were in the midst of a labor strike, volunteered to shuttle passengers to schools converted into shelters. One market stayed open on a 24-hour basis to help handle shelter needs. Local television stations made sure that the temporary accommodations had cable lines. The whole town seemed committed to caring for their guests. As Jim Defede chronicles:

> The Salvation Army was in charge of gathering supplies and acting as a central clearinghouse for the shelters. The local radio station and public-access television started running announcements asking folks in town to donate food, spare bedding, old clothes—anything the passengers might need. At the town's community center, a line of cars stretched from the front door for two miles as people brought sheets, blankets, and pillows from their homes for passengers.
>
> Local stores donated thousands of dollars worth of items.
>
> *(Ibid: 57)*

Unique anecdotes of care by the Gander community are too numerous to entirely recount. The golf course allowed passengers to play for free; townspeople lent them clubs. Many Gander residents volunteered to give people rides or have them come to their homes to take showers, as many of the makeshift shelters had no shower facilities. Tired, scared, and inconvenienced, the international travelers came to recall the community's response fondly.

Gander was not extraordinary regarding care resources, education, or disposition. Nevertheless, ordinary human beings put their skills of care on display. Defede concludes,

> Given all those human frailties, what happened in Gander is still remarkable. And perhaps the lesson isn't that these acts of kindness occurred because Gander is a magical place, but rather that these people came together in a time of crisis regardless of their own personal shortcomings. And if that's the case, then it offers hope that all of us have the ability within us.
>
> *(Ibid: 261)*

Gander's history is replete with tragic events to which the town responded, and their hospitality and compassion are legendary even when there is no tragedy. Like Defede, Canadian philosopher Trudy Govier finds a caring capacity exhibited even among ordinary people. Nothing is astonishing about Newfoundland residents, which makes the potential for further replication of the care ethos an inspiring idea.

> Yes, human beings want power. But even power requires relationships with other people, and besides, it's not the only thing we want. We also seek such things as knowledge, a sense of worth and achievement, and happiness—all of which require decent relationships with other people. We care about other people—how they are faring and how they respond to us. Our own happiness depends on theirs; and theirs depends on ours. We want to connect with them and have them want to connect with us. Moving stories about care for strangers illustrate these basic facts about human nature. The people in Gander and Lewisporte, Newfoundland [another site for landing planes on September 11, 2001], behaved with energy and generosity, and they were wonderful in a crisis, which is good news, and we should appreciate good news when we hear it. But there's even better news: these capacities for sympathy and kindness are shared by human beings everywhere.
>
> *(Govier, 2006: 396)*

The actions of the Gander community in the fallout from the 9/11 disaster can be viewed as instances of event-driven moral heroism that humans have repeatedly demonstrated in the face of fires, hurricanes, earthquakes, and floods. However, a moral commitment to care existed among the people of Gander before this tragedy and remained afterward. For example, years later, the city became deeply involved in Syrian refugee resettlement (Antle, 2018).

The caring response of the people of Gander is the kind of inspiring, feel-good story that has captivated audiences through multiple books, documentaries, and a Tony-nominated Broadway musical (*Come From Away*). Can people adopt the commitment to care exhibited at Gander more regularly? This question focuses

**28**  Thinking about Better Care

attention on moral social norms. Ethical expectations around helping others are unwritten standards of behavior that people internalize and adjust. Our moral agency is exhibited in that adjustment. Walking by a homeless person may be socially acceptable, but that does not preclude someone from conversing with someone on the street, figuring out what they need, and helping them acquire it. Actions above accepted moral norms are labeled "supererogatory": there are no ethical expectations that people engage in such acts. They are considered above and beyond the call of moral duty. However, as I indicated in the Introduction, care has an imaginative dimension. We can imagine and enact higher personal expectations of understanding, connection, and acting on behalf of others. We have the power to instantiate a more excellent personal standard for care. No one could have morally faulted anybody who lived in Gander if they did not work 20-hour days to help all the distressed travelers. However, as many have indicated, the citizens of Gander demonstrated an ethos of care that allowed them to imagine a higher order of care. *In the face of all those suffering, is it possible to enact a greater commitment to care more widely and more often?*

Of course, it is the hope and argument of this book that the answer to the previous question is yes. This chapter briefly discusses an ethic of care and moves on to its central theme of the skills of good care. Care is a relational approach to morality essential to human survival, and it radiates from and develops out of our bodies' capacities. Like any ethic, a "care ethic" is a systematic consideration of care's morally normative properties (although I also contend that care has supra-normative properties). An ethic of care interrogates how and why it is moral to care personally and collectively. Good or effective care is dictated by the circumstance and assessed as to its quality by those receiving care. What constitutes good care cannot be predetermined. The people of Gander anticipated basic human needs but then adapted to the emergent requirements of their unexpected guests as they met and got to know them. Although the specifics of good care cannot be determined in advance, the methodology for good care, its skills or habits, can be characterized. This chapter focuses on the processes of good care, and the subsequent chapters of the theoretical portion of the book address issues of normativity, commitment, and ethos.

### An Ethic of Care

> We need to recognize how care is central to human well-being, to citizenship and to security, and how this recognition should change our theories and our practices.
>
> —Virginia Held (2015: 52)

Many outstanding books are foundational for the study of care ethics,[2] and the list is growing. First named in the 1980s by feminist theorists drawing upon the historically underappreciated experiences of women's ideas and work, an ethic of care is a relational approach to morality with critical normative implications, i.e., what is the right thing to do? Care theory offers a more comprehensive view of morality beyond solving moral problems. Although the standard description of feminist care ethics ascribes its origins to the works of Carol Gilligan and Nel Noddings, alternative genealogies posit proto-care ethical writing in the work of David Hume (Baier, 1989), John Dewey (Leffers 1993), and Jane Addams (Hamington, 2009b). The care ethical critique of traditional ethical approaches circulated in the intellectual imagination before Gilligan's *In A Different Voice*.

One overlooked source of care theorizing can be found in the writings of Latinx feminist philosophers. Gloria Anzaldúa and María Lugones, both of whose work predate Gilligan and Noddings, address a relational care ethic. Andrea J. Pitts describes Lugones's 1978 dissertation, *Morality and Personal Relationships*, as a precursor to feminist care ethics (Pitts, 2021: 152). In her dissertation, Lugones is critical of the impersonal abstraction found in moral rules and principles (1978: 2). Her words resonates with the particularism of care theory when she argues that personal relationships allow us to view the other as a unified whole rather than categories or stereotypes (Ibid: 12). Similarly, Anzaldúa develops a rich relational ontology of *nos/otras* and spiritual inquiry or *conocimiento* that is explored later in Chapter 2. Unfortunately, the standard history of the development of feminist care ethics omits the works of Latinx feminists. My comments are not intended to suggest that Lugones's project is the same as care ethicists or should be appropriated, given the differences in context. Still, it is unfortunate that her pioneering work is not recognized in the care literature.

Furthermore, various indigenous and non-Western moral traditions place care at the forefront, and these traditions existed long before contemporary feminist care theory. A few of these traditions are discussed in Chapter 4. It is Western hubris to claim the discovery of care ideals. However, in an act of resistance to the dominant moral narratives, the work of feminist scholars established care as a viable intellectual subject for Western academicians.

In an early work of feminist care ethics, philosopher Peta Bowden acknowledged the difficulty in defining care as indicative of the flexibility and liminality of an ethic of care. She is content with a vague definition of care ethics because she views a narrow construction of normativity as one of the errors of traditional moral theory: "Caring highlights the ways in which ethical practices outrun the theories that attempt to explain them" (1997: 2). But, of course, for academics who characteristically specialize in categorical precision, this presumed complacency with vagueness is anathema. Writing almost 20 years after Bowden, philosopher Stephanie Collins, displeased with the nebulousness of care theorists, endeavored to bring care ethics into conversation with analytic philosophy, a hyper-rational and precise form of philosophy. Her concern was that "care ethics remains a somewhat shadowy entity at the outskirts of debates in analytic moral philosophy, often mentioned in connection to feminism and virtue ethics, but without a definitive statement of precisely what its advocates

**30** Thinking about Better Care

are committed to—without a slogan" (2015: 2). Although Collins's project is admirable in bringing more attention to care theory, I do not focus on a more precise definition of care ethics given the existing body of scholarship. Instead, I focus on the skills and components of good or effective care.

### Good Care

> Good care is the proper aim of caregiving.
>
> —Asha Bhandary (2017: 13)

Why do I focus on good or effective care? Aside from the concern for pervasive carelessness, or even a crisis of care, a great deal of poor or ineffective care exists. We not only need to take care of one another, but we also need to take *better* care of each other. There is understandable antipathy toward the concept of care in some communities, given the damage invoked in the name of care. For example, two Canadian disability scholars describe, "Care is a dirty word in our Mad[3], disability, queer activist communities. It is used euphemistically to refer to precisely those unpleasant, embarrassing, or violent arrangements where (the best versions of) care rarely flourishes" (Eales and Peers, 2021: 170). Accordingly, the advocation for greater attention to care found in this book should not be confused as a call for quantity without concern for the quality of care. A commitment to care should entail wanting to be effective at it, i.e., humble, understanding, and responsive.

Many theorists might object to naming good care because care is contextually driven. They are correct. In *Care Aesthetics: For Artful Care and Careful Art*, James Thompson explicitly states that he does not present a case for good care because care is always "embedded in certain cultural norms and expectations" (2023: 2). However, although we may not be able to preemptively and universally name what good care is, that does not mean that we cannot find patterns of behavior or practices or habits that lead us toward better care. The focus here is not on universally defining good care but on naming the skills of improving care: learning, connecting, and responding. The distinction between *a priori* describing good care and recognizing that there are actions that can lead to better care is crucial. Thompson implicitly recognizes the difference as he endeavors to shine "a firm light on those practices of exceptional virtuosity" (Ibid: 4) in his exploration of care aesthetics.

Aesthetics draws our attention to sensation, perception, and the body. Good care starts with the body. A commitment to care entails an awareness and sensitivity to our corporeal existence that becomes the basis for care. As French philosopher Christine Leroy explains, "Everything starts from the body; but not a somatic body, but rather a body woven of affects lived carnally. To care is therefore not only to care for a *sôma*, but to consider above all this affective and embodied fabric which calls for care" (2021: 14). Similarly, in *Embodied Care*, I argued that the contours of care could not be fully understood and appreciated without considering care's embodied basis. I extended the claim of Maurice Merleau-Ponty that our bodily perception gives us our lifeworld, asserting that our bodies give us our moral world through care. That embodied care comprises capacities that can be developed and habituated through will and iteration.

The Western philosophy tradition overlooks embodiment's centrality to our cognitive and rational claims about ethics. As political theorist Hollie Sue Mann writes,

> The activity of practicing care is crucial for acquiring the precise techniques and habits of caregiving. We cannot develop the proper affective, physical, and cognitive skills appropriate to giving care if we are not first habituated to that activity. Mastering knowledge of the right tones of voice, forms of touch, methods and techniques for bathing, feeding, nursing, changing bedpans, cleaning and dressing wounds, and simply comforting the sick requires participation in caring relationships. Further, these are skills that must not only be developed and sharpened through habituation, they must be preserved in and through ongoing practice. The more we care for others, the more we discover about the caring needs of human beings, and the more we discover about our own potential needs.
>
> *(2012: 210)*

Mann appropriately integrates a relational ontology that frames the moral activity of care as more than an exchange between individuals, seeing it as a dynamic interplay with the potential to leave all parties to the care experience changed by their encounter.

One of the reasons that the definition of care ethics is vague by philosophical standards is that it involves both moral goods and emergent normativity. An ethic of care has implications for what is right and thus can help us answer questions about what is ethical, but caring is also a good to be pursued—it has value and beauty. Its embodied nature gives care, texture, and feel. As James Thompson describes, "Remembering the shape and sensation of mutual care, is a direct invitation to imbue that feeling, that aesthetics of care, in all places where we believe our work is seeking to negotiate positive change" (2020: 48). Thompson aptly employs the word "negotiate" because care is also a skill of embodied performance. Those authentically intending to care must respond to the particular people and circumstances confronting them. Thus, care is a skill of improvisation,[4] making it challenging to predetermine normative action with any precision. Accordingly, I focus on the competence involved in effective care rather than pushing care ethics toward a more precise language of definition than I have already offered. Joan Tronto described competence as her

## 32  Thinking about Better Care

third dimension or phase of care ethics. She points out that emphasizing good care pushes the discussion to a form of moral consequentialism, but not in a utilitarian sense (1993: 133). Care is as much a methodology as it is an ethical theory. Care theory is nonideal and process-oriented, directed toward building competencies.[5]

In the Introduction, I described effective care as bolstered by inquiry, connection, and action. Of course, anyone can claim to act out of caring, but these activities or habits of care move superficial caring to a deeper, more meaningful, and effective experience. Here, I explain the inquiry-connection-action processes of care by adding qualifiers to the terms. Good care consists of humble inquiry, inclusive connection, and responsive action. (Figure 1.1)

These characteristics can proceed in any order and often simultaneously. There is no precise formula for good care. Care theory suggests a process morality that guides improvement and does not seek the determination of specific claims to good care. For example, one might form a connection with someone before getting to know them. Because of circumstances, one might engage in activities on behalf of someone and later get to know them (or perhaps not at all) and potentially connect with them.

Furthermore, sometimes the elements of effective care are not in equal proportion. Of course, "good" or "effective" are subjective terms on a degree continuum. Much of the discussion that follows considers the processes of good care. Perfection is seldom, perhaps never, achieved, yet one can continually improve their care by examining and strengthening these constituent processes or habits. What ensues is an examination of each of these aspects of good care. Analogous to Tronto's work, they can be described as phases, but I am wary of the sequential connotation of phases.

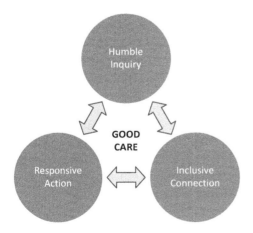

FIGURE 1.1  An Open-ended Heuristic for Good Care.

## Humble Inquiry: Generalized and Concrete

Effective care often but not always begins with knowledge. Perhaps claiming that effective care starts with knowledge appears elitist if it suggests that formal education is needed to care. However, there is no way around the significance of information in delivering good care. The knowledge required for good care can be characterized as general and particular.[6] Specifically, a broad understanding of the need and the particular context of the one in need is optimal for good care (Hamington, 2018). For example, if someone presented themselves to me as hungry and needing food, general knowledge of food preparation or access to food is helpful. However, I can raise the quality of care further by inquiring into the individual's dietary restrictions or other contextual circumstances to fulfill the need better. Pursuing both generalized and contextualized knowledge raises the potential for effective care. This two-factor approach to inquiry does not suggest that one form is superior to the other or which form of inquiry must come first. Context drives knowledge considerations. Professional generalized knowledge is crucial in healthcare settings, but that does not preclude the significance of particular knowledge. The acquisition of knowledge regarding specific patients demonstrates respect for the individual. It can yield vital information that can be interwoven with generalized knowledge to form a better basis for good care.

The humble inquiry I associate with effective care combines a notion of epistemic humility with the active pursuit of knowledge implied in the term inquiry. Epistemic humility is a relatively simple concept—a self-awareness of the limits of one's knowledge. Yet, humility appears to be in short supply in an era of easy access to information and political narratives of assertive bravado. Inquiry implies an active rather than a passive pursuit of knowledge: one seeks to understand better. Numerous care theorists have commented on the significance of humility in the care relation. Writing before the advent of feminist care theory, Milton Mayeroff devoted a section of his book, *On Caring*, to humility, straightforwardly claiming: "An attitude of not having anything to learn is incompatible with caring" (1971: 23). For care theorists, humility is bound up with attentiveness and listening to others.

Similarly, Noddings finds listening a moral obligation of care and the best way to learn. She advocates a humble "listening to believe" as a receptive path to understanding (2003a: 21). In her early work, Noddings argued that care entailed "engrossment," which raised some eyebrows but revealed a disposition of active, attentive inquiry (1984: 17). In several articles, Sophie Bourgault argues that listening is at the heart of the moral ideal of care (2017: 314). It represents a humble willingness on the caregiver's part to challenge held knowledge and change. This way, listening to the other means a commitment to mutual vulnerability (Bourgault, 2020). Here is where traditional moral categories are inadequate to capture care. Humble attention to the other is an

**34** Thinking about Better Care

informational-gathering practice. Yet, it is also a moral good as the one listened to often perceives being heard as inherently an experience of care.

The term "inquiry" connotes the active responsibility to learn. The effective caregiver is a lifelong learner of generalized evidence-based knowledge and particular knowledge of those cared for. John Dewey employed the term inquiry in an active and experiential sense consistent with its use here: "Inquiry and questioning, up to a certain point, are synonymous terms" (1988: 109). Larry Hickman notes that for Dewey, "Inquiry is thus a reflective activity in which existing tools and materials (both of which may be either tangible or conceptual) are brought together in novel and creative arrangements to produce something new" (1998: 169). Dewey characterized inquiry as not an abstract approach to knowledge production but a project in service of social amelioration. Effective care includes humble inquiry for better understanding, resulting in better care. Note that Hickman suggests creativity is involved in inquiry. Such inquiry requires an active and imaginative engagement with an openness to new possibilities. Imaginative openness resonates with a spirit of care.

The caregiver's quest for knowledge or inquiry is writ large and can include numerous sources. Historically, when Western theorists consider knowledge acquisition in epistemology, it is usually framed as propositional knowledge or knowledge that can be formed as declarative statements such as facts. However, the ongoing inquiry suggested here is expansive and inclusive outside propositional knowledge. Canadian philosopher Alexis Shotwell argues that implicit understanding or knowledge beyond the propositional is crucial for interpersonal and political considerations across identity boundaries. She does not create a hard border between propositional knowledge and implicit knowledge but instead finds propositional knowledge enmeshed in other forms of understanding (2011: x). Shotwell offers four kinds of understandings: 1) Skill-based "know-how," which is obtained through practice and experience. 2) Implicit understanding, at the nexus of the visceral and the cognitive or felt knowledge, adds experiential texture to conceptual ideas such as "feeling good." 3) Tacit knowledge is information not now reducible to symbolic representation but, with effort, might be put into words, such as a unique experience that takes time and reflection to describe. 4) Affective knowledge or feelings as an implicit understanding. Shotwell makes it clear that these four forms of implicit understanding are interrelated and vital for relationality:

> These four facets of implicit understanding are always experienced in co-constituting relation with one another. We will not have affect without bodily being, both social and skillful, and feeling may point to or be the nascent form of something that could be put into words—and the same can be said for any configuration of implicit understanding in which we prioritize one of these four.
>
> *(Ibid: xiii)*

Since the 1960s, evidence has indicated that the information conveyed through nonverbal communication outweighs verbal communication. For example, according to Albert Mehrabian and Susan R. Ferris: "Attitudes inferred from two-channel facial vocal attitude communications are a linear function of the attitude communicated in each component, with the facial component receiving approximately 3/2 the weight received by the vocal component" (1967: 251). Although the relative significance of verbal versus nonverbal communication can be debated, there is little question that a substantial amount of knowledge is unspoken. Shotwell argues that sensuous or implicit knowledge felt in our bones is a crucial linkage for a co-created personal and social transformation. As she describes, "sensuousness, stitching together sociality and embodied experience names one aspect of the complex, agentful living implicit in flourishing" (Shotwell, 2011: 15). Shotwell does not use the language of care. Still, she employs relationality to gain the understanding necessary to bring hope to a divided world.

An example of sensuous and tacit knowledge can be drawn from healthcare. Although it may be necessary for a healthcare professional to review a patient's health history to find particular knowledge of the one cared for, the information is limited to propositional evidence—facts and dates of illnesses, symptoms, and procedures. Healthcare professionals gain significant additional knowledge through face-to-face somatic encounters and time spent with patients through office visits or checkups. Presence (Klaver and Baart, 2011), time, and attention communicate care and respect, revealing further propositional knowledge. Still, it also opens the potential for embodied learning, a tacit wellspring of information between embodied beings (Hamington, 2012). Our bodies can capture extensive implicit understanding about another person even if we cannot readily thematize or articulate the information gained. Posture, voice inflection, smell, and facial expressions can all be revelatory if we take the time to attend to another person.

Furthermore, caring inquiry is a never-ending process. We can always learn more about others, and a caring ethos is an openness to the possibility of new knowledge. For many years, practices in higher education, as espoused by John Dewey and others, have advocated the goal of not simply educating students for a limited number of years in college but motivating them to become "lifelong learners." The idea is that we should learn and grow as individuals and as a collective throughout our lives. Such continuous growth is healthy for both the individual and the community.

Similarly, the inquiry required for good caregiving is never-ending as we can always learn more to be better caregivers, including about the plight and experiences of others. For example, as a healthcare worker, I want to keep up with the latest medical science to ensure I bring the best-generalized knowledge to my patients. Furthermore, if my community has, for example, a large influx of Syrian refugees, I also want to learn more about their cultural practices and

**36** Thinking about Better Care

values. This particular knowledge assists me in being a better healthcare provider. Such inquiry takes many forms, including direct encounters, literature reading, and engaging art and performances that explore and celebrate the human condition. Of course, knowledge does not guarantee good care; there is also the need for a motivational connection and responsive action. Care is knowledge work in the sense of active, ongoing, and broad inquiry (Hamington and Rosenow, 219: 28–30).

### Inclusive Connection: Attuned Empathy

The notion of "connection" employed here is appropriately ambiguous. Our connection to others can be very strong or weak. Ties to family and friends are often perceived as committing us to care more than with unfamiliar others. However, our imaginative abilities can raise perceived weak connections to a stronger sense of linkage regarding caring. Consider, for example, genealogy. If I discover a living sixth cousin twice removed while exploring my family tree, I might perceive a connection given that we share a tiny bit of DNA. Such familial discoveries have social meaning, given the pervasive narrative that "blood is thicker than water." However, the reality is that distant relatives are no more or less connected to me than any other human being. The commonality that genealogy creates is primarily a social construction of reality through which we imaginatively invest deeper meaning.

Sophie Lewis makes a compelling argument that the contemporary narrative of the family is patriarchal, exploitive, capitalist, and "a miserable way to organize care" and thus should be abolished (2022: 11). The modern notion of a "chosen family" has reinforced the idea that "family" is a malleable construct. Physical and emotional proximity create a caring support structure regardless of lineage. Accordingly, there is a linkage between caring and the designation of who constitutes a family. Given the history of care theorists presupposing heteronormative familial constructs, the use of "family" in this book is intended to be expansive and inclusive of supportive others or kinship as designated by the one cared for. As Hil Malatino points out, "the feminist literature on care labor and care ethics are steeped in forms of domesticity and intimacy that are both White and Eurocentered, grounded in the colonial/modern gender system" (2020b: 7). No matter what our identity is, there are those who are closer to us who we rely upon and trust. The political challenge of care is to go beyond these familiar others to care for the less-familiar others. A perceived familial connection can spur greater care for an individual. Although this domestic care is good, nothing precludes us from making caring connections to unfamiliar others. Intentional inclusivity raises the moral weight of caring beyond parochial concerns.

For this reason, I attach the adjective "inclusive" to the term "connection." Such broader connections are what create an "ethic" of care. Extending a moral good to someone else, particularly unfamiliar others, rather than simply considering self-interest, ease, and comfort is an ethical practice. Care is always a moral choice we make, even on behalf of a person close to us, but it is a more challenging and more profound moral choice when we take steps to care for someone known less well. Tronto makes the political necessity of inclusivity explicit: "Caring in a democratic society is highly participatory, and, at the very least, depends upon honest inclusion of everyone's perspectives" (2013: 140). I suggest that inclusion is not only essential for democracy but a generalized theory of care as well.

Raising the value of inclusivity as part of a moral commitment to care suggests self-reflexivity regarding biases and assumptions in developing care theory.[7] Several contemporary scholars have correctly highlighted that care theorists often have not problematized the power, privilege, and lack of awareness in their premises and examples. One, but not the only, critical scholar is Mia Angélica Sosa-Provencio. Aiming to construct a *Mexicana/Mestiza* ethic of care (2017) and/or a "*Revolucionista* Ethic of Care" (2016), Sosa-Provencio is concerned that "decades of care ethics scholarship continue to center White feminist frameworks wherein care is feeling with another and reminiscent of intimate maternal relationships" (2017: 7). The work of care ethicists such as Hil Malatino, Kanchana Mahadevan, Sarah Munawar, and Vrinda Dalmiya has endeavored to encompass diverse voices and subject positions. However, the concern about white heteronormative Eurocentrism should continue to be taken seriously. Employing qualitative social scientific methods, Sosa-Provencio engages the *testimonios* of Mexican-American educators to draw out themes of care in the context of cultural marginalization and its resistance. These *testimonios* reveal "a Revolucionista Ethic of Care is a reframed social justice revolution—an undertaking of love planted and harvested in unseen spaces for the educational attainment and dignity of Mexicana/o students" (2017: 4). Attending to testimonials is an example of the humble inquiry so important for caring. Sosa-Provencio values care theory and desires to make it more inclusive and responsive to the lives of oppressed peoples. I share this goal of inclusive connection in constructing a commitment and ethos of care along with their radical provocations; however, I recognize that I can and do fall prey to my privilege-induced deficiencies.

Nel Noddings distinguishes between "natural caring" and "ethical caring" to interrogate care's inclusive potential. Natural caring can be described as the more accessible and expected care relations with family and friends, our first experience with care. Ethical caring consists of the care practices we engage in with less-familiar others—the care that takes more work and risk. Noddings is careful not to create a moral hierarchy between the two but finds them in an imaginary relationship with one another: "Natural caring is the motivating force behind ethical caring. In our relational encounters, we want to restore or maintain natural caring when something goes wrong (or might go wrong). To

**38** Thinking about Better Care

do this, we draw on what I have called our 'ethical ideal,' our memories of caring and being cared for" (2013: xvi). Hopefully, we have experienced the good of caring and draw upon that knowledge to extend it to others. Much of that care knowledge is tacit and found in our bodies. Most, but not all, individuals have embodied experiences to draw from and leverage to the benefit of their moral imaginations.

The subtitle of this section is "attuned empathy" because the inclusive connection often takes the form of an empathetic connection to someone else. The suggested attunement entails having the humility to reflexively check our imagined link and understanding against what we learn through inquiry.

Empathy is not simply a trait of some people and not of others. People generally have empathic capacities that they can develop if they make an effort. After years of experimental work and engaging with the latest neuroscience scholarship, psychologist Jamil Zaki claims, "empathy and kindness are partially genetic, but there is still room for non-genetic factors—experiences, environments, habits—to play a crucial role" (2019: 23). No matter how easy or difficult it might seem to care about someone, it is always, at some level, a choice. This caring volition is also true of the components of care: inquiry, connection, and action. Philosopher Roman Krznaric is direct in his advocacy of empathy and the fact that if we desire to be more empathic, we can do it:

> The first habit of highly empathic people is to "switch on your empathic brain," by which I mean embracing this more sophisticated understanding of human nature. It is about recognizing two things. First, that the capacity to empathize is part of our genetic inheritance, with roots deep in our evolutionary pasts. And second, that empathy can be expanded through our lives—it is never too late to join the empathy revolution.
>
> *(2014: 3)*

The message of human agency in developing caring habits and practices is emerging from many disciplines. Accordingly, Zaki concurs with Krznaric:

> In any given moment, we can turn empathy up or down like the volume knob on a stereo: learning to listen to a difficult colleague, or staying strong for a suffering relative. Over time, we can fine-tune our emotional capacities, building compassion for distant strangers, outsiders, and even other species. We can free our empathy from its evolutionary bonds.
>
> *(2019: 15)*

Krznaric goes so far as to claim that humans are *"homo empathicus*—wired for empathy" (2014: xiii). Similarly, economist and social theorist Jeremy Rifkin finds that empathy has been overlooked in the history of humanity and that we are amid an emerging "Empathic Civilization." However, the actualization of this empathy depends on our choices: "Only by concerted action that establishes a collective sense of affiliation with the entire biosphere will we have a chance to ensure our future" (2009: 616). Thus, viewing attuned empathy as a choice is an element in understanding a commitment to care as a fundamentally moral act.

The role of empathy in care ethics has been the subject of significant discussion. Some theorists have favored sympathy and others empathy (Engster, 2007: 197–98). To further confuse the matter, sometimes, the terms are used interchangeably in the literature. For example, Noddings initially did not wish to employ the word "empathy" out of fear that the individual empathizing would project too much of their feeling onto the one cared for. However, through an intellectual dialogue of academic journal articles, Michael Slote convinced her that empathy was an acceptable approach (2017: 266–67). There is also no clear preference among care theorists for cognitive (an intellectual understanding of someone else's emotions) or emotional empathy (a visceral knowledge of someone else's emotions). Rather than dismissing such equivocations as sloppy thinking, I suggest that the lack of categorical thinking results from the complexity of the human condition. Good care requires emotional intelligence, an intelligence for which natural capacities can be developed and habituated. Understanding someone else's context means grasping their emotional state, which may require an inkling of emotional resonance within one's self and a cognitive grasp of their feelings. The capacity for attuned empathy allows one to avoid the pitfalls of runaway emotional connection while leaving room for affective reverberation.

Eva Kittay makes a similar argument regarding the need for connection when she argues that dependency labor requires an affective connection. Some who work as professional caregivers might balk at this observation as it seems to connote the burden of emotional labor that has so often historically burdened women and underburdened men. However, Kittay acknowledges an affective dimension in the competent carrying out of caring responsibilities: "Caring about the welfare of persons for whom you are responsible and for whom you are caring is entailed in normal and *effective* caring. The failure of much-institutionalized care-taking is traceable to the difficulty of evoking this thick involvement on the part of the caregiver; that is, the caregivers often *don't care*" (1999: 94–95). Care theorists appear to share a concern that effective caring must be more than transactional. Good caring is affective at some level.

The idea of empathic connection is significant to good care for several psychological and philosophical reasons. Finding a connection to someone else provides at least three interrelated components for improving care: a *motivational* impetus for acting on behalf of the other engages *imagination* for better understanding and creates the circumstances for *revelatory* opportunities.

A caring connection engages our relational ontology and activates our embodied capacities for care. In other words, we naturally desire to connect and

**40** Thinking about Better Care

are generally skilled at it.[8] Therefore, this vague term" connection" is intended to have intellectual and emotional elements that can be described as an empathetic linkage. However, a caring connection is neither strictly emotional nor intellectual but rather a dynamic mix of both. As such, these connections take the form of empathy.

An "attuned" empathy involves emotional connection and is tempered by acquired knowledge. Accordingly, inquiry is not mutually exclusive of connection.[9] As a motivational impetus, a connection drives us to make the time and effort to care for someone. As noted earlier, we commonly feel connected to family and friends; therefore, although caring is always a choice, it's a much easier choice for those we are close to. The fundamental problem for a political theory of care is extending some of that care from familiar to unfamiliar others—to widen the circle of our caring. If I can feel at least a modicum of connection to unfamiliar others, the chance that I will more effectively care for them increases. Noddings refers to the emotional displacement when someone becomes sympathetic to another person's plight (2002a: 17–19).

Similarly, our imaginative capacities are initiated when we perceive a connection to someone else. We actively explore our experiences and feelings to understand each other better. Of course, our imagination can be wrong, for example, in thinking that someone else's experiences are the same as ours. In this regard, a caring connection is the opposite of alienating someone by othering them. To connect is to resist moral echo chambers and the strict dichotomies of "us versus them."

Social scientist Joshua Greene argues that finding a "common currency" is crucial for overcoming what he refers to as the "moral tribalism" that divides humanity (2013). Tribalism, a term used to describe strong loyalty to a social group, is a long-standing human phenomenon with significant implications for morality and bias (Clark et al., 2019). Contemporary Western use of this term has racist overtones and does not reflect the reality of its indigenous history in Asia, Africa, or in the United States (Mungai, 2019). In recent decades, "political tribalism" has characterized antagonistic political divisions, which can exacerbate differences and amplify distrust and hate (Kornacki, 2018). Drawing on the commonality of human experience, Greene argues for the shared values found in utilitarianism. Noddings finds a resonance between care theory and utilitarianism in the concern for the real-world outcomes of decisions. Still, she draws the line between a calculative and abstract approach to morality (2010: 239–40). Greene's conclusions regarding utilitarianism born from human experience are better captured through the commonality of embodied care. No matter our moral echo chamber or tribe, we have bodies with interdependent needs for care.

Women and gender studies scholar M. Jacqui Alexander concurs, arguing we "need to adopt, as daily practice, ways of being and of relating, modes of analyzing, and strategies of organizing in which we constantly mobilize identification and solidarity, across all borders, as key elements in the repertoire of risks we need to take to see ourselves as part of one another, even in the context of difference" (2006: 265). Caring involves creatively reaching out to understand the behavior and feelings of those unfamiliar to us rather than dismissing them. When we "other" someone, we deny connection: they are a different category than us, and thus we claim that they are incomprehensible in some way. Identity-based stereotypes are one means of othering someone, making it easier to not care about them. Finding an avenue of connection open keeps the possibility for further inquiry and understanding alive. In the vignette described in the Introduction's opening, consider the role that making a relationship with Derek Black played. What began as a closed mind with an othering narrative regarding many races and cultures slowly relented to the imaginative possibilities that the discriminatory narrative was flawed. Connection made the epiphany a reality.

### Responsive Action as Caring Practice

Knowledge and connection blossom into care when people take action on behalf of the other.[10] Responsiveness is crucial to caring efforts. Without responding to the specific needs of the one cared for, caring actions can be disrespectful, ineffective, and even harmful. There is a consensus among care theorists that care describes a practice. In other words, care is more than a disposition or sensitivity. It must be enacted. However, that action should respond to the inquiry and connection. For example, when increased crime in a community generates a greater police presence armed with greater weaponry, likely, the actions are not responsive to the needs and voices of the community. Historian Elizabeth Hinton documents a long-standing pattern in the United States of "over-policing" in black neighborhoods, which results in resistance that escalates to violence and rebellion in response to increased "law and order" tactics (2021: 20). In these instances, the actions are not in reaction to the community's needs but in service of maintaining white privilege and acquiescing to white fragility (DiAngelo, 2018). Care is not fully considered under such circumstances. Tronto has argued that care and democracy exist in a symbiotic relationship, each needing the other. Accordingly, while democracies must address how caring responsibilities are assigned, care practices must be carried out democratically (Tronto, 2013: 29). Democracy's need for care partly ensures that government policy and procedures are responsive to collective needs. Perhaps the image of the 45th U.S. president throwing paper towels at victims of a deadly hurricane is an extreme example of unresponsive care, an action demonstrating a lack of sensitivity to the needs of devastated people (Nakamura and Parker, 2018).

Malatino describes the theory and practice of responsive care as "an infrapolitical ethics of care" (2019: 131). Recognizing the fundamentally political nature of care in the power and privilege of care systems and practices that help some people more than others, Malatino focuses on the experience of care in the trans community. For Malatino, care engages in the vital work of repair for those who experience "profound recalibrations of subjectivity and dependency" (2020b: 3). This approach is congruent with the definition of care offered by Tronto and Fisher. However, Malatino challenges presumptions of heteronormative gender dimorphism by attuning the needed care to the circumstances of the marginalized trans community. They theorize that for those undergoing profound and sometimes reviled identity shifts, one responsive action of a caregiver might be to "witness, hold space for, and, when appropriate, amplify and intensify their anger, especially if this amplification serves the greater purpose of keeping one another alive" (2019: 131). Supporting anger is not a common understanding of caring action, particularly for those whose identity and subjectivity are not problematized in society. However, caring actions are improvisation responses to the needs of another. Responsive action demonstrates another way that care theory is unlike traditional ethical systems.

Underdeveloped elements of what is described as good care can result in poor or ineffective care. Estelle Ferrarese characterizes bad care as "care that responds to a request that was not made, or was but in different term … a misinterpretation of another's needs, an inapt adjustment or an insincere concern" (2018: 97). Ferrarese's description can be interpreted as a weakness in the humble inquiry, inclusive connection, and responsive elements of good care. But, of course, care seldom manifests in a simple binary of presence or absence. Instead, iterations of care can be fine-tuned for impact and effectiveness as they aim toward the growth and flourishing of others, whether individually or collectively. Inquiry, connection, and action represent micro-practices of care that reveal human agency. As embodied beings, we can engage in these activities, habituate them, and improve them individually and collectively as a society.

## Participating in Good Care

If care allows humanity to move forward together, it should be at the heart of morality. As defined by humble inquiry, inclusive connection, and responsive action, good care represents the ongoing process of living a moral life. This moral life is not static; it is centered on relational striving to do better, to be better at caring for one another.

The elements of good care described in this chapter characterize a feminist relational heuristic—an open-ended guide to the process of caring well. "Heuristics" are employed in various ways and are sometimes considered "shortcuts." Accordingly, heuristics can be reductive, as witnessed by my critique of traditional ethical systems of adjudication that can be game-like in their procedural emphasis. Moreover, some have criticized heuristic thinking as sacrificing existential complexity for the allure of clarity and security

Good Care **43**

(Nguyen, 2021). However, others have suggested that heuristics can offer relational (Stainton and Papoulias, 1985), playful, and feminist (Kimura, 2012) approaches that spur imaginative methods for addressing human complexity. In the latter spirit, the heuristic of good care is suggested as particularly fitting given the process nature of caring. Of course, the people of Gander, like most people who provide good care, did not apply a heuristic in 2001. Instead, they had established caring habits and participated in a spirit of care to respond to the challenge of human needs. Nevertheless, in elevating care discourse in society and valuing care processes and practices, an open-ended heuristic of care can be a valuable tool for reflective and imaginative consideration.

If care theory describes a process morality or *ethic*, then it has significant implications for normativity—the standards of morality. We are used to fixed moral norms: "What is the right thing to do?" However, care methods and practices suggest a different path to understanding moral normativity. The next chapter addresses how care theory shifts the framing of ethical norms.

## Notes

1 Although the circumstances were rather chaotic, the closing of borders to US borders to international flights forced neighbor countries to accept the perceived terrorist risk that the United States was unwilling to undertake. If there were a threat of further terrorism, were these other countries better equipped to contain it? It might be argued that the United States foisted its ethical responsibility upon its neighbors. Did the US leadership exhibit care for the countries it borders?

2 A representative sampling, but by no means a complete list of books that address the definition and character of care ethics: Brugère, 2021; Engster, 2007; Gilligan, 1982; Held, 2006; Kittay, 1999; Kittay, 2019a, 2019b; Mortari 2022b; Noddings, 1984, 2002a, 2010; Pettersen, 2008; Puig de la Bellacasa; Pulcini, 2009; Robinson, 1999, 2011; Sevenhuijsen, 1998; Slote 2007; Stake and Visse 2021; Thompson, 2023; Tronto, 1993, 2013.

3 Mad studies is an umbrella term for scholarship and social activism for those who identify as mentally ill, neurodivergent, and disabled. Employing crip theory analysis, the field resonates with but differentiates itself from disability studies.

4 Given the embodied nature of caring, there is much to be gained by care theorists in collaborating with dramaturgical scholars given the latter's intense focus on corporeality and emotion. Both character acting and improvisational acting entail embodied skills that are applicable to improving habits of care (Hamington, 2015, 2020).

5 I thank care scholar Maggie FitzGerald for pointing out that sometimes I refer to care ethics and other times care theory despite my expressed preference for the latter term. I think of care theory as the more encompassing term but that is not to say that it negates care ethics. Rather, one might picture a Venn diagram of concentric circles with the larger circle being labeled "care theory" and the smaller circle being "care ethics."

6 The epistemic idea that good care entails both generalized and concrete knowledge is based in part on the work of Seyla Benhabib. She argues that one of Carol Gilligan's contributions to moral theory is to suggest that traditional moral theory has focused on the "generalized other" to the detriment of considering the "concrete other." Similar to my argument about inquiry, Benhabib contends that both

**44** Thinking about Better Care

approaches are necessary: "From a meta-ethical and normative standpoint, I would argue, therefore, for the validity of a moral theory that allows us to recognize the dignity of the generalized other through an acknowledgment of the moral identity of the concrete other" (1987: 168–69).

7  Care scholar James McMaster appropriately challenged my use of the term "inclusive" here because it can imply a parochial and limited sense of joining, i.e., "inclusion into what?" With this concern in mind, I intend inclusion to suggest an openness or disponibility to humble inquiry and responsive action that earnestly endeavors to eschew colonial or paternalistic inclusion. The concept of disponibility is discussed further in Chapter 9.

8  I realize that invoking the term "natural" in philosophical circles is a fraught approach as it is difficult to separate socially constructed proclivities from innate ones. Furthermore, challenging socially constructed narratives of prejudice preoccupy a great deal of the work of care. Nevertheless, humans have an "innate disposition to care for others" (Engster, 2015: 227).

9  It may appear that I am not embracing empathy in the same way as Zaki, Krznaric, or Rifkin in that I have argued that empathy is a necessary but insufficient condition of care as it also entails inquiry and action. However, a careful reading of Zaki, Krznaric, and Rifkin reveals that they too offer an enlarged notion of empathy that includes other elements. For example, Krznaric suggests that the habits of highly empathic people include, "radical listening" and "sheer courage." Roman Krznaric, *Empathy*, 98. In my formulations of good care, radical listening is a form of inquiry and courage is needed to act on behalf of the one cared for. Thus, although these and other researchers address empathy and I focus on care, we are really addressing the same moral phenomenon with different emphases.

10  Although not a care ethicist per se, Bruno Latour's process and relational approach to understanding the complexity of human activity and society supports the notion that knowledge and connection can blossom into care (Flower and Hamington, 2022).

# 2

# CARE AND NORMATIVITY

### Prologue: Transforming Society's Moral Norms

Activist and community organizer Alicia Garza has worked to change society's norms and values her whole life. At 12, she fought for better sex education regarding birth control in her California middle school (Garza and Hayes, 2019). While attending college at the University of California, San Diego, Garza participated in campus efforts to raise the pay for the university's janitors. Later she organized the first Women of Color conference at the university. After college, Garza joined a grassroots organization called People Organized to Win Employment Rights (POWER). There, she engaged in community organizing to improve the lives of a Black community, Bayview Hunters Point in San Francisco (Garza, 2020: 58). The list of her activism is long. So, Garza was already an experienced organizer when she, together with Patrisse Cullors and Opal Tometi, formed the Black Lives Matter project in 2013, which shortly after became part of the Movement for Black Lives.

Garza honed her caring skills in a manner that resonates with the cycle of humble inquiry, inclusive connection, and responsive action through her early community organizing. During her time working for POWER, Garza engaged in personal exchanges with individuals and listened to their stories:

> I would spend my afternoons going from house to house, sitting with folks at a kitchen table or leaning on a porch, talking with a resident as they peered through a thick screen door at me. I would run through a set of questions designed to get to know them better and learn more about what they cared about.
>
> *(Ibid: 61)*

DOI: 10.4324/9781003368625-4

**46** Thinking about Better Care

Garza describes replicating these neighborhood encounters hundreds of times. She demonstrated care through listening and learning, leveraging individual interactions into a movement of social and political care.

Accordingly, relationality permeates Garza's philosophy and methodology of organizing. For Garza, working to change social norms and practices is not a compartmentalized activity:

> For me, organizing is as much about human connection and building relationships as it is about achieving a political goal. The work feeds me. It's embedded in who I am. But the idea of building relationships with our neighbors and others in order to accomplish things in the world is embedded in all of our lives: It's part of all the things we do every day to survive, to feed ourselves, to express ourselves, to restore ourselves. Humans are social creatures; connection is at the core of who we are. And organizing is connecting with a purpose. When we connect to others, we learn about them and about ourselves. And that understanding is the beginning of real political change.
>
> *(Ibid: 47–48)*

Without employing the technical language of feminist philosophy, Garza has expressed care's personal, political, ontological, and relational nature. Furthermore, she endeavors to inspire a caring ethos in the movements she has helped to create.

Garza, Cullors, and Tometi articulate care at the heart of the Black Lives Matter organization. In particular, the inclusivity of care is evident in the stated goals of the movement:

> **We are expansive**. We are a collective of liberators who believe in an inclusive and spacious movement. We also believe that in order to win and bring as many people with us along the way, we must move beyond the narrow nationalism that is all too prevalent in Black communities. We must ensure we are building a movement that brings all of us to the front.
>
> **We affirm the lives** of Black queer and trans folks, disabled folks, undocumented folks, folks with records, women, and all Black lives along the gender spectrum. Our network centers those who have been marginalized within Black liberation movements.
>
> **We are working** for a world where Black lives are no longer systematically targeted for demise.
>
> **We affirm our humanity**, our contributions to this society, and our resilience in the face of deadly oppression.
>
> *(Black Lives Matter)*

This care mission extends to the methods and organization of Black Lives Matter. Garza describes building solidarity in the movement through listening, asking questions, and being there for one another (2020: 157). The organization is also intentionally decentralized, which Garza characterizes as "leader-full" to not create a movement around the cult of personality. Finally, the Black Lives Matter movement consciously values care as an internal and external value. Garza claims the best way to care for ourselves is "to connect with each other in ways that propel all of us toward care for ourselves and one another" (Ibid: 288).

The founders of the Black Lives Matter organized differently than many recent civil rights movements. Rather than religion or an iconic figure at the center, it places fundamental norms of human existence at its core. Political theorist Deva R. Woodly also finds the Movement for Black Lives striking a tone that signals a shift in political organizing and thinking. This approach draws from the history of civil rights resistance efforts but manifests differently. Woodly describes this novel approach as "radical Black feminist pragmatism." In a compelling argument, Woodly views the care found in radical Black feminist pragmatism as both an embodied and a political value that offers answers to today's challenges in a manner that liberalism and socialism cannot. She claims care is the "backbone of the political philosophy of radical Black feminist pragmatism" and a radical departure from the political norm (2021: 125). Specifically, she offers three observations about what makes this caring approach novel. First, because it begins with contextual particularity and experience, "this inductive approach puts the question of what people's lives are actually like at the center of conceptualizing political problems" (Ibid: 126). Second, narratives of fairness take a back seat to "the view that because people matter, they are entitled to care, and, as such, care must be the main subject of governance" (Ibid). Finally, humanity's physical, embodied nature must remain at the forefront of political thinking, including "adequate income, housing, food, and education, but also to exceed these material items and include psychological health and well-being" (Ibid). For Woodly, the Black Lives Matter movement signals a shift in social and political thinking to one rooted in care.

The simple tweet, "Black Lives Matter," that Garza sent out in 2013 amidst the brutal violence perpetrated against Black men is a clarion call for altering social norms. Black lives have not mattered throughout much of US history. Changing rules and rights to foster greater care and justice is essential yet unlikely adequate to bring about the broader and deeper norms of care that can sustain social change. Garza views her movement as entailing a social shift toward higher norms of caring for one another. These new norms emerged from previously ignored needs of the people—particularly the oppressed.

This chapter interrogates aspects of care as a moral norm. First, there is a brief review of the nature of moral norms, followed by introducing "emergent normativity" as a concept best suited to address how care operates as a standard or guide for ethical action. Next, a discussion of seeking the good versus seeking the right is offered. Pursuing the good leads to discussing care as a process morality that is more skill-based and methodological than adjudicative. Because care is a responsive process, need is addressed as the motivation for

**48** Thinking about Better Care

caring. Given all the harm historically justified in the name of care, colonialism, and paternalism are engaged. Finally, the contested notion of self-care is discussed. The many topics in this chapter reflect the multiple aspects of care normativity.

## Moral Norms

The *Oxford Encyclopedia of Philosophy* describes a norm as a standard of behavior, the violation of which results in some form of censure (Blackburn, 1994: 265). Although ethics and aesthetics can be categorized as value theory (e.g., how do we come to value some things over others?), adjudication and the assessment of normativity have dominated contemporary ethical theorizing. James Fieser describes normative ethics as "arriving at moral standards that regulate right and wrong conduct. In a sense, it is a search for an ideal litmus test of proper behavior" (2015). Norms are our moral expectations for ourselves and others (Nistelrooij and Visse, 2019). The suggestion is that care has significant normative aspects, although not in the manner that ethical responsibilities and expectations are traditionally framed. Care normativity blurs the distinction between is and ought in a co-created, relational manner.[1] Accordingly, accounts of normativity in care theory cannot be abstracted from contextual or relational reality.

Standard conceptions of normativity are primarily *a priori*. Accordingly, people often want to know the "right" thing to do, but the basis for determining the answer is abstracted from the situation or with the barest details of the context. When principles or a rubric of morality guide our ethics, such as "always act to create the greatest happiness for the greatest number of people," the engendering of normative response to a specific experience is eschewed or placed in the background in favor of this abstract structure. In other words, the experience must fit into the structure of moral assessment rather than the experience shaping the normative analysis. Such morality assumes that the agents and circumstances are interchangeable (Benhabib, 1992). For example, in a Kantian principle-based approach, the standard of "one should never lie" ostensibly is applied in all situations. Such rule-based systems often become legalistic, sometimes including certain exemptions or contentions that, under some circumstances, negate the demand. In this sense, rule-based approaches have a normativity that focuses on actions taken. Still, even then, some situations can negate the rule, for exceptions are limited and generalized such that they are to be made known before subsequent events (i.e., thou shalt not kill, *except* in war or self-defense). Accordingly, because the morality proposed is offered as objective, the rubrics of normativity should be objective.

A consequentialist approach is more responsive to experience, given the effort to maximize positive future experiences from the standpoint of a particular context. Indeed, consequentialism, virtue theory, and rule-based ethics

Care and Normativity  **49**

share some resonances with care approaches. For example, feminist philosopher Julia Driver substantially defends "sophisticated consequentialism" as addressing some contextual partialism that characterizes care ethics (2005). Still, a consequentialist approach assumes an *a priori* utility calculation that is not always possible (i.e., can we know that dropping an atomic bomb on Hiroshima and Nagasaki prevented more harm than not doing so?). As Virginia Held claimed in her early work on care:

> Utilitarians suppose that one highly abstract principle, the Principle of Utility, can be applied to every moral problem no matter what the context. A genuinely universal or gender-neutral moral theory would be one that would take account of the experience and concerns of women as fully as it would take account of the experience and concerns of men. When we focus on women's experience of moral problems, however, we find that they are especially concerned with actual relationships between embodied persons and with what these relationships seem to require.
>
> *(1990: 330)*

For care theory, particularity translates to intersectional individuality and identity such that knowers are not interchangeable even in a particular context. Nevertheless, our fundamental relationality ensures that we are never entirely incomprehensible to one another. As previously suggested, care is messy and challenging, requiring the hard work of inquiry, connection, and responsiveness.

Analytic philosophers often support the paradigm of *a priori* norms partly through concerns over relativism. Perhaps one of the strongest epithets in philosophy, the claim of "relativism" signals that there is no systematic ethics, nor can there be because morality becomes perspectival. In particular, subjectivism is of the most significant concern. Can anyone simply claim whatever they are doing is moral? Claims of relativism or subjectivity are frequently bipolar, suggesting that anything less than objective moral truth is considered a slippery slope to "anything goes." The emergent norm of care described here is neither objective truth delineated before experience nor is it simply a claim anyone can make about characterizing any activity as care (particularly given the heuristic of good care—humble inquiry, inclusive connection, and responsive action). Thus, *emergent normativity* occupies the interstitial space between the alternatives of a fixed objective moral structure and a relativistic complete lack of structure.[2] Care is morally prescriptive while still being contextually based. The emergent norms of good care are behavioral—humble inquiry, inclusive connection, and responsive action—rather than rule or outcome-based.

Explicit treatments of normativity in the care ethics literature are inconsistent at best. In many ways, care theorists have taken a pragmatist approach to normativity. They have correctly chosen to dwell more on what works in the

**50** Thinking about Better Care

world rather than taking a position on objective moral truth and its adjudication. Yet, normativity has always been in the background if not explicitly discussed. For example, Carol Gilligan's founding work on care ethics was motivated by Lawrence Kohlberg's early assessment of women and girls' "inadequate" ability to make moral decisions (Gilligan, 1982: 18). Gilligan does not address issues of normativity. Instead, she identifies a different imaginative position (the "different voice" of care) pervasive among, but not exclusive to, women based on developmental experiences. Accordingly, the different imaginative position of women motivates a caring normative assessment (Ibid: 62–63).

Implicit normative language found expression in personal and political theorizing of care. In her groundbreaking work on the politics of care, Joan Tronto defined care as a disposition and a practice (1993: 104) while situating it in the long tradition of contextual ethics that challenge universalistic morality (Ibid: 27–28). Tronto does not directly address normativity but indicates that as a contextual morality, care maintains that "more is necessary to describe morality than the delineation of moral rules and the requirement that humans will use their reason to understand and apply these moral rules" (Ibid: 28). Although Tronto emphasizes the extra-rational aspect of care, in one of the most explicit treatments of care normativity, Michael Slote indicates that the moral sentimentalism of care has a norming component. He denies that "moral claims or judgments *are* normative" as a matter of "rational force or authority" (2007: 107). Instead, Slote contends that moral approval and disapproval are "affective states" (2020: 7). For Slote, "Empathy and concern for others are built into the meaning of terms like *right* and *wrong* (and also *just* and *unjust*)—they are part of how the reference of such terms is conventionally, semantically, fixed" (Ibid: 106). Slote's concern is how care can make conventional assessments of right and wrong. Noddings' responsive conception of care points to a more liminal sense of normativity drawn from inquiry into circumstances.

### Emergent Normativity

Normativity is a bedrock concept of Western philosophy.[3] The central concern for moral normativity, "What is the right thing to do?" is a common-sense question and the source of endless theorizing. In what follows, I suggest that care theory approaches normativity with a trajectory or disposition rather than prescribed action. Thus, care alters the concept of normativity that is typically employed. For care, as theorized by Noddings and others, specific activities or responses only emerge out of the context, relationship, and knowledge of the individuals involved. Thus, a caring character guides these actions in a non-predetermined manner.

Still, so much contemporary moral thinking hinges on a preordained notion of right and wrong that is disengaged from the particulars of human experience, given concerns regarding partiality and bias. I introduce the idea that care has an "emergent normativity" because the best moral action must respond to the context. A notion of emergent normativity is a radical departure that further supports the idea that care theory is not merely an alternative form of ethics but represents a paradigm shift in conceptualizing the nature of morality. In forming the Black Lives Matter movement, Garza did not attempt to employ a universal structure of moral rules but instead responded to the needs of communities on the ground. Caring norms are grounded in ethical commitments but as norms of action that emerge from the situation.

I propose that within a care approach, normativity—what one ought to do—emerges or unfolds as knowledge of the other and their context increases. Accordingly, care has an emergent normativity. "Emergent" is appropriate for characterizing care as a process morality. Ends and means, methods, and goals are interlaced. Good or effective care involves practices of humble inquiry, inclusive connection, and responsive action—all in a continual dynamic that, if attended to, can help us care better. Garza's activism and community organizing do not start with the answers but develop direction and action after being immersed in and understanding the community. Accordingly, norms don't lord over experience but are clarified and sharpened by experience. Care is the categorical imperative, but particular norms of moral behavior are entangled with life and thus emerge from context.

This notion of emergent normativity is consistent with philosopher Seisuke Hayakawa's temporal understanding of moral agency. Dissatisfied with standard accounts of agency as static, Hayakawa argues for a process-oriented description of agency:

> In our temporally extended lives, empathic receptivity is not only associated with an event at a single moment but also with a dynamic process unfolding over time. In my view, such diachronic receptivity helps us to deepen our understanding of others' perspectives, and in so doing, to reflectively examine our own ways of thinking and acting from different angles that we have not previously recognized.
>
> Given that our agency unfolds temporally, practical rationality appears to be partly a matter of how we can develop our reflective capacity conducive to continuous learning from others.
>
> *(2016: 235)*

Seisuke grounds agency in the complexity of the human condition rather than as an abstract universal. This complexity includes epistemic and temporal considerations as we grow and learn. Similarly, a caring normative response is not an *a priori* decision or calculation but rather the result of a relational process that includes reflecting and learning.

**52** Thinking about Better Care

Care is a process of discovery often described by geographic metaphors. For example, the teacher and student enter a rich educational journey with a sense of direction and purpose. Despite the teacher's planned curriculum, the routes they take together may vary, and what they learn and do along the way cannot be entirely known in advance. Noddings claims, "Caring teachers listen and respond differentially to their students" (2005: 19). Learning will take place, but the character of that learning cannot be entirely predefined. Similarly, the caregiver knows that they will be responsive but does not know what particular moral action will be warranted until they check out the particulars. They must be willing to enter the journey together before knowing the precise destination.

This responsive caring relationship has a postmodern element to it. Our language often has categorical limits, so when I write the "caregiver" and the "one receiving care," it appears single-directional. However, we know that is not the case given, for example, the broad approaches to reciprocity discussed among care theorists (Sander-Staudt, n.d.). How often have teachers expressed the idea that teaching is the best way to learn about a subject? How many times have teachers learned from students in profound ways? The responsive relationship is also a reciprocal one. Caregivers can also receive a great deal, growing and flourishing along with the one receiving care. As Noddings has described, the caring relationship can be marked by great joy and satisfaction for those involved. Teachers can initiate something akin to a "care spiral." If, instead of leveraging positional power to make learning a hierarchical transaction, teachers authentically listen to students, adapting to their needs, students often respond by taking an interest in the curriculum and returning the care and concern to the instructor. Again, if the teacher–student relationship is our model for other relationships, caring relationships benefit the one caring in sometimes-unexpected ways. Emergent normativity may compel those receiving care to respond in kind as part of a caring spiral.

Emergent normativity may take more work on the part of the ethical agent than traditional normative approaches, but it also has some distinctive advantages. Normative thinking within traditional frameworks has the potential for "gaming" because morality is structured as a problem to be solved with the right rule or the correct formulation of outcomes (Hamington, 2009a, 2015). Although principle-based and outcome-based ethical approaches are ostensibly the result of objective and abstract moral analyses, they are fraught with human bias and partiality that influence the choice of rules and language in the application. Adjudication can become a game of applying rules, loopholes, and formulas. For example, witness the ethical machinations invoked to justify the US involvement in the Gulf Wars. Given the complexity and high stakes involved, the metaphor of ethics-as-game falls short; life is simply not a game, because of the complexity and high stakes involved.

Noddings has described caring as non-formulaic in its application (1984: 46–47). Care theory reframes morality. It mitigates the calculating and legalistic approach and the accompanying game-playing that can occur. Thus, morality includes a continuum of relational discovery that is authentically focused on the well-being of the other rather than determining an objective right or wrong response. As Noddings is fond of noting, care is a moral ideal, and thus, humans will invariably fall short. Certainly, caregivers can have biases and make terrible mistakes. Still, they should continually check the integrity of their actions with the growth and flourishing of the other—learning and acting in the process. Caring norms are emergent and changeable, but good care—based on humble inquiry, inclusive connection, and responsive action—is the guiding light.

## Pursuit of the Good

> The ultimate moral good can be found in relationships marked by love and care. These are good in themselves, good for participants and good for society.
>
> —Jonathan Herring (2021: 98)

Although care norms may be emergent rather than static, they exist. These emergent care norms are not aimed at fixed ethical standards but move toward a moral good: care. For example, Luigina Mortari describes the entanglement of care, ontology, and the pursuit of the good,

> Care is ontologically essential; it protects life and helps make existence possible. Good care keeps one's being steeped in goodness, and it is this goodness that gives shape to the generative basis of our being and that structures the layer of being, keeping us securely among things and among others. Practicing care is therefore putting ourselves in touch with the heart of life.
>
> *(2021: 145–146)*

One of the tensions in moral philosophy is whether ethics is directed toward "the good" or "the right." Good is often juxtaposed with evil, and right is set against wrong. This distinction may be another false dichotomy, but in the Western tradition of philosophy, ethics has been emphasized in the pursuit of the right as associated with a deontological or rule-based morality. A conflation of legality with morality as well as divine command theory, which ascribes morality to a god's will in legalistic versions of Christianity as manifested in biblical authority, has served to propel "doing what is right" as the goal of ethics in the popular imaginary (see Chapter 7). However, pursuing the good is not without its challenges, as this approach is often associated with a utilitarian form of consequentialism. Although maximizing the good, as in utilitarianism, is a reasonable moral approach, it can become distorted by an "ends justifies the means" rationale, which sometimes supports atrocious and uncaring behavior as moral, including war and violence.

**54** Thinking about Better Care

Given the complexity and variation in humanity, there is no one way or right way to care. Still, there are suitable methods to increase the well-being of self and others: humble inquiry, inclusive connection, and responsive action.

## A Process Morality

The previous discussion addressed care as "a pursuit" of the good. The emphasis is on the journey and the means rather than the ends. I claim that care theory represents a process morality whereby one seeks to improve care through iterative mind-body habits of humble inquiry, inclusive connection, and responsive actions. Care's process nature does not suggest that care is without normative implications (as this book's invitation/provocation section explores). However, within good care, means and ends are intertwined. As philosopher Estelle Ferrarese describes, care activities "generate the sensitivity they require: concern for others arises from the practical activity of caring for their needs" (2021: 79). Just as Garza spent time with communities in Oakland to understand and connect prior to organizing a personal and political response, care is a process (perhaps better stated in the plural, processes) rather than just an endpoint and thus requires the hard work of presence and time. Process theory has historically focused on metaphysics and ontology rather than morality. Similarly, the care ethics literature implies care as courses of action and practices without explicitly naming it a "process morality."

In process theology, the metaphysical premise is no god is omnipotent, omnibenevolent, and all-knowing but rather a being in process: learning and growing (Cobb and Ray, 1953, 1976). Similarly, process philosophy is steeped in the metaphysics of the universe's dynamism. Accordingly, all beings are becoming rather than static; our philosophy must match this reality (Seibt, 2022). In modern Western philosophy, process thinking traces to the work of Alfred North Whitehead, who in turn acknowledges a process tradition, including Heraclitus, Gottfried Wilhelm Leibniz, Henri Bergson, C. S. Peirce, and William James, among others (Rescher, 2000: 4). Process philosophy offers an alternative to dominant forms of metaphysics that emphasize static and discrete enduring objects. Nicholas Rescher provides a five-fold description of the fundamental propositions of process philosophy:

1. Time and change are among the principal categories of metaphysical understanding.
2. Process is a principal category of ontological description.
3. Processes are more fundamental, or at any rate not less fundamental, than things for the purposes of ontological theory.
4. Several, if not all, of the major elements of the ontological repertoire (God, Nature as a whole, persons, material substances) are best understood in process terms.

## Care and Normativity   55

5.  Contingency, emergence, novelty, and creativity are among the fundamental categories of metaphysical understanding (Ibid: 5–6).

Note the compatibility of process thinking with relational care thinking. Relationships are thoroughly dynamic. The individuals involved are growing and changing, and sustained relationships adapt to those changes. Caring relationships forefront attentiveness, empathy, and responsiveness.

Although care ethics has not been described as a process ethic in the care literature, a few scholars have recognized the resonance between feminist theory and process thinking. In particular, several feminist scholars of religion find process theory conducive to a relational worldview. Theologian Carol P. Christ notes,

> Process philosophy asserts that feeling, sympathy, relationship, creativity, freedom, and enjoyment are the fundamental threads that unite all beings in the universe … In process philosophy, all beings are connected in the web of life. Process philosophy makes no absolute distinctions between human and other forms of life … For process philosophy, the whole universe is alive and changing, continually co-creating new possibilities of life.
>
> *(2006: 292–293)*

Accordingly, the universe is dynamic and inherently relational as all beings participate in a co-created experience. Note Christ's use of an emotional connection and idea consistent with care theory, particularly regarding empathy. Thus, process philosophy appears well suited for care theory. For example, Nancy B. Howell argues that a Whiteheadian process philosophy can help construct a feminist theory of relationality (1988). However, Howell recognized that feminist thought includes an embedded critique of power dynamics (particularly identity-based privilege) absent in Whitehead. Neither Christ nor Howell employs the language of care, but their work supports how we have been framing care as a process morality. Just as our world is in process, so is our morality.

As philosopher Maggie FitzGerald describes, "Care can never be finished, it can only be engaged in over and over again to the best of our abilities and revised when necessary" (2022: 205). Fitzgerald captures the iterative nature of care. One is not generally labeled as "caring" over a single act of kindness, as we can name plenty of people with patterns of uncaring behavior who occasionally respond meaningfully to others. As with any embodied activity, caring can be improved through practice and reflection if we value care in our lives. A care ethic is a process morality in our lives, describing how we approach others. We respond to the needs of others using the methods of good care.

## 56 Thinking about Better Care

### Need as an Impetus for Care

> Obligations, whether unconditional or relative, eternal or changing, direct or indirect with regard to human affairs, all stem, without exception, from the vital needs of the human being.
>
> —Simone Weil (2002: 6)

As Weil suggests, arguably all morality stems from human needs. However, some philosophers would not agree, particularly given the lack of precision that the term "need" entails (Brock and Miller, 2019: 2). A need is a condition that must be met if a person is not to suffer (Ibid: 19). The care of others comes into play because many needs cannot be fulfilled without the assistance of other people. One of the agreed-upon qualities of care ethics is that good care requires responsiveness. That is to say, responsiveness to another person's needs. Within the cycle of what I describe as effective care, inquiry-connection-action, the process involves identifying, understanding, and responding to another's needs.

To care is to meet someone's needs (including our own needs in self-care). Of course, not all needs are as urgent as others. Moreover, there is a distinction between "needs" and "wants," but these distinctions are not always clear. For example, philosopher Peg Tittle offers a tongue-in-cheek quip that suggests that the need/want division is anything but obvious:

> And here we get to the infamous "needs/wants" distinction. Many people call a "need" what is really a "want." For example, contrary to popular opinion, one doesn't need sex. Of course, the crucial question is, "Need for what?" My answer is pretty basic – "for survival": if you can live without it, you don't really need it, you just want it.
>
> *(2000)*

Caring is about meeting someone else's needs and perhaps some of their wants as well. Implicitly, care ethics has always been about meeting needs. In her 1984 groundbreaking work, *Caring*, Noddings describes, "When we care, we consider the other's point of view, his objective needs, and what he expects of us" (1984: 24). The notion of meeting needs seems indispensable to an ethic of care. Still, Sarah Clark Miller provides the first comprehensive exploration of the linkage in *The Ethics of Need: Agency, Dignity, and Obligation* (2012).

Miller develops an ethics of need to redress a historical failure of philosophy to address human needs in a nuanced manner. Accordingly, Miller delineates a variety of distinctions among needs. Significantly, some needs are fundamental and trigger what Miller describes as a duty to care (Ibid: 5–9). She brings a Kantian approach to care ethics that applies Kant's appeal to reason. Miller argues that in light of human finitude and fundamental interdependence and because "rational beings, as rational, will their own continued existence, that finite rational beings must help one another in cases of need as they practice the duty to care" (Ibid: 55). Miller offers six features of a duty to care, including multiple manifestations of caring rather than one prescribed approach, practical love that allows for a variety of feelings rather than a singular high standard of familial love, balancing self-sacrifice with the commitment to others, a demand for action rather than mere sentiment, eschewing paternalistic forms of care, and an acknowledgment of human finitude in the reality of multiple and competing needs (Ibid: 63–64). With some differences, Miller's features of a duty to care resonate strongly with what I offer as the characteristics of a commitment to care in the next chapter. We return to her illuminating analysis there.

Although need is often the impetus for care, as it should be, there is the danger of framing care as only responsive when there is an expressed need. However, care can also be proactive or anticipatory. Such anticipation is a tricky and nuanced understanding of the temporality of care because we cannot overly plan for caring. Time must be allowed for responding to the other in dialogue. As Estelle Ferrarese describes, "Caring for others ... if it is to be caring, presupposes an attention to the needs, expressed or silent, of that person there, in their uniqueness" (2021: 17). Excessive anticipatory care of a particular sort bypasses that attention. Relatedly, Noddings discusses the distinction between "assumed" and "expressed need." Care is likely warranted when there is an expressed need (i.e., I need shelter, I need asylum from violence, I need refuge from domestic abuse). However, sometimes we assume the needs of others in anticipation of their needs, such as developing an education curriculum, a workout regimen, or a course of therapy for someone. Such practices demonstrate good organization for care. However, too much planning can foment passive responsiveness—waiting for the expressed need to become so great as to be destructive. For example, for too long Western medicine has emphasized cure over care. Accordingly, we have developed systems for helping people once they are in a health crisis. Yet a better form of anticipatory care might include consulting with individuals regarding lifestyle medicine that encourages healthy eating, exercise, and mental exercises, which can mitigate or avert the need for crisis interventions.

Similarly, someone might extend a friendly or caring action to you even when an explicit need is not expressed or perceived. These, too, can be care. But conversely, overly anticipatory preemptive care can result in unjustified paternalism. Indeed, paternalism is so significant to care theory that it warrants its own discussion.

## Care, Colonialism, and Paternalism

There is a dark side to the invocation of care in history. Power differentials have created opportunities for care to be utilized as a source of abuse and oppression. Settler colonial actions "for the good" of indigenous people are tragic examples of the abuse of power under the guise of care. Philosopher Uma Narayan

**58** Thinking about Better Care

describes how the discourse of care historically provided a moral cover for the economic interests of colonial oppression: "Justifications for colonialism and slavery in terms of crude self-interest alone seem to have been rare. These enterprises were made morally palatable by the rhetoric of responsibility and care for enslaved and colonized Others" (1995: 134). This so-called care was not a responsive action intended to promote the growth and well-being of the cared for but rather a gross form of paternalism motivated by unacknowledged self-interest. However, even if the aim was genuine care, disposition alone is not a testament to good care. The effort cannot be described as good care when actions contribute to harm. As Tronto describes regarding care theory: "Good intentions are no defense if the end result of one's intellectual work is to create forms of domination" (2020: 182). Such "care" fails the test of adequate humble inquiry, inclusive connection, and responsive action. Colonialism is a collective form of inappropriate paternalism.

The moral conditions of paternalism are an abiding topic in philosophy. Gerald Dworkin defines paternalism as "the interference with a person's liberty of action justified by reasons referring exclusively to the welfare, good, happiness, needs, interests or values of those being coerced" (1970: 120). The association of paternalism with coercion has given it a negative moral connotation. One of the challenges of paternalism is that paternalistic acts exist on a normative continuum, with some practices easily condoned, others summarily condemned, and a whole range of ethically disputable actions in between. No one ethically faults the paternalism of a parent grabbing a child against her will to prevent that child from running into a busy street. However, at the other end of the spectrum, acts of violence to prevent adults from practicing their religion witnessed in the history of colonialism are paternalistic actions easily criticized as morally reprehensible (as in the case of the well-documented activities of canonized California missionary Junipero Serra[4]). Moral philosophers have developed nuanced understandings of paternalism to address the broad range of moral gray areas. For example, "hard" versus "soft" paternalism hinges on the extent to which an individual knows and understands the harms they face (Dworkin, 2020). The topic of paternalism is complex and fraught, but the challenges do not warrant abdicating a fleshing out of the parameters of acceptable paternalism.

Among care theorists, paternalism receives significant attention because caregivers often hold power over those receiving care and are thus able to make decisions for them. Care inevitably entails paternalism from time to time. Eva Feder Kittay describes: "An ethics of care walks the line between the Scylla of paternalism or domination and the Charybdis of neglect" (2019b: 183).

In healthcare, informed consent for medical intervention can be complicated, and paternalism plays a role, given the healthcare providers' psychological, social status, and information advantage. In addition, the vulnerable who need care, including everyone at one time or another, are often treated paternalistically in their time of need. Just as a political history of colonization has tainted the notion of care as a moral motivation for some, so has the experience of paternalized individual care soured the notion of care for others.

Appropriately, feminist theorists have addressed the contested relationship between care and paternalism. Noddings, although recognizing the fundamental tensions between the two, contends that paternalism is acceptable in a caring relationship when it is tempered by "attentive love," which she contrasts with "self-righteous love:" "attentive love listens, it is moved, it responds, and it monitors its action in light of the response of the cared for" (2002a: 136–37). Noddings' claim—listening, being moved, and responding—corresponds to what I have described as effective care: humble inquiry, empathetic connection, and responsive action. In other words, an earnest effort at good care leaves open the possibility for paternalism, not as an authoritarian or colonial paternalism but within a responsive relationship. Sarah Clark Miller points out that paternal actions may become necessary under certain circumstances because people can be in error regarding what they need: "They can either believe they need things that they actually do not, or conversely, believe that they have no need for something that they actually do need. Thus, individuals cannot always be self-determining what regard to their own needs" (2012: 66). However, Clark couches this claim that being cared for should not entail the loss of agency. Once again, the strict dichotomy of actions being framed as paternalism or not paternalism is inadequate to the reality of complex circumstances and the liminal potential of care.

Furthermore, paternalism is a significant consideration for a political approach to care because it addresses the circumstances under which a government can require actions in the name of care. Political philosopher Marion Smiley suggests that traditional applications of paternalism assume an individualistic and context-independent understanding. Such a worldview removes individuals involved from the reality of the web of relationships within which we all exist. Accordingly, Smiley finds a flattened conception of "paternalism" that reinforces libertarian ideals by emphasizing personal choice (2020: 99). Moreover, highlighting an internal locus of control allows those with privilege to alienate those in need by blaming them for their lot rather than acknowledging the complexity of the human context (including how influential sheer luck is in individual human success (Frank, 2017)).

By contrast, Smiley argues it is only possible to see "paternalism" in a positive light if we require a sense of relationality as the state of our being. Caring or relational paternalism suggests a more significant connection among people than the paternalism at play in a world of libertarian individuals. Smiley advocates breaking free of the libertarian understanding by reframing state care in nonauthoritarian ways, emphasizing universal participation rather than paternal practices/policies that subordinate and stigmatize particular groups (2020: 112–13). For Smiley, compelling examples of caring state programs include

**60** Thinking about Better Care

social security, home mortgage support, consumer protection programs, and unemployment insurance (Ibid: 111). These infrastructure programs do not succumb to libertarian pronouncements of paternalism which mark some people as "incompetent." Another way of viewing Smiley's proposal for promoting the caring state is to reinvigorate discussions of the common good through care. The notion of the common good is significant in the latter part of this book when issues of the radical implications of care are taken up.

The issue of paternalistic morality becomes further amplified when considering social policies that are not universally supported. At what point can practices of the caring good be imposed on those who reject them? For example, many in the United States resisted seat belt laws in the 1970s and 1980s. One state official who proposed mandatory seat belt regulations received hate mail that compared him to Adolf Hitler. Resistance to seat belt laws even led to a challenge brought to the U.S. Supreme Court. Today, seat belt resistance has largely waned.

A similar concern about paternalism was raised during the Covid-19 worldwide pandemic with angry protests over mask and vaccination mandates. Do such acts of regulatory paternalism overstep their bounds? I suggest establishing a "reasonable caring person standard" as an ethical construct rather than deferring the issue to law or even popularity (hence democratic voting). Under such a standard, rather than avoid discussions of regulations needed for the public good, such issues would be addressed straightaway and with warranted complexity. A reasonable, caring person standard would entail an inclusive, deliberative, and democratic process and, as such, could not be invoked by an autocratic leader. Standards for its use would be established at a high threshold, including validated evidence such that its use would be for agreed-upon public safety issues of grave concern. Respect for individual freedom would not be trampled on, but its invocation will not always be popular. Given the Western world's terrible legacy of hiding abuse behind care language, the reasonable care standard requires many safeguards. This reasonable caring standard exemplifies how state-sponsored paternalism might be morally sanctioned in the name of care.

### Self-care

Paternalism can be described as disproportionate hubris exerted in the name of care. Yet, pure altruism is also problematic as a disproportionate other-directedness of care, mainly when such altruism connotes no care for the self. Historically, women in patriarchal heterosexual marriages were often asked to care selflessly for their husbands and families (Groenhout, 2003: 155–58). This altruistic expectation significantly diminished the lives of many women resulting in psychological harm and a loss of well-being. For Carol Gilligan, altruism is what patriarchy demands:

In the gendered universe of patriarchy, care is a *feminine* ethic, not a universal one. Caring is what good women do, and the people who care doing women's work. They are devoted to others, responsive to their needs, attentive to their voices. They are *selfless*.

*(2011: 19)*

One of the challenges for care theorists is to valorize that which has been historically degraded for being feminine and care, while not replicating women's oppression. In other words, lifting the values and practices without repeating the gender essentialist burdens. Subsequently, Gilligan affirms that caring does require "paying attention, seeing, listening, responding with respect," but she explicitly declares, "It is not selfless" (Ibid: 23).

Good care should not require pure altruism in its motive or practice because such a standard is unrealistic, nearly impossible to determine, and, as Gilligan suggests, potentially damaging for the caregiver. Instead, care is better understood as mixed-motive altruism or a weak form of altruism (Kraut, 2020). Accordingly, no neat binary between care/not care maps onto self-directed/other-directed behavior or self-interested/other-interested motives. The human experience requires a healthy balance for care work between caring for the self and caring for others. Here, I agree with philosopher Tove Pettersen's notion of mature care:

Mature care is considered to be a developed disposition; it is a mean between two vices. The excessive extreme can be comprehended as selflessness, the deficient selfishness ... Mature care is characterized by its intermediate position, it is the mean between too little and too much concern for others (or for oneself).

*(2008: 125)*

Pettersen's use of the term "maturity" is appropriate because balancing care for self and others is an acquired skill that, like all care skills, is not perfectible. Nevertheless, we can improve this balance through iterative experience and reflective practice. Significantly, despite the conventional moral bias favoring purity of intention, the moral quality of care is not tarnished by self-interest in care practices. Purity of interest is not a goal or standard of good care. If care ethics is enacted by need, then the caregiver's needs cannot override the needs of the cared for. The relationship requires a mutuality of interests, often intertwined. Raising the profile of care entails valuing and paying attention to self and others.

A topic related to self-care is self-sacrifice. The two concepts are in dynamic tension with one another but can coexist. In several publications, Inge van Nistelrooij has comprehensively interrogated the relationship between sacrifice and care. The selflessness of the caring women described above often demanded

**62** Thinking about Better Care

a high level of self-sacrifice. Care theorists, like Gilligan, have criticized the burden of sacrifice. Nistelrooij endeavors to find equilibrium. She argues that self-sacrifice is not anathema to caregiving. On the contrary, she claims that sacrifice is inherent to all moral theories and that sacrifice does not automatically imply oppression (2014: 520). A caring commitment is a commitment to take on some level of sacrifice for others. However, much like Pettersen's notion of mature care, proportionality plays a vital role, as sacrifice is not an unmitigated good. As Nistelrooij describes,

> Self-sacrifice is not intrinsically good, but nor is it to be rejected as mere stupidity or mere heroism. Self-sacrifice is and must remain ambiguous: we would rather not see it, but sometimes a sense of belonging, of relatedness, of mutuality, is worth and may even require self-sacrifice. It must have this purpose and may never be sought for its own sake.
>
> *(Ibid: 528)*

Although self-sacrifice can be bounded in individual acts chosen by the one caring, selflessness is a global term of altruism often considered morally praiseworthy.

Part of the historic drive to morally overvalue selflessness in moral theory might stem from the traditional individualized ontology of Western philosophy. Ethical behavior is primarily prized for its other-directedness, assuming individual agents. However, the social ontology of care theory reframes the self as always participating in relationships—we are all second persons. Thus, we are fundamentally both self and other (Hamington, 2020b). Melissa Silverman observes that a relational ontology finds selflessness is more like "self-fulness." She suggests that when we realize how much we need one another, reciprocity completes the circle of care (2012). Self-care is intimately tied to caring for others when we see ourselves as interconnected. Milton Mayeroff argues that self-care is a prerequisite for the habits of caring. He claims only the person "who understands and tries to satisfy [their] own needs for growth can properly understand appreciate growth in another; for I relate to other people in the same general way in which I relate to myself" (1971: 48). In other words, how can one care for others when they do not care for themselves?

Some theorists have warranted concerns that self-care does not necessarily lead to improved care for others (Myers, 2014: 23). They are correct. Sometimes self-care leads to a narcissistic and individualistic personal concern with limited regard for others (Thompson, 2023: 36). Tronto refers to the results of failed interpersonal connection as "privileged irresponsibility," which exists when social advantage creates a parochial care understanding (1993: 121). Self-care is valued by the wealthy and powerful, but their privilege and perceived lack of vulnerability make it easier not to recognize the need for self-care in others. Empathetic imagination and reflection are crucial to the inclusive connection necessary to move from caring for the self to caring for others. As in an aesthetic of care, the naming, valuing, and attending to care practices can strengthen the possibility that self-care leads to improved other-directed care. Still, it is by no means a foregone conclusion. Such a connection is the thoughtful effort needed in relational morality.

Unfortunately, the notion of self-care is often co-opted by the marketing of products purported to bring succor or fulfillment. Although some of these products provide a measure of care for the self, the category often includes luxury goods or experiences intended to appeal to a sense of desert. As Lenora E. Houseworth describes, "If you go by social media, it's easy to think self-care is simply a series of Instagram posts, candles, bubble baths, and yoga pants mainly accessible to well-off young people in expensive urban areas and the suburbs" (2021). She points out that self-care is an estimated $10 billion-a-year industry. However, self-care can also be a form of resistance against oppression, as witnessed, for example, by the work of the Black Panthers to care for a community under siege.

Relatedly, self-care is denigrated within a neoliberal paradigm emphasizing productivity and labor's instrumentality. Several liberatory theorists have recognized the radical nature of self-care. Audre Lorde, for example, claimed, "Caring for myself is not self-indulgence, it is self-preservation and that is an act of political warfare" (2017: 130). As always, when it comes to care, context matters. Self-care is imperative for oppressed people who don't have access to the time, resources, or treatment that accompanies privilege.

This brief foray into self-care is a bit of a diversion from the general discussion of care and normativity. However, considering the role of self-care is a reminder of complexity of care. The relational entanglements of this ethical approach mean that simple labels and value judgments are not in the offing. Committing to care entails doing the hard work of seeking the right balance between the needs of others and the needs of the self because each is enveloped in the other. Bringing attention to and valuing care for self and others means raising the norms of good care in society.

## Norms of Good Care

Alicia Garza is among many leading a charge to change the norms of society to care more about the previously uncared for. For Garza, this goal is achieved by a process of caring for oneself and those in the movement while advancing a more caring society. This change in norms is a revolutionary undertaking. A project engendered not by violently overthrowing a government (although some institutions may have to transform) but rather through changing the hearts and minds of citizens. The quest is not other-worldly utopian. On the contrary, the care revolution leverages the embodied care that we are capable of and puts care into practice on personal and political fronts.

**64** Thinking about Better Care

This revolution includes adjusting notions of moral responsibility from concerns about external mandates (norms of expectations for others) and internal agency (individual ethical standards) to co-created ones. Inge van Nistelrooij and Merel Visse, applying the work of French phenomenologist Jean-Luc Marion, observe that to be responsible is to respond.

> There is a 're-active' dimension to responsibility, that seems to make sense in caring practices: one becomes responsible for something or someone by receiving a 'call.' This call appears within a relational practice with someone who is in some kind of need for care.
>
> *(2019: 285)*

Nistelrooij and Visse emphasize that this moral reactivity cannot be disentangled from the caregiver's context. Like Garza, we can be the catalyst for advancing care norms, but it must be co-created through relationships.

Philosopher Tove Pettersen concurs that we collectively advance social norms. She dismisses the idea that a more caring society is a naïve desire, arguing, "If hope and vision for a better future do not exist, and if faith in the possibility to change ordinary lives is not present, a normative theory is certainly defective" (2011: 63). For Pettersen, morality is more than determining the rightness or wrongness of choices in ethical dilemmas. Consistent with the social transformation described in this book, she finds care to be a "mature normative ideal that can ultimately guide human interaction" (Ibid). However, care has a novel approach to normativity. A process morality engages the relational skills of humble inquiry, inclusive connection, and responsive action that take time[5] and reflection to develop. The norms of action emerge from context and needs.

The second section of this book explores some possibilities if norms of good care become more profound and widespread. However, before we get to those ethical provocations and invitations, a caring commitment is discussed in the next chapter as an enduring moral motivation, followed by reflecting on the power of a shared spirit or ethos of care in Chapter 4.

## Notes

1 The violation of the is/ought distinction is particularly egregious to analytic philosophers who apply logical form to the normative question (Pigden, 1988). In a technical logical sense, the distinction holds but once the human experience is interjected, the barrier seems less relevant (Greene, 2003).

2 As Michael Flower pointed out to me, many theorists are finding binary analytic notions of relativism untenable. For example, influential scholar Bruno Latour argues, "We must learn to find in relativism, or, better, in relationism, that is, in the establishment of networks of relations, the fragile help that will allow us to advance in the inquiry, feeling our way without going too far astray" (Latour, 2013: 95). Thus, the liminal space of care's contextuality I describe above is a place of

uncertainty, reflection, or as Latour describes, a "hiatus" rather than a space of either/or.

3 Normativity can also be a source of oppression when social expectations diminish individual agency and expression as in heteronormative social beliefs (Shotwell, 2012). The aim here, given the context of good care (humble inquiry, inclusive connection, and responsive action) is that advancing norms of care can be accomplished in helpful rather than oppressive ways.

4 Grzegorz Welizarowicz describes the self-proclaimed justification of Junipero Serra's actions against indigenous people: "The fugitives are to be taught a lesson because, despite previous instruction and punishments, they have not yet shown improvement.... Serra and his cadre served as spiritual and civil leaders, and ultimate judges; they assessed the Indian progress toward the ever elusive divine, civil, or individual (rational) norm" (2018: 271).

5 Although the process morality of good care can be slow, it does not preclude quick caring judgments, such as in an emergency like that experienced at Gander. However, even quick decisions are informed by iterations of skill and habit.

# 3

# A CATEGORICAL COMMITMENT TO CARE

### Prologue: Lifelong Inclusive Activism

The precious, intangible gems like happiness, satisfaction, self-respect, and pride—they are the thanks to the people who come into your life. Life is not what *you* alone make it. Life is the input of everyone who touched your life and every experience that entered it. We are all a part of one another.

—Yuri Kochiyama (2004: xxi)

The March 5, 1965, issue of *LIFE* magazine carried a story about the murder of Malcolm X that occurred two weeks prior (*LIFE* Magazine Staff Writers, 26–31). In a photograph depicting one of the chaotic moments following the assassination at the Audubon Ballroom in New York City, Malcolm X is lying on his back, and people are attempting to address the wounds in his chest. In the photo, a bespectacled Asian woman cradles Malcolm X's head. That woman was Yuri Kochiyama. She had been sitting in the audience, and in the frenzy following the gunshots, she ran on stage. Kochiyama saw that Malcolm X was having difficulty breathing, so she elevated his head, but it was to no avail (Fujino, 2005: 159). The moment was tragic and extraordinary, and Kochiyama had a history of caring activism that extended from her twenties until her death at age 93 in 2014.

Born Mary Yuri Nakahara in Los Angeles, a second-generation Japanese immigrant, or *Nisei*, she enjoyed a middle-class upbringing. Her social consciousness began to change with the advent of World War II. Kochiyama experienced forced removal from her home and incarceration with 110,000 other West Coast Japanese during the war (Fujino, 2009: 296). Her racial consciousness

DOI: 10.4324/9781003368625-5

A Categorical Commitment to Care **67**

further developed when she moved to New York and married Bill Kochiyama, whom she had met during incarceration at an Arkansas concentration camp.[1] She experienced class, gender, and racial injustice as the couple struggled to survive while raising six children. Kochiyama began inviting civil rights leaders to her home for weekly social gatherings. She met Malcolm X in 1963. Although she first rejected his critique of integration in favor of the more harmonious vision of Martin Luther King and the Civil Rights Movement, Kochiyama eventually found his politics of self-determination and autonomy compelling. After Malcolm X's assassination, she engaged in a whirlwind of activism across identity lines. Kochiyama brought a "culture of caring" to Black militancy (Fujino, 2009: 299) but also participated in actions on behalf of Japanese Americans and in the Puerto Rican independence movement (Fujino, 2005: 224–29). Kochiyama demonstrated a commitment to care through her openness, willingness to learn about the plights of others, and her emphasis on building relationships.

Asian American Studies scholar Diane Fujino describes Kochiyama's leadership as grounded in tireless relational action and presence. Rather than invoke her official hierarchical authority in activist organizations: "Her practice involved being an on-the-ground grassroots organizer who talked to people one-on-one, recruited through personal networks, and welcomed people into her home" (Fujino, 2009: 300). For Kochiyama, hospitality was crucial for providing interpersonal learning opportunities and the relationships necessary to sustain a movement. Fujino describes Kochiyama as masterful at humanizing the struggle and believing that "there's more that unites us than divides us" (Ibid: 303). Kochiyama's granddaughter, Akemi Kochiyama-Ladson, describes her grandmother taking her to a Hiroshima Day protest when she was six years old:

> I remember that the moment we got to the demonstration site, it seemed like she knew everyone: these people were her extended family. She was in her element, greeting, embracing, and introducing her colleagues to one another, all the while handing out leaflets to every person she encountered. Meanwhile, she quickly obtained a sign from someone and hung it around my neck. The sign was about as tall as I was, and twice as wide. It read "MEET HUMAN NEEDS."
>
> *(1994: 33)*

A commitment to care can manifest in different ways. Kochiyama's extraordinary life seems beyond what is attainable for most people. Yet, Kochiyama would likely describe her choices and actions in ordinary terms of caring for others rather than exceptional acts. When Kochiyama was 18 years old, long before she entered public life as an activist, she wrote a moral creed for herself. She prefaced the declaration by stating, "What type of person I was, am, or become, or whatever others think of me, I hope to live by this one creed that

**68** Thinking about Better Care

which, not I alone, but all others I have ever come in contact with, formulated for me. I say 'others' because I am only a part of all I have met" (2004: xxiv). Kochiyama demonstrates an implicit understanding of the relational ontology of care in her moral creed and through her encounters with others. The statement addresses respectful, humble relations with others that she describes as "my philosophy of life" (Ibid: xxv). Few people engage in an exercise of developing a moral vision for themselves, let alone at such a young age. This creed symbolized Kochiyama's commitment, manifested in a life of hospitable and caring yet forceful community activism. The statement was an instrument for Kochiyama to live what philosophers advocate regarding the examined life. Kochiyama put thought into developing the creed[2] and felt it was significant enough to reprint in her memoir. If she engaged the creed at various times, it may have acted as a touchstone for a moral reflection and a reminder of her commitment to care.

There is no morality in this world unless people enact it. Murder, slavery, and oppression can be deemed unethical, but the approbations are somewhat hollow unless people are willing to take action. It is one thing to identify what is morally good, and it is another thing to enact the pursuit of that good. A moral commitment provides the psychological impetus for taking action on behalf of care, not replacing it. Such was the case for Kochiyama's commitment to turning words into action.

In this chapter, I address the nature of a moral commitment to care. I then suggest that care is a categorical commitment—the foundation of our moral selves and an expression of our relational humanity. Our ethical commitments are contextual and have entanglements. If care is a process morality, then a commitment to care is an abiding investment in improving care personally and in society. Accordingly, I conclude the chapter by addressing the concomitants of care and the ideas that accompany a dedication to care. Specifically, I consider commitments to learning and truth, sympathetic and empathetic understanding, and acting on behalf of others. These associated commitments flesh out the overall commitment to care by clarifying the expectations of a trajectory toward meaningful care. They set the stage for the radical moral provocations and invitations in Section 2 of this book.

## Why a Moral Commitment?

There are many ways to frame the ethics of caring, such as a duty, obligation, or responsibility, so why describe it as a commitment? The short answer is that a commitment connotes a strong sense of personal will and a focus on moving forward to take actions that improve the world rather than looking back to assign moral blame. Accordingly, the obligation to care is less imposed from the outside upon the individual (which is not to say that one is not externally influenced). Instead, a commitment leans into caring as an exercise of will and autonomy. The idea of a commitment to care does not oppose a duty or responsibility to care. In fact, it shares many of the same elements. Often care theorists describe caring duties or responsibility with a notion of volition in mind that makes what they are addressing very similar to a commitment to care. And so, we first examine formulations of a duty to care and care responsibilities prior to returning to the idea of a commitment to care.

Philosopher Sarah Clark Miller develops a compelling case for a duty to care. She both employs and critiques a Kantian understanding of duty. In particular, she argues that a Kantian duty of beneficence is the foundation for a duty to care (2012: 48). Beneficence—good actions are distinguished from benevolence—well-meaning dispositions. Accordingly, the needs of others exert a normative force that obliges us to act on their behalf. Miller builds a deontological argument for care. She argues that the imposition of duty helps overcome the error of the naturalistic fallacy. Just because people *can* and *do* care does not necessarily mean they *ought* to care. Miller is concerned that care theorists have not provided sufficient moral argument to move from the "is" to the "ought."

Miller draws on the paradox of the present care crisis amidst such potential to care as a reason for seeking a moral obligation:

> The question is: Must I care? And if I must, why must I care? ... care ethicists build their project on a rather large assumption that humans will care for one another by responding to present needs. Still, human reactions of indifference to need are widespread. The level of willingness and ability to care for others inevitably differs from human to human. Care ethics would therefore be well-served to establish an obligation to care for one another, that is, a duty to care. If a person must care because it is his or her duty to do so, then care ethics, instead of beginning from the empirical observation some humans do care, can rest on the foundation of a universal obligation to care.
>
> *(Ibid: 50–51)*

Miller is meticulous in building an argument that includes recognition of the objections many care theorists might have to a Kantian approach. Ultimately, Miller's approach to a duty to care is so nuanced that its challenge to care theorists' skepticism of obligation is mild: "Principles are not meant to tell us exactly what to do in every situation. They are a guide of sorts ... " (Ibid: 70). This position is very similar to what I have described as the emergent normativity of care, where the circumstances dictate the caring actions. We might call this "the emergent duty to care." Miller wants us to understand that principles are at play, even if they are more like guides, and we are not always aware of them. There is an implication that rules are not enough to achieve robust morality. As previously described, care ethics is not opposed to rules, but moral rules are shortcuts, and good care requires that we do the hard work of inquiry, connection, and responsive action in each circumstance.

**70** Thinking about Better Care

Political theorist Daniel Engster also makes a rational appeal for a duty to care based on mutual vulnerabilities and moral consistency:

> *Since all human beings depend upon the care of others for our survival, development, and basic functioning and at least implicitly claim that capable individuals should care for individuals in need when they can do so, we should consistently recognize as morally valid the claims that others make upon us for care when they need it, and should endeavor to provide care to them when we are capable of doing so without significant danger to ourselves, seriously compromising our long-term functioning, or undermining our ability to care for others.* [italics by the author] Capable individuals who refuse to honor this principle violate the logical principle of noncontradiction and behave hypocritically.
>
> *(2007: 49)*

Like Miller, Engster recognizes that care theorists have been reluctant to embrace traditional moral languages such as rules and rights because of resistance to the idea of external and abstract ethical obligations (Ibid: 53). Also, like Miller, Engster softens or equivocates the terminology in such a way as to acknowledge the liminal and nontraditional approach of feminist care ethics: "The notion of a right to care is simply a shorthand way of indicating that individuals in need can justify their claims on others for care, and consequently, that capable individuals have an obligation to care for individuals in need when they can do so" (Ibid). Finally, both Miller and Engster are concerned about the lack of care exhibited in the world and desire to justify a higher degree of care among those seemingly unwilling to provide it.

Joan Tronto is intentional in her use of the term "responsibility" rather than duty or obligation when it comes to an ethic of care:

> Compared to obligation, responsibility has both a different connotation and a different context. It seems at first to be a more sociological or anthropological, rather than a political or philosophical, concept. Responsibility is a term that is embedded in a set of implicit cultural practices, rather than in a set of formal rules or series of promises.
>
> *(1993: 131–32)*

Tronto is attracted to "responsibility" because of its ambiguity. Thus, responsibility implicates a more general role in morality than can direct and clear lines of cause and effect suggested by duties or obligation. For example, in asking what responsibility I have to assist Afghan refugees fleeing oppression, the lack of a direct causal line from me to their circumstances might imply that I have none in a formal ethical sense. However, according to Tronto, the flexibility of the term responsibilities means that I can be understood as morally responsible

A Categorical Commitment to Care **71**

to them. Caring responsibilities are crucial to Tronto's understanding of the linkage between democracy and care. She claims, "Democracy is about assigning caring responsibilities" (2013: 11). Tronto is utilizing the term responsibility in a particular manner.

Tronto points out the roots of the term responsibility in the word "response," a central characteristic of care. She points out that responsibility can be used in an adjudicative manner, to assign blame, which is not the main focus of care. Tronto emphasizes the temporal trajectory of traditional moral uses of responsibility versus caring ones: the former looks back, and the latter looks forward (Ibid: 50–51). A care ethic and a care ethos are primarily concerned with responding to the moment at hand with actions that address needs and assist people in growing and flourishing. For Tronto, responsibility is a means for someone to enter into a caring relationship rather than simply a tool to locate the source of moral failure.

## A Caring Commitment as *Taking* Responsibility

Miller, Engster, and Tronto use the terms duty and responsibility in nuanced ways that resonate with the term commitment employed here. However, this book examines the radical implications of a commitment to care rather than a duty or responsibility to care. Perhaps Virginia Held offers a framing of care responsibility that aligns with commitment when she describes "taking responsibility." The action verb "taking" suggests turning the table on moral motivation. Rather than an assignment or delegated obligation, taking responsibility is recognizing and seizing a moral burden. Held acknowledges that the functioning of a complex society that requires some degree of holding people accountable for their actions or inactions is necessary. Still, she wants to shift the ethical emphasis: "I wish to argue, however, for a shift of focus, from ascriptions of responsibility to recommendations to *take* responsibility. Instead of concentrating on holding persons or groups responsible for purposes of blame or compensation and the like, we ought, I am suggesting, to pay attention especially to arguments for *taking* responsibility" (2018: 401). On the one hand, care ethics can sometimes be viewed as a bit passive in that it is responsive to the needs of others. However, taking responsibility points to a proactive element where one decides to own a moral task. A commitment to care describes a disposition or posture of openness to taking responsibility.

Held views care ethics as promoting taking responsibility. In justifying this claim, Held employs language that closely matches the humble inquiry, connection, and responsive action I describe as good care. She explains, "Understanding what will best respond to actual needs can require subtle and empathetic understanding, reliable empirical findings, and respect for all involved. The ethics of care will call for these" (Ibid: 402). In other words, taking responsibility is caring. However, "taking responsibility" can be applied narrowly for a particular need or

**72** Thinking about Better Care

a limited time. A commitment to care connotes a more abiding and less limited approach. The categorical commitment to care is an enduring openness to taking responsibilities—the plural recognizes the wide range of a care commitment.

An intriguing aspect of Held's argument for taking responsibility is that she is making it in the context of addressing substantial social problems, such as global poverty, as well as the challenge of parsing the moral responsibility of collectives such as corporations. Both significant problems and collective social structures represent ethical challenges. For the former, no single individual can take responsibility for solving the problem (no one individual can solve global hunger). For the latter, collective organizations vary in character and goals, making taking responsibility a complex and challenging but not impossible task. Social and structural problems are particularly exigent for ethical theory because of the diffuse sense of responsibility. In social psychology, this is referred to as "social loafing." Held argues that of all the moral theories, care offers the most holistic approach to taking responsibility in an age when it appears that moral responsibility is elusive: "Care requires us to take responsibility, now, for responding to urgent needs, and doing so effectively" (Ibid: 410). An abiding commitment to care makes *taking* responsibility a real possibility. It is more challenging, although sometimes necessary, to assign responsibility to others.

Furthermore, an ethical commitment is a forward-facing assent to a moral direction. Commitments also have a unique type of moral force or salience: they are not as compelling as requirements, yet more compelling than reasons (Shpall, 2014). Commitments are escapable under certain circumstances or reasons, yet they should not be abrogated willy-nilly. As Bernard Williams describes, "A commitment has a high deliberative priority for us if we give it heavy weighting against other considerations in our deliberations … it outweighs most other considerations" (1985: 183). Commitments exist in a liminal space of moral compulsion.

Philosopher Cheshire Calhoun provides a helpful taxonomy and definitional interrogation of commitments that help us situate a commitment to care. Commitments have utility. They inform self-understanding and can contribute to a life lived well. Although there can be passive commitments, ones we find ourselves in because of circumstances, the focus here is on intentional commitments. As Calhoun describes,

> *Active commitments* are ones that one takes on by making a decision to commit and often by using a commitment convention—promising to others, contracting, pledging, enlisting, volunteering, signing up for, officially adopting, promising oneself, or making a resolution.
>
> *(2009: 616)*

Calhoun also describes the persistence of commitments. They provide stability but not without effort. Commitments must be sustained by the one committed

(Ibid: 622). Furthermore, commitments give purpose and meaning to one's life by providing an abiding character. They participate in our identity (Ibid: 631 and Williams, 1981: 11). Similarly, philosopher John Davenport argues that the combination of caring and commitment makes up what he describes as the "striving will"—a state of firm resolve that constitutes our character (2007: 4). Caring is thus a manifestation of an individual will, a personal commitment.

The significance of the active intention found in a commitment cannot be overstated. A chosen commitment has an enormous psychological and motivational advantage over a duty or obligation. Philosopher Shay Welch describes how the relational aspect of commitments transforms the disposition of the one committed:

> Commitment both relates to, and differs from, obligation and responsibility. Responsibilities exist as given via relationships and memberships in communities. They exist, whether one wants them or not, by virtue of the associations the individual chooses to maintain or communities within which she is embedded. For an individual to have a commitment, though, requires more from her than mere recognition of those responsibilities. When relationships become central, the person more fully understands those responsibilities and sees them as needs, not ones that require grueling attention, but ones that are satisfying to fulfill.
>
> *(2012: 119)*

Welch offers a "commitment framework" that provides an intriguing insight into the nature of moral compulsion. On the one hand, rules and duties seem stricter in their requirement for adherence than commitments, but Welch points out that volition matters. Actions taken due to mandated requirements, such as in the exchange of labor for compensation, can be viewed as a necessary evil with implications for effort, quality, and avoidance behavior (Ibid). However, actions taken within a chosen commitment, even when challenging, are likely to elicit a more positive disposition. One ironic twist is that even if duties or rules are seen as more absolute in their demands, the internal motivational force behind a commitment might elicit a higher level of action, perhaps even supererogatory actions, on the part of the one committed.

Thus far, I have addressed the notion of commitment on an individual basis: an intentional decision by a person. Albeit less studied in the literature, there is a corollary notion of collective or joint commitment. Given our social nature, philosopher Margaret Gilbert characterizes joint commitments as central to human life. She describes a joint commitment as "the wills of two or more people impose the commitment on the same two or more people—as one" (2015: 18–26). Although the definition is simple enough, a multi-subject commitment's complexity remains. Gilbert describes the need for both common knowledge and open communication to create the conditions for a joint commitment. She refers to this as "readiness" for collective commitment (2014: 65). Such mutual commitments morally constrain each member; an individual cannot end the overall commitment. Like Welch, Gilbert recognizes the significant psychological dimension of the commitment process (2015: 18–26). Accordingly, participating in a collective commitment is a dynamic negotiation of psychosocial forces and the will of individuals. A collective commitment never stops being an individual commitment, but it is influenced and participates in the agency of others. The notion of joint or collective commitment has implications for a commitment to care and participating in an ethos of care, discussed in the next chapter.

In summary, commitment has a unique status in the lexicon of moral philosophy. Commitments have the potential to be relational, voluntary, future-oriented, abiding, and identity-forming. In many respects, we are the sum of our commitments. Although the bonds of commitment are not absolute, escaping a commitment is not an arbitrary decision and is only acceptable under certain circumstances and with reflection. Everyone has commitments that they have entered into, some more important than others. This book contends that a moral commitment to care is within everyone's capacity, regardless of political, cultural, religious, or social identity. Furthermore, we should seize and develop this commitment to address much of the pain and suffering in the world. Finally, commitment is an appropriate framework for thinking about the morality of care given care's focus on meeting needs and repair rather than judging participants in ethical dilemmas. The following section focuses on the nature of a commitment to care.

## Committing to Care

Interestingly enough, the terms care and commitment have long been associated. Although care and commitment are not the same, it is understood that the objects of care give rise to our commitments (Blustein, 1991: 38). As Harry Frankfurt describes, "The formation of a person's will is most fundamentally a matter of his coming to care about certain things, and of his coming to care about some of them more than about others" (1982: 268). Frankfurt highlights how care is the experiential driver of will or agency development. In other words, care and commitments are intermingled and can feed one another. We are, first and foremost, relational beings, and therefore our cares mostly begin with other beings. Committing to care alters the moral focus from caring about individuals, the object/subject of care, to caring about care, the practice. Most ethics literature centers on caring about others, whether familiar, unfamiliar, or collective beings. For example, in considering nursing and educational settings, philosopher Joseph P. Walsh claims, "to describe care as involving a commitment to the cared for is to point out that care will not be arbitrarily discontinued by the caregiver" (2018: 619). He describes care itself as a type of commitment.

A Categorical Commitment to Care **75**

Although this is an appropriate application of a commitment to care, it is individual-based: care is directed toward a particular other. I want to consider a general commitment to care as participating in an ethos or way of being rather than focusing on specific agents cared for.

One might object to a generalized commitment to care because such an approach violates the particularism of care ethics. Earlier, I described good or effective care as entailing, in part, inquiry into the specific circumstances and contexts of concrete others. So, how can I endorse a commitment to care absent the specific one cared for? The fulcrum for a general commitment to care is the moral imagination's vacillating between particular experiences and broader concerns. Accordingly, a commitment to care draws upon extending my past and present care experiences, not in a route mapping onto new circumstances but as creatively attuned to them. Care, as Noddings and others have claimed, is a moral ideal, but it is a moral ideal grounded in experience. A commitment to care is abstract in that the forms are abstract for Plato. If you ask me to think of the form of a chair, I will draw upon all my images of chairs from personal experience. Similarly, if you ask me to commit to care, I will refer to the experiences of care that I have had or witnessed. This imagined care will be limited and imperfect, so we must inform our imaginations with robust care experiences (through personal encounters, the arts, etc.). A commitment to generalized care for others may entail abstraction, but that abstraction is always in the shadow of experience.

Philosopher Jeffrey Blustein defines a commitment to care, or caring about caring, that suggests how intimate the general and particular should be: "To care about caring is to care about one's ability to care deeply about things and people in general, to invest oneself in and devote oneself to something (or someone) or other" (1991: 61). Terms like "invest oneself" and "devote oneself" are manifestations of commitment. A commitment or chosen path implies a higher degree of persistence in pursuing care in the face of inevitable constraints. Ideally, a commitment to care integrates an ethic and ethos of care. The commitment indicates that one desires to deliver effective care and is open to new and novel care opportunities.

A commitment to care can be (and has been) fraught with pitfalls of misinformed and misguided actions that can do more harm than good if we are not vigilant in fine-tuning our imaginations' abstractions. Eva Feder Kittay addresses the issue of abstraction and attunement regarding care by drawing upon an analogy with the work of Josiah Royce on loyalty to loyalty (1936). Royce recognized that loyalty, like care, can have a dark side if expressions of loyalty remain unchecked.[3] Kittay replaces Royce's concept of loyalty with care:

> If we believe that care is a supreme good, one can make a similar argument for care. Efforts at care that destroy or create conditions that destroy

**76** Thinking about Better Care

the possibility of care for others destroy the very value we honor when we care for another. This recognition requires the self-reflective moment in the practice of care. Is my caring for this person or persons such that it allows or destroys the possibility that others can give and receive care? How do we arrange our social and political life to care about care in this sense? Such self-reflection requires us to acknowledge our ignorance of the many possible consequences of our actions, and to attempt to gain knowledge from others to see whether our acts of care impinge on the ability of others to care—knowledge only available from others and most especially those over whom we have power and who occupy less privileged positions.

*(2019a: 861)*

Just as one can have a general commitment to loyalty that is tempered by self-reflection, so too can a person have a broad commitment to care.

Kittay begins her claim above almost off-handedly, "If we believe that care is the supreme good." This is not a trivial proposition, as the social revolution called for in this book is found in the sustaining morality of humanity. Care is the supreme good that animates the quest for all other moral goods, such as justice, rights, fairness, etc. This is an essential primary claim because we want to commit to the highest ideal, realizing that we will likely fall short. That is why the discussion of good care is so relevant. Quite different than a compliance orientation—endeavoring to comply with some minimal standard of the good—the moral commitment is directed at the ideal of good care. Some philosophers might be concerned that such a claim smacks of monism,[4] a singular notion of moral good. The danger of such an approach is a type of reductionism whereby diversity is squelched.

Caring is the ideal advocated. However, caring is an indefinite goal, the general direction that we pursue, but its expression can be as different and varied as there are contexts and relationships. Tronto describes the co-existential tension within care around general morality and specific practices: "Conceptually, care is both particular and universal. The construction of adequate care varies from culture to culture" (1993: 109). For example, mothering as the paradigm of care practice is a Western construction with presuppositions about race and class that may be unfamiliar to other communities. Care as the ultimate good must remain intersectional in its manifestation while staying true to its humble responsiveness to the needs of others. As Tronto claims, "the meaning of care varies from one society to another, and from one group to another, care is nonetheless a universal aspect of human life … care is not universal with regard to any specific needs, but all humans have needs that others must help them meet" (Ibid: 110). Later, we extend the efficacy of care to nonhuman life as well. Process care ethics and an ethos of care should suggest an open-ended array of caring actions dictated by the context and emergent needs.

## A Categorical Commitment

I propose that a commitment to care should be the highest and most central moral commitment: a categorical commitment for individuals and collectives. Kant offered a categorical commitment (formulated in various ways) as a universal and absolute rule. I am employing the idea of a categorical commitment in a postmodern manner. The modifier "categorical" is intended to indicate the primacy of this commitment among all other moral commitments. Still, care ethics does not have the burden of characterizing absolutes regarding how such an approach should be applied. However, it does suggest that all other moral concepts, such as justice, fairness, rights, and virtue, have care at their foundation and/or are enhanced through effective care. For example, human rights are significant symbols or totems of care. They signal a society's values and can help argue for minimum protections and provisions. Such rights are nevertheless abstractions, external moral impositions that require the enactment and follow-through of individuals and societies to become a reality. For example, no one argues that civil rights laws are essential to combat injustice directed at Black Americans. Yet, similarly, no one suggests that passing civil rights legislation ended racial injustice and oppression. The existence of rights did not extinguish the racist and exclusionary practices of people. Paradoxically, external socially constructed markers such as rights and the internal commitment to ethical relations are needed to enact moral progress. Realizing racial justice can only come when people genuinely care for one another. Laws help but cannot bring about moral behavior on their own. Thus, it is argued in this book that developing the skills and ethos of care are the highest priority for creating an ethical community.[5]

Dutch philosopher Knud Ejler Løgstrup described the radical demand of morality as the experience of other people's needs that we must fulfill. He, too, described a categorical moral imperative that is open-ended and dictated by circumstance:

> The demand implicit in every encounter between persons is not vocal but is and remains silent. The individual to whom the demand is directed must him or herself in each concrete relationship decide what the content of the demand is. This is not to say that a person can arbitrarily and capriciously determine the content of the demand ... And since the demand is implied by the very fact that a person belongs to the world in which the other person has his or her life, and therefore holds something of that person's life in his or her hands, it is therefore a demand to take care of that person's life. But nothing is thereby said about how this caring is to be done.
>
> *(1997: 22)*

Løgstrup was not a feminist care ethicist, and his scholarship has significant points of departure from care theory (Skærbæk, 2011). However, his

**78** Thinking about Better Care

influential work on the fundamental ethical demand portrays the relational reality of interdependence found among care theorists. Løgstrup calls for something akin to a caring commitment to meet the radical demand of others' needs, and he leaves open the precise choices to be made to meet that demand. Caring is an improvisational performance that responds to the needs of the other. The commitment to care is a willingness to engage in such improvisations.

Løgstrup's notion of the ethical demand has similarities to Noddings' notion of commitment arising from a care disposition. Noddings describes the "I must" of caring as prompting commitment: "Caring requires me to respond to the initial impulse with an act of commitment: I commit myself either to overt action on behalf of the cared-for ... or I commit myself to thinking about what I might do" (2013: 81). What Noddings suggests may be accurate; however, I am suggesting that in the spirit of being moral people, we commit to care up front and then allow ourselves to be open to where this commitment takes us. The moral life can present us with a complexity of care commitments. A foundational commitment to a life of caring pushes us toward humility, inclusion, and action that can enact individual commitments.

What does it mean to hold a commitment to care? How do we know if we have an individual or collective commitment to care? The simple answer is that it has to be a living idea for us. Of course, there are implicit and explicit forms of commitment, and it is possible for a commitment to care to seep into one's psyche and identity through social reinforcement, such as participating in a community committed to care. However, to effect significant personal and social change, more explicit means of engaging the morality of care are likely more effective. Such straightforward means might include increased discussions of care in schools, churches, and organizations; care education curricula in K-12 and college; and training in care practices for professionals.

Furthermore, symbolic markers of care can offer greater social instantiation of care as a value. For example, physicians recite the Hippocratic oath. Similar statements addressing care could become part of other professional ceremonies. We keep ideas alive and allow them to grow by talking about them. A national narrative regarding care could be developed in politics and the media. Histories of care (and not just healthcare) can be written. We have many histories of national military events, so why not histories of national care traditions? None of these methods ensures an internalized commitment to care. Still, their existence could raise the potential for people to align themselves with care, not as a subversive inculcation of an external ideal, but as a means to engage with a vital capacity of humanity.

In describing a new politics for an age fraught with crisis, writer, political and environmental activist George Monbiot explains the need for a new repeated story to replace the old neoliberal narrative of humanity that collective efforts failed and only individual achievement leads to progress. There is a living story of care that is infused within society that needs to be highlighted and retold. Monbiot writes,

> If our purpose is to create a kinder world, we should embed within the political story we tell the intrinsic values that promote this aim, empathy, understanding, connectedness with other people, self-acceptance, independent thought and action.
>
> *(2017: 9)*

A commitment to care is not merely a private matter of belief but should infuse our political narratives and the stories we tell about ourselves and our ideals. When Monbiot desires to characterize a kinder world, he employs the language of effective caring: inquiry, connection, and action. Monbiot suggests that those seeking to shift the political paradigm could learn something from organized religion in knowing one's values and then evangelizing through powerful narratives. A commitment to care is just such a powerful narrative.

The Care Collective, academics in the United Kingdom from various disciplines who authored *The Care Manifesto*, describes the story of care in terms of promiscuity. For the Care Collective, care promiscuity is another term for an indiscriminate and widespread commitment to care. Such promiscuity is not superficial and casual as in the transactional care of free-market capitalism. Instead, it means "caring *more* and in ways that remain experimental and extensive by current standard" (2020: 41). An ethos of care can be instigated through institutions that embrace a care narrative. The authors are careful not to invoke any over-prescriptive form of care but rather the more general disposition that allows for diverse manifestations. They describe a social commitment:

> To encourage promiscuous care means building institutions that are capacious and agile enough to recognize and resource wider forms of care at the level of kinship. But Promiscuous care should also inform every scale of social life: not just our families but our communities, markets, states, and our transnational relationships with human and non-human life as well.
>
> *(Ibid: 44)*

This statement coincides with the purpose of this project. Furthermore, The Care Collective's notion of caring beyond the general standard points to the radical provocations in Section 2 of this book.

In what follows, I describe three concomitants of care that correspond to good care habits: humble inquiry, inclusive connection, and responsive action. These associated commitments assert that if one commits to care, one wants to improve. So each of these is an element or sub-commitment of a categorical commitment to care.

## 80 Thinking about Better Care

### *A Commitment to Learning and Truth*

> A reliable sign of real caring is the intolerance of ignorance about the current state of what we care about … a sign that a person or cause is not merely important to one, but one which one cares about, is the need for constant contact with and news about the welfare of what is cared about.
>
> —Annette Baier (1982: 274)

What does committing to care as a central moral value and trajectory mean? As claimed in Chapter 1, good care involves knowledge work. Although that knowledge work can sometimes take the form of traditional educational methods such as studying and reading, the knowledge work of care is more expansive. For example, it includes engaging the arts or simply being open to listening and learning about the plights of others. In addition, the knowledge necessary for effective care has practical wisdom and respect for experience.

Political philosopher Michael J. Sandel makes a potent argument regarding the alienation and division created by a meritocracy that views education as a credentialing process. For Sandel, neoliberal meritocracies supported by the political left and right have made the university a symbol of "credentialist privilege and meritocratic hubris" (2020: 104). Of course, universities can be the locus of tremendous growth, understanding, and solidarity. However, as Sandel points out, formal education can also be weaponized to distinguish winners and losers, thus fostering social division. Good care cannot succumb to such distinctions. The knowledge necessary for care work comes from multiple sources through various means. One does not need a college education to be an effective caregiver, but one must be willing to learn and grow.

To claim that care is knowledge work is not to claim that a fixed set of learning objectives will lead to better care. One of the perplexing things about care is that it is a practice—labor that occurs in the world—but it is also a disposition that impacts the practice. Thus, in addressing a commitment to learning as part of the categorical commitment to care, the manifestation of the commitment is witnessed in intellectual, emotional, and physical practices. For example, presence is a physical practice that can facilitate caring knowledge. However, active listening is an intellectual practice, and compassion is an emotional disposition that aids in caring knowledge development as well. The practice of being present can assist with the knowledge work of care, but it is amplified with a compassionate disposition.

There is a role for facts or justified true belief in caring. Garnering propositional knowledge is often a significant step in caring knowledge. For example, understanding the history of indigenous oppression in Canada or the United States is a path toward caring. Knowing the scale of death and disease, dates of broken treaties, or forced labor provides an essential backdrop to current conditions. Facts matter, but there is more to the truth than just propositional knowledge and statistics. Being present or witnessing testimonials of indigenous people offers a subtle form of knowledge that can communicate values and emotions. Furthermore, a caring disposition that entails an emotional openness makes learning and witnessing more than simply recording information. It allows us to imaginatively inhabit (but not own or claim) the experience of others, allowing us a clue or glimpse into their lived experience. Thus, the commitment to learning is holistic, intended to foster an abiding and comprehensive sense of learning and growing.

Because caring is so tied up in what it is to be human, it is difficult to disentangle the various aspects of care (hence my claim that care defies categorical thinking). Philosopher Vrinda Dalmiya expresses a sense of the holistic part of the pursuit of knowledge in service of care by developing a care-based epistemology: "The intertwining of caring and knowing in a care-based epistemology is not just the causal connection of the latter arising from the former[6] ... Rather, the claim is that there is a certain 'way of being'—a certain character that centrally involves the trait of humility—and this is the source for ensuring the goals of both caring and knowing" (2016: 18). Dalmiya names humility as the disposition needed for caring knowledge production. Similarly, I described, "humble inquiry" as required for effective care. Dalmiya finds "the character trait of relational humility" as "the root from which both good caring and good knowing flow" (Ibid). In this respect, we once again describe a spirit of care rather than a strict ethic as traditionally understood. A spirit of openness and humility are essential to a commitment to learning in service of care.

Although perhaps not the first trait one thinks of when imagining philosophers, humility in inquiry is not foreign to modern philosophy. The feminist philosophers who have developed care theory not only value epistemological humility, but as feminists, they are attentive to the power differentials that foster epistemic oppression and injustice.

Some might find the notion that caring is knowledge work surprising, particularly given how care is popularly associated with emotion. But, conversely, epistemology has sought objectivity in its scientific and analytic manifestations. Lorraine Code, for example, notes the link between care and knowledge production while challenging the quest for abstract objectivity. Code argues that epistemic responsibility to "real-world, situated knowledge projects" requires a personal investment in outcomes (2015: 3). Continuing the feminist scholarly assault on an objective "view from nowhere," Code is not arguing for epistemic relativism. Instead, resonating with care theory, she eschews the objective/relative binary in favor of caring as a "vital component" of meaningful inquiry into the issues with the most significant impact in the world today (Ibid: 18).

Note that I titled this section a commitment to learning *and* truth. The pursuit of truth is not easily separated from the quest for understanding. Dalmiya describes care as a reliabilist epistemological virtue (2002: 34). Reliabilism is a philosophical term that includes a range of epistemological theories regarding knowledge or the justification of belief by considering the process of knowledge

**82** Thinking about Better Care

acquisition (Goldman, 1979). In plain language, reliabilism addresses how trustworthy a knowledge acquisition process is. Reliabilism counters extreme forms of skepticism. So although Descartes' claim that the senses can be wrong is correct, generally speaking, our senses are reliable sources of information. Dalmiya notes that care should be added to other trustworthy wellsprings of information, including "sight, hearing, memory, introspection, deduction, and induction" (2002: 42). Dalmiya addresses the complexity of the care relationship in its mix of ethics and epistemology. "Care-knowing" is reliabilist for Dalmiya because the particularity of care for the other allows for a careful and nuanced understanding of the other, resulting in a trustworthy source of knowledge or truth (Ibid: 43). When we care for others in rich and meaningful ways, we know them. Reliable truth emerges.

Furthermore, the terms reliable and trustworthy are relational. Caring relations rely on truth-telling. Deceit on significant issues can damage the relationship, thus mitigating trust and respect. A robust commitment to care needs an associated commitment to knowledge and truth. Recall that care theory is non-binary and does not demand perfection. Accordingly, an individual untruth may not diminish the care trajectory in a relationship; however, an overall commitment to truth is essential. One can care for a serial liar, but there is damage to the trust in the relationship that keeps interaction circumspect.

### A Commitment to Inclusive Sympathetic and Empathetic Understanding

Committing to care entails being devoted to pursuing knowledge and truth while connecting with others. This is perhaps the most controversial of my proposed concomitants of care because of this commitment's personal and possibly emotional nature. The idea of connection is less valued in traditional philosophy and is not particularly valued in modern neoliberal society. I suggest that connection includes sympathetic and empathetic understanding to emphasize this approach's intellectual and emotional dimensions. Furthermore, the commitment must not be parochial. Caring for loved ones is admirable, but enlarging care to its political and social potential requires more inclusive care relations. Imagination plays a crucial role in caring at all times. However, it is acutely necessary to care for less familiar others. Using imagination in ethics is a fraught subject with some deserved concerns, as knowledge gaps cannot be avoided.

Drawing on the idea of humanity's relational ontology—as beings, we are not isolated individuals but existentially intertwined—the notion of connection needed for effective care, as I am framing it, has cognitive elements, emotional/visceral elements, and involves imagination. In the spirit of a postmodern, non-binary approach to care theory, I am invoking sympathy and empathy into the concept of connection. Although the distinction between sympathy and empathy is not always as straightforward as some would like, generally, sympathy is regarded as feelings of understanding and concern about the circumstances of others. Empathy is understood as experiencing an inkling of the emotions of others, often with visceral affect. In other words, through sympathy, one can feel pity and regret *for* another person's distress. However, through empathy, one can feel at least a portion *of* the sorrow of the other.

Perhaps one of the best expressions of the complexity of our connection with others that considers social and political contexts is the work of Gloria Anzaldúa. Anzaldúa employs the term "nos/otras" to describe the artificial nature of social tribalism, which divides humanity into factions of them and us. Anzaldúa navigated the experience of multiple oppressed identities, including disability, lesbian, and being a Tejana/Chicana borderland dweller. Anzaldúa's influential work addressed the postmodern reality of liminal existence. Her work of resistance drew upon her experiences to theorize about oppression, but it also reveals a great deal about human connection. Anzaldúa describes her linguistic signification of human interconnectedness:

Living in a multicultural society, we cross into each others' worlds all the time. We live in each other's pockets, occupy each other's territories, live in close proximity and intimacy with each other at home, in school, at work. We're mutually complicitous—us and them, white and colored, straight and queer, Christian and Jew, self and other, oppressor and oppressed. We all of us find ourselves in the position of being simultaneously insider/outsider. The Spanish word "nosotras" means "us." In theorizing insider/outsider I write the word with a slash between nos (us) and otras (others).

*(2000: 254)*

Anzaldúa's work supports a relational ontology. As Andrea J. Pitts describes, Anzaldúa rejected the individualism of traditional Western philosophical and moral theory (2021: 33). Anzaldúa also eschewed the mind/body dualisms in favor of a more holistic and embodied approach to human flourishing. Anzaldúa finds hope in the interconnectedness that meshes with a care ethos spurred by a commitment to inclusive understanding:

Hopefully sometime in the future we may become nosotras without the slash. Perhaps geography will no longer separate us ... the future belongs to those who cultivate cultural sensitivities to differences and who use these abilities to forge a hybrid consciousness that transcends the "us" vs. "them" mentality and will carry us into a nosotras position bridging the extremes of our cultural realities.

*(2000: 255)*

Care is a relational way of being. Committing to care entails exploring, valuing, and improving one's ability to connect with others.

**84** Thinking about Better Care

### *A Commitment to Moral Action*

Ultimately, all care is experienced. It must be enacted as a phenomenon in the physical world. Whether personal or institutional, care engages the body. Somebody has to pick up the crying baby, tend to the gunshot wound, teach in the overcrowded school, and grow the food that will feed the community. Although there are many rational and intellectual elements to knowing and connecting with others, responsive action requires doing. Care is a practice that has an aesthetic for which we can choose to participate through our actions or stay on the sidelines. Care must be enacted.

First proposed a quarter of a century ago, enactivism represents a cluster of theories in the study of mind drawn from Buddhism, cognitive science, evolutionary biology, phenomenology, and psychology (Varela, Thompson, and Rosch, 1991). Since then, a variety of approaches have been taken to enactivism. Yet, they share some common elements, often referred to as the 4Es of cognition:

> Embodied—the mind is not just a brain but a fully integrated part of the body.
>
> Embedded—the mind and its cognition are interrelated with its environment and cannot be extricated from its situatedness.
>
> Enacted—the mind is actualized in what it does through the body. The mind is inter-active. Cognitive processes partially acquire meaning through their role in the context of action. We are what we do.
>
> Extended—cognition reaches into its environment. Enactivist approaches emphasize cognitive systems' extended, intersubjective, and socially situated nature.

Sometimes it is also argued that enactivism entails ecological, empathic, and affective dimensions (Gallagher, 2017: 28). Enactivism is a transdisciplinary approach to questions of agency, autonomy, and value through a lens of interaction that challenges that the mind is simply the manipulation of mental representations of the world.

Enactivism engages the embodied mind in a manner similar to the way feminist physicist Karan Barad discusses the intra-activity of matter. For example, Barad argues that the measurement process alters what is being measured (2012: 77) (Barad's work is further discussed in Chapter 4). Similarly, enactivist thinkers view cognizant embodied subjects as impacting the meaning of experience and not simply gathering external information (Di Paolo, Rohde, and De Jaegher, 2010: 39). In other words, the actions of agents co-constitute their world.

In several articles, philosopher Petr Urban has argued that care ethics resonates strongly with enactivism. Urban claims the two approaches share

A Categorical Commitment to Care **85**

a "rejection of individualist, disembodied and rationalist accounts of human agency, cognition, society, and morality" (2015: 127). He views the two fields as potentially benefiting from further interchange. In particular, enactivist theorists have developed a rich exploration of how interaction creates meaning beyond representational and propositional knowledge. At the same time, care ethics retains its feminist concern about power, privilege, and politics. Urban's analysis is helpful in this project because of enactivism's emphasis on relational activity. Accordingly, responsive actions are not simply transactional moments but provide meaning. Caring practices participate in creating a more caring society. A care revolution will occur through many responsive acts of care.

In Chapter 1, I described good care as consisting of humble inquiry, inclusive connection, and responsive action. In Chapter 2, the idea that care is a process morality that responds to the emergent needs of others was addressed. This chapter has translated the three elements of good care into the sub-commitments of an overarching commitment to care. In committing to care, we should strive to improve these three areas.

## A Commitment to Care is an Ethical Imperative

> Those relationships formed by consent and manifested as care are the center of community. It is this consenting care that is the essence of our role as citizens. And it is the ability of citizens to care that creates strong communities and able democracies.
>
> —John McKnight (1995: ix)

Community scholar and activist John McKnight echoed the voice of Jane Addams from a century earlier when he framed care as a function of civic engagement. For McKnight, "care is the consenting commitment of citizens to one another" (Ibid: x). A care revolution is a manifestation of such a commitment.

Commitments to care help us respond to a myriad of circumstances. Those who commit to care do not have to be extraordinarily skilled or in any particular profession. However, such a commitment can be lifesaving and imbue life with meaning and hope. Like Yuri Kochiyama, when we commit to care as a way of life or an openness to the possibility of caring once the moment arrives, we participate in the greater good of society.

At the close of *Trans Care*, Hil Malatino shares the story of their youth when they were a gender outcast, including marginalization from their biological family. Malatino made a family with another gender outcast, eventually creating a caring network among "similarly trans and queer and broke and traumatized and disassociated" folks (2020b: 71). Amidst dramatic transformation, Malatino names a commitment to care as the ability to "make a space for one another's becoming" (Ibid). Thus, deep, genuine care is marked by abiding moral responsiveness, "a commitment to showing up for all of those folks engaged in the necessary and integral care work that supports trans lives, however proximal or distant, in the ways that we can" (Ibid: 72). The commitment to care that Malatino describes was born out of extreme need and survival. The challenge for a care ethos is whether we can make space for one another's becoming across the socially constructed boundaries that divide us by identity and politics.

One could justifiably refer to the present moment as the golden age of care ethics. Only a few decades after it was first named, care theorists worldwide and across many disciplines are advancing the idea of care in novel and meaningful ways. This intellectual work is critical and bears fruit. Along with the scholarly reflections on care, an accompanying popular movement fueled by a spirit of care will help realize the promise of care ethics. An attractive care ethos, something we desire to participate in, can draw a sense of shared commitment along with the resulting sense of hope. Of course, we can individually commit to care, but that care exponentially multiplies if shared. The following chapter addresses the nature of commitment care, which can build a shared ethos. A revolution entails much more than a manifesto—the ideals must be taken to heart. Next, we discuss how to co-create that spirit.

## Notes

1 Although we tend to use euphemisms such as "relocation camps" to describe the experience of Japanese Americans during World War II, they were incarcerated in concentration or prison camps.
2 Kochiyama refers to this creed as "Creed 22" which suggests that she wrote 21 versions prior to this one (Kochiyama, 2004: xxiv).
3 For an analysis of loyalty to care based on Royce's work, see Hamington, 2014.
4 I thank Gregory Fernando Pappas for interrogating me on this issue of monism.
5 It should be understood that care is a moral ideal and that a commitment to care is not to imply that a utopian society is possible. However, a commitment to care is a vital way forward as we are all capable of caring and capable of improving our care for others. Care is an ideal built on the reality of our tremendous capacity for understanding, connection, and responsive action.
6 I would expand Dalmiya's concern about caring not necessarily giving rise to knowledge to include that knowledge does not necessarily give rise to care. Care and knowledge are inexorably intertwined and although not causal, often caring can elicit better knowledge and better knowledge can lead to greater caring.

# 4

# A CARE ETHOS

## Prologue: A Spirit of Support

Umoja means "unity" in Swahili and is the principle celebrated on the first day of the secular celebration, Kwanzaa.[1] In 2004, drawing on the term's cultural value, Umoja was the name given to a high school-based mentoring and leadership program in New York City High Schools that focuses on the holistic development of young men of color (Jackson, Sealey-Ruiz, and Watson, 2014: 397). Although each school's program evolved differently, they share many objectives and practices. Ostensibly, the general goal of Umoja is to diminish the education gap between the achievement and graduation rates of Black and Latine[2] youth and their White counterparts. The program focuses on developing leadership and improving academic outcomes. Ingrid Chung, who became principal of the Urban Assembly School for Applied Math and Science (AMS), describes their Umoja program:

> We target our most at risk boys in high school from grades nine through 12th grade. The guys are all leaders, and it is a cohort model. So as seniors graduate, we add a new batch of freshmen (20 per year) into the program, and it is designed to ensure that students who are young men of color can exercise their leadership skills in a way that will make them college and career ready and be able to impact their community both inside and outside of the school. So, whatever they do becomes contagious to others.
>
> *(Chung quoted in Workman, n.d.)*

DOI: 10.4324/9781003368625-6

**88** Thinking about Better Care

Empirical evidence indicates a positive impact on the Umoja participants. Upon entering the program, male students of color show academic promise but either have high absentee rates or have not completed enough credits to keep pace with their grade level. According to Iesha Jackson, Yolanda Sealey-Ruiz, and Wanda Watson,

> The young men who become members are overage, under-credited (OA/UC) transfer students from traditional high schools where they did not experience academic success. The OA/UC student population is defined as students who are at least 2 years behind their peers in age and credits earned toward a high school diploma
>
> *(2014: 398)*

These students are deemed "disengaged" and are thus at risk of failing to graduate high school and possibly getting swept into the systemic oppression of the school-to-prison pipeline (Melgar, 2020: 6 and 11).

Umoja provides students of color with a community of support comprised of young men who share identity-based discrimination. Umoja students meet on Tuesdays after school and Saturday mornings to discuss academic and non-academic issues during the school year. One Umoja student, Sarshevack Mnahsheh, describes, "I'm from the South Bronx, so my whole life I've had to make the choice of whether to do well in school or be a part of the street life" (Su-Yeung, 2017). The Umoja community is referred to as a brotherhood by its members. As another participant, Carlos, claims, "There's just unity here, like we're all united, and no matter what, no matter what each and every one go through, I got your back, that's how it is" (Watson, Sealey-Ruiz, and Jackson, 2016: 994). However, the experience of brotherhood at school does not inoculate the young men from the harsh realities of racism. After class one day, Umoja member, Johnny, was caught up in the fraught "stop and frisk" practices of the New York police department at the time. Johnny's resistance led to his mistreatment and arrest (Ibid: 998). When Johnny returned to school, the next session of Umoja was devoted to members sharing their stop-and-frisk experiences as well as comforting Johnny. In 2016, a 19-year-old member of the Umoja brotherhood, Joseph Jimenez, died of gunshot wounds while walking to his girlfriend's house in what the police described as a mistaken identity. In the aftermath, the Umoja community consoled and drew strength from one another: "The members started checking in on each other more frequently, and the brotherhood reached a new level of importance" (Su-Yeung, 2017).

The Umoja program created a community of care. The elements of good care are present in the activities of the group. Members learned about one another through proximity and storytelling (inquiry); they found personal resonances with one another through shared experiences of hardship (connection), and they actively listened and reassured each other when their brethren were in need (responsive action). The academic gains from the Umoja program are entangled with its relational nature.

Social researchers Iesha Jackson, Yolanda Sealey-Ruiz, and Wanda Watson describe Umoja as fostering an ethos of care: "We found that a distinct ethos of care encouraged the young men to bring their full selves—triumphs and challenges—to the mentoring space" (2014: 398–9). An ethos of care does not provide specific prescriptions for how to respond to the challenges of the community, such as how to survive and thrive in racially oppressive and tension-filled neighborhoods. An ethos is not the same as an ethical system of adjudicating moral dilemmas. However, it establishes the human groundwork for the moral work of care: the spirit and disposition that make care practices possible and desirable. Jackson and her colleagues delineate their use of the term ethos:

> We define an ethos of care as an intangible spirit of personal interest in and responsibility for others. This ethos rests at the center of united communities that actively pursue the individual and collective well-being of their members. We use an ethos of care to acknowledge that for the community to flourish, individuals must recognize their interconnected relationships to one another. Stated differently, an ethos of care is rooted in an understanding that an individual's success can only be measured in relation to the success of his or her community.
>
> *(Ibid: 399)*

This care ethos negotiates the tension between the general moral good of care and the community's particular needs. Jackson, Sealey-Ruiz, and Watson argue for culturally relevant care (CRC) that is appropriate for the community and culture involved yet does not trample the individual humanity of its members. They are balancing the general moral need for care with particular local circumstances. Jackson, Sealey-Ruiz, and Watson somewhat surprisingly describe CRC as a practice of freedom:

> CRC as a practice of freedom involves a process of building mutual trust in which all community members not only recognize each other's humanity and full capacities, but work collaboratively to tackle injustices big and small, encountered by community members.
>
> *(2016: 998)*

This care practice is a "freedom to" support one another emotionally rather than a "freedom from" the demands of caring relationships. Such relational freedom is compatible with social and political care theorists' work. Although an ethos of care may start as a generalized disposition, attunement to specific circumstances allows caring norms to emerge. Context matters, and so does the spirit of care in the community.

**90** Thinking about Better Care

The claim here is not that Umoja is without foibles and is the ultimate model for a caring ethos.[3] Instead, Umoja represents a context-driven, responsive effort at spreading a disposition of care that can have a lasting impact on the flourishing of those involved.[4] In a world where narratives of masculinity often devalue caring, the Umoja program in New York City schools incubates a caring ethos. It has a moral tone without moralizing, the ethos is co-created and sustained by the community of young men, and it has an emotional dimension with an impact that can affect the members beyond the program. The program's name is an intentional connection to ancient moral traditions lost to Western modernity.

## An Ethotic Approach to Care

In Chapter 1, I focused on the character and contours of an ethic of care, emphasizing what constitutes effective care. Subsequent chapters addressed care normativity and the significance of a care commitment. In this chapter, I attend to a personal and communal disposition or spirit of care, named here as an *ethos of care*. I suggest an ethotic approach to care not as a replacement, somehow superior, or even separate from an ethic of care. Instead, I contend that an ethos of care is a means for capturing a broader spectrum of the care experience. Earlier, I stated that care is more than a disposition, which is true. However, care can have a disposition or spirit that extends the possibility of new caring opportunities and the depth of care. In this section, I highlight the disposition of effective care in a manner not given significant attention in the care theory literature.

Although Sandra Laugier does not explicitly address an ethos of care, she finds something sacred in the very ordinary activities of care that moves it beyond assessing standards of behavior: "Care then appears as one of the existent paths toward a genuine ethics, one that is concrete, attentive to actual practices and forms of life, and not only normative" (2020: 39). Perhaps one way to find that path is through an ethos of care. I have indicated that an ethic of care has normative and extra-normative elements. Still, the notion of an ethos of care diffuses care's adjudicative and normative role even further. A spirit of care can act like a positive contagion that infects an individual and spreads to others.

"Ethos" is a contested term and yet is being invoked more than ever (White, 2009: 113). Some have even referred to the "ethotic turn" in contemporary critical theory (Hatzisavvidou, 2016). For this book, I am not describing ethos within the rhetorical paradigm of *logos* as rational argument, *pathos* as emotional persuasion, and *ethos* as an appeal to authority. Instead, I draw from modern analyses that seek to move beyond Aristotelian notions of ethos.[5] Nevertheless, ethos, like care, remains a somewhat vague concept. Definitions of ethos can be paradoxical and contradictory (Baumlin, 1994: xi–xxvii). English scholar Marshall W. Alcorn goes so far as to declare that Aristotle's formulation of ethos is outdated, given the difference between Greek society and contemporary society (1994: 17).

A Care Ethos **91**

I apply three significant elements of modern ethos theorizing to care in this chapter. First, contemporary thinkers view ethos as an open-ended moral trajectory rather than a prescribed ethical structure, as in an ethical system such as consequentialism. Second, many applications of ethos employ an identity-building moral alignment between the speaker and the speech act co-created by the individual and society. Finally, ethos describes the integration of emotional/visceral and cognitive commitments. Following this threefold application of ethos, I focus on three traditions of care often lost in modernity: indigenous concepts of moral spirit in African *Ubuntu* and Cree *Wâhkôhtowin*, hospitality traditions, and Gloria Anzaldúa's notion of *Conocimiento*. The last two sections address why a care ethos is so significant and the political dimension of a care ethos.

### Ethos as an Indefinite Moral Commitment

An ethos connotes a dynamic moral trajectory rather than a fixed structure of adjudicative ethics. To endorse or claim an ethos is to make a moral commitment or participate in the moral commitment of a community, but not in a narrowly prescribed manner. Ideally, if one responds out of an ethos of care, they do not know in advance what choices they will make in any given situation; however, they are committed to performing care—to inquire, connect, and act. This generalized commitment exhibits the tension between a caring ethos and an ethic of care. The latter suggests a normative framework, whereas an ethos is a disposition more comfortable with the ambiguity of *a posteriori* moral decision-making than is an ethic. Care entails an emergent process of normativity and disposition.

Maria Puig de la Bellacasa is one of the few care theorists to employ the term ethos with depth. Her work has been particularly concerned with extending care beyond human relations. Puig de la Bellacasa explains the liminality and flexibility of an ethos of care:

> A feminist ethos of representing care is not reduced to the application of an established theory but it has to be constantly rethought, contested and enriched. Thinking of matters of fact as matters of care does not require translation into a fixed explanatory vision or a normative stance (moral or epistemological), it can be a speculative commitment to think about how things would be different if they generated care. This is a commitment, because it is indeed attached to situated and positioned visions of what a livable and caring world could be; but it remains speculative as it won't let a situation or a position – nor even the acute awareness of pervasive dominations – define in advance what is or could be. In this sense, too, what care can mean in each situation cannot be resolved by ready-made explanations.
>
> *(2011: 96)*

**92** Thinking about Better Care

There is a hint of the radical nature of care in Puig de la Bellacasa's framing of ethos. A care ethos is a "speculative commitment" that refuses to define moral action before the encounter. Moreover, Bellacasa's approach supports the process methodology of care in her claim of constant rethinking and contestation.

Bellacasa employs ethos as a methodological commitment to recognize the posthuman implications of care theory. Hil Malatino applies Bellacasa's understanding of care ethos to the responsive work of a community: in this case, the trans community. In *Trans Care*, Malatino describes the morality of an ethos as strikingly different than that of an ethic:

> When I invoke the question of ethos, I'm calling attention to collective ways of doing and the norms and principles that emerge from such ways of doing. This is a very different conception of ethical behavior than one that proceeds from ethical rules or first principles and features a moral agent who has maximal agency and unmitigated choice in the actions they take. An ethos emerges from an ensemble of practices; when we shift collective practice, we reconfigure ethos. Practices of care are always part of an emergent ethos. Because care isn't abstract, but only ever manifested through practice—action, labor, work—it is integral to our ways of doing.
>
> *(2020: 40–1)*

Malatino emphasizes the co-creative and communal aspect of care (as well as the political which I return to at the end of this chapter). The care Malatino describes is embodied: fleshed out in practices that contribute to a collective spirit that is just as much ontological as ethical. A care ethos has the potential to imbue our relational identity

Puig de la Bellacasa and Malatino highlight the indeterminate commitment to care that coalesces around the emergent knowledge of the other's needs. This responsive morality shifts ethical authority from abstract rules, rights, or formulas to the revelation of relationships. In this manner, individuals reclaim their moral agency through the improvisation needed to meet the needs of the others (Hamington, 2020). This "speculative commitment" is essential to a caring ethos.

Part of a care ethos's speculative and indefinite nature can be found in its dynamic processes. Because care is highly contextual, it must be reformulated anew in every situation, although with the help of habituated care practices. Given its relational underpinnings, an ethos of care undergoes continuous adaptation. As Puig de la Bellacasa describes, care requires hard work because it has to be rethought and adapted to each circumstance (2017: 59–60). Thus, an ethos of care means being open to involving oneself in the burden of care should needs present themselves. A care ethos entails a tenuous prescription to care, yet with a critical edge. For Puig de la Bellacasa, care is anything but a feel-good approach. Instead, its attention to oppression can lead to disagreements and conflicts by questioning how issues are assembled (Ibid: 61). To paraphrase *Star Trek*, a care ethos prompts us to "go boldly" in our daily voyages of relational discovery, leaving the possibility of care open and not determined.

### Ethos as a Co-created Moral Identity

"Ethos" is also employed as a dynamic product of individuals engaging with social understandings. An ethos may have a social expression and force; however, it is not fixed by artificial moral constraints. This co-creative aspect of care gestures toward a shared or interactive notion of agency. In their introduction to a special issue of the journal *Humanities* on *History of Ethos: World Perspectives on Rhetoric*, James S. Baumlin and Craig A. Meyer admit to the challenges of narrowing the meaning of ethos given the variety of contemporary usages. However, they conclude that "any adequate 'map' or model of ethos will include *a version of self* and its relation to culture and language" (2018: 2). Philosopher William McNeill offers a Heideggerian (and Foucauldian) notion of ethos as a dynamic way of being that exists in terms "of our stance and conduct in the moment of action," thus how we dwell in the moment and how that moment is part of "our more enduring way of Being" (2006: xi). The ethotic commitment has ontological implications as an act of self-authorship in relation to society.

For McNeill, ethos is an integration of ontology and ethics understood as rooted in ways of being that shift "our understanding of 'ethics' away from a set of theoretically constructed norms, principles, or rules governing practice" (Ibid: xii). In this manner, ethos is not permanent and unchanging but continually transitioning as we negotiate time and context. Yet, it finds continuity in the agency of our relational selves (Ibid: 13). Ethos suggests a dynamic triangulation between one's moral performance, society's moral norms, and moral self-identity. Accordingly, ethos offers a postmodern deconstructive element that blurs the categorical distinction between the one-caring and the cared-for when applied to the caring relation. Like nomadic subjects (Braidotti, 1994), the caregiver and receiver co-create one another's moral identity through caring processes. Still, even that dyad is not truly distinct from the moral milieu in which it operates. Social norms also tug and push at the caring relationship and thus also participate in identity formation. An ethos of care suggests entering the triangulation with an indeterminate commitment to care while maintaining agency over particular practices.

What I described above as a "triangulation" of caring ethos is not limited to three distinct parties of caregiver, care receiver, and the social normative context but rather a postmodern intertwining of fluid and dynamic forces. Puig de la Bellacasa describes, "An ethos of care in knowledge politics cannot be reduced to the application of the theory of good care; it has to be continuously tested and rethought" (2017: 59–60). One pertinent analogy can be drawn from

**94** Thinking about Better Care

Maurice Merleau-Ponty's concept of the "hyper-dialectic." In endeavoring to move beyond the dialectical tradition, Merleau-Ponty offers the term "hyper-dialectic" (1994: 94) to account for a humble, self-reflective interrogation of perceptual experience through all of its interactions. Merleau-Ponty is well known for leveraging his Husserlian-trained phenomenology to develop a philosophy of the body. His notion of the "hyper-dialectic" is another window into our relational ontology.

Furthermore, although Merleau-Ponty never explicitly develops an ethical philosophy, the hyper-dialectic implicates a sense of wonder in inquiry for diverse, intersectional experiences. This process suggests an emergent normativity rather than *a priori* ethical structures typically used in moral theory. Such emergent normativity has a robust contextual basis that contradicts a universalizable Kantian moral standard. Merleau-Ponty situates the hyper-dialectic as a "good dialectic" compared to the standard Hegelian approach. Michael Berman describes,

> The good dialectic is the hyper-dialectic that criticizes itself (in self-reflection, self-correction, and *verstehen* ). ... By viewing without restriction, the hyper-dialectic does not totalize experience from the disconnected distance of high altitude thinking. Instead, it inhabits that openness that we have to the world through our perceptual experiences.
>
> *(2003: 410)*

Merleau-Ponty implicitly grounds a morality of primary empathy (Daly, 2016: 225) within the framing of the hyper-dialectic. The human propensity for reflective meaning-making comes through our participation in the flesh of the world (Merleau-Ponty, 1994: 248–51) and is facilitated by our perceptual reversibility (as we touch and are touched) (Ibid: 254–7). Merleau-Ponty's constellation of thoughts surrounding the hyper-dialectic supports a rethinking of how moral identity is formed—as the activity of an independent individual's agency *and* co-created through deeply intertwined and related agents (Hamington, 2020). Co-created moral relationality is an element of an ethos of care. The presumption of a relational ontology has been central to the work of care ethicists (Robinson, 1999: 2), and an ethos of care places that presumption at the forefront. Furthermore, relationality, vital to feminist philosophy, has become increasingly significant across a spectrum of theoretical arenas.

Karen Barad, a feminist physicist and philosopher, has applied the interconnectedness of quantum physics to advance the interrelatedness of all things within her study of posthumanism. In particular, Barad extends the work of Nobel Prize-winning physicist Niels Bohr to suggest a relational ontology for all matter without jettisoning the notion of agency. To accomplish this, Barad constructs a lexicon of terms to address liminal understandings that exist between phenomena. Two such terms pertinent to this discussion are *intra-activity* and *agential realism*. Grounded in Bohr's physics of entanglement, for Barad intra-activity is the source of phenomena but in a manner that is contradictory to the Cartesian assumptions of distinct subjects and objects. Intra-activity "queers the familiar sense of causality" (2012: 77) because there is no discrete source of agency.

Nevertheless, distinctions can be made within the intra-active phenomenon: "intra-actions enact 'agential separability'—the condition of exteriority-within-phenomena. So, it is not that there are no separations or differentiations, but that they only exist within relations" (Ibid). Thus, "humans" are emergent phenomena of intra-activity (2007: 338). Barad's term, agential realism, draws upon feminist, queer, scientific, cultural, and critical social theory insights. Barad uses agential realism as an explicitly political repudiation of representational humanism. The concept brings together several forces in a dynamic and relational understanding of the world whereby matter fully participates in the doings of existence. Rather than the product of subjects or objects, phenomena are co-created: "Agency is the enactment of iterative changes to particular practices through the dynamics of intra-activity" (2003: 827). Agential realism reflects a process ontology as the universe is constantly becoming: "The world is a dynamic process of intra-activity in the ongoing reconfiguring of locally determinate causal structures with determinate boundaries, properties, meanings, and patterns of marks on bodies" (Ibid: 817) Such acknowledgment of intra-activity is not an abdication of human moral responsibility but rather a call to take that responsibility within a shared and enlarged understanding of humanity as entangled with one another and the matter of the universe. A process ontology matches the process morality of care.

Merleau-Ponty's phenomenology and Barad's extension of quantum physics point to a complex relational form of moral identity compatible with the notion of ethos proposed here. Similarly, Johanna Schmertz offers a feminist definition of ethos that entails the relational as well as the liminal space of ethos: "I ultimately want to define ethos for feminism as neither manufactured nor fixed, neither tool nor character, but rather the stopping points at which the subject (re)negotiates her own essence to call upon whatever agency that essence enables" (1999: 86). Care theorists have always posited a relational ontology. Still, an ethos of care suggests a form of relational moral agency that bears witness to flourishing within our humanity through collectively participating in a commitment to care.

### Ethos as an Integration of Emotional, Visceral, and Rational Commitments

A third aspect of contemporary ethotic thinking posits it as more than just a rational process. The modern ethotic turn incorporates emotion such that the

**96** Thinking about Better Care

distinction between thought and feeling is blurred. Some propose that emotion and reason were not mutually exclusive in Aristotle's formulation of ethos (Yoos, 1979: 48). As Stephen K. White notes, "Ethos is peculiarly aligned with both practical reason and affect, or emotion" (2009: 113). Coupled with the idea that ethos helps co-create identity, the depth of a commitment to care suggests an emotional component. People do not merely apply propositional elements regarding ethical decision-making; they have feelings reinforcing the action trajectory. For example, philosopher Werner Marx develops a non-metaphysical ethic with a phenomenological ethos. For Marx, ethos includes emotional attunement crucial to breaking out of a transactional approach that plagues the world with apathy. He claims that emotional attunement can "liberate man from the imprisonment constituted by the *indifference* towards his fellow-man and the community" (1992: 34). According to Marx, emotional attunement helps humanity constitute a sociopolitical ethos (Ibid: 69).

Contemporary applications of ethos often assume an enlarged understanding that integrates emotion with rational commitments. In addressing the mental health of school children in the UK, education scholar Jo Warin argues for a whole-school ethos of care that entails emotional investment and explicit concern for the emotional well-being of students (2017). In discussing a democratic political ethos drawn from the work of political philosopher Michael Oakeshott, Luke Philip Plotica finds emotion to be a shared resource for democratic discourse. Accordingly, Oakeshott suggests a "flow of sympathy," which includes a "stock of emotions, beliefs, images, ideas, manners of thinking, languages, skills, practices and manners of activity" that [people] draw upon as practical resources in conversation" (Plotica, 2012: 293). Care theorists have argued for a strong connection between care and emotions, as indicated above in the discussion regarding empathy and compassion as the connective elements of care. For example, Fabienne Brugère states, "The ethics of care cannot be separated from emotional factors" (2020: 37). Much like other habits of care, emotions can be cultivated (Ibid: 42). Without utilizing the term ethos, Brugère hints at the ethotic nature of care through its mutual emotional impact as a caregiver and care receiver "each affect and are affected by the other" (Ibid). Ultimately, despite analytic approaches that mitigate the significance of emotion, humans are always "affectively situated" (Bourgault and Pulcini, 2018: 4) in their web of social relations. The emphasis on emotional participation foregrounded in an ethos of care is an aspect of its spirit.

What is less common in the care literature is the role of the body in the emotional and cognitive experience of care. Perhaps this lack is partly due to the artificial divide between care ethics and care labor scholarship. The latter is more likely to address the particularities of embodiment in its fleshy form. For example, economists Mary Phillips and Alice Willatt explore the activist practices of a community kitchen in the south of the United Kingdom to argue that embodiment is an essential element in lived relationships of care (2019).

In particular, one of their conclusions is that "embodied learning involving felt emotions and physical experience disrupts our settled preconceptions of 'the ways things are,' so that movements between embodied emotions/actions, and 'care-ful' imagination and understanding, are iterative and mutually reinforcing" (Ibid: 212). The mutually reinforcing notion of disruption is pertinent to constructing an ethos of care. Emotions and their visceral expressions—rapid heartbeat, sweaty palms, a mirrored inkling of pain, and such—disrupt us in ways that draw our attention as if to remind us that there may be something important to care about. An ethos of care represents holistic participation in a caring commitment.

Emotions find their expression and visceral experience through embodiment, so it is crucial to remember the corporeal aspect of care, not just in health care but all forms of care. An ethos of care is not merely a relational commitment of cognitive assent; it is felt in the body. Philosopher Christine Leroy addresses "kinaesthetic empathy" as the internal sensation of movement when we observe the movement of others (2021). Our bodies capture and understand care in muscle memory. Leroy discusses how kinesthetic empathy can result in a sensual contagion for those who watch dance performed. Spectators not only feel but grasp an internalized inkling of the performance. Choreographer Susan Leigh Foster explains:

What do we feel, kinesthetically, when we watch a performance? This chapter's trajectory suggests that our experience is contingent, in part, on the conception of the body that pervades our historical moment. The dancing body's "contagion" can impel our bodies as outward manifestations of an interiorized psyche, to mimic its movement, and, as a result, feel its feelings. Or it can prompt an active engagement with physicality, enlivening our perception of our own bodies' articulateness. Or it can beckon us to try out/on various scenarios for moving.

However it moves us, it does affect our bodies".

*(2008: 57)*

Accordingly, non-theater caring actions can also be witnessed and internalized. The spirit of care can spread if this valued activity is iteratively observed and reflected upon. Valorizing and acting out of care can build collective momentum.

By participating in an ethos of care, we are moved *to* care for others *by* our ethotic commitment. The heart, mind, and hand draw together to participate in an uplift of spirit. A care ethos is an idea that is gaining momentum in today's social and political organizing.

For example, as discussed in Chapter 2, contemporary race activism, exemplified by the Movement for Black Lives, takes a more holistic approach to social change (Woodly, 2022: 138–9). Similarly, restorative justice scholar,

**98** Thinking about Better Care

social activist, and law professor Fania E. Davis envisions a transformation in race relations driven by an indigenous moral ethos characterized by the African philosophy of *Ubuntu*. For Davis, a less race-oppressive society is possible, but to get there, hearts and minds will have to shift, as well as policies and practices. A veteran of civil rights efforts, Davis observes that her experiences of social change efforts focused on single-issue goals and seldom created healthy relationships for activists (2019: 50–1). She finds today's activism driven by a younger generation seeking a complete social transformation.

> My dream is that restorative justice, as a worldview inspired by indigenous insights and as a medium of holistic change—on intrapersonal, interper sonal, intragroup, intergroup, and systemic levels—might help move us from an ethic of separation, domination, and extreme individualism to one of collaboration, partnership, and interrelatedness.
>
> *(Ibid: 115)*

Davis does not invoke the language of care theory, but her vision resonates with an ethos of care. This resonance is particularly true of her emphasis on relationship representative of a social ontology of care. In addition, her honoring indigenous ways of being as a counterpoint to Western individualism is essential groundwork for an ethos of care and a topic that receives further exploration in the next section.

### A Care Ethos, *Ubuntu*, and *Wâhkôhtowin*

As indicated above, ethos is a complex and somewhat indeterminate notion. Those of us living in industrialized countries might find it difficult to imagine a generalized ethos of care, except perhaps in crises where we see people and communities rising to the occasion. For example, the experience of the pandemic in the 2020s witnessed an outpouring of care in some communities but also widely publicized pockets of uncaring where some shielded themselves behind individual rights to avoid the inconvenience and sacrifice needed in a caring community. In this respect, nations of the "developed world" have much to learn from the moral culture of other peoples, including indigenous communities. Two examples include the *Ubuntu* tradition of southern Africa's Zulu, Xhosa, Tswana, and Venda people (among others) and the *Wahkohtowin* tradition of the Cree First Nations of Canada.[6]

Several scholars have addressed the resonance between care ethics and *Ubuntu*. Sinenhlanhla S. Chisale describes *Ubuntu* as "synonymous with care ethics" (2018: 1). Yusef Waghid and Paul Smeyersand claim that *Ubuntu* is "a particular formulation of an ethic of care" (2012: 6). There are significant differences given that *Ubuntu* is deeply embedded in the religious culture of Africa,

A Care Ethos **99**

and care ethics has been broadly secular.[7] Nevertheless, *Ubuntu* is frequently described as a "worldview" or "way of being" (Gouws and van Zyl, 2016: 173–4; Chisale, 2018: 3) and thus shares the spirit-like quality of an ethos. Previously, I described care as rooted in our relational ontology or being, which makes care theory a path to recapturing our humanity. Similarly, *Ubuntu* can be characterized as a journey toward our shared humanity. As philosopher Augustine Shutte understands the term:

> The concept of UBUNTU embodies an understanding of what it is to be human and what is necessary for human beings to grow and find fulfillment. It is an ethical concept and expresses a vision of what is valuable and worthwhile in life. This vision is rooted in the history of Africa and it is at the centre of the culture of most South Africans.
>
> *(2001: 2)*

Out of sensitivity to presumptions of Western primacy, and given that *Ubuntu* existed long before care theory, perhaps one could flip the Waghid and Smeyers statement to suggest that care theory is merely a particular formulation of *Ubuntu*.

Like care theory, *Ubuntu* enmeshes the personal, social, and political. Before the oppression of colonialism, *Ubuntu* was a long-standing, even ancient, communal ethic of hospitality, generosity, and compassion that imbued many African communities. However, the creation of a post-colonial state and the rebuilding of society brought *Ubuntu* to the fore once again, particularly in South Africa, through the work of the Truth and Reconciliation Commission. The nation was looking for a way forward from the devastation of apartheid. Ubuntu offered a return to traditional indigenous values that could provide comfort and meaning in chaotic times.

Desmond Tutu, who led the TRC, describes the ethotic nature of *Ubuntu*:

> *Ubuntu* is very difficult to render into a Western language. It speaks to the very essence of being human. When you want to give high praise to someone we say, "*Yu, u Nobuntu*"; he or she has *Ubuntu*. This means that they are generous, hospitable, friendly, caring and compassionate. They share what they have. It also means that my humanity is caught up, is inextricably bound up, in theirs. We belong in a bundle of life. We say, "a person is a person through other people" (in Xhosa *Ubuntu ungamntu ngabanye abantu* and in Zulu *Umuntu ngumuntu ngabanye*). I am human because I belong, I participate, and I share. A person with *Ubuntu* is open and available to others, affirming of others, does not feel threatened that others are able and good; for he or she has a proper self-assurance that comes with knowing that he or she belongs in a greater whole and is diminished when others are humiliated or

**100** Thinking about Better Care

diminished, when others are tortured or oppressed, or treated as if they were less than who they are.

*(1999: 34–5)*

It can be challenging to appreciate the intimate personal/social/political ensemble that others experience in the unity that Tutu describes. *Ubuntu* is an intriguing moral spirit for those in the West whose ethical traditions are much more individualistic and adjudicative. There is hubris in not recognizing the value and opportunity to learn from indigenous moral philosophies.

An ancient indigenous moral concept that has not received as much attention as Ubuntu among care theorists is the Cree notion of *Wâhkôhtowin*. The Cree are the largest group of First Nations people in Canada. Among the Cree, the Metis are people of mixed ancestry, specifically French and aboriginal lineage. Like *Ubuntu*, *Wâhkôhtowin* is accorded a community spirit or ethotic status with religious undertones. However, *Wâhkôhtowin* emphasizes a high degree of relationality among all things, including non-human objects. Consistent with other formulations of the definition, Matthew Wildcat offers a threefold understanding of *Wâhkôhtowin*: (1) the relatedness of humans to one another and everything in this world; (2) everything, including animals and other objects, is animate and has a spirit; and (3) there is a proper way to be in good relationship with others and all the animate objects in the world (2018: 14). Applying Western philosophy, the first two claims establish an ontology, and the third indicates morality. Wildcat quotes Metis elder Maria Campbell's definition of *Wâhkôhtowin*:

> There is a word in my language that speaks to these issues: "wahkotowin." Today it is translated to mean kinship, relationship, and family as in human family. But at one time, from our place it meant the whole of creation. And our teachings taught us that all of creation is related and inter-connected to all things within it.
>
> Wahkotowin meant honoring and respecting those relationships. They are our stories, songs, ceremonies, and dances that taught us from birth to death our responsibilities and reciprocal obligations to each other. Human to human, human to plants, human to animals, to the water and especially to the earth. And in turn all of creation had responsibilities and reciprocal obligations to us.
>
> *(2007: 5)*

Cree legal scholar Harold Cardinal offers an example of the holistic relationality of *Wâhkôhtowin* in describing how a respectful relationship can still entail drawing sustenance from the natural world:

> What I would call the doctrine of *Wahkohtowin* speaks to the laws that we have as nations that govern the conduct of our relationship with each other

and with all things in life. There are laws, there are teachings that go with how, for example, if you are a fisherman with what your duties are to the fish you take, what relationship you have to respect if you are going to continue to be able to feed your family from that fish. How that relationship is two way, our laws teach us that because not only are we related to that particular species but that species is related to us.

*(2009: 93)*

Like my treatment of Ubuntu, this is a very short and superficial acknowledgment of the rich tradition of *Wâhkôhtowin*. There are, for example, supporting doctrines of *Wâhkôhtowin* that specifically address various forms of familial relations (LaBoucane-Benson, 2009: 293–8). Colonial imperialism damaged Cree relationships in violation of *Wâhkôhtowin*, but it could not destroy the relational spirit of the people (Flaminio, 2013: 14).

In referencing *Ubuntu* and *Wâhkôhtowin*, I hope to indicate that a long-standing and deep caring ethos in a community is possible and has existed for millennia. In a capitalist society, a spirit of care appears to be a fantasy and difficult to foster, but human history demonstrates that it can be done. For the indigenous nations discussed here, the ethos reflected their understanding of the world and values and was reinforced and maintained through language, symbols, and education. While honoring indigenous traditions, there should be healthy pragmatic skepticism. Accordingly, honoring should not be the same as romanticizing. Of course, not everyone in these communities always lives up to *Ubuntu* or *Wâhkôhtowin*. They are moral ideals. Furthermore, given care theory's concern with context, any Western manifestation of a care ethos today is unlikely to mirror the indigenous communal spirit. Nevertheless, these stories can spark the moral imagination to envision a different way of being with one another and the world.

Shay Welch, drawing upon the work of indigenous scholars, reminds us that in hoping to find wisdom in the morality and practices of First Nations people, we can fall into the trap of forgetting how different our contexts and presuppositions are. This failure to recognize the foundational difference is sometimes called a problem of incommensurability (2013: 216). For example, the Enlightenment liberal underpinnings of feminist care ethics differ from the cultural origins of *Ubuntu* or *Wâhkôhtowin*. Incommensurability is a warranted concern, and we must remain wary of potential overreach in comparative analysis and skeptical of casual appropriation. However, *Ubuntu* and *Wâhkôhtowin* possess qualities that Western society can learn from in promoting a care ethos. In this regard, I agree with Welch's conclusion:

Much of traditional feminist philosophy requires a restructuring and reconceptualizing of core European foundational principles to reach more inclusive and realistic accounts of the autonomous self in diverse communities.

**102** Thinking about Better Care

My claim is this ethical and philosophical battle will remain insurmountable so long as feminist theory does not incorporate and draw on the diversity of ideas of the world to theoretically facilitate specifically nonliberal, pluralistic analyses and prescriptions for sociopolitical exchanges.

*(Ibid: 219)*

As Welch points out, while feminist ethics shares much with indigenous morality, this specific morality is only native to indigenous peoples. Colonial settlers of the West will have to work harder to overcome the socially constructed narratives of division and individualism to build an ethos of care that comes more easily to people who live out and value their relational ontology. The spirit and practice of *Ubuntu* and *Wâhkôhtowin* can show us the way to an ethos of care. Some cultures express an ethos of care through hospitality.

## A Care Ethos and Hospitality

Specific communities and cultures harbor a reputation for outstanding hospitality. How does one garner such a reputation? Iterations of welcoming and compassionate encounters contribute to an abiding narrative. For example, Fauzia Ahmed describes Bangladesh's tradition of hospitality as "an ever-present priority in daily life" and as "extravagant, spontaneous, and, at times, overwhelming" (2010: 109). The spirit and openness of hospitality are part of what I advocate in an ethos of care. Hospitality is not simply a unidirectional activity. Good hospitality benefits and comforts the guest but can also accrue significant value to the host. Encounters of hospitality are opportunities for reciprocal sharing, vulnerability, and growth (Sander-Staudt, 2010). In terms of the humble inquiry necessary for good care, welcoming someone into their home or space and generously meeting at least some of their needs can be a powerful means to learn about the plight of others for better understanding that can, in turn, foster further care. Ultimately, good hospitality entails all the elements of good care enumerated earlier. A good host brings the one welcomed into proximal space. Such hospitality provides opportunities for learning and connection while simultaneously meeting the embodied needs of the guest. Hospitable encounters may, but not always, lead to further caring actions on the part of the host or the guest.

Jacques Derrida takes up the notion of hospitality in various published works (Derrida and Dufourmantelle, 2000). Derrida appears to be gesturing toward what we are describing as an ethos of care when he claims that hospitality is "not simply some region of ethics" but instead considers it "ethicity itself, the whole and the principle of ethics" (1999: 50). Derrida frames the care about others manifested in hospitality as the heart of morality.

An ethos of care and hospitality share much in common. Through hospitality, we confront an unfamiliar or less familiar other in a space that increases comfort and potentially lowers barriers, thereby creating the possibility of reciprocal exchange and better understanding. Hospitality not only describes a set of practices, it also characterizes a disposition. To be hospitable is to welcome others to put them at ease. There are strong associations between hospitality and embodied ministrations of food and drink or perhaps the offer of a place to sleep. Ostensibly, such care is not given simply out of obligation or exchange, although historically, there have been ritualistic displays of hospitality in specific contexts.

South African theologian Robert Vosloo views an ethos of hospitality as precisely necessary at the present moment in history. Arguing that people are seeking a common moral language in light of the contemporary crisis of care, Vosloo agrees with Derrida that a spirit of hospitality is needed to lead a moral life today: "Without an ethos of hospitality, it is difficult to envisage a way to challenge economic injustice, racism, and xenophobia, lack of communication, the recognition of the rights of another, etc. Hospitality is a prerequisite for a more public life" (2003: 66). Vosloo has in mind a holistic sense of ethos that is embodied through visceral understanding. He claims,

While an ethos of hospitality, as openness to the other and otherness, challenges the mindset of enclosed and stuffy identity, it is not to be equated with a liberal, romantic openness toward otherness in which the other is viewed as an abstract ideal that serves to satisfy our aesthetic appetite for strangeness.
*(Ibid: 67)*

Vosloo does not mention care and shows no sign of being familiar with feminist care ethics. Still, he notes that hospitality has a temporal and spatial dimension consistent with what I have described as embodied care. He argues against treating hospitality as an abstraction, stating instead that it requires "embodiment in time" (Ibid: 67) in a manner that disrupts the neoliberal demands of contemporary life.

Vosloo repeatedly suggests that an ethos of hospitality is needed for public morality. It is indeed a public morality that an ethos of care supports, although not to offer a dichotomy between private and public morality. One of the early criticisms of feminist care ethics was its focus on the interaction of dyads—a personal morality between those caring and the cared-for. The rise of political feminist care ethics has led to the dissipation of such criticisms. An ethos suggests a blurring of the personal and the political. I address the political dimension of care further in the conclusion.

## A Care Ethos as Care Spirituality or *Conocimiento*

"Spirituality" can be a vexing term. Secular philosophers and theorists like me are not always comfortable with the word because of its close ties to religious conviction. As a religious studies graduate student, when someone said

**104** Thinking about Better Care

to me, "I am concerned about your spiritual life," they meant that they were worried that I did not attend church or have a religious affiliation. In addition to the association with religiosity, the word "spirituality" invokes seemingly contradictory journeys of self-discovery entailing either confronting the transcendent, that which is bigger than me, or an internal looking within oneself to discover truths. Therefore it is not surprising that few care theorists have developed a care spirituality (van Nistelrooij, Sander-Staudt, and Hamington, 2022). I contend that an ethos of care is akin to a care spirituality—a metaphysical disposition and motivation regarding our connection with others and the world experienced individually yet supported communally.

One care theorist who has addressed spirituality is philosopher Luigina Mortari. She is concerned that care theory is often too materialist: "Care ethics is based on an embodied conception of care and forgets the immaterial dimension of human life, but also the immaterial life requires care" (Mortari, 2022a: 122). The current crisis of care is usually invoked regarding providing basic physical needs. Here, "spiritual" is an inclusive term describing people's metaphysical needs. She describes human ontology as both spiritual and physical, and accordingly, "care not only requires providing material things (biological resources, home to inhabit and where to live in the shelter of weather, and therapeutic gestures of cure) and provide immaterial things that can nourish the spiritual life" (Ibid).

Nel Noddings addresses spirituality in several places outside of her work on ethics. For example, in *Happiness and Education,* Noddings draws on Martin Buber to suggest that spiritual experiences of encounter are essential and positive aspects of life (2003c: 168–78). Not surprisingly, Noddings offers a relational account of spirituality that stems from encounters with people and also with animals, plants, objects, or events that can lead to wonder and contentment. Noddings describes,

> I have come to a skeptical spirituality. I think that we have much to learn from personal accounts of spirituality and from music, poetry, nature, fiction, and loving interpersonal relations. But religious claims to knowledge are all suspect.
>
> *(2003b: 224)*

Noddings' approach mentions the communal aspect of spirituality but remains primarily centered on individual experience. However, the work of Chicana feminism scholar Gloria Anzaldúa on political spirituality and *conocimiento* perhaps best captures a care ethos as personal and political.

Anzaldúa might be the most significant scholar whose work can substantially contribute to care theory yet has not been applied. Her publications are widely read in feminist studies and foundational to Chicanx, queer theory, and feminist theory. Furthermore, Anzaldúa's writings are currently enjoying a renaissance of interest—or perhaps the interest never really waned. Nevertheless, care permeates her scholarship without necessarily using "care" as care ethicists do. In introducing the notion of a care ethos, a co-created, embodied spirit of care, Anzaldúa's work appears remarkably prescient. Anzaldúa's philosophy aims at a more caring society through spiritual and political activism. Anzaldúa deserves a complete treatment of her work's intersection with care theory, but a brief overview is offered here.

Anzaldúa is best known for her intersectional work on identity. In her much acclaimed, *Borderlands, La Frontera: The New Mestiza*, Anzaldúa pushes the edge of feminist thinking by weaving personal experience with ontological and epistemological insights in a holistic method incongruent with the neat categories of modernist analytical theory. She describes straddling physical, psychological, sexual, and spiritual borders and the oppression and joy stemming from such a position (2007: 19). Many of Anzaldúa's concepts are pertinent to a care ethos. Still, I restrict myself to two: *nos/otras* and *conocimiento*.

Relationality is at the heart of Anzaldúa's thinking. She makes the significance of relationality explicit in her use of the term "*nos/otras*," where she problematizes the categorical distinction between them and us:

We all of us find ourselves in the position of being simultaneously insider/outsider. The Spanish word "nosotras" means "us." In theorizing insider/outsider I write the word with a slash between nos (us) and otras (others). Today the division between the majority of "us" and "them" is still intact. This country does not want to acknowledge its walls or limits, the places some people are stopped or stop themselves, the lines they aren't allowed to cross. ... [But] the future belongs to those who cultivate cultural sensitivities to differences and who use these abilities to forge a hybrid consciousness that transcends the "us" vs. "them" mentality and will carry us into a nosotras position bridging the extremes of our cultural realities.

*(2000: 254)*

Anzaldúa's political theory includes *nos/otras* as an ontological foundation that is both hopeful in its potential for healing yet morally weighty and demanding in its implication for shared responsibility in oppression. *Nos/otras* diminish everyday social psychological practices such as scapegoating and othering essential to moral parochialism. As philosopher Andrea Pitts describes, *nos/otras* is a "critical relation politics that seeks to interrogate the many economic, political, and otherwise normatively laden sites of separation and construction of difference among Chicanx and Indigenous communities" (2021: 142). Earlier, I claimed that care theory has a postmodern element because it resists commonly employed philosophical categories. Anzaldúa raises the political stakes by challenging categories and claiming that such distinctions are a legacy of oppression and colonization (Zygadlo, 2017: 213).

**106** Thinking about Better Care

For Anzaldúa, *conocimiento* is a practical epistemic term of art. A Castilian Spanish word meaning "knowledge," Anzaldúa employs it in various interrelated ways to suggest a subversive and holistic knowledge practice. Pitts describes Anzaldúa's *conocimiento* as "a state of embodied awareness that equips one with a capacity to act and to create by locating the muliplicitous relations in which one is embedded" (2021: 37). Anzaldúa offers seven stages of conocimiento. These stages are a reflective practice consistent with living the examined life with a holistic, political, and embodied dimension.

Anzaldúa's moral analysis is sophisticated and multidimensional. Publishing up to her passing in 2004, Anzaldúa's work predated much of the expansion of care theorizing beyond its formative years. Her exclusion from the care literature may be explained by unconscious bias, or a writing style not aligned with dominant theoretical approaches. This exclusion is unfortunate, given that her spiritual/political philosophy is potentially beneficial in shaping the vision of a care ethos. Anzaldúa's liminal and holistic understanding matches the co-creative aspect of ethos employed here. For example, Pitts finds Anzaldúa's concept of nos/otras as underlying a notion of "multiplicitous agency" that troubles inclusion and exclusion distinctions in ways that can assist in creating a "relational agency that aids in coalition efforts" between communities resisting oppression (Ibid: 133). Effective care as humble inquiry, inclusive connection, and responsive action are practices of relational agency that begin with an abiding disposition or spirit of care.

## Conclusion: The Significance of A Care Ethos

> We feel the urgency for a new ethos of civilization, a new ethos that enables us to give qualitative leaps in the direction of more cooperation in our living together.
>
> —Leonard Boff (1999: 11)

Sometimes revolutionary ideas appear to have a life and momentum of their own and emerge from various sources as if emerging from the atmosphere. For example, when care ethics was first introduced to the Western world in the 1980s, Carol Gilligan, Nel Noddings, and Sara Ruddick were not actively collaborating yet developed a similar relational framework. The time was ripe for alternative thinking about the relational nature of morality, ontology, and epistemology. Similarly, as care theory matures, numerous publications have posited the need for a broad-based care movement (Stone, 2000; Tronto, 2005; Engster, 2010; Hamington and Flower, 2021). The social movement sought in this book is a care revolution. This revolution must be fueled by something more than propositional and rational changes. As African American Studies scholar Ruha Benjamin states, "The facts alone will not save us" (2022: 36). The political theorists of care are correct: practices, laws, and responsibilities must change to foment caring. Yet, the care movement is not sustainable or sufficiently robust if the culture or social imagination does not change. A care ethos provides the psychosocial momentum to fuel, drive, and maintain the movement even when systems fail.

The work of the aforementioned Hil Malatino is an example of seeking to intertwine a cultural spirit of care with political urgency. Recall that Malatino is one of the care scholars who has invoked the need for a care ethos. Focusing on the oppression of the trans community, they reject the distinction between the political and the ethical, a la Tronto. However, Malatino has in mind a supportive co-created moral spirit that connects the personal and political in what they describe as "an infrapolitical ethics of care."

> it is a form of care that circulates among a beloved community that enables both political resistance and intracommunal survival and resilience. … one of the central aspects of an infrapolitical ethics of care is to support vulnerable and traumatized persons in the context of a break: to witness, hold space for, and, when appropriate, amplify and intensify their anger, especially if this amplification serves the greater purpose of keeping one another alive.
>
> *(2019: 131)*

Although care theorists have always held space for emotion in ways uncommon in analytic philosophy, Malatino complicates a care ethos by suggesting that for oppressed people, supporting and fueling rage may be essential for individual care and supporting a movement of care. Rage as an expression of care in service of social change is an idea that Malatino shares with philosopher Myisha Cherry who argues that rage can be indicative of who we care about (2021: 32). For Malatino, healing and repair are the ultimate goals of this spirit.

In *A Paradigm of Care*, Robert Stake and Merel Visse argue that a care paradigm or zeitgeist is a generalized idea or spirit to give and receive care (2021: xv). Without employing the term "ethos," there is an understanding that an effective care movement requires society's empathetic imagination. As Stake and Visse describe, the zeitgeist of care is an expression and culmination of humanity:

> A paradigm of care exists among people with widely different experiences and values, even among those with contentious views of care practice and recovery but sharing the aspiration that the medium of caregiving be made better.
>
> A paradigm of care is an expression of humanism, an increasing devotion to the sanctity of life nearby and afar, an investment in compassion, an attitude of benevolence.
>
> *(Ibid: 142)*

**108** Thinking about Better Care

Allowing this "aspiration" to flourish is the goal of a care movement and a care revolution. We have seen that an ethos is co-created; thus, we need the community for the care we require and for better assistance in caring for others. Philosopher Seisuke Hayakawa describes this as "a more inclusive epistemic-empathic community" (2021: 134). For Seisuke, such a community seeks to liberate those who carry excessive epistemic burdens in self-sacrificial care. These burdens are borne disproportionately by oppressed and disadvantaged people.

Infrapolitical relations intertwine epistemology, ontology, and morality. A paradigm of care, the care zeitgeist, requires an ethotic understanding to help traverse these human-made boundaries.

A care ethos may go against the grain of popular narratives steeped in individualism, acquisition, and revenge. Still, an ethos of care returns us to our fundamental relational and embodied humanity. Carol Gilligan finds care subsumed into the ideology of ethics as adjudicative justice that imposes morality on people rather than drawing it from their being:

> Once the ethic of care is released from its subsidiary position with a justice framework, it can guide us by framing the struggle in a way that clarifies what is at stake by illuminating a path of resistance grounded not in ideology but in our humanity.
>
> *(2011: 43)*

Thus, the spirit of care is paradoxically challenging because of its unfamiliarity in popular narratives of morality and politics. Yet, it is oddly comfortable because it resonates with who we are. Adopting an ethos of care returns us (ideally) to childhood, family (broadly construed), and friends, where the neoliberal stranglehold of competition, merit, and individualism are not as strong. Thus, an ethos of care is familiar but sometimes elusive. It combines emotional and intellectual rationalities: heart and mind. By naming and valuing a care ethos, we hope to curate a caring spirit in our lives and transform society for the better.

One might object that a care ethos does not impact bad actors—those who choose to care little and take advantage of others' care for them. Joan Tronto identifies the aforementioned phenomenon of "privileged irresponsibility," whereby a sense of entitlement or lack of awareness allows some people to shirk caring responsibilities (2013: 103–6). Accordingly, the objection would be that a bad actor would not participate in the spirit of care. To this objection, I raise two responses. One is to suggest that a community imbued with a care ethos makes it more challenging not to participate. Some will still avoid caring but lifting social norms means outliers must resist the tide. Care can be a physical and dispositional contagion. My second response is to recall that care is non-binary. Everyone cares, but we often fall short of what we have described as good care. A process ethic of care means that all can improve at caregiving.

Some may be less enthusiastic caregivers, yet they may incorporate aspects of good care in their lives if it becomes an essential participant in the social imagination.

The aim of the care theory literature valorizes care to make the world a more caring environment. Care thinking is not an ideal theory with the unattainable goal of perfect caring. Human limitations and frailty make such an outcome unrealistic. Nevertheless, the nature of care as a process morality means that improvement in caring is possible. Changing policies, practices, laws, rules, and institutions is essential, and as I have pointed out, care theorists have offered tremendously valuable suggestions and arguments in that direction. However, society will only achieve a higher standard or norm of care through the interplay of a caring state and caring people. People makeup society's institutions, including its governing bodies, and these institutions are ultimately responsible to them. Accordingly, a care ethos is vital. The combination of a care state with rights and practices that ensure its people's needs are met, a caring populace that supports one another, and the procedures that ensure care is a potent blend capable of moving society forward in lateral progress. Without a care ethos, a widespread spirit of care, state-sponsored care such as healthcare, education, disaster relief, and disaster preparedness will be undermined by narratives of division witnessed in the ascendancy of neoliberal ideas.

Just as witnessed and experienced by the students in the Umoja program, a spirit of care can buoy our relational connection in a precarious world.

## Notes

1  Umoja is also the name of a matriarchal village in Kenya founded for women who were survivors of violence and girls running from child marriages.
2  As of the writing of this book, there remains disagreement over how to use non-binary language to describe the Latina/Latino population. Both "Latinx" and "Latine" have been suggested as alternatives, however, employing non-binary language is still a minority position and not favored by everyone. My use of Latine and Latinx are intended to be gender inclusive.
3  One of the less-thematized aspects of Umoja is how it infuses feminist values into a male community. The terrible oppression imposed on men of color has led to a form of hyper-masculinity as a defense mechanism. This masculinity is marked by heightened disaffection. Umoja is a program about caring. The terms of compassion and understanding used by the Umoja Brotherhood could be viewed as unmasculine within a hypermasculine framework. A further examination of masculinity takes place in Chapter 5.
4  A follow-up article on Sarshevack Mnahsheh written post-high school graduation and three years after his previous testimonial about Umoja finds him taking care of and mentoring his younger five (of seven) siblings while his mother works during the day. He describes helping them be prepared for school and life. It is not much of a stretch to speculate that the habits of care Mnahsheh garnered through the Umoji program influenced his care for his siblings. (Kirsch, 2020).
5  Even standard interpretations of the Ancient Greek understanding of ethos have been challenged to be more expansive. (Yoos, 1979: 43).

110   Thinking about Better Care

6 As a settler living on lands stolen from indigenous people, my use of these terms may strike some as another cultural appropriation. I accept this criticism. I do not claim an authoritative position for their use nor the deep understanding of one who lives their values. However, I humbly employ these terms to honor and learn from them and the people who developed them. All scholarship includes appropriation of others' ideas: a standing on other peoples' shoulders. I utilize *Ubuntu*, and *Wahkohtowin* to open a space for Western scholars to seek further knowledge and appreciation of these ideas. Ideally such research comes from indigenous scholars.

7 In addition to the religiosity of Ubuntu, another difference with care ethics is that it has been criticized by some for sexism (Kai, Tait, and Lauw, 2013).

# SECTION 2

# Invitations and Provocations

## Imagining Transformative Possibilities

Section 1 laid the theoretical foundation for viewing care theory as a personal and social transformational driver, understanding care as a process morality with the aim of ethical betterment through humble inquiry, inclusive connection, and responsive action. The latter are skills that prepare us to care well in a nimble and improvisational manner to respond to emergent needs. A care morality is thus a commitment that is best when internally driven rather than externally imposed. Adopting such a commitment to good care entails related concomitants that lead to seeking improving care through better knowledge acquisition, empathy, and practices. Ultimately, an ethos of care can be collectively engendered—a spirit that drives a shift in social values. Care has been essential for sustaining humanity, and raising the attention, value, rhetoric, and instantiation of care is a moral imperative for the challenges before us.

Section 2 represents an opportunity for stretching the imagination. The four chapters in this section offer invitations to think about some radical positions differently, specifically as caring possibilities. Thus, while I invite you to consider these positions as caring directions, I recognize they are also provocations. If you find the ideas in the first section persuasive, this section asks what possible practical implications result. In other words, how does a commitment to care translate into our personal and social practices? This commitment should entail openness to at least considering new ideas. Although they are not the only provocative areas of caring responsibility I could offer, the four I have chosen are significant: feminism, socialism, humanism, and veganism. The discussions of these areas are not comprehensive, but aspects of each area are utilized for these imaginative flights.

DOI: 10.4324/9781003368625-7

**112** Invitations and Provocations

Chapter 9 offers a conclusion and a return to the idea of a care revolution. In particular, I claim that care as a process morality can lead to a process revolution that opens the opportunity for moral progress.

## Cargo

*By Greg Kimura*

You enter life a ship laden with meaning, purpose and gifts
sent to be delivered to a hungry world.
And as much as the world needs your cargo,
you need to give it away.
Everything depends on this.

But the world forgets its needs,
and you forget your mission,
and the ancestral maps used to guide you
have become faded scrawls on the parchment of dead Pharaohs.
The cargo weighs you heavy the longer it is held
and spoilage becomes a risk.
The ship sputters from port to port and at each you ask:
"Is this the way?"
But the way cannot be found without knowing the cargo,
and the cargo cannot be known without recognizing there is a way,
and it is simply this:
You have gifts.
The world needs your gifts.
You must deliver them.

The world may not know it is starving,
but the hungry know,
and they will find you
when you discover your cargo
and start to give it away.

Used by permission. www.cargopoem.com

# 5

# FEMINISM AND RESISTING TOXIC MASCULINITY

## Prologue: Challenging Masculine Tropes

Australian anthropologist Aaron J. Jackson describes how his life as a caregiver for his son, Takoda, took a tragic and unexpected turn in the summer of 2011. Takoda, only four months old then, began having frightening tonic-clonic (grand mal) seizures. He was diagnosed with Global Developmental Delay and later declared severely intellectually disabled (Jackson, 2021: 6). Takoda had multiple episodes daily, and trips to the hospital were fraught with fears that he might not return home (Ibid: 27). Jackson understandably felt pain and anguish from his son's physical state. He also recognized the disruption to his sense of masculinity. Jackson acknowledged that men are not socialized to care in the ongoing intimate manner this disability requires. Care for Takoda now became the center of Jackson's world. Utilizing his skills as an anthropologist, Jackson engaged in autophenomenology to bring his experience with Takoda into a study of men who find themselves caring for severely disabled children. Jackson, along with his wife, Kim, and his two children, Takoda and India, traveled to the United States in 2015 to engage at length with eight fathers of children who "require a high level of hands-on care and are considered by their respective carers as severely or profoundly disabled" (Ibid: 11). The resulting autoethnographic work is both moving and insightful regarding many aspects of care, including gender differences, embodiment, and disability.

One of the straightforward declarations of those engaged in feminist theory is that "gender matters," and this understanding is an essential aspect of Jackson's exploration. He observes, "Fathers' worlds of care are shaped by an attunement to prevailing cultural notions of masculinity that often emphasise the subordination of empathy, the risk of vulnerability, and the value of control and recognition"

DOI: 10.4324/9781003368625-8

**114** Invitations and Provocations

(Ibid: 80). Patriarchy, the idea that society is organized around men and male values, is operant in both explicit and subtle ways. Ironically, a commentator once questioned my use of the word "patriarchy" in a journal article because he thought I was using terminology that was a relic of a feminist analysis whose time had passed.[1] However, such is not the case; Jackson clarifies how necessary feminism is to combat patriarchy and heteronormative thinking in the present.

For example, one of the fathers that Jackson worked with, Ethan, cared for his son, Jack. Ethan's son suffered from childhood epilepsy and was diagnosed with Pervasive Development Delay and autism. Ethan had left his job and was selling rare toys on eBay to be more available for his son. Ethan, like Jackson, had suffered abuse and abandonment as a child and struggled to determine the path toward being a good parent, particularly how to be a good father. On the one hand, Ethan was present in Jack's life. Still, on the other, he has not achieved a masculine record of individual hierarchical achievement, such as climbing the corporate ladder that he prized so much. Jackson describes the tensions and contradictions Ethan feels: "he is wedged by the fact that the ideals of manhood and fatherhood he is drawn to implicitly clash and even devalue the care labour he is engaged in" (Ibid: 87).

If the circumstances were not challenging enough, Ethan began reading the works of Christian counselor and author John Eldredge. Like many Christian leaders I discuss in Chapter 7, Eldredge advances traditional, heteronormative roles for men and women in the family and society. Published in 2001, his *Wild at Heart: Discovering the Secret of a Man's Soul* was the most popular Christian work on masculinity of its time. Eldredge advocates for an essentialist and wilder form of masculinity than did the previous formulation of masculinity by the Promise Keepers. This evangelical organization peaked in popularity in the 1990s and focused on having men keep their heteronormative familial commitments. Part of the modern "muscular Christianity" movement, Eldredge characterizes all men as seeking a battle to fight, an adventure to live, and a beauty to rescue (Harper, 2012). Unfortunately, Eldredge's words heightened Ethan's sense of failure to be a proper man. Ethan desired to be a primary caregiver in his son's life. Jackson describes the psychological toll that Eldredge's vision of masculinity has on Ethan:

> The felt weight of these moral gender expectations press in on Ethan's everyday experiences of fatherhood and caregiving, squeezing out their potentiality for an analytic reworking of his thoughts and emotions, or alternatives for thinking himself out of difficulty—rendering problematic his relationships with his wife and children in the process.
>
> *(2021: 87)*

Jackson turns to the intersectional analysis of feminist theorists such as Linda Alcoff and bell hooks to negotiate the dynamics of Eldredge's manifestation of a masculinity we can describe as toxic. Alcoff frames identity as an "interpretative horizon" that she links to embodiment (2006: 92–113). Accordingly, identifying as male brings significant meaning in a society concerned with gender but also calls forth a hermeneutic and a value system. hooks describes a dominant form of masculinity that "socializes males to believe that without their role as patriarchs, they will have no reason for being" (2004: 115). Jackson points out that he and Ethan share the experience of having a father who perpetuated an ethic of domination with masculinity that eschewed care, portraying it as the role of women and a sign of weakness (2021: 83). Given his childhood experience of masculinity and the contemporary social messages from people like Eldredge, the struggle Ethan feels in coming to terms with his identity as a caregiver takes a personal toll but is also an opportunity for rethinking social norms.

Jackson's analysis navigates the tension between norms of extreme masculinity and the demands of caring fatherhood. The experience of Ethan and the other participants in his study are refracted against Jackson's self-identity and challenges in taking care of Takoda.

Amid the relational burden, Jackson also finds the joy and power of embodied care. In this instance, I am not using the term "power" as something to hold over another but as an energy that can be shared and enliven experience. Care is not just an ontological reality in a rational sense, but it goes to the core of our embodiment. In one poignant incident, Jackson straps his son's legs to his own for Takoda to experience playing soccer.

> My feet are fastened to Takoda's in a pair of joining sandals. I stand and adjust the tension in the straps so that our bodies are positioned correctly and are in alignment. I look down at our bodies coupled by a web of material, Velcro, and plastic. It is a strange sight for me to see him stand so upright. I wonder how tall he is in comparison to his peers. I take a step and his leg follows mine. I can feel his hesitation and the weight of his leg through my own, so I wait for him to initiate the next step. He does. My leg follows his through space. Slowly, we find a rhythm and begin moving as one. I must deliberately alter the length of my stride but otherwise we achieve synchronization. There are reversibilities at play. At times I lead. At others I trail. I am both passive and active. I am mover and moved. Sometimes we move in unison and it's hard to differentiate. We kick a soccer ball: I swing our legs and our feet make contact with the ball, which hurtles across the room. "Hey," I beam. He squeals and looks up at me. His face is awash with joy and his eyes are full.
>
> *(Ibid: 63)*

Jackson's account of caring for Takoda epitomizes how care's burden, joy, and sacrifice can go hand in hand. Western moral theory has difficulty accounting for such embodied care. However, feminism has provided an intellectual space for revaluing and reconsidering corporeal experience. Jackson is navigating toward a feminist-informed caring masculinity. Many men, even privileged

**116** Invitations and Provocations

men, have been alienated from the joy of embodied caring through narratives of masculinity that eschew relational caring.

The prolific care theorist Eva Feder Kittay has written extensively about caring for her severely disabled daughter, Sesha. Kittay's description and analysis of her relationship with Sesha features the reciprocity of a caring relationship. Kittay does not offer a unidirectional understanding of caregiving despite the differences in physical capacity but instead addresses how much she has learned within the caring relationship. Kittay claims that Sesha taught her about joy (2019b: xx–xxi). For Kittay, the joys of caring add motivation to human being: "With joy, life has a point, a reason to be, a perfection of what it is to be" (Ibid: 71). Kittay also realizes the centrality of embodiment to the care experience, and she credits feminism for that sensitivity:

> We always know each other only through body, but we pretend otherwise. It has been the wisdom of feminism to reveal the displaced body that lurks with the mental, the repressed emotion that lurks with the "rational," the hidden dependence within in-dependence.
>
> *(Ibid: 248)*

Feminism brings a particular set of tools for living the examined life. Just as Socrates asked questions that unsettled the powerful of society, so too are feminist philosophers today questioning the sources and sustenance for identity-based power and privilege. The list of those marginalized under patriarchy is long, including those disabled and anyone queered by not meeting the impossible standards of heteronormative gender binaries. As Jackson demonstrates, even white males who dare to place care as a primary value suffer from the critical eye of dominant masculinity.

Care theory is an original contribution of feminist theorists born out of women's experience as the bearers of care in society. No matter how popular care ethics becomes across disciplines and worldwide, one cannot disentangle its development from its feminist roots. However, as is argued in this chapter, feminism is also a viable outcome of a commitment to care for all people, not just women and not just cis-gendered white women. In other words, a commitment to care, with its attending commitments to inquiry, connection, and action, should make feminism a worthwhile moral option. In this chapter, I define what I mean by feminism—a modern, inclusive, critical race feminism, and explain why being a feminist, particularly as resistance to dominant forms of toxic masculinity, is so vital to creating a caring society. There are many reasons feminism contributes to a more caring world, and writing about them would fill a book. In what follows, I focus on feminism as an integral approach to challenging the hegemony of a particular character of uncaring manliness that permeates patriarchy. Of course, feminism and feminist scholarship offer much more than simply resisting misogyny; however, this chapter's subject is that resistance.

## Inclusive, Decolonial, Transnational, Critical Race, Queer and Trans Affirming, Intersectional Feminism

> Feminism: how we pick each other up. So much history in a word; so much it too has picked up.
>
> —Sara Ahmed (2017b: 1)

> My own definition of a feminist is a man or woman who says, "Yes, there's a problem with gender as it is today and we must fix it, we must do better."
>
> —Chimamanda Ngozi Adichie (2012: 48)

"Feminism" remains a complex and dynamic term. When I offer an introductory lecture on feminism to undergraduate students, I describe the word in a tripartite manner, including describing it (1) as naming historical movements, (2) as a lens of analysis and consciousness, and (3) as a position of advocacy rather than merely a neutral field of study. I also point out that the singular "feminism" belies the varied cultural, historical, and intellectual reality of the "feminisms" that exist. However, these complexities are just the tip of the iceberg, and there is always more to say about feminism, including naming the critical and ground-breaking work that feminists have done in the academy. For example, care theory is just one of feminism's many intellectual contributions. In what follows, I characterize how I am employing feminism as an inclusive, decolonial, transnational, critical race, and intersectional approach (in both disposition and practice) that renders awareness and resistance to unfair power and privilege. The vision aligns with Gloria Anzaldúa's claim, "In this millennium, we are called to renew and birth a more inclusive feminism, one committed to basic human rights, equality, respect for all people and creatures, and for the earth" (2011: xxxix).

Feminism, like care, also has a dark side. The term is sometimes invoked in racist, transphobic, and exclusionary ways. As Bonnie Mann, Erin Mckenna, Camisha Russell, and Rocío Zambrana observe in their inaugural essay as editors of *Hypatia*, the premier journal of feminist philosophy,

> Racism, colonial control, reinforcement of modes of material inequality, political exclusion, and social sanction sometimes travel under the banner of "feminism," are sometimes entangled with feminist thinking and practice, and sometimes appropriate feminist demands for their own ends. While the word "feminism" is associated with hope and renewal in some contexts, at some times, for many of us, it also carries historical associations of betrayal, dismissal, privileged indifference, and willful ignorance in relation to crossed relations of power
>
> *(2019: 395).*

For many feminist thinkers, the misuse of feminism is not enough to dissuade them from the transformative potential of the feminist movement. For example,

**118** Invitations and Provocations

given their oppressive academic experiences, countless feminist scholars of color have had every reason to walk away from the label "feminist." However, many notable scholars have found a value in the ideal of feminism that motivates them to resist oppressive applications and reclaim the moniker in its most inclusive form. Gloria Watkins, better known as bell hooks, could have fled from feminism given her academic experiences of discrimination. However, she maintained that "feminism is for everyone" and that despite recognizing multiple forms of identity oppression, she advocated feminism (2000:31). Although hooks popularized the straightforward definition that feminism is "the struggle to end sexist oppression" (Ibid: 26), she clarifies that she means a broader resistance to patriarchal domination. hooks is an outspoken proponent of inclusive feminism. Sarah Ahmed left her position at Goldsmiths, the University of London as the inaugural director of the Centre for Feminist Research because of the failure of the university to address the problem of sexual harassment on campus. Ahmed describes finding many traditional works of feminist theory disappointing because they "did not engage with the questions of racism and sexism in the academy" (2017a). However, Ahmed does not sour on the feminist ideal, and her work has elevated and promoted intersectional feminism: "I am not a lesbian one moment and a person of color the next and a feminist at another. I am all of these at every moment" (2017b: 230).

Although critical of Western feminism, political theorist Chandra Talpade Mohanty, like hooks, maintains a commitment to feminism while endeavoring to give it a more transnational form. Her project is to argue for decolonizing feminist theory and creating solidarity that neither loses sight of entrenched privilege nor forgets history. Mohanty claims, "Third world women have always engaged with feminism, even if the label has been rejected" (2003b: 50). She explicitly connects the kind of feminism she envisions to the groundbreaking work of Cherrie Moraga and Gloria Anzaldúa on Latine feminism in the United States (Ibid: 50–1). Mohanty emphasizes the importance of history and not forgetting the legacy of intersectional oppression—the "simultaneity of oppression" that women under colonial hegemony have faced. Mohanty also faced intellectual oppression when as a graduate student at the University of Illinois, she wrote: "Under Western Eyes" (1988). The article addresses how "'women' as a category of analysis is used in western feminist discourse on women in the third world to construct 'third-world women' as a homogeneous 'powerless' group often located as implicit victims of particular cultural and socio-economic system" (Ibid: 66). Mohanty describes the "disbelief and hostility" she received in some circles which contrasted with the "relief and recognition she received from postcolonial and US women of color" (2013). Mohanty perceived that she was "cast as the 'nondutiful daughter' of white feminists" (2003a: 55). Nevertheless, she advances the notion of inclusive feminism that is anti-racist, postcolonial, and anti-capitalist in resisting identity-based oppression.

Drawing upon the transnational themes in Mohanty and adding particular attention to intellectual colonialism, philosopher Serene Khader advocates for a nonideal feminist universalism—an acute understanding and sensitivity to power and privilege that is part of the vision of feminism needed in care theory. In *Toward a Decolonial Feminist Universalism*, Khader points to a modern theoretical conundrum in the tension between universalism and relativism. Feminists and other scholars who challenge hegemonic Western ideas and methods are often accused of being relativists. She notes that many feminists have overcompensated in avoiding the relativistic claim by constructing a feminist moralism grounded in Western assumptions. Thus morality inadvertently takes on an imperialist character to "save" non-Western societies. Khader labels this approach "missionary feminism" in that it is well-meaning but not self-aware in its grounding in "ethnocentrism, justice monism, and idealizing and moralizing ways of seeing that associate Western culture with morality" (2019: 23). Khader claims that the authentic source of concern should be idealization rather than giving up on developing universalizing theory. She is mainly concerned with asymmetrical moralism, a naturalistic fallacy that makes Western ideals normative. An "objective" critique implicitly carries the assumption of the colonizer. Khader suggests that a nonideal universalizing theory that pays attention "to the nonnormative assumptions held by those likely to adopt it and the effects normative concepts will produce if adopted under existing social conditions" (Ibid: 32) is a superior approach to engaging in theory. Regarding feminism, Khader is attracted to hooks's framework of describing it as an opposition to sexist oppression rather than offering specific cultural formulations as the solution to patriarchy. Khader has engaged in the difficult work of opening a conceptual space for feminism that is universalist but not missionary in nature (Ibid: 46).

Khader's sharp analysis has significant implications for care theory, and the feminism embraced in this chapter and this book. Care ethics can and has fallen prey to missionary feminism sometimes (I include my work as subject to this criticism). Implicit bias favoring Western forms of care can neglect the myriad approaches to care manifested in various communities and configurations worldwide. For example, Kanchana Mahadevan finds that Carol Gilligan's work on care "does not theorize Western feminism's position of privilege" (2014: 224). Perhaps no one's care theorizing is riper for cultural-centric criticism as missionary feminism than that of the late Nel Noddings. In her early work, Noddings draws heavily on mother-child relationships and the home as paradigmatic of care. Although many of the insights translate to other cultures, she assumes Western configurations. However, Noddings is not alone. Many years ago, when my daughter was very young and I was developing the concepts of embodied care, I recounted an anecdote about washing my daughter's hair and the nonverbal care communicated in the proximal experience (Hamington, 2002). My phenomenological analysis did not problematize cultural, gender,

**120** Invitations and Provocations

and class assumptions (i.e., cultural mores regarding a father washing a daughter's hair and the privilege of time to care for my daughter). In other words, I did not use "queer phenomenology" as Ahmed suggests to interrogate the underlying circumstances of my perception (2006). Given the emphasis on experience in feminist care ethics, the potential for implicit bias and Western normative assumptions is fertile. That is why it is incumbent upon the one committed to care to be vigilant in their humility and efforts to learn and grow.

Perhaps nowhere has contemporary feminism demonstrated more of an exclusionary posture than toward trans identity. Philosopher Hil Malatino has documented the rationale, history, and power of "trans rage" as "a telling reaction to the failures of feminism and gay liberation movements to substantively include trans subjects" (2021: 835). This trans exclusion is physical—at venues open to women but not trans women, and intellectual—in feminist language that reinforces gender dimorphism. A self-identified intersexed scholar, the abandonment of feminism is particularly hurtful because Malatino is strongly influenced and has benefited from feminist thinking. Their dissertation advisor was the groundbreaking and influential Latinx feminist philosopher Maria Lugones (Malatino, 2020a). For Malatino, rage is communal energy that can fund transformation, a force for good if appropriately channeled (2021). Collective and self-care are essential outlets for rage, particularly for those oppressed as much as the trans community. Care becomes a mode of resistance, survival, and healing. Therefore, despite the harm done, Malatino remains hopeful about the possibility of a transfeminist coalition. The ideals of feminism remain powerful in resisting patriarchy, even if the applications and assumptions have sometimes been damaging.

*Revolutionary Care* endeavors to negotiate the balance between universalism and normativity that Khader addresses, particularly regarding the open question of feminist identity. Care means resisting patriarchal forms of masculinity that harm people and their relationships. However, the particular means for fighting sexism and misogyny are context-driven. Feminism is one of this book's four applied provocations, but none are prescriptive in an absolute sense. Still, they should remain a distinct possibility for anyone committed to care.

My references to the works of hooks, Ahmed, Mohanty, Malatino, and Khader suggest that the feminism one must consider if they are committed to care is broad and inclusive. The feminism of care cannot be just that of biological females, white women, middle-class women, or the women of northern nations (Wing, 2000). Arbitrary exclusion is a barrier to relationship and is patently uncaring. Furthermore, the inclusive feminism I have in mind here is not merely theoretical. At times, feminist theory can be complex and somewhat abstract despite its basis in experience. Committing to care involves knowledge and action. Angela Davis warns, "Global sisterhood in the twenty-first century will be a failed venture if it is imagined primarily as a project of generating knowledge—whether anthropological or legal—about similarities and differences among northern and southern women" (Davis, 2000: xi–xiii). Similarly, care cannot simply be a mental exercise but must manifest in people's lives.

Good care involves responsive action, and an ethos of care suggests that such efforts can occur on an individual and/or collective level. In addition to her highly regarded status in the academy, hooks endeavored to build a grass-roots feminist movement. She intentionally wrote *Feminism Is for Everyone: Passionate Politics* in an accessible and inclusive manner. For example, she argued that feminism benefits men by releasing them from the "bonds of patriarchy" (2015: xiii). Hook's argument was advanced over 30 years before Jackson's ethnography was published, with the latter suggesting a similar conclusion. Although not the mass resistance movement hooks would have liked, the term "feminism" has come a long way from being the pariah it was only a few decades ago. A Pew Research Study conducted in the United States in 2020 found that about 61% of women indicated that "feminist" described them very or somewhat well. This number is even higher (71%) for those with a bachelor's degree. Over 40% of those surveyed indicated that feminism benefited them, and most Republicans and Democrats felt that the Equal Rights Amendment (ERA) should be passed. These numbers show a positive trend even from Pew studies conducted only three years prior. Of course, popular feminism is not the same as academic feminism, and, likely, many who invoke the term feminism are not using it in the inclusive, transnational, critical race, and intersectional manner I have described. Nevertheless, the increased acceptance of the term means that it is not now as radical for those who commit to care to embrace it as it was when Phyllis Schlafly publicly denigrated feminism. Schlafly, who spearheaded efforts resisting the passage of the ERA in the United States, noted the enmity between feminism and patriarchal masculinity:

> If American women want to know where all the manly men have gone, they can blame the feminists. Not only can men no longer hold the door open for women, they can't even save a woman's life and get a gracious thank you. Feminists have destroyed the relationship between men and women. Most women like big, strong, John-Wayne-type men. They want men who bravely put out fires, fight in combat, protect their wives and children against intruders, and save damsels in distress. But feminists have made a lot of men afraid to be manly. It's time to say, we love manly men.
>
> *(2012)*

If all men ever did was open doors and save lives, they could be pardoned. However, ideals of chivalry mask inequitable power relations in toxic masculinity that is particularly antithetical to caring relations. Inclusive feminism remains a necessary rebuff against a virulent manly identity that impacts more than merely men's behavior but broadly influences contemporary relational understanding.

**122** Invitations and Provocations

## Masculinity and Toxic Masculinity

> I see feminism as one of the great liberation movements in human history. It is the movement to free democracy from patriarchy.
>
> —Carol Gilligan (2011: 176)

Given popular misconceptions, distinguishing between "men" and "masculinity" is warranted. Male students have occasionally accused me in my introduction to women's studies courses of "picking on men" (despite my presentation as a cis-gendered man). The distinction between identifying as a male and identifying with masculinity is significant but not popularly recognized consistently. Judith Butler argues that male representation as gender is a chosen performance or a stylized repetition of behaviors (1999). Butler's performative approach to gender negotiates a liminal ground between biological and social constructive determinism that maintains individual agency. However, more often than not, gender is viewed as a manifestation of biology. Masculinity, or masculinities, are archetypes or ideals that some men strongly identify with. In a gender-binary dominant society, masculinity has been assigned a great deal of value. Masculinity is a social construction of reality—a set of meanings attached to an ideal of manliness. Gender studies scholar and long-time editor of *Feminist Studies,* Judith Kegan Gardiner, describes the conceiving of gender as a social construction as the most significant accomplishment of 20th-century feminist theory (2004: 35). Men do not have to be masculine in any particular way. Still, there are social pressures to conform to certain norms of masculinity from childhood through adulthood. The masculine ideal may shift and vary, but ask any group of people what the norms of masculinity (or femininity) are. A relatively consistent list of characteristics emerges because modern society places so much stock in the gender binary. Queering that binary allows progress in challenging the boundaries of masculine and feminine care, but the social inertia keeping them in place has been strong.

For example, one research study compared how three categories of British and Americans, men, women, and society as a whole, perceived traditional masculine norms as defined by ten variables: restrictive emotionality, self-reliance through mechanical skills, negativity toward sexual minorities, avoidance of femininity, the importance of sex, dominance, toughness, disdain for homosexuals, self-reliance, and pursuit of status. The researchers found men perceived that other men valued traditional forms of masculinity while women and society did not. This value conflict caused the researchers to speculate about how men handle the tension and the adaptation and coping behaviors. Social norms of masculinity are being challenged, but not in a homogenous manner. From the standpoint of building a more caring society, this conclusion indicates that men's groups are likely to have the most entrenched anti-relational values (Iacoviello et al., 2021).

Feminism and Resisting Toxic Masculinity **123**

Those committed to care should be provoked to consider identifying with feminism to resist the detrimental impact of masculinity on people and their relationships. There are three critical terms regarding the manifestations of masculinity to be considered: patriarchy, sexism, and misogyny. Misogyny is extreme hatred of women. Kate Manne refers to misogyny as the shocking acts of harm that reinforce sexism and patriarchy. For Manne, sexism is "the theoretical and ideological branch of patriarchy: the beliefs, ideas, and assumptions that serve to rationalize and naturalize patriarchal norms and expectations" (2020: 7). Patriarchy is the social system of control, power, and authority that men exert in society resulting in male entitlements. Regarding care practices, patriarchy allows men to be cared for but exonerates many privileged men from care work. Joan Tronto describes the discrepancy: "Patriarchal societies inscribe men's control over women's daily activities, but not the need to engage in those activities as both a responsibility and privilege of their superior gendered location" (2013: 71).

Some might argue that masculinity is evolving for the better regarding relational sensitivity, but that evolution is slow and inconsistent. Manne, for example, acknowledges that much progress has been made in terms of manifestations of misogyny in society, but masculine entitlement persists. She argues that women are still socially restricted from taking "masculine-coded goods" from men while being compelled to give men "feminine-coded goods." Masculine-coded goods include leadership positions, authority, influence, money, and other forms of power, as well as social status, prestige, and rank (2019: 113). Feminine-coded goods include respect, love, acceptance, nurturing, safety, security, and safe haven—goods associated with care work (Ibid: 130). Patriarchal entitlement creates social norms where dangerous masculinity can manifest. Tronto is concerned with the way modern society has distributed care responsibilities. She finds patriarchy assigning men a "pass" on caring responsibilities predicated on men engaging in certain types of valued care activity, leaving women to shoulder the daily care duties.

Tronto offers two categories of passes: protection and production. The protection pass has a distinctly masculine character in that the work of police and military, even when women are among their ranks, has a masculine nature. To need protection is to be feminized (2013: 72–6). According to Tronto, the second pass given to men is for production, as witnessed by the persistent gendered dichotomy between "breadwinners" and "caregivers." Even when men are the private sphere, caregivers, they are socially feminized (Ibid: 80–2). Tronto recognizes that such categories are dynamic and changing. Patriarchy may be entrenched, but it remains a social construction that leaves open the possibility for change toward a more inclusive feminist future.

Social construction can be relatively benign, as in the association of warning with red and yellow. However, many of the popular narratives attached to masculinity are harmful. As Gilligan describes, "manhood [or masculinity]

**124** Invitations and Provocations

can easily become a license for carelessness .... But it is absurd to say that men don't care" (2011: 24). As a social construct, masculinity is also a malleable ideal. Bonnie Mann writes, "Any particular mode of masculinity is constituted through time, realized over the course of events" (2014: 48). The masculine ideal has taken different forms in different contexts. Sociologists Sara L. Crawley, Lara J. Foley, and Constance L. Shehan concur, noting that no singular form of masculinity exists. However, there are exemplars or iconic men in Western culture, such as John Wayne or Ronald Reagan, whose qualities are held up as a male fantasy. The authors describe, "These heroes symbolize force, power, control over others, individualism, wealth, and ability to enforce their individual wills" (2007: 54). Crawley et al. cite the work of R.W. Connell, who claims that although there may be many forms of masculinity, the aforementioned social narrative about masculinity reinforced in popular culture forms a "hegemonic masculinity." This hegemony does not only assert itself over other masculinities but over femininity as well (1987: 183). Thus, concern about masculinity's impact on relationality is not just a problem for cis-gendered men, but because of its popular valuation, it becomes a problem for everyone.

Although Nancy Chodorow brought psychoanalytic feminism to theorizing about masculinity and femininity four decades ago, Judith Kegan Gardiner finds that her approach remains persuasive today. Gardiner recounts Chodorow's findings regarding Western masculinity; it is "emotionally impoverished, competitive, and fearful of intimacy" (2013: 115). Chodorow notes that although ideals of masculinity may be relationally truncated, social institutions such as market capitalism and Christian organizations do not require greater relationality but valorize the emotional deficits. Dispassionate demeanor, abstract objectivity, and transactional relations held sway as authoritative values. Historian Kristin Kobes Du Mez, who meticulously traces the connection between modern Christian evangelical movements and the clinging to a particular vision of masculinity, finds late 20th-century evangelicals

> looked to a rugged, heroic masculinity embodied by cowboys, soldiers, and warriors to point the way forward. For decades, militant masculinity (and a sweet, submissive femininity) would remain entrenched in the evangelical imagination, shaping conceptions of what was good and true.
>
> *(2020: 12)*

Far from being universally condemned, harmful forms of masculinity are celebrated in some circles of society.

Given the damage that certain forms of masculinity can do to caring relations, a commitment to care entails an openness to inclusive feminism that resists patriarchy. Before moving on, I offer a brief discussion of toxic masculinity.

Toxic masculinity is a contested term and a source of concern for feminist scholars. One of the challenges is how to characterize what behaviors are toxic within the broader category of masculinity. Toxic masculinity describes aspects of values associated with a manliness that is particularly harmful in society—to relationships and specifically to women. Toxic masculinity has no definitive characteristics. However, it is often associated with misogyny, homophobia, aggression, bullying, sexual assault, and domestic violence (Harrington, 2021). As one might expect, the term is malleable with no monolithic understanding. Political theorist Bryant W. Sculos lists norms, beliefs, and behaviors associated with toxic masculinity:

> Hyper-competitiveness, individualistic self sufficiency (often to the point of isolation nowadays, but still, and more commonly in the pre-Internet days, in a parochial patriarchal sense of the male role as breadwinner and autocrat of the family), tendency towards or glorification of violence (real or digital, directed at people or any living or non-living things), chauvinism (paternalism towards women), sexism (male superiority), misogyny (hatred of women), rigid conceptions of sexual/gender identity and roles, heteronormativity (belief in the naturalness and superiority of heterosexuality and cisgenderness), entitlement to (sexual) attention from women, (sexual) objectification of women, and the infantilization of women (treating women as immature and lacking awareness or agency and desiring meekness and "youthful" appearance). (2017)

The term "toxic masculinity" first appeared in the 1990s at the dawn of the development of the "mythopoetic" men's movement. Since then, "toxic masculinity" has received numerous scholarly and popular applications. The modifier "toxic" suggests that although masculinity is harmful and normative in the culture, it is curable (Harrington, 2021: 347). Some feminist theorists criticize this distinction indicating that some manly behaviors are localized, which exonerates other masculine activities. Relatedly, claims of toxic masculinity may undermine the critique of the underlying patriarchal system by framing the problem as one of individual men. Moreover, the label "toxic masculinity" requires further intersectional analysis. Terms such as "machismo" suggest men of color are the worst offenders of toxic masculinity. Such labels intertwine identity-based oppression with masculine privilege.

For example, Erik Morales finds "These stereotypes of aberrant masculinities justified the racial oppression Black and Chinese communities experienced, as many white Americans believed they were unfit for American modern life" (2015: 7). Morales acknowledges the complexity of popular narratives such as machismo in that although they may fuel a racist stereotype. Such labels influence male ideals and sometimes result in behavior that manifests to fulfill the characterization.

Sociologist Carol Harrington argues that we should only use the term "toxic masculinity" in a narrow descriptive sense and not as a broader analytic category.

She is concerned that some men can disavow toxic masculinity as a problem due to unenlightened men but not themselves. For Harrington, toxic masculinity dangerously "individualizes the problem to the character traits of specific men" (2021: 350). Thus some men can distance themselves from some acts while the systemic privileges that men accrue are "systemically obscured." Australian sociologist Andrea Waling goes so far as to claim that the men and masculinity studies field is not as engaged with feminist thought and methodology as it purports. Bucking the trend of pluralizing identities to capture the diversity of manifestations better, Waling prefers the singular "masculinity" over "masculinities" in the context of post-structural analytics of fluidity. Like Harrington, Waling views "toxic masculinity" as positioning men as victims and masculinity as "the only expression of gender that men and boys can engage, but also, deflects attention from forms of female and non-binary masculinity" (2019: 363).

Criminologist Michael Salter, who studies violent crimes against women and children, is also concerned that "toxic masculinity" can mask other social forces at work. Salter notes that there are financial interests that welcome a focus on toxic masculinity to obscure their role. He notes that studies indicate liquor store density can be correlated with violence, but the alcohol industry welcomes the attention given to toxic masculinity (2019). A similar argument could be made about the prevalence of guns in male violence associated with toxic masculinity. However, Salter does note that there is a role for the term "toxic masculinity" when he quotes Raewyn Connell, "when the term toxic masculinity refers to the assertion of masculine privilege or men's power, it is making a worthwhile point. There are well-known gender patterns in violent and abusive behavior" (2019). Waling, Harrington, Salter, and Connell point to the limitations of the label "toxic masculinity." Those interested in care must be willing to engage with the messiness of human existence, and there are no simple single-variable answers to endemic social challenges. Furthermore, the radical implications of care are interdependent. Thus, we find many intersectional connections between masculine, religious, economic, and other narratives that suppress care.

In advancing a more caring society, individual acts of male violence and repression that harm relationships and systemic patriarchal practices that mitigate caring must be resisted. Feminism provides tools for identifying, analyzing, and countering masculinity. However, the oppression is pervasive on both a personal and political level. bell hooks describes patriarchy as the most life-threatening social disease, defining it as

> a political-social system that insists that males are inherently dominating, superior to everything and everyone deemed weak, especially females, and endowed with the right to dominate and rule over the weak and to maintain that dominance through various forms of psychological terrorism and violence.
>
> *(2004: 18)*

Despite the desire to relegate patriarchy to the past, we cannot underestimate its virulence. Although I began this section by describing the difference between men and masculinity, social narratives don't always make this distinction.

For example, Sculos describes the level of identification with masculinity by both men and women in specific conservative communities: "The reaction on the Right to discussions about toxic masculinity are inherently confrontational because they assail something tied to a self-perceived identity, one they were likely conditioned with from a very young age" (2017). In recounting his own experiences of publishing his social analysis addressing Disney's "Beauty and the Beast" to explore the contemporary relationship between toxic masculinity, capitalism, social responsibility, and transformational politics, Sculos found tremendous popular resistance from conservative media. Furthermore, he received hateful and mocking emails and voicemails, sometimes referencing personal information. He expresses particular surprise given that the article was published in a "relatively obscure academic journal." Sculos believes the extreme reaction is partly due to large swaths of the general population (men) identifying with many aspects of toxic masculinity (2017).

Toxic masculinity is another version of misogyny—the hate of women. Patriarchy, misogyny, and toxic masculinities can be nuanced to describe different phenomena or actors, but they each share a repressive force on caring relations. Manne provides a comprehensive analysis of misogyny. She frames patriarchy as a political phenomenon "dependent on there being norms and expectations of a patriarchal nature" and misogynist hostility as "anything that is suitable to serve a punitive, deterrent, or warning function, which (depending on your theory of punishment) may be anything aversive to human beings in general, or the women being targeted in particular" (2019: 67). While women are the primary focus, Manne does not limit misogynist hostility to women alone. Patriarchy is one system of domination interwoven with other methods of oppression, with toxic masculinity being one manifestation (2019: 12). Also, as an entrenched institution, Manne points out that everyone in society is complicit in its perpetuation at some level (2020: 8). For this project's purposes, traditional masculinity values, toxic or otherwise, undervalue or undermine the humble inquiry, empathetic connection, and responsive action of good care, and therefore a commitment to care suggests adopting the feminist mantle.

## A Care Ethos and a Feminist Consciousness

In Chapter 4, I described a care ethos as the spirit or spirituality of care. A feminist consciousness can be an essential participant in a caring ethos. What does it mean to have a feminist consciousness? Feminist historian Gerda Lerner described such consciousness as a group's awareness of oppression, drawing upon Marxist notions of class consciousness (1993: 284). Even though Lerner

**128** Invitations and Provocations

acknowledged the complexity of oppression, understanding that the oppressed can also be the oppressor, I seek to describe a feminist consciousness beyond understanding one's personal oppression.

In the spirit of empathetic attunement, I suggest a feminist consciousness participates in an ethos of care and is available to all, regardless of identity. A care ethos only requires an adequate will and effort toward openness. Caring is not a pretense to fully knowing someone else's circumstances, including their oppression. On the contrary, the non-binary, liminal nature of care theory indicates moving away from a dichotomous sense of understanding the other as all or nothing—knowledge/no knowledge. The feminist consciousness employed here is grasping the pain of others, not colonization of it. Perhaps Nigerian feminist psychologist and social theorist Amina Mama best describes the feminist consciousness sought as a participant in a caring ethos:

> Conscientisation is a dynamic dialectical relationship between radical thinking and action. It takes integrity and courage to listen across boundaries, to hear and respect the multiple languages of gender and sexuality, marked by the striations of other dimensions of power and status. Unless we link collective organising with coherent feminist consciousness informed by sound theories of gender oppression and change, we easily become subject to an identity politics that will keep us divided. By strengthening feminist consciousness, we strengthen the collective "will to change" that we express through activism.
>
> *(2017: 1)*

Mama has historically been concerned with issues of identity. She identifies as feminist and challenges prevailing Western thought by claiming that feminism originates in Africa.[2] Her view of feminist consciousness is expansive, intersectional, and linked to making change. One can see the language of ethos ("dynamic dialectical relationship") and good care in the statement above.

Feminist consciousness-raising groups were a significant component of the 1960s and 1970s second wave of feminism. We can learn much about fomenting an ethos of care from the feminist consciousness-raising experience and philosophy. There were no rigid rules for feminist consciousness-raising other than a commitment to listening honestly to women's experiences, learning from one another, and co-creating a spirit of change that translated into action. Although the language of care was not explicitly prevalent within the writings of consciousness-raising groups, it was entailed in the process. Social work scholar Deborah Western describes a multi-phase transformation in consciousness-raising groups. First, women shared their stories of oppression under misogynistic patriarchy, including experiences of sexual harassment, rape, domestic violence, and unequal pay. However, the personal and political connection becomes apparent in sharing stories, and a narrative emerges (2013: 47). This consciousness-raising is a co-created transformation of self and community in an ethos of care. Inquiry, connection, and action infused with tangible and intangible spirit.

The point is that a commitment to care should also lead one to value and be open to the wisdom of feminism. Consciousness-raising can be co-constitutive of an ethos of care. For those privileged individuals who are not directly experiencing the pain and suffering of particular identity-based oppression, the empathetic and imaginative work to have one's consciousness raised will be more challenging but certainly within the capabilities of embodied human beings.

## A Path Forward for Men: Caring Masculinities

> Part of what we have to do is to expand our notions of manhood and power so that providing people health care and caring for children and being good stewards of the environment, that's what men do ….. As opposed to just going to war and making lots of money and, you know, telling other people what to do.
>
> —Barack Obama (2021)

The ultimate goal of this book is to envision and enact a more caring world through moral commitment and a spirit of care—a revolution. I have suggested that such a commitment should open one up to radical ideas and labels inferred from a moral life of caring. Feminism is one of those radical potentials. Feminism is radical not in the sense that it is an absurd or crazy idea but because patriarchy is so entrenched at the center of civilization that rethinking the values of heteronormative masculinity appears to be a form of blasphemy. Some might argue that it might be best to do away with the notion of masculinity, given that it reflects an inaccurate binary connotation for the human condition and so many toxic and misogynistic manifestations. However, some theorists propose that perhaps a more realistic feminist task is reimagining masculinity, as Barack Obama recommends above, thereby providing men with a more relational and life-affirming masculinity as a set of ideals. Recalling that hegemonic masculinity is a socially constructed narrative, it is not deterministic—it can be resisted and changed despite its historical appearance as immutable.

Sociologist Karla Elliott argues for a "practice-based" caring alternative to dominant forms of masculinity. For Elliott, "practice-based" means leveraging the caring practices and behaviors that men already engage in to expand the possibilities of caring masculinities (2016: 241). The challenge is that men must change their relationship with power and privilege. For example, men would have to relinquish traditional masculine notions of competence and mastery as dominance over the family and relationships in favor of understanding competence as mastery over relational skills. She remains hopeful that such change is

**130** Invitations and Provocations

possible because, given the opportunity and will, men have exhibited successful, caring experiences. Elliott cites numerous studies demonstrating the self-reported positive responses and benefits men receive when engaging in caring activities. For example, she draws from the interviews of Niall Hanlon, who found that men described care work as making them feel self-respect, competency, and pride, as well as happiness and joy (2012: 137). More important than simply providing positive reinforcement to men who engage in caring masculinity, Elliott finds a more significant personal and social impact for men embracing the role of caregivers: "An ethos of affective, relational, nondominating care ... motivates people to support care. In other words, an ethos of care helps to cultivate more care in people. Care begets care" (2016: 254–255). For Elliott, toxic masculinity is not a forgone conclusion despite its intransigent history.

Political philosopher Asha Bhandary addresses masculinity in her thoroughgoing liberal defense of care as an individual choice made within a Rawlsian justice framework. This approach separates Bhandary from many care theorists who criticize liberalism, yet she holds their other intellectual commitments regarding promoting care in society and concern regarding masculinity. She recognizes that some manifestations of masculinity devalue care and that the dominance of masculine values must change to imbue society with greater care. Trained as a philosopher rather than a sociologist, Bhandary shares Elliott's optimism that caring masculinity is possible: "Teaching caregiving skills to everyone and restructuring institutions will result in a society where caregiving is subjectively valued" (2020: 152). Bhandary takes a voluntaristic approach with expectations that many people will choose not to care but that an ethos of care can be built that will be generally attractive. She even suggests the possibility of a "care corps" of young people that would be trained and work as caregivers, thus infusing the country with systematic exposure and education in care processes (Ibid). In addition, there are examples of care awareness and activism programs that positively impact advancing more feminist forms of masculinity.[3] Accordingly, as Aaron Jackson observed, men can find joy and connection in the process of caring.

On the one hand, challenging toxic masculinities and patriarchal power is essential to building a caring society. On the other hand, confronting the gender binary is also part of a commitment to care. Keeping in mind that care work is not afraid to engage with complexity, there are no single-variable or quick-fix cures for the masculine repression of care. However, feminism has made clear that gender/s matters. Gender is not the only thing that matters but it is a powerful force in our society. We all participate in the construction and reinforcement of norms. A commitment to care includes a spirit or ethos that should make us more sensitive to how personal and political power dynamics play out. In *We Should All Be Feminists*, Chimamanda Ngozi Adichie says clearly,

Gender matters everywhere in the world. And I would like today to ask that we should begin to dream about and plan for a different world. A fairer world. A world of happier men and happier women who are truer to themselves. And this is how to start: we must raise our daughters differently. We must also raise our sons differently.

*(2012: 25)*

## Notes

1 Kate Manne discusses how feminist analysis is often framed as obsolete: "There is often a sense that misogyny is a thing of the past … I doubt that this is true though, and it defies considerations of parsimony. Although a patriarchal order is something broader than misogyny, the latter is a ubiquitous and arguably causally necessary aspect of the former, insofar as it serves to enforce patriarchal norms and expectations" (2017: 101).
2 Mama was asked if she was a "womanist" employing the term coined by Alice Walker to distinguish white feminist from black feminism. Mama replied that such a distinction was not needed in the African context: "white women have always looked to Africa for alternatives to their own subordination …. African feminism dates far back in our collective past—although much of the story has yet to be researched and told" (Mama, 2001).
3 For example, The MenEngage Alliance is an international organization that works with men and boys to transform unequal power relations and dismantle patriarchy by, "Transforming patriarchal masculinities and rigid, harmful norms around 'being a man.' Working with men and boys on gender justice through intersectional feminist approaches. Building inclusive collaborations from local to regional to global levels. Developing joint actions in partnership with and accountability to women's rights, gender- and other social justice movements" (MenEngage Alliance, n.d.).

# 6
# SOCIALISM AND CREATING A CARE ECONOMY

## Prologue: Economic Care from Kolkata, India to Seattle, Washington

Karma Kutir is a voluntary social welfare organization providing women's vocational training in India. The operation was founded in 1961 by the pioneering Indian social activist Phulrenu Guha (1911–2006), who deserves attention as a significant feminist leader of the 20th century. She advocated for women and the oppressed on many fronts, including sex education, rights for sex workers, and literacy (Sur Ray, 2017). Karma Kutir reflects Guha's philosophy of integrating economic empowerment with intellectual development in a holistic manifestation of care. The organization serves marginalized and impoverished women through handicraft training, production, marketing, and self-employment preparation. Karma Kutir maintains a central showroom and offices in the West Bengal city of Kolkata, India, and opened additional training centers in the rural communities of Aamtala, Bisnupur, Mahmudpur, and Palliunayan. Over six decades, Karma Kutir has helped thousands of women obtain self-sufficiency and meaningful labor. However, Karma Kutir is more than a transactional educational facility that contributes to labor productivity: it also models a caring approach to labor and economics.

Context drives Karma Kutir's work. India is a country of wealth extremes. Like the United States, the disparity between the rich and poor is striking. The top 1% of the wealthiest Indians own over 42% of the country's assets (a higher percentage than in the United States). In comparison, the bottom 50% of the country's population owns less than 3% (in this regard, the United States is somewhat better) (Ghatak, 2021). Furthermore, women's social and economic plight in India is precarious, particularly for those not in the wealthy class.

DOI: 10.4324/9781003368625-9

Socialism and Creating a Care Economy **133**

According to the World Economic Forum's Global Gender Gap Report for 2021, India ranked 135th out of 140 countries surveyed for the index, which employs an array of social indicators to determine relative well-being. The reasons for this low rank are small labor participation rates for women, poor health and survivor statistics (an indicator of possible intimate partner violence), and an average compensation rate of one-fifth of a man's salary (Press Trust of India, 2021).

The accomplished American Journalist, Moni Basu, describes the conditions in Kolkata (the location of Karma Kutir), near where she grew up. On a trip to India, Basu chronicles the plight of an old acquaintance, Amina, against the backdrop of the wealth disparity in the region. Amina had worked in Basu's childhood home, and Basu tried to visit her on her trips to India. Approximately 80 years of age (well beyond the average lifespan in India), Amina's plight mirrors the precariousness of poor women in India. Amina lives in a slum near the gleaming Quest Mall, where India's wealthy shop. Her meager living space, made possible by the generosity of a son-in-law who pays the rent, is shared with her grandchildren and sometimes a daughter. Amina has been a domestic worker from a young age, often holding multiple jobs. Although hobbled by decades of strenuous physical labor, Amina must continue to eke out a meager existence. Basu quotes Amina in exemplifying the hopelessness of the impoverished masses, "I will always be a poor person. ... There is no way out for people like me" (2017). Karma Kutir endeavors to interject hope through the prospect of economic advancement and caring for people ignored by society.

Philosopher Bindu Madhok employs Karma Kutir as a case study regarding how care ethics can provide a unique theory-practice nexus instrumental in addressing human poverty. Madhok points out that Karma Kutir operates a holistic approach to vocational training rather than an oppressive "banking method" (Friere, 2005: 109) of education which frames students as passive receptors of information. Karma Kutir offers daycare, preschool, and after-school programs, where children receive school uniforms, meals, health checkups, medications, and lessons (Madhok, 2019: 25). They also provide funds for transportation and lunch for trainees. In addition, Karma Kutir also responds to the community's specific needs by offering training and placement programs for impoverished young adults and supplementary teacher training on computer use. Madhok interviewed women who had participated in Karma Kutir's training programs at various facilities. Through these interviews, one can witness an abiding ethos of care beyond the numerical success of Karma Kutir's trainees. For example, one woman offered how the community responded by allowing her to take homework when her father fell ill, and she had to stay home (Ibid: 26). Other women relayed similar expressions of communal support. Madhok explains, "They don't view Karma Kutir simply as a place of training or employment but more so a nurturing environment where they feel safe, cared for, and trusting of one another and their supervisors" (Ibid: 27–8). Many of Karma Kutir's program graduates feel so attached to the community that

**134** Invitations and Provocations

they decide to stay and work or volunteer for the organization (Karma Kutir). For Madhok, the community at Karma Kutir exemplifies how care theory has advantages over other ethical frames:

> Ethical approaches which prioritize maximization of utility, individual autonomy, or rights on the other hand, fail to make the necessary relational connections between poverty, vulnerability, security, and care responsibilities in their context-specific forms and thus fall short in comparison to an ethics of care approach.
>
> *(2019: 29)*

For Madhok, care ethics has a contextual reality or "bottom-up approach." This aspect of care is why it is a non-ideal theory (realistic about implementation rather than just focused on moral perfection) and represents the ethical thinking needed at the present moment.

What if society, through its economic distribution and business operations system, provided the grassroots care Karma Kutir offers its community? In her article on Amina, Basu hints at this possibility of interjecting the care found at Karma Kutir into economic thinking by mentioning the work of progressive economists such as Thomas Piketty (2020: 359–61) and Raj M. Desai (Desai and Joshi, 2013). These economists have been critical of the disparities and sexism in India and have offered solutions that involve a more fair distribution of resources. Many economists, some of whom are addressed in this chapter, have suggested that changes need to be made to economic practices to make them fairer and more sustainable. However, although aligned with such approaches, this chapter somewhat shifts the ethical telos or goal. Although I am entirely supportive of fairness, the priority taken here is care—making sure everyone in society has their essential needs provided for. A caring economy would also be fairer than those dominant ones in society today. However, my point is this: care comes first. The provocation of using the term "socialism" in the title of this chapter is not predicated solely on a fairer distribution of wealth but rather on fulfilling the essential needs of those in society so that they may thrive and flourish. In other words, an ideal of a particular standard of income equality is not as compelling as ensuring that people are adequately cared for, even if these concepts are not mutually exclusive.

Some 850 miles west of Kolkata is the city of Pune, India. Pune and later Mumbai were the childhood homes of economist turned politician Kshama Sawant of Seattle, Washington. As a young person, Sawant was obsessed with the problems of hunger and poverty (Jaffe, 2015: 23) that she witnessed. This obsession drove her to obtain an economics PhD in the United States. During her graduate studies, she was troubled by the stark examples of homelessness and poverty in the face of enormous wealth (Kamb, 2013). Her PhD project was an empirical study addressing elder labor policies and support for those like

Amina described above. The dissertation highlighted the need for various state programs to support older adults. Relatedly, one cannot assume that living in an extended family (as is frequently the state narrative) alleviated all the suffering (Sawant, 2009: 222–3). Sawant moved to Seattle, Washington, and in 2014 was elected to the city council. She served in that capacity for four terms and withstood recall efforts through 2023.[1] Sawant is the first member of the Socialist Alternative party to hold public office. She has spearheaded the fight for a $15 minimum wage and curbs on corporate power and environmentally damaging projects. Sawant views socialism as a means to care for the community:

> People would ask me, especially when we were running the campaign, "Aren't you worried about the 'S' word?" … Certainly, there is truth to that because of the Cold War–era propaganda and everything. But with the recession and the collapse of the idea of the American dream among generations of American young people who are going to have worse-off standards of living than their parents for the first time in American history— for them it's not so much about the "S" word. It's the "C" word. "Capitalism" is the dirty word.
>
> *(Sawant, 2015)*

Does a commitment to care translate into advocating socialism? As found in the work of Karma Kutir, should we ensure people experiencing poverty have gainful employment, education opportunities, and a caring infrastructure to pursue one's life goals?

Several clarifications are warranted. Of course, capitalists—people who engage in the market for profit—can and do care. The wealthy, hedge-fund managers, industrialists, and CEOs exhibit care under particular circumstances. However, socialism, as outlined here, provides a more systematic approach to providing for the needs of society members. *Revolutionary Care* is not merely about offering policy recommendations. The notion of socialism suggested here includes a care ethos whereby the commitment to care includes a spirit of wanting the members of our society to be cared for. Thus, caring might include a different disposition toward socialism. I flesh out a particular notion of socialism in the following section.

Like all the provocations and invitations to care in the book's second section, economics is much too large a topic to be addressed comprehensively. So instead, I focus on a few central economic issues. First, I define how I employ socialism given its various meanings. Socialism has a technical definition among trained economists, but I broadly discuss it as *an economy providing for society's essential needs*. Next, I briefly review emerging literature integrating care ethics into economic theory. The works in this field are not extensive, but some themes emerge. Next, I consider what it would mean to construct a needs-based sustainable economic system drawing from the existing works

**136** Invitations and Provocations

of care theorists and others. Then, I take on three particular economic areas: unionization, taxation, and debt. Labor organizing and progressive taxation have declined in the last half-century, and I suggest this is to care's detriment. Furthermore, debt has become an overarching burden that can make work appear like servitude for many. Finally, I conclude the chapter by discussing a moral revolution in economic thinking where caring infrastructure for people and the environment is the goal.

## Socialism Defined for this Context

Socialism is generally a bad word in the United States. Between 2010 and 2021, the Gallup organization polled Americans about their attitudes on economic terms. Capitalism received a favorable rating from 60% of survey respondents in a relatively stable popular assessment, while socialism received a substantially smaller 40% positive review. In assessing these findings, Senior Editor Jeffrey M. Jones observes that the definition of socialism is malleable depending upon one's disposition toward the idea. Those who favor it tend to associate socialism with "a fairer, more generous economic system, and how socialism would build on and improve capitalism." In contrast, those critical of socialism find it "undermining Americans' work ethic and building an increased reliance on the government, along with mentions of the historical failure of socialism when adopted in other countries and how socialism does not complement the U.S. government system" (Jones, 2020). Socialism has a public relations problem in the United States. Some politicians, such as Bernie Sanders, have raised the favorable profile of socialism, but powerful and well-funded narratives remain that denigrate socialism. Setting aside the rhetoric, I am framing socialism as *an economy that makes a substantial investment in caring infrastructure to meet the needs of its citizens*. It can also suggest an attitude of economic care for others that should pervade individual and business operations.

Contemporary narratives always juxtapose socialism with capitalism. The latter is associated with neoliberalism, freedom, democracy, and being on the right side of history (given the "fall" of communism). The capitalism/socialism dichotomy is false because there has never been a clear social experience of absolute capitalism or socialism. Some countries are more socialistic, and others are more capitalistic, but all economies are "mixed" to some extent. For example, although the United States has numerous capitalistic tendencies (competitive markets, limited government intervention, and capital accumulation), subsidies, minimum wages, rent controls, health, and safety laws, public services, taxation, and many other practices familiar to Americans separate the country from absolute free-market capitalism.

Furthermore, as economist Nancy Folbre points out, capitalism always relies on a hidden economy of relational care to function: "Even in the United States, a country widely considered the epitome of modern capitalism, more than half of all the work performed on a daily basis is unpaid, involving the provision of goods and services for oneself or others" (Folbre, 2020: 221). Given the lessons of history, no one would earnestly desire that the country become a purely free-market economy as such a life would be treacherous and perhaps, nasty, brutish, and short. Under a "more" free-market economy of the 19th century, labor was perilous. For example, the mill workers in Paterson, New Jersey, worked 13.5-hour days until labor actions prompted a reduction (Loomis, 2018: 21). Long hours were just one of the consequences of the unregulated capitalism of the era. At the turn of the century, losing a limb on the job typically cost the loss of employment and came with no compensation. In contrast, socialistic cooperation, industrial laws, pooling of resources, collective bargaining, and distributive justice have led to many labor protections and comforts we expect in the modern economy. Yet, these protections ebb and flow as many workers continue to toil in precarious and oppressive jobs.

This chapter does not advocate socialism over capitalism per se but instead supports *economic policy and practice that exhibits caring* that appears more closely aligned with socialistic ideas. Sociologist Anthony Giddens offers the following general definition of socialism:

A socialist society involves a combination of industrial democracy and central direction of economic enterprise. Government control of economic life is needed to control economic fluctuation and redistribute wealth. More extensive democracy, covering industry as well as the political sphere is necessary to make sure that government power is not used to suppress individual liberties.

*(Giddens, 1989: 651)*

Giddens invokes democracy twice in the above statement. Democracy or inclusionary participation is a central aspect of how I frame socialism, as is the notion of wealth redistribution. This socialistic redistribution is for the care and flourishing of society and can manifest in several ways. Accordingly, I offer no one precise definition of socialism. Economist Thomas Piketty also employs an amorphous understanding of socialism but is adamant that an alternative to free-market capitalism, or "hypercapitalism," is needed. Piketty suggests a new manifestation of socialism that he describes as "participatory socialism," characterized as "participative and decentralized, federal and democratic, ecological, multiracial, and feminist" (2021: 2). Piketty's emphasis on decentralization conflicts with Giddens's traditional definition of socialism. Some centralized control seems necessary to prioritize caring for the well-being of citizens but not, as Giddens points out, suppressing individual liberties. Piketty makes a refreshing nod to how any reconceptualization of the economy must consider feminist and multiracial concerns. He acknowledges that historical manifestations of socialism were not immune to patriarchal, colonial, and racist elements

**138** Invitations and Provocations

(Ibid: 22). This claim starkly contrasts defenses of the "colorblind" rationality typically associated with economic theory.

The care economy socialism envisioned here must be inclusive—an essential element of effective care described earlier. Such an understanding of caring socialism is close to Piketty's definition, except perhaps for my emphasis on caring over fairness. The theme of the unfairness of current capitalistic practices, such as wage disparity and taxation, pervades Piketty's assessment of capitalism, and I agree. However, I am interested in fairness to the extent that it advances caring. Those committed to care should desire to proffer care to other members of society.

Reconceptualizing economics in terms of care priorities means challenging the dominant values of capitalism. For example, capitalist assessment of the economy emphasizes constant growth. The microeconomic objective of increasing a company's market share, sales, and profits parallels the macroeconomic goal of growing gross national product and wealth. Capitalism is admittedly the most productive economic system in history. Even Karl Marx acknowledged the wealth-producing capabilities of capitalism (1969: 17). However, wealth creation neither ensures fair distribution nor guarantees care for the masses. Economists have long pointed out that growth statistics under capitalism have limited value as indicators of general well-being (Piketty, 2021: 274–5). Richard Easterlin is a leading figure in well-being or happiness economics. One outcome of his research is that positive economic growth is informative of but not necessarily correlated to human happiness: "Economic growth in itself does not raise happiness. Evidence for a wide range of developed, transition, and developing countries consistently shows that higher growth rates are not accompanied by greater increments in happiness" (2013: 13). However, he does observe "full employment and safety net policies do increase happiness." Furthermore, he believes the latter is not utopian but an achievable objective for almost all countries worldwide. Happiness correlates imperfectly with care. One can be cared for and still not be happy. For example, if I have a terminal disease, I may feel I am getting excellent care but still not be pleased with my overall circumstance. Nevertheless, being cared for often does raise one's happiness and sense of well-being. We need new narratives and ways of thinking about economics to place and maintain care at the center of our endeavors.

For those committed to care, socialism is not a mandated belief. Still, it is hard to imagine a personal commitment to care that does not desire the economy to serve the people in creating robust social goods. Such an economy is a socialistic one.

### Care, The Commons, and Mutual Aid

The common is our only shot at a liveable future.

—Neil Vallelly (2021: 179)

Peter Kropotkin was a Russian-born polymath who suffered imprisonment for labor-organizing activities considered subversive. He lived in exile from Russia for 41 years, spending most of that time in Europe but traveling the world. His 1902 book *Mutual Aid: A Factor in Evolution* became part of a counter-narrative to Social Darwinism, the notion that evolution destined some people to rise to the top because they were the fittest of the species. Social Darwinism twisted biological theories of evolution to reinforce the presumed morality of social inequality and comfort the egos of the super-wealthy. A legacy of Social Darwinism, supported by Ayn Rand and others, still exists today as billionaires receive unearned credibility and esteem in fields far removed from their expertise. Kropotkin was part of what historian Eric M. Johnson describes as "Socialist Darwinism" as a manner of thinking that contrasted with the Social Darwinists: "The Socialist Darwinists emphasized the principles of cooperation and solidarity while the Social Darwinists emphasized competition and individualism" (2019: 204). Johnson suggests that Socialist Darwinism was the original social narrative to emerge from evolutionary biology and that Social Darwinism was a response to support maintaining existing power structures (Ibid: 339). Kropotkin wrote that the lesson of evolutionary biology was practicing mutual aid as "the surest means for giving to each and to all the greatest safety, the best guarantee of existence and progress, bodily, intellectual, and moral" (1902: 48).

Political researcher and author Shane Burley finds Kropotkin inspirational for today's mutual aid networks that are emerging to fill the care gaps in society:

> A sort of alternative to the charity model of servicing, with mutual aid, communities provide systems of care out of a mutually beneficial relationship, with *solidarity* as the operative term. This mutual aid intends to transform disconnected relationships into real, working, and personal community bonds, creating an alternative to the often disjointed neighborhoods we come from.
>
> *(2021: 26).*

Note the language of a care ethos embedded in this quote. Amidst the despair of today's care crisis, Burley remains hopeful because of grassroots mutual aid efforts. He quotes social worker and organizer Stephanie Noriega who works on mutual aid programs in Tucson, Arizona: "Mutual aid is important because it normalizes and reminds us how to be in community again, how to look out for our neighbors and how to recenter ourselves in the values of justice, service, and relationship" (2021: 26). Mutual aid is significant because it represents an alternative to economic discussions based on macro-decisions made at government policy levels. As a result, material change that meets the needs of community members can develop locally and collectively, as in the case of Karma Kutir.

**140** Invitations and Provocations

Legal scholar and activist Dean Spade has become a champion of mutual aid. He defines mutual aid as "collective coordination to meet each other's needs, usually from an awareness that the systems we have in place are not going to meet them" (2020: 7). As this definition suggests, Spade's approach is grassroots and antiauthoritarian. Spade is quite wary of dominant neoliberal thinking; he believes the only antidote is for communities to organize to meet needs regardless of what the government is doing. Spade finds government programs too fragile to rely on. He is modeling care-in-action. Spade advocates for mutual aid groups to foster a culture of participation, feminism, and anti-racism (Ibid: 67). Such groups manifest a caring ethos. My provocation of socialism is perhaps more agnostic about whether the care comes from the grassroots or the government. I suggest a "both-and" approach that advocates care permeating all levels of society. Moreover, integrating decentralized decision-making with economic policy leads to compatibility with notions of mutual aid. Such a combination suggests a grassroots, participatory, and caring socialism held together through an ethos of care.

In its various manifestations, care is the lifeblood of humanity; it is a shared need, albeit diversely and to different degrees at different times. In Joan Tronto's words, we are *homines curans* (caring people) (2017). Sharing society's resources is one way to bring care to the masses, but the concept of the commons is more than a structure of public ownership as in the short definition of communism. The commons have a *physical* and a *spiritual component*. The physical aspect of the commons consists of the structures and systems jointly owned and widely accessible.[2] Highways, national parks, hospitals, and the like represent physical and systemic commons. However, a spirit or ethos of community and cooperation supports the commons in the public imagination. Economist Robert B. Reich laments the loss of a sense of the common good in the United States, declaring it "no longer a fashionable idea" (2018: 14). For Reich, the common good is founded on human vulnerability and the need for one another.

Although each has its nuance and technical definition, the terms *infrastructure*, *welfare state*, *mutual aid*, and *building the commons* share an economic impetus of open access to caring in society. These are systems and assets held by society for the good of society with little or no transactional cost. Each meets needs and is an example of social care. However, such programs and processes cost time, material, and attention. A commitment to care implies that such socialistic practices warrant the expense.

It bears repeating that I am not advocating any particular economic system of socialism per se, but relatively greater regard for socialistic thinking—concern for society's general well-being—that delivers and foments a broader care experience for all. Although one can find plenty of caring within capitalism, more free-market policies will not inspire the care economy sought here. Tronto describes "neoliberal care" as steeped in personal responsibility and driven by

Socialism and Creating a Care Economy   **141**

the market, whereby people bear the care burdens claimed as having resulted from their individual decisions (2013: 38–9). Capitalism focuses on productivity and profitability with a sometimes hoped-for by-product of meeting the caring needs of the community (if the invisible hand of the market finds a place for care). More often than not, care is ignored and becomes part of an unnamed and underappreciated support for a capitalist economy. A caring economy begins with essential needs satisfaction; thus, there is no diversion from or delusion of the care goal.

## Care Theory and Economics

> Economists have traditionally taken care for granted, seeing it as an expression of natural or biological altruism located in the family, quite distinct from the pursuit of individual self-interest in the competitive marketplace.
>
> —Nancy Folbre (2014: 3)

There have been several feminist scholars who have addressed the relationship between care ethics and economics. Economist Nancy Folbre has an impressive corpus of work on care labor, gender oppression, and the failures of capitalism. Folbre is critical of capitalism on many fronts, notably its patriarchal origins. She notes that the word "socialist" is derived from the Latin term for "friendliness" and was invoked in the English-speaking world by Robert Owens, the founder of the utopian community of New Harmony, Indiana. However, gender concerns quickly clouded the vision as Owens advocated for socialism that mirrored traditional family relations. Owens' contemporaries, British journalist Anna Wheeler and Irish political philosopher William Thompson, were concerned that families were far too patriarchal as a model for society (Folbre, 1993: 95). Both Wheeler and Thompson advocated for cooperative socialism as a manifestation of social solidarity over the prevailing competition model of the economy (Ibid: 99). Similarly, Folbre assesses other forms of socialism, such as those of August Babel, Friedrich Engels, and Karl Marx, as imperfect steps toward more feminist-friendly and inclusive economic visions.

Joan Tronto concurs with Folbre in a tepid endorsement of socialism. A care economy is not identical to socialism, but there are features of socialism that honor the relationality and interdependence of care. Tronto writes, "Care is not simply a new cast for old models of socialism, though it is probably anti-capitalistic because it posits meeting needs for care, rather than the pursuit of profit, as the highest goal" (1993: 175). One of the challenges for Tronto, particularly in *Caring Democracy: Markets, Equality, and Justice*, is that she argues that care and democracy are intertwined and interdependent such that social caring needs democracy and political democracy depends on social care: "democratic caring is not only better because it is more democratic, it is better because it

**142** Invitations and Provocations

provides better care" (Ibid: 155). She makes a compelling case. While recognizing that modern democracy is too strongly associated with capitalism, Tronto argues that we must alter the connection. For example, she suggests markets should not be veridictive in a democracy.

> I want to argue that what we currently call "politics" is wrong, and that our obsession with market-foremost democracy distorts what should be the most fundamental concern: care. The market can't make ethical decisions about who receives what care, yet we've organized our democracy to leave large segments of the polity priced out of the markets that would make us better when we are ill, educate us when we are ready to learn, let us spend time with our children if we have them, and ensure the safety of our loved ones.
>
> *(2015: 2)*

Care theorists find current economic priorities misplaced and wish to recenter them around care, which means meeting the needs of society.

## A Paradigm Shift to Need-Based, Sustainable Economics

Care theorists are not the only scholars advocating for a significant shift in economic thinking toward a more relational approach. They may not all name care as a prime commitment of their financial recommendations, but the congruence with the socialistic thinking advocated here is evident. In this section, I take a closer look at the work of Kate Raworth of the UK. Like Piketty, Raworth has endeavored to influence mainstream thinking and policies and, in doing so, does not simply engage with other economists.

In her 2017 *Donut Economics: 7 Ways to Think Like a 21st Century Economist*, Raworth rails against static thinking in dominant market-based economics. In particular, Raworth charges that economic thought lost its way in the 20th century. She laments that Adam Smith, who professed that the economy should aim to supply revenue or subsistence for the people and fund the state to provide public services, became known as the father of free-market thinking (2017: 29).[3] Raworth describes economic growth, specifically growth in the Gross Domestic Product, as the emergent faux economic objective that garnered hegemonic status. Raworth shares a criticism of idealizing economic growth with Piketty and others. Raworth labels it a "cuckoo goal" that we should knock from its lofty status (Ibid: 30–7). Growth does not ensure human provisioning. Rather than an image of an ascending arrow on a chart of ever-growing economic output, Raworth offers the metaphor of a donut, where two concentric circles represent an economy of equilibrium between various elements. The inner circle represents the social foundation or minimum necessary to care for the needs of society, and the outer circle is the ecological ceiling or the upper limit of ecological sustainability. The goal is to function between the two concentric circles, a "dynamic balance" of providing for society while not exceeding environmental capacities (Ibid: 44).

Raworth recognizes that humanity must think about itself differently to achieve this dynamic balance. Rather than assenting to the myth of rational humanity, the notion that people efficiently maximize self-interest in transactions, she suggests that society should more accurately see itself as an assembly of reciprocating, adaptable, and flexible beings. Like Tronto, she jettisons *homo economicus* as an accurate description of human identity. Raworth offers five critical shifts needed to construct a more comprehensive image of humanity:

> First, rather than narrowly self-interested, we are social and reciprocating. Second, in place of fixed preferences, we have fluid values. Third, instead of being isolated, we are interdependent. Fourth, rather than calculate, we usually approximate. And fifth, far from having dominion over nature, we are deeply embedded in the web of life.
>
> *(Ibid: 88)*

Raworth does not explicitly advocate socialism, but she supports distributive justice, greater public services, and emphasis on investment in the commons—shareable resources (such as knowledge and open-source code) governed by the public. Raworth's image of a donut economy resonates strongly with a caring economy that valorizes meeting the needs of individuals and the environment over wealth accumulation.

Raworth suggests that a sustainable economy is a balancing act. Care in meeting society's essential needs—of all the community members and not just privileged individuals—is the goal of a caring economy. The donut represents the inherent tensions in maintaining a macro balance rather than an unsustainable endeavor to outrun need by producing even more—a fantasy once described as "trickle-down economics."[4] Growth-based, neoliberal, trickle-down economics has led to an increased disparity between the wealthy and the poor rather than improving the lives of everyone. The United States instituted egalitarian programs post-World War II, including a more progressive income tax, low-cost, widely available education, and social programs that mitigated income disparities. However, the Reagan era (and Thatcher era in the UK) ushered in policies and practices that have increasingly benefited the wealthy up to the present day. The economic approaches Raworth suggests (or those of Piketty or any other economist) will not end wealth accumulation; however, they would widen the circle of economic care.

## The Metaphoric Fallacy and Opening Up the Caring Imagination to Create a Care Economy

Imagination is an unsung hero of caring. First, we use our imagination to leverage what we know about others to speculate about their conditions. We use

**144** Invitations and Provocations

our imaginations to create connections of understanding and empathize with others. Finally, we use our imaginations to determine the best courses of action (or inaction) to care for others. However, faulty ideas can limit our imaginative possibilities by creating self-imposed limits, unconscious bias, and stereotypes. The philosophical mandate to live the examined life continues to be imperative to interrogate our ideas to see if the boundaries we place on our thinking and actions are still warranted. In previous publications, I offered the notion of the "metaphoric fallacy" as one of those errors in thinking whereby a powerful rhetorical narrative becomes so ingrained that the metaphor (a similar means of explanation) is mistaken for equivalency or definition. In particular, I have significant concerns about applying game metaphors to business, politics, and ethics as definitional (rather than allegorical), resulting in a reductionist moral understanding that masks the significance of these realms in people's lives (Hamington, 2009a, 2015). Regarding creating a care economy, some economic theorists claim that political leaders and the general public commit a metaphoric fallacy in our essential understanding of how the national economy works. These economists espouse modern monetary theory (MMT), asking us to rethink how we approach federal spending, particularly as it applies to public infrastructure projects.

The most visible and heralded of these MMT economists is Stephanie Kelton, who acknowledges the truncated imagination inherent in dominant economic thinking: "MMT gives us the power to imagine a new politics and a new economy" (2021: 12). That economy is a care economy. Kelton has taken particular aim at what she refers to as the deficit myth that stems from a faulty metaphor of the federal economy operating like a household economy. For example, the common claim that the government has limited resources and cannot afford the programs that would allow members of society to survive and thrive is a neoliberal narrative. Accordingly, the government could not afford universal healthcare, free college education, and job guarantee programs without imposing heavy taxes on the populace. Kelton, a trained economist, challenges the premise. She points out that households use currency while the US federal government is a currency creator, particularly since going off the gold standard in 1972. Households can run out of money and go into debt. However, as appealing as it seems, the metaphor does not hold for the federal government.

> The truth is, the federal government is nothing like a household or a private business. That's because Uncle Sam has something the rest of us don't—the power to issue the US dollar. Uncle Sam doesn't need to come up with dollars before he can spend. The rest of us do. Uncle Sam can't face mounting bills he can't afford to pay. The rest of us might. Uncle Sam will never go broke. The rest of us could. When governments try to manage their budgets like households, they miss out on the opportunity to harness the

power of their sovereign currencies to substantially improve life for their people.

*(Ibid: 8)*

Suppose the federal government wants to accomplish something, fight a war, fund a space program, or underwrite a pandemic aid package. In that case, it can do so by issuing the money for those efforts and balancing them with government-issued bonds people purchase and hold in their savings. Kelton indicates that our metaphors are all wrong. Rather than think of government spending as debt, it's an investment in society. Furthermore, these expenditures are NOT paid for by taxes. They are simply political decisions. MMT is not a utopian dream. There are still real limitations in terms of inflation, but the limitation is not income. If the government wanted to provide a free college education for everyone in the country, it could make that happen. There are still good reasons to tax, but it is not to fund the government.

The household metaphor for federal spending has been destructive because it deprives society in the name of resource scarcity. For example, discredited international austerity programs (Elliott, 2016) can wreak havoc on countries, as they did in Greece and Spain, resulting in unnecessary suffering. In *Care Ethics in the Age of Precarity*, Michael Flower and I described what we termed "neoliberal precarity" as creating unnecessarily precarious lives amidst enormous economic wealth. The language of financial limitation on the national level had fostered unnecessary suffering through crushing student debt, patchwork healthcare, and lack of disaster and pandemic preparation. If we value needs over budgets and jettison the household metaphor at the federal level, we can fund infrastructure that diminishes precarity.

Several MMT economists have argued that we can create a care economy if our society better understands it. By dropping the household economy metaphor, there is no longer a concern about how to pay for these programs, although inflationary pressures do have to be monitored. Pavlina R. Tcherneva outlines a Job Guarantee Program in the tradition of Franklin Roosevelt's Bill of Economic Rights (2018). The federal government can fund the jobs guarantee, but local communities administer it. Anyone who wanted to work would get a minimum living wage and benefits while gaining the skills and experience to seek other jobs. These workers would build the commons by contributing to the care infrastructure through local projects. Tcherneva refers to this as a National Care Act and names three strategic care arenas: care for the environment, community, and people. The Job Guarantee is an investment in people that would help the unemployed and underemployed who already draw significant resources through various programs. However, this approach has moral, psychological, and material benefits that would pay dividends in many ways. An ongoing program, a jobs guarantee, would set a floor for wages and benefits that would influence the private sector while offering a buffer against the vicissitudes of economic cycles.

**146** Invitations and Provocations

Note that MMT theorists do not employ the "s" word of socialism, which has so much narrative baggage that it can be a distraction. Nevertheless, they argue for building a commons and a caring infrastructure that resonates with the broad-based manner in which I am employing the term. Although Kelton utilizes Marxist analysis to a point, modern socialist thinkers generally reject MMT as not challenging the underlying structures of capitalism (Beams, 2020). Nevertheless, my primary concern is advancing a caring society, so I seek economic approaches that bring infrastructure and distribution of goods that meet needs no matter the economic framework. Socialism is the word I have chosen to mark a society-oriented economy.

In the following sections, I delve deeper into three aspects of a caring economy, one that is much more socialistic than capitalistic but, most importantly, more caring. The first area is taxation and infrastructure. A caring economy needs a robust progressive income tax to fund programs that systematically benefit the general population and mitigate the advantage of privilege. Taxation is unpopular in modern society but effectively organized as it was for a time in the mid-20th century in the United States, taxes can be a powerful tool for enriching the lives of most people in society. The second area I explore is the role of unionization in a caring economy. Like taxation, unionization has become anathema among neoliberal values. However, through their relationality and democratic possibility, collective bargaining organizations can be powerful tools of caring socialism. Like taxation, union activity can be poorly and ineffectively implemented, or it can be a positive means for widespread involvement and improving the labor experience of workers. Third, I examine rethinking debt relationships given the devastating effect of high debt on people and nation-states. I am suggesting that a commitment to care should result in a greater openness to socialistic ideas in the economy, including, but not limited to, advocacy for progressive income tax and support for labor unions. Consider the following three sections as examples of what a commitment to care means to economic thinking rather than a thorough list of relevant topics.

## Taxation for Infrastructure: An Economic Care Ethos

As noted, "taxes" is a word generally disliked in the United States on par with "socialism." Complaining about taxes is an American tradition. Samuel Clemens purportedly claimed, "The only difference between a tax man and a taxidermist is that the taxidermist leaves the skin." Will Rodgers described income tax as making "more liars out of the American people than golf has." In some ways, the abhorrence of taxes cuts across ideological lines. Conservatives criticize taxation ostensibly because it interferes with the free market, inhibits the ability of those who wish to invest in the economy, and contributes to big government. Perhaps the contemporary epitome of this view is Grover Norquist, the head of Americans for Tax Reform; he created a pledge—signed by many government officials—to oppose all taxes (Americans for Tax Reform). Of course, some progressives have a tradition of tax resistance as a statement in opposition to the funding of military action. For example, the National War Tax Resistance Coordinating Committee has organized boycotts and campaigns such as One Million Taxpayers for Peace (National War Tax Resistance).

In general, taxation is merely a system for a government entity to garner the resources needed to fund collective efforts. The history of taxation parallels the history of civilization, with the United States first implementing a national income tax in 1861 to fund the Civil War effort. Taxes support public goods as well as harmful activities, and they have been implemented in just and unjust ways. There is nothing inherently good or caring about taxes. However, if structured and employed with an ethos of care, they can be a powerful tool for a caring economy. Higher taxes characterize socialistic economies.

Two elements to consider in the moral assessment of taxation are the *purpose* for which the government collects them and the *method* by which tax is applied. First, the purpose of taxation can be viewed as caring when it serves to meet the community's needs, such as in funding infrastructure. Infrastructure is defined as systems and resources widely available to society. We usually think of infrastructure as physical—for example, roads, bridges, railways, hospitals, etc. However, for our purposes, infrastructure also includes social and emotional support encompassing such services as education, mental health, crisis intervention, and addiction treatment (Hamington and Flower, 2021: 281–304). Such infrastructure contributes to a broader sense of Social Security consistent with Fiona Robinson's notion that national security is more than weapons and systems of defense against war, as has historically dominated security studies (2011: 1–15). Infrastructure signals that the community is there for mutual support: it expresses an ethos of care.

For example, public education is an infrastructure. This infrastructure provides free education through 12th grade in the United States. However, the infrastructure could be more robust and caring if it included a college education. Unfortunately, dominant neoliberal narratives in the country have framed education as a commodity and a practical means to an end: a job. That may be an essential function of higher education, but it is a reductionist understanding of learning. A college education can be more than the path to economic security. It can provide an opportunity for personal growth, improve the civic capabilities of citizens, and expose students to alternative identities, ideas, and ways of being. Remember that effective care consists of humble inquiry, inclusive connection, and responsive action. Education can foment such inquiry. Yet in the United States, a college education today is most often viewed as something to be completed quickly with a minimum of extraneous courses and a view to its economic benefits.

Journalist Sarah Jaffe describes an unfortunate shift in the perception of college education: "Rather than being considered a social good that people undertake to become better informed, more engaged members of society, education is increasingly perceived as a commodity, something that you purchase to increase your value to an employer" (2016: 55). Jaffe claims that the high cost of higher education in the United States is a labor-market problem—not enough high-paying and meaningful jobs and a funding problem—education costs have shifted from state budgets to tuition income (Ibid). Heather McGhee documents the withering commitment of the US federal government to fund education, but states social priorities shifted as well: "By 2016, eighteen states were spending more on jails and prisons than they were on colleges and universities" (2021: 45). Thus, the federal and state governments were complicit in depleting the infrastructure of higher education in the United States. If college were free or inexpensive in the United States and did not come with the burden of massive debt, its commodification could be weakened. More students would participate and be more likely to explore interests in an environment less fettered by the fear of debt. One might assume that free college tuition is a pollyannish notion, but the cost of eliminating the economic incumbrance is minuscule compared to other government programs.[5] Parents may not have the wherewithal to fund their children's education, but as part of a caring relationship, they do not wish their children to be saddled with crushing debt. The state paying for a college education is a socialistic and caring practice.

Building such infrastructure is not mutually exclusive from developing "the commons," and they can support one another.

Care may be a relational approach to morality and living, but it is not limited to engaging humanity. Infrastructure is another term to describe a relational reality between humans and their environment. Things such as a bus or a park matter; they are a part of our relational existence and become matters of care. Infrastructure is another term to describe a relational reality between humans and their environment. The idea of national parks, which originated in 1872 with the status given to Yellowstone, is an example of a commons or infrastructure with rich relational meaning. Anyone who has watched the Ken Burns documentary, "The National Parks: America's Best Idea" (2009), comes away understanding that these designations were not just about the land and its inhabitants or the making of recreation for millions of visitors but rather a negotiated common and living heritage that participates in the community's self-understanding.

A second element to consider regarding the caring morality of taxation is its implementation. If taxation is a method for funding infrastructure that can help care for the community, who and how should people be taxed? Although many economists focus on the inequality of the current moment and point to tax policy as a means of combating inappropriate wealth distribution, care theory remains focused on meeting the needs of society. Because the two goals are not mutually exclusive, the distinction between seeking equality and providing care may appear minor, but it is essential to maintain concentration on care. Engster explains:

> Care theory is not an egalitarian theory in the sense that it aims to limit income differentials as an end in itself. It justifies taxing the income and resources of individuals only for the sake of supporting the care of others. Once the government has accumulated sufficient resources to support caring practices at adequate levels, individuals should be allowed to keep whatever additional resources they earn or possess. Since the costs of caring are fairly high, income and wealth differentials are nonetheless likely to remain within a moderate range in a caring society.
>
> *(2007: 150)*

Taxation to support a caring infrastructure or commons remains a thorny issue. As with much that has to do with care, liminality and imaginative flexibility must participate in sorting out the distribution of responsibility.[6] Many economists concerned with runaway income disparity have suggested an emphasis on changing tax policy to include more significant progressive income taxes, wealth taxes, unearned income taxes, estate taxes, or the closing of tax loopholes. However, no single approach to funding a care infrastructure in society is likely adequate. Instead, a comprehensive suite of progressive, rather than regressive, taxation reforms is required.

From a care perspective, changing the policies and practices of taxation is essential. However, a change in disposition consistent with a caring ethos should also participate in the solution. Changing attitudes toward taxes is no small feat, given the antipathy they elicit. However, if taxes are a method of caring for our sister community members, perhaps feelings about taxation can change in the social imagination. There is some evidence that such attitude change is possible. Behavioral researchers Abigail B. Sussman and Shannon M. White have dissected the general aversion to paying taxes and have found widespread misunderstanding, a lack of connection to benefits, and a lack of agency contributing to the adverse reaction (2018). Their concern is that poor attitudes lead to tax evasion and avoidance.

Sussman and White's policy change recommendations include eliciting taxpayer feedback on their tax forms. Giving taxpayers a voice makes the act of taxpaying more participatory rather than one-sided and might thus contribute to a sense of agency. A second recommendation is explicitly tying tax payments to their social benefits, i.e., what taxes pay for. Understanding the connection between actions (taxation) and outcomes (social infrastructure) is essential to a personal motivational force (Hamington, 2009a). Finally, Sussman and White suggest changing the norms surrounding paying taxes. The negative voices regarding taxation currently dominate, but perhaps there could be a positive voice regarding a sense of pride and support for the community in the act of

**150** Invitations and Provocations

paying taxes.[7] About one-third of US taxpayers currently express a strongly positive attitude toward paying taxes, driven mainly by receiving a refund (Motel, 2015). This positivity could be leveraged into a more widespread feeling of the moral importance of paying taxes. For example, those with high earnings could be recognized for their generous contribution to society through taxation (assuming more significant progressive changes to the tax code could be implemented). Furthermore, rather than resisting the paying of taxes, large megachurches (which, as religious institutions, are not required to pay taxes in the United States) could embrace paying taxes to support their community. The taxation for infrastructure needs policies that distribute the care responsibilities fairly across those who can help the community. It also requires an associated disposition or ethos to instill this practice's moral importance and concrete implications.

## Caring Unionization and the Operation of Businesses

A commitment to care that recognizes the relational value of socialism might also manifest in a positive attitude toward unionization. Traditionally, collective bargaining and labor union organizing have been a conflict-based resistance movement necessary for workers to challenge the domination of capital since the industrial revolution. The labor movement has successfully won concessions in the workplace that are taken for granted today, including increased compensation, improved safety conditions, protection against harassment, reasonable work time, and greater workplace control. These gains positively effect all workers and not just those in the union. Labor unions seek to help workers meet basic needs and provide a sense of security, both hallmarks of care.

Nevertheless, labor union membership in the United States has declined as a percentage of the total workforce. In 1964, approximately one-third of all laborers were unionized: as of this writing, the share had fallen to just above ten percent (Bui, 2015). Several factors have contributed to this decline, including globalization, technological changes, mistakes made by labor leaders, and the rise of service and contingency labor, where worker organizing is more challenging. Preventative tactics by corporations and hostile government practices are additional influences. Union busting involves numerous tactics to prevent workers from entering the collective bargaining process, including spying on employees (Canales, 2020), closing locations with unionizing potential (Pichi, 2015), and strong-arm tactics to intimidate potential collaborative efforts (Nagarajan, 2021). Labor historian Erik Loomis notes that periods of union thriving often depend on whether federal and state governments have favorable collective bargaining dispositions and practices. The US government is currently in an extended period of opposition to labor unions that began with the Professional Air Controls Organization (PATCO)'s demise under the Reagan Administration in 1981 (Loomis, 2018: 186–92).

I suggest that labor unions can be considered compatible with a vision of a more caring society because of their relational nature. Business organizations can be thought of as systems of relationships. These relationships are generally hierarchical (hence the pyramid shape of organization charts) for efficient, productive work and clear lines of responsibility and power. Business culture, the system of shared meaning any institution or collective has, tends toward the patriarchal, imbuing the organization's head with extra privileges and control. Homes, by contrast, are systems of relationships ostensibly organized to meet human needs, although they can be patriarchal, matriarchal, or egalitarian.

Unions consist of collegial relationships intended to address unmet worker needs. Ostensibly, the caring potential for collective bargaining units is present as members work in solidarity for shared benefit.[8] Unions bargain for greater pay, improved benefits, and job security so that members can have meaningful work, stability, and assistance when unable to work. The American philosopher and social organizer Jane Addams, whose publications foreshadowed feminist care ethics (Hamington, 2009b, 2023) developed a half-century after her death, argued for labor unions' social and relational significance. Addams viewed labor unions as moral endeavors because of their efforts to bring "more democratic relation[s] to the employer" (2007: 149). Similarly, she viewed democracy as both fundamentally relational and moral. Addams worked closely with numerous labor unions and pioneered support for women union members.

Feminist philosopher turned union organizer Sam Sumpter eloquently reconciles the conflictual nature of collective bargaining with the caring purpose of labor unions. In a blog post titled "Organizing from and for a Radical Ethics of Care," Sumpter appears to advocate an ethos of care in her juxtaposing of caring for the individual and the community:

> More than ever, the current moment calls for a radical application of an ethics of care to our organizing. For one, it is incumbent upon us to take seriously that caring for any individual entails caring for their community. None of us is empowered alone nor supported in a vacuum, somehow apart from the social others with whom our fates are inextricably intertwined. As with care ethics work, our organizing must come packaged with meaningful attention to the agent-as-whole, the agent-as-situated-in-their-community, and thus, also to the community itself. And here the agent-community distinction blurs even more. The community is the body that makes possible the agent's organizing; the community is not separate from the organizer nor from the organizing but instead is comprised of organizers, informs organizing, produces organizer/ing.
>
> *(2020)*

The blog post emphasizes the interdependency, trust, and respect unions depend on for success. Sumpter suggests that unions are care-based, whether explicitly characterized as such or not.

**152** Invitations and Provocations

Although perhaps not in an overt manner, social science seems to support Sumpter's connection between care and labor unions. In a study of national perception and participation in labor unions, Gangaram Singh found that countries with cultures testing high for masculinity tended to have lower union membership rates. Singh suggested that unions were associated with "a high priority on quality of life and caring for others" (2001: 333). Although this work tended to set up essentialist dichotomies of masculine and feminine, the salient point is that unions are perceived as inconsistent with the masculinist rugged individualism and neoliberal paradigms that dominate masculine cultures like that of the United States.

Although labor unions receive very little attention in the care literature, their collective efforts at meeting workers' needs can be viewed as caring. When unions engage in antagonistic tactics to achieve that care, it is a form of economic self-defense to keep its members from harm.

## Rethinking Debt Relationships

High levels of debt can be crippling to the well-being and care of people at the individual and national levels. A survey of 2000 US consumers in 2018 indicated that about 40% of consumers with credit card debt said it affected their general happiness, and one-third stated that debt negatively affected their standard of living. Furthermore, one in five respondents suggested debt harmed their health (Dickler, 2018). These are subjective self-reported responses, but the narrative of oppressive personal debt is supported on many fronts. Loans are generally viewed as transactional: one party receives goods or services, and the other gets a promise to be paid for those goods. The transaction is framed as contractual, with rights and responsibilities on both sides. However, a "transaction" does not describe the full implication of loan or credit card debt. Human beings are engaged in these transactions. There is usually a power differential between the two parties to a loan, with the debtor typically in a weaker position. Perhaps society no longer enslaves people or indentured servants, but debt can feel crushing and balloon into an overwhelming burden that simulates servitude. Ostensibly, debt is entered voluntarily; however, how voluntary is the debt when participation in society increasingly demands expensive goods, such as a vehicle, housing, education, and telecommunications? A care economy that resurfaces the relationality of debt can challenge the reduction of such relations to transactions.

Most personal loans are unproblematic. However, having large debt can be seen as a personal moral failure: one cannot live within one's means and thus requires help from others. Such reliance can be a concern in a society that stresses individual independence. Philosopher Rocio Zambrana criticizes neoliberalism for its "affirmation of personal responsibility. Debt crises represent, at once, the fulfillment *and* failure of personal responsibility" (2021: 25). Furthermore, to force responsibility, austerity becomes a neoliberal value imposed upon individuals in ways that constrict freedom. According to Zambrana, such austerity "binds debt and guilt. … The indebted man is an abject subject" (Ibid: 44–5). There can be a sense of shame from heavy debt[9] or bankruptcy. Neoliberal narratives promote the notion of individual economic agency; thus, those who enter into debt relationships must deal with the consequences. This extreme view of autonomy fails to consider the myriad factors that can impact debtors in the debt relationship, including poverty, unexpected tragedy, illness, mental illness, and unfair and uninformed lending practices. Furthermore, debt can and does support spiraling consumerism.

Zambrana interrogates the transformative properties of extreme debt. She is particularly concerned about how nation-state debt extends coloniality into modernity, but her insights help understand personal debt. Zambrana claims that debt serves "as an apparatus of capture, predation, dispossession, and expulsion" (2021: 11). Debt chains people across time and space by foreclosing futures and creating servitude. Furthermore, for Zambrana, debt instantiates racial and gender hierarchies of oppression and maintains white supremacy.

What if personal loans were made within the auspices of a caring relationship? Those with more power and privilege might take on greater responsibility in the debt relationship, and such obligation would be more than just regulatory. Creditors would assume a caring ethos. Such a disposition does not mean sacrificing financial solvency, but it might translate into forgoing maximizing profits in the extreme. In 2021, US banks recorded earnings of $279 billion (Schroeder, 2022). There appears to be room for flexibility in debt management without requiring financial losses on the part of banks. Care in the debt relationship could manifest as a commitment to more significant financial education, concern for the success and well-being of the debtor, and flexibility as circumstances dictate. This new debt relationship might include genuinely informed consent to the debt marked by education and understanding rather than a perfunctory agreement. Ongoing connection through the term of debt might come with open lines of communication and a willingness to adjust the terms of debt (caring action) depending upon the borrower's circumstances. Paths to debt forgiveness might also be a possibility. Of course, predatory lending practices and exorbitant lending rates must be eliminated. Debt does not have to be an oppressive barrier to caring relationships.

## A Moral Revolution in Economic Thinking

> Someone once said that it is easier to imagine the end of the world than to imagine the end of capitalism. We can now revise that and witness the attempt to imagine capitalism by way of imagining the end of the world.
>
> —Frederic Jameson (2003: 76)[10]

**154** Invitations and Provocations

The dismal science of economics focuses too extensively on human limitation and not sufficiently on human imagination and possibility. Care thinking is imaginative thinking. If we commit to care, we might consider being open to a socialistic economy centered on the well-being of society and its members, thus moving beyond the artificial barriers we have constructed that hinder human flourishing. Joan Tronto insightfully began her groundbreaking work, *Moral Boundaries,* by asking the reader to notice self-imposed narratives of social boundaries and imagine an alternative vision of life, "one centered on human care and interdependence" (1993: x). A more caring economy is not utopian but rather an ongoing struggle for improving the lives of our communities that can be motivated by an abiding commitment to care and manifested in a care ethos. We know that a caring economy is possible because we have flirted with its possibilities in the past.

In the 1940s, the United States came close to setting the nation on a path to a more socialistic, caring economy but ultimately balked. In his State of the Union Address on January 11, 1944, Franklin Delano Roosevelt offered what he referred to as the Second Bill of Rights. He viewed the Allied success in World War II as a step toward international security. Moreover, like Fiona Robinson's argument regarding rethinking and expanding the idea of security in terms of taking care of people, Roosevelt believed that new domestic programs were required to bring security home to everyone's daily life.

The New Deal instantiated care programs, including Social Security, labor union protection, and welfare programs. Moreover, legal scholar Cass R. Sunstein contends that Franklin Roosevelt also engaged in profound public transformation. In *The Second Bill of Rights: FDR's Unfinished Revolution and Why We Need It More Than Ever* (2004), Sunstein claims that Roosevelt attempted to initiate *constitutive commitments.* Sunstein describes a "constitutive commitment" as a widespread underlying belief that may or not be maintained by ordinary law but is viewed as so fundamental that it is difficult to change. Social Security is an example. The Constitution does not protect Social Security but is so widely supported that it is entrenched in the American identity.[11] Sunstein views Roosevelt's Second Bill of Rights proposal in this manner. On January 11, 1944, Roosevelt's 1944 State of the Union speech included the notion that American citizens could not be free unless they were free from want. Sunstein calls this a "declaration of interdependence" (12). Roosevelt went on to delineate eight rights that included a right to a job, food-clothing-recreation, a decent return for farmers, businesses free from unfair competition and monopolies, every family to own a home, medical care, economic support during old age, sickness, and unemployment and finally to a good education. According to Sunstein, Roosevelt was less concerned that these rights became law as much as they contributed to a collective responsibility to care. Here is an extended excerpt from Roosevelt's speech:

We have come to a clear realization of the fact that true individual freedom cannot exist without economic security and independence. "Necessitous men are not free men." People who are hungry and out of a job are the stuff of which dictatorships are made.

In our day these economic truths have become accepted as self-evident. We have accepted, so to speak, a second Bill of Rights under which a new basis of security and prosperity can be established for all regardless of station, race, or creed.

Among these are:

The right to a useful and remunerative job in the industries or shops or farms or mines of the Nation;

The right to earn enough to provide adequate food and clothing and recreation;

The right of every farmer to raise and sell his products at a return which will give him and his family a decent living;

The right of every businessman, large and small, to trade in an atmosphere of freedom from unfair competition and domination by monopolies at home or abroad;

The right of every family to a decent home;

The right to adequate medical care and the opportunity to achieve and enjoy good health;

The right to adequate protection from the economic fears of old age, sickness, accident, and unemployment;

The right to a good education.

All of these rights spell security. And after this war is won we must be prepared to move forward, in the implementation of these rights, to new goals of human happiness and well-being (1944).

Note the strong resonance with care theory, including meeting needs and recognizing interdependence. Furthermore, Sunstein describes Roosevelt as altering the nation's care ethos through its commitment to Social Security. Roosevelt pushed the nation toward a more caring infrastructure, and many countries took the notion of a welfare state further. My goal in this chapter has not been to lay out a series of specific policy recommendations but rather to reclaim the idea that a caring economy—one that not only has socialistic practices but is driven by a spirit of care—is possible. Rethinking debt relationships, empowering greater employee unionization, reimagining progressive taxation, and breaking free of artificial limitations on monetary policy are examples of what can be done if we collectively commit to care.

## Notes

1 In 2023, Sawant announced she would be retiring from the Seattle City Council to pursue labor activism. (Sawant, 2023).

2 *Widely accessible* commons or infrastructure does not mean *perfectly accessible* as efforts to monetize everything under the aegis of neoliberalism have resulted in many encroachments on the social contract of the commons including tolls, fees, and other forms of privatization on otherwise common goods.

3 Besides economics, Adam Smith also authored influential works on ethics including *The Theory of Moral Sentiments* (1759) which have been linked to an extended genealogy of care theory (Slote, 2010: 33–4).

4 Trickle-down economics, the notion that if the wealthy were economically successful, that success would lead to economic gains by everyone in society has been widely discredited, and yet the idea persists within neoliberal narratives under a variety of guises (Raworth, 2017: 145).

5 The calculation of free tuition varies depending on how the notion is structured. "What Is Free College Tuition and How Much Would it Cost?" (Peter G. Peterson Foundation, 2021b). In a 2020 projection of the most expensive plan to eliminate college tuition, it was estimated that the cost would be $75 billion in the first year Carnevale, Jenna R. Sablan, Gulish, Quinn, and Cinquegrani, 2020). By comparison, in fiscal year 2020 the United States spent $725 billion on national defense according to the Office of Management and Budget. $139 billion of that total was spent on weapons procurement and $100 billion on weapon research and development (Peter G. Peterson Foundation, 2021a).

6 Recall that Joan Tronto suggests a caring democracy requires a rethinking of the distribution of responsibilities and particularly care responsibilities (2013: 53–5).

7 A study of German taxpayers reveals that although the context is quite different from the United States under the right circumstances of perceived moral importance, high income earners will support higher taxes. Hennighausen and Heinemann (2014: 255–89).

8 Labor unions do not always exhibit inclusive care. Historically, many labor unions have exhibited exclusive behavior, including misogyny, racism, and homophobia and thus not caring in the ways I have described in this book (Jaffe, 2016: 144; Loomis, 2018: 65–6).

9 In a 2019 study of over 1000 debtors in the United States found that three-fourths of people with medical debt felt ashamed of their financial situations and 57% of home owners felt ashamed of the debt they had accumulated from buying their homes. This is self-reported data but it points to the strong feelings that come from the debtor relationship (The Ascent Staff, 2019).

10 Jameson's derivation of this quote is the subject of some discussion, but the point here is regarding the social normative function of popular imagination rather than sources (Beaumont, 2016: 79–89).

11 Similar to Sunstein, I suggest that care can be a constitutive commitment of the United States (or any country's) citizens thus creating a social momentum toward relational moral progress.

# 7

# HUMANISM AND BALANCING THE PRIMACY OF CARE WITH RELIGIOUS AUTHORITY

## Prologue: A Social Vision without Religion

> I have devoted my time and fortune to laying the foundation of a society where affection shall form the only marriage, kind feelings and kind action the only religion, respect for the feelings and liberties of others the only restraint, and union of interest the bond of peace and security.
>
> *Frances Wright (n.d.)*

Imagine a speaker so incendiary to social sensibilities that to prevent their public presentation, someone would set a barrel on fire at the venue's entrance (Morris, 1984: 186). That was the case of groundbreaking feminist Fanny Wright (1795–1852). Born in Dundee, Scotland, Wright made her first visit to the United States when she was 23 years old, and she would leave her mark on the American social narrative. As a child, tragedy forced Wright to mature quickly. Her father, a college-educated liberal who corresponded with the likes of Adam Smith, and her mother both died before she was three years old. Wright was sent to England to be raised by an aunt. She was a serious child who used the family library to study history and philosophy. Despite her privilege, she developed class consciousness early and applied her egalitarian ideals about the fundamental equality of humanity throughout her life (Baker, 1963: x). Wright envisioned a caring society grounded in intellectual inquiry and eschewing religiosity.

Like many European liberals, Wright was fascinated with the American experiment and determined to experience it first-hand. Wright and her sister traveled to the United States for the first time in 1818. This journey represented her strong-willed nature as she told few people of her excursion, and women traveling without male escorts were somewhat scandalous. During her visit, she

DOI: 10.4324/9781003368625-10

**158** Invitations and Provocations

produced her play, *Altorf.* This tragedy was performed briefly in New York to positive acclaim, even garnering a favorable review from Thomas Jefferson. On a subsequent visit, Wright toured the country and visited social reformer Robert Owen's utopian community of New Harmony, Indiana. She was enthralled with Owen's communitarianism's inherent anti-hierarchal nature and progressive thinking. Owen's vision of structured social improvement strongly influenced her political philosophy.

The correspondence from her American visits was collected and published in 1821 as *Views of Society and Manners in America*. European liberals hailed the book because of its positive portrayal of American character and success. Wright described a proud people who identified with their democratically elected government and had little poverty and oppression. Wright's ideology likely drove this overly optimistic view, but she soon sobered to the significant problems in the United States, particularly slavery. As she notes in *Views and Manners in America*, the evil of slavery was an issue that plagued Wright, and she put considerable energy into combating it.

The success of her publication brought her friendship with Jeremy Bentham and his cohort of philosophical radicals as well as the war hero Marquis de Lafayette. Wright met many influential people in the United States and Europe who became impressed by her intellect and insight. She parlayed her writing success into a speaking career. A powerful orator who spoke without notes, the 5'11" Wright wore a "masculine" knee-length tunic and "Turkish trousers," which made her a radical spectacle given the heteronormative attire of the time (Jarrett, n.d.). Like a modern-day professional wrestler villain, crowds wanted to witness the "manly woman" who spoke of radical ideas that they loved to hate. However, behind the visage was a well-spring of social philosophy and activism.

Inspired by Owen's New Harmony experiment, Wright attempted to create a utopian community to free at least a few enslaved people. In 1825 she purchased 2,000 acres in western Tennessee, near Memphis, for the Nashoba settlement. In what she termed the "gradual emancipation of slaves," Wright planned to purchase families of enslaved people from their owners and have them come to Nashoba, where they would learn various trades and become part of a cooperative community. Slave families could be kept together while they worked off the cost of their purchase. These formerly enslaved people would eventually resettle outside of the United States. Given the tumultuous history, Wright believed whites and blacks couldn't live harmoniously in America. Although modern sensibilities reveal various latent racist assumptions in her plan, Wright viewed Nashoba as mediating between the extremes of complete abolition of slavery, which she saw as forcing too much sudden economic upheaval, and continuing with slavery, which she viewed as a heinous crime against humanity. Like Owen's New Harmony, Nashoba lasted only a few years, partly because of public condemnation of Wright's advocacy of "free love," defined as relations outside of marriage. The Nashoba community allowed sexual relations between people regardless of race or marital status. Despite this setback, Wright continued her public activism on behalf of women, enslaved people, and working people as a lecturer, author, and newspaper writer/editor. She died in 1852 alone, in poverty, and somewhat forgotten.

During her lifetime and thereafter, it was not unusual for commentators to refer to Wright as "notorious" and "radical" in a swipe that addressed her provocative ideas and scandalous lifestyle. Furthermore, Wright broke gender norms by being a powerful and outspoken orator and maintaining fluid personal relationships, uncommon for women of her era. A *New York Daily Times* obituary captured the public perception of Wright.

Her "free-thinking" and infidelity ... caused a prodigious stir, and made her name a by-word and a hissing among the better class of people. She wrote numerous political tracts too and was no less famous as a politician than as an infidel.

*(1852)*

Commentators indicate that the commonly applied term "infidel" referred to an interrelated mixture of her lack of lasting devotion to a particular man and her lack of fidelity to Christianity (Ginzberg, 1994: 205). In either case, *The New York Daily Times* correctly stated that her name became synonymous with radicalism. "Fanny Wrightism" was invoked to marginalize political or economic reform efforts viewed as extreme.

Historian Jan L. de Jong argues that Wright offers a comprehensive feminist theory rooted in a philosophy of social transformation. She brings a feminist sensibility to her work, including a wariness of authority, particularly the authority of religion. de Jong describes the "interconnected structure of her theory is an actual part of [its] political and moral foundation" (2012: 118). Although her philosophy emerges from her other publications, the most comprehensive and linear study can be found in the *Course of Popular Lectures* collection; the first volume was published in 1829, and the second in 1836. These are transcripts of lectures she gave in major cities on the east coast of the United States. Wright's subjects include knowledge acquisition, religion, and morals. Wright is not a care theorist by today's standards. Instead, she is strongly influenced by utilitarianism and virtue theory. Wright was mentored by Jeremy Bentham, who described her as "the sweetest and strongest mind that ever was lodged in a female body" (Bentham, 1992: 3). Her concern for relationships, the well-being of society, and sympathy for others resonate with care theory.

Wright argues that inquiry leads to a better understanding of our interconnectedness. Thus relationality is the essential character of epistemology:

**160** Invitations and Provocations

Thus related, as we are, to all things, and all things to us, how interesting a theatre that in which we stand! How calculated to awaken our intellectual faculties, and excite our moral feelings! Our sympathy is attracted to every creature, our attention to every thing. We see ourselves in the midst of a family endlessly diversified in powers, in faculties, in wants, in desires; in the midst of a world whose existence is one with our own, and in whose history each mode of being is an episode.

*(Wright, 1829: 64)*

This quote about inquiry underscores connection and sympathy for others, moving beyond morality as calculus.

Furthermore, Wright emphasizes reflection, experience, and engagement as leading to greater moral proficiency. Her claims reflect the process of good care found in humble inquiry, inclusive connection, and responsive action.

This cultivated sensibility, variously called by philosophers the moral principle, emotion, faculty, or sympathy, and in the figurative language of Friends, *the light within, the spirit of truth, or God within the breast*, may, I think be distinguished by every self observer, as existing apart from the purely intellectual powers, though always demanding their guidance.

*(Ibid)*

Wright acknowledges that morality engages both rational and emotional faculties. Moreover, her reference to the Quakers is intriguing as a recognition of the pervasive religiosity of her audiences. Still, Wright bucks the trend of most feminists of her era because of her forthright humanism.

Referred to by some ministers as the "High Priestess of Infidelity" (Morris, 1984: 184), Wright considered religion divisive, wasteful, and grounded in an unprovable foundation. Wright questions the veracity of religious claims in her published lecture on religion, given that religious institutions lack empirical evidence (1829: 98). For Wright, this deficit is exacerbated by the claim that a divine presence is behind the truths of religions. Furthermore, she questions why religious knowledge tends to be held by the few at the heads of these religions: "Does their God of wisdom open worlds to the observation of a few especial ministers?" (Ibid: 99). Perhaps influenced by her utilitarian connections, Wright claims that too much financial resources and time are spent on religions that lack epistemological legitimacy. She often claimed that people waste $20 million annually on faith. However, most of all, Wright views religion as advancing a questionable morality that has been marked by violence and division:

The rivers of earth run blood! Nation set against nation! Brother against brother! Man against the companion of his bosom; and that soft companion, maddened with the frenzy of insane remorse for imaginary crimes, fired with the rage of infatuated bigotry, or subdued to diseased helplessness and mental fatuity, renounces kindred, flies from social convers, and pines away a useless or mischievous existence in sighings and tremblings, spectral fears, uncharitable feelings, and bitter denunciations. Such are thy doings, oh religion Or, rather, such are thy doings, oh man!

*(Ibid)*

In concert with her fiery critique of religion, Wright sought to create a humanistic society based on mutual aid and understanding—a caring society. Despite her concerns, Wright maintained hope for the moral progress of the United States. She was unapologetic regarding her objective,

practical equality, or, the universal and equal improvement of the condition of all, until, by the gradual change in the views and habits of men, and the change consequent upon the same, in the whole social arrangements of the body politic, the American people shall present in another generation, but one class, and, as it were, but one family—each independent in his or her own thoughts, and all cooperating, according to their individual taste and ability, to the promotion of the common weal.

*(1977, 126)*

Wright sought the kind of change advocated in *Revolutionary Care*, and for her, religion would have to take a back seat to our intelligent and inclusive regard for one another. Wright provides relevant provocation for considering this chapter's juxtaposition of religion and care ethics.

## A Bevy of Belief

Francis Wright spoke and wrote at a time of strong Christian fervor and barnstorming revivals in the United States—and she responded in kind to that zeal. There are parallels to the present moment. Care theory has ascended at a time of cacophonous religious belief. Population growth and diversity of religion have made any generalization about current public religiosity challenging. Although secularism is rising, religious enthusiasm remains high in many communities. Furthermore, one cannot assume individuals hold any particular religious identity, given the increasingly cosmopolitan nature of the world. Nevertheless, religion is a primary aspect of identity for many, and all religions carry significant moral pronouncements. Hence, this chapter addresses the relationship between care and religious faith to reconcile religious and caring commitments.

Readers are invited to consider that if one is committed to care, at moments when caring morality comes into conflict with religious beliefs, care must prevail. I first define the terms used to lay the foundation of this argument.

**162** Invitations and Provocations

In particular, I describe *secularism, atheism*, and *humanism*. As in the other provocation chapters of this section, the scope of the discussion is limited. The philosophy of religion is a vast subject and cannot be comprehensively delineated in a single chapter. However, we take up several issues. After defining the terrain, the question of whether one can be moral without religion is addressed. Care has a robust anti-authoritarian element, which often puts moral norms at odds with theologically based morality. There is literature where care theorists have engaged religion and mined it for central themes. Perhaps the best opportunity for rapprochement is that religious morality declarations regarding care and compassion are rampant. However, social, and moral progress toward inclusion, acceptance, and connection is often stymied by the conservative nature of religious institutions and their traditions. Ultimately, I invite the reader to consider that the primacy of a care commitment leads to an openness to humanism and secularism that coexists with religious belief. However, when faced with moral challenges, care should hold the center.

"Secularism" is an overarching term to describe non-religious social philosophy and practices. Philosopher A.C. Grayling emphasizes that secularism "is the view that Church and State (religion and national government) should be kept separate" (2007: 32). Since the Enlightenment, much of the world has become more secular. Still, this phenomenon is neither linear nor globally consistent (Zuckerman and Shook, 2017: 1–20). Through the Enlightenment's great thinkers, Locke, Voltaire, and Rousseau, secularism entered the public imagination and slowly transformed daily life in Europe and the United States (Jacobs, 2019). Recent history has witnessed the acceleration of secularism. Although the United States is still predominantly Christian, research suggests that from 2007 to 2021 alone, religious affiliation has declined by 12%.[1] Secularism is an observable trend for social scientists. However, the term holds a negative connotation for many Christians who associate non-belief with a lack of moral values. This chapter interrogates the relationship between religion and morality, arguing for the primacy of care rather than a repudiation of religion.

One who is agnostic holds that the reality of a supernatural being is unknown. An agnostic is noncommittal regarding the existence of a god. Here, I use the term in a more general sense. I suggest that *care theory is agnostic about religion and spirituality*. Care does not require religion, nor is it opposed to it. Instead, this chapter argues that care supersedes theologically based morality, particularly when religious ethics impedes relationality with socially constructed restrictions (i.e., prohibitions of homosexuality) or inhibits the flourishing of individuals (i.e., sexist approbations). In other words, religion can foment or repress caring, and when it does the latter, those who are committed to care should be open to a more humanistic approach.

Frances Wright was a Freethinker and closely aligned with atheism. Atheism is a species of secularism that argues that there is no god.[2] Atheists contend that science is the best way to understand humanity. However, I have chosen to emphasize that a caring commitment entails an openness to humanism in matters of morality rather than an openness to atheism. My choice of "humanism" is not to denigrate the caring potential of those who identify as atheists but rather to draw upon a term that expresses the value of disbelief in the positive, recognizing the centrality of humans in building our reality, as opposed to atheism which defines itself in the negative: not believing in the supernatural. This distinction is nuanced and perhaps a matter of optics and should not obscure the commonalities between atheism and humanism.

Furthermore, atheism comes in different forms. For example, the so-called "New Atheism" movement is associated with the work of Madalyn Murray O'Hair, Sam Harris, Richard Dawkins, and Daniel C. Dennett. It is unclear how New Atheism differs from other forms of atheism (Taylor, 2022). However, a faction of the New Atheists exhibits an abrasive critique of religion which is sometimes masculinist in disregarding relational concerns (Torres, 2021). This characterization does not preclude the growing number of feminist atheists (Trzebiatowska, 2019).

Some have endeavored to reconcile theistic and atheistic philosophies. For example, Julia Kristeva argues that humans have an inherent desire to believe, and atheists should not fear that aspect of the human psyche. Moreover, Kristeva claims, "The history of Christianity is a preparation for humanism" (2009: 83). Similarly, philosopher Richard Kearney offers a middle path between extreme theism and atheism under the term "anatheism." Kearney frames the anatheistic approach as engaging humility and imagination to find existentially and intellectually satisfying interpretations of religious traditions. For Kearney, hospitality is an essential anatheistic moral disposition (2010: 47). Hospitality is a tradition and a temperament imbued with care (Hamington, 2010).

Before addressing humanism, it bears repeating that care theory is indifferent to individual claims of theism, atheism, or anatheism. Religion can be an ally or foe to good care, and it is often both. When religious leaders leverage moral authority in uncaring or destructive ways, those committed to care should consider resisting religious morality in favor of humanistic responses.

Although atheism defines itself purely in contrast to religious belief, philosopher Joachim Duyndam contends that humanism is a critical tradition that has co-existed with religious tradition and has sometimes been embraced by liberal factions within religions (sometimes referred to as religious humanism). As a critical tradition, humanism is anti-authoritarian in its resistance to dogmatism. However, Duyndam suggests that humanism is not just an alternative to religious belief and has its own content:

1.  The principle that all humans are entitled to human dignity and that, based on this, people should treat each other as equals;

**164** Invitations and Provocations

2.  The belief that all religious and worldview orientations in knowledge and deed are context-sensitive constructs—even if those orientations themselves do not acknowledge this—and are, as such, hermeneutically accessible products of culture;
3.  The responsibility of people to use their freedom to develop themselves in relation to others (*Bildung*) and to seriously engage in caring for themselves and others, as well as for nature and the environment, and in so doing, develop their personal abilities and talents; and
4.  The belief that life is ultimately all about the fate of specific, unique, physically and mentally vulnerable, and irreplaceable people who can love and be loved and are trying to find meaning in life. (2017: 711–12)

The moral way of being that Duyndam describes as the substance of humanism has much in common with care. Note the lack of thoroughgoing condemnation of religion in Duyndam's description of humanism. He finds humanism in religious traditions such as the Ten Commandments. However, religious practice cannot run roughshod over humanistic morality.

A.C. Grayling's account of humanism is similar to that of Duyndam, including a caring morality and respect for those who maintain a religious identity. He characterizes humanism as humble regarding knowledge, contrasted to the certainty that often accompanies religious fervor. Above all, Grayling views humanism as valuing the natural world:

> For that is what humanism is: it is, to repeat and insist, about the value of things human. Its desire to learn from the past, its exhortation to courage in the present, and its espousal of hope for the future, are about real things, real people, real human need and possibility, and the fate of the fragile world we share. It is about human life; it requires no belief in an afterlife. It is about this world; it requires no belief in another world. It requires no commands from divinities, no promises of reward or threats of punishment, no myths and rituals, either to make sense of things or to serve as a prompt to the ethical life. It requires only open eyes, sympathy and the kindness it prompts, and reason.
>
> *(2007: 64)*

Aligned with secularism, humanism connotes a moral stance that advocates for human agency, freedom, and progress without religious entanglements. As with Wright's critique of religion, humanists emphasize rationality, including but not limited to scientific methodology. Modern feminist care theory is humanistic in origins as none of the founding mothers of the field emphasized religion as a basis for care; however, care has been part of religious teachings for millennia.

Finally, a note about posthumanism: counterintuitively, care theory can also be a posthuman project. Posthumanism refers to decentering existential theories from their tradition of positing humans as exceptional and the only source of agency. A posthuman approach does not entirely negate humanism but addresses its speciesism and hubris regarding humanity. Anthropocentrism, which has led to the devaluing and destruction of nonhuman life and the environment, is an example of humanism run amok. Thus, posthumanism is an extension of the humanistic project. Humanism suggests that the supernatural is not the arbiter of truth, while posthumanism indicates that humans are not, either. Some care scholars, such as Maria Puig de la Bellacasa and Vivienne Bozalek, have argued that the relationality of all matter, including nonhuman animals, reflects a posthuman care theory (Puig de La Bellacasa, 2017; Bozalek, 2021). Accordingly, one committed to care should be open to humanism *and* posthumanism.

The discussion of veganism in the next chapter takes up posthumanism as manifested in our relationship with animals. Although we are finite embodied beings, our ability to care is quite expansive. It is not a zero-sum game. Caring for other humans does not preclude us from caring deeply about the nonhuman: animals, trees, the environment, etc. So the discussion regarding humanism in this chapter is aimed at recentering religious morality around inclusive and responsive care and should not be construed as reinforcing anthropocentrism.

## Morality without Gods

One persistent social narrative is the perceived necessity of god to sustain morality. This issue manifests in several debates. An ongoing concern in the philosophy of religion and religious studies is what determines morality. Is an action moral because a deity pronounced it so, or was the moral declaration made to coincide with universal moral truth? Long before Christianity, Plato portrays Socrates as framing a dilemma, "Is the pious loved by the gods because it's pious, or it is pious because it is loved?" (Euthyphro: 10a). Relatedly, Christian theologians have an enduring discussion about whether the norms of "Christian ethics" should differ from those of secular ethics. Morally speaking (rather than authoritatively speaking), what normative content differentiates Christian ethics from morality that would be best for all of society? (Clem, 2023: 11–31).

A major Pew Research study regarding popular beliefs on the connection between belief in a god and morality found significant geographic differences. Less than half of the world viewed faith in god as necessary for morality, but the overall association was still high (nearly 45%) (Tamir, Connaughton, and Salazar, 2021). Philosopher Elizabeth Secord Anderson, like many other philosophers, is critical of the idea that a god is necessary for morality in the world. Focusing on Christianity, Anderson finds the religious claim rooted in needing an "authoritative commander" to raise specific moral claims above the rest. Anderson is not arguing for care ethics, but she finds no compelling evidence supporting the need for a god in any ethical approach. Looking at the Christian bible in terms of its alleged divine revelation, Anderson observes

**166** Invitations and Provocations

inconsistencies and support for heinous actions (Anderson, 2007: 228). She contends that morality has always rested with humanity as scriptural teachings are insufficient and poorly suited to meet the complexity of ethical challenges (Ibid: 216).

By contrast, care ethics is anti-authoritarian. Recall the discussion in Chapter 2 regarding emergent normativity. Accordingly, the caring moral response stems from the context and needs of the one cared for. Anti-authoritarianism does not mean that the claims of moral authorities should be summarily dismissed, but whether the content of those claims is caring remains paramount to their significance. Religions, law, and cultural traditions may have moral insight, but that insight must be weighed against how to best care in the circumstances. My point here resonates with the logical fallacy of "appeal to authority" (Dowden, 2022). Appealing to authority is not a sufficient condition for making any argument valid.

Furthermore, religious moral authority is demonstrably susceptible to questioning. Religions often make extraordinary claims to moral clarity in the name of a deity. Accordingly, moral authority should not be tarnished by grave inconsistencies. No one is morally perfect, but relatively few institutions claim absolute ethical insight like religions do. As Anderson discusses, Christianity is replete with historical and moral missteps. Catholicism, for example, claims that the pope can promulgate moral teaching with infallibility. Such claims are problematic because the teachings of a deity are mediated through fallible human beings. It is virtually impossible to know the extent of the harm from the sexual abuse perpetrated by Catholic clergy against children. Still, one estimate places the number of cases between 1950 and 1970 in France alone at 330,000 children (Associated Press, 2021). These abuses demonstrated severe moral hypocrisy. Such actions are not the only damage to institutional Catholic morality. The Roman Catholic Church had centuries of positive, progressive social teachings on labor, unionization, and war that point to a caring society. However, it squandered moral goodwill gained from these issues by condemning contraception and abortion to the point that even Catholics do not generally adhere to its sexual morality. For example, according to recent studies, 99% of Catholic women have used contraception, and 24% of women receiving an abortion identify as Catholic (Jones, 2020).

## The Catholic Church and Abortion

The issue of Abortion offers significant insight into how religion can perpetuate uncaring policies and practices. A comprehensive discussion of abortion morality could fill volumes. However, a brief overview in light of Catholic teaching is offered here. In the 1995 papal encyclical, *Evangelium Vitae*, Pope John Paul II reiterated the declaration of predecessor Paul VI as a unified and eternal position on the morality of abortion,

# Humanism and Balancing the Primacy of Care with Religious Authority    **167**

Given such unanimity in the doctrinal and disciplinary tradition of the Church, Paul VI was able to declare that this tradition is unchanged and unchangeable. Therefore, by the authority which Christ conferred upon Peter and his Successors, in communion with the Bishops—who on various occasions have condemned abortion and who in the aforementioned consultation, albeit dispersed throughout the world, have shown unanimous agreement concerning this doctrine—I declare that direct abortion, that is, abortion willed as an end or as a means, always constitutes a grave moral disorder, since it is the deliberate killing of an innocent human being. This doctrine is based upon the natural law and upon the written Word of God, is transmitted by the Church's Tradition and taught by the ordinary and universal Magisterium.

*(1995)*

However, no amount of reiterating an appeal to authority makes the statement true. First, despite the veneer of perpetual infallibility, the Catholic moral teaching on abortion has changed throughout its two millennia of history (Monk, 2020). Second, grounding authority in biblical teaching is of little help and usually involves theological gymnastics, given the absence of biblical attention to abortion. As biblical scholar L. William Countryman describes, "The Bible contains nothing helpful on the subject [of abortion]" (1988: 255). Similarly, religion scholar Gerald Laure indicated, "In the modern controversy over abortion neither side can draw directly upon biblical verses to support its position" (1983: 123). Finally, and relatedly, Jesus did not teach about abortion (although abortion existed) (Depierri (1968)).

Many have speculated that the motivation for the absolute position on abortion taken by conservative churches is political rather than trying to achieve morality. For example, Kristin Kobes Du Mez points out that evangelical churches in the United States were lukewarm in resisting abortion until reproductive rights became a visible part of the women's movement. Then, a patriarchal resistance to women's empowerment seemed to galvanize the position into a moral rallying cry (2020: 68).

The divisiveness of the abortion debate around legalization misses an opportunity for moral rapprochement between secular and religious interests. Feminists and church leaders could join forces to reduce the number of abortions through support for better sex education and contraception access. Feminists are not endeavoring to increase the number of abortions. Instead, pro-choice advocates wish to empower women with greater agency and autonomy. However, the insistence on criminalizing abortion means extensive time and energy expended on legal and political maneuvering rather than working to meet the needs of women.

Finally, one might appropriate care ethical language to claim that church teaching merely expresses care for an unborn fetus (Zagar, 2022). Although

**168** Invitations and Provocations

one can care for an unborn fetus in an imaginative and projective manner, the difference between the two circumstances can be found in juxtaposing coercion and the depth of care commitment. Legal scholar Jonathan Herring argues that abortion is a public good because it facilitates ending unwanted pregnancies and thus prevents people from caring for those they do not want or are unable to care for. Herring leverages the notion of coerced pregnancies to make a legal case for abortion (Herring, 2019). Supporting Herring's claim is the depth of care required to raise a child. For example, we may wish to compel a health practitioner to care for someone they find morally objectionable because it is their chosen social role to which they commit. Such care may be transactional and limited. However, coercing a woman to care for a child is forcing a depth of care that is long-term and consuming. Furthermore, Herring points out that coercive care tramples the mother's ability to care for herself.

Many women desire to maintain their Christian identity and find reproductive freedom the more caring choice for society (Eggebroten, 1994). Abortion is not only morally acceptable from a care standpoint, but it may be the best care for someone and future children that a woman may choose (or not) to have. Evangelical Christian Anne Eggebroten claims,

> If we cared about poor women, we would make a society where they had the economic resources to provide for all the children they wanted to bear, but until we get to such an ideal world, we must not require them to bear children for whom they have no economic resources.
>
> *(Ibid: 228)*

Some pro-choice advocates would not necessarily frame their arguments this way, but the message here is that there is room for agreement among differing identities when care is valued. For Eggebroten and others, insufficient caring is not an acceptable religious ethical position.

## Care Theory and Religion

Published in 2022, *Care Ethics, Religion, and Spiritual Traditions* is the first book-length consideration of the relationship between care theory and religion (van Nistelrooij, Sander-Staudt, and Hamington, 2020). Engaging Christian, Indigenous, Islamic, and Jewish experiences, contributors to this volume address issues including masculinity, moral authority, sex education, spirituality, environmentalism, and peace. *Care Ethics, Religion, and Spiritual Traditions* is neither a condemnation nor endorsement of religion but a discussion of the relationship of care ethics to religiosity. Before this book, the general lack of attention to the relationship between care ethics and faith is surprising, given the ubiquitous value of care in religious moral teaching. I flesh out a few instances when care theorists confronted religion in what follows.

# Humanism and Balancing the Primacy of Care with Religious Authority  **169**

In *Caring: A Feminine Approach to Caring and Moral Education*, Nel Noddings makes a naturalistic argument regarding care when she distinguishes between "natural caring" and "ethical caring" (1984: 79). She contends that humans naturally care for familiar others—family and friends—with whom we share proximity and time.[3] Such caring is not always easy, but it is so expected and routine that it appears natural. Noddings gives natural care an originary position that takes more significant effort and imagination to extend to unfamiliar others through what she names ethical caring. Although social institutions often place ethical caring as a moral ideal, they often fall short because "they demand loyalty, insist upon the affirmations of certain beliefs, and separate members from nonmembers on principle" (1984: 117). In particular, religious institutions claim "frequent insistence on obedience to rules and adherence to ritual contributes to the erosion of genuine caring" (Ibid). Subsequently, Noddings authored *Women and Evil* (1989), engaging the feminist theology of Mary Daly, Rosemary Radford Ruether, and Elisabeth Schüssler Fiorenza to interrogate the underlying social narrative that associates women with evil. Noddings focuses on institutional gender oppression. Religion is roundly criticized. Noddings does not advocate atheism; however, she finds much harm throughout the history of organized religion. For example, she claims that religion contributes to a form of "othering" that can incite violence and war:

> The notion that salvation rests in our relation to God and not in our relation to other human beings has often led to a devaluation of persons and a tendency to place those with whom we differ outside the moral community.
>
> *(1989: 204)*

In 1991, Noddings delivered the annual John Dewey Lecture on "Educating for Intelligent Belief or Unbelief." Although the speech does not explicitly address care ethics, Noddings recommends that all public schools should teach religion (1993: xv) and give students positive and negative information, as well as the tools to assess the teachings of religion in an evidence-based manner (Ibid: 139–44). Noddings is wary of religious morality as inconsistently pro-caring but not dismissive or discounting of religion.

Noddings focuses on the connection between religion and violence as she develops a social and political philosophy of care in *Starting at Home: Caring and Social Policy*. Accordingly, she criticizes Christianity for making certain forms of suffering acceptable: "Christianity has—in both its theological traditions and ordinary pulpit preaching—promoted the idea that pain is deserved" (2002a: 196). The book's premise is that social policy should take its cues from the ideal caring relationships associated with home and family life. Thus, for Noddings, a concept like eternal damnation does not make sense in the moral relationships found in the home where, ideally, forgiveness and compassion should reside. Noddings recognizes that many Christians have fallen away from

**170** Invitations and Provocations

strict beliefs regarding hell and eternal damnation, but the legacy of these religious constructs remains.

In *Educating Moral People: A Caring Alternative to Character Education*, Noddings expresses concern regarding recent efforts to instill character education in schools that focus too strongly on virtues. Although care ethics is often associated with virtue theory, given that care is neither deontological nor utilitarian, she finds virtue ethics too individualistic. For Noddings, care's relational ontology distinguishes it from virtue theory. Thus any character education that emphasizes traditional virtues is missing the significance of the fundamental relationality of humanity (2002b: xiii). Accordingly, she argues that religious character education contains an implicit endorsement of problematic masculine virtues. For example, Noddings criticizes the valorization of a warrior model marked by individualism, hyper-competitiveness, and hierarchical thinking (Ibid: 110). Likewise, although she finds the peace and compassion-oriented teachings of Jesus compatible with care, an implicit masculine enforcer exists: "Jesus, while counseling his followers against violence, promised that God would mete out justice in destruction of the wicked" (Ibid: 104).

One scholar who seemingly bridged care thinking and religious themes is Catherine Keller. In *From a Broken Web: Separation, Sexism, and Self*, Keller does not explicitly name an ethic of care, but her discussion of ontological relationality resonates strongly with the work of care theorists. Keller weaves gender, sexuality, mythology, and religion into a lament about how the social imagination has valorized separateness from various sources, ranging from popular conceptions of god to the patriarchal differentiation of men and women (1986: 35 and 38). Keller's analysis is thorough and nuanced; however, it is not a critique of religion and spirituality per se. Instead, her concern is with dominant institutional and theological manifestations of religion. She argues that religion can be a potent force for connectedness among people under different conditions (Ibid: 225). However, according to Keller, religious institutions and their theologies have more often than not reified separateness: "Religion defining holiness as separation has made itself into the bearer of barriers, of disconnection, of exclusion" (Ibid: 219). This separateness runs counter to our composite identity. Keller declares, "I *am* many" (Ibid: 228) in affirming the web metaphor of self as multiplicity: "my many selves as the fabric of other persons, plants, places—all the actual entities that have become part of me" (Ibid: 227). Keller concludes her argument on a hopeful note by integrating the notion of relational ontology with a process theology in claiming that rather than a detached and abstract omnipotent and omnibenevolent deity, the possibility of a god constantly becoming and unfolding in the web of existence exists (Ibid: 248–52). This process theology matches the process ethics of care. Keller's work represents a type of proto-care ethics that recognizes the significance of spirituality in people's lives.

Relational ontology was also at the center of a discussion in 2007 at a symposium sponsored by *The St. Thomas Law Review* titled "Workplace Restructuring to Accommodate Family Life." One panel included Roman Catholic feminist legal scholars and Eva Feder Kittay, a prolific and highly regarded care philosopher. Kittay was invited to represent a secular feminist position. During the presentations, care ethics was framed as a secular approach over and against religious methods. In her presentation, Kittay made it clear that there is much she values in the feminist religious tradition. Still, there is a distinction in how she approaches human dignity, and care plays a central role in that distinction:

> I really do welcome the writings of religious feminists who emphasize love, care and human vulnerability, an emphasis that stands in contrast to an often constricting and obsessive valuing of the human capacity for rationality. Contrast the conception of dignity that predominates in philosophy with the one dominant in religious traditions. Philosophical treatments of human dignity tend to be based on our ability to reason. Human dignity as conceived within religious traditions derives from the idea that we are all created in the divine image, that we are all children of God. While I feel an affinity to attributions of dignity that are not based on the capacity for reason, I don't think that appeal to a personal deity is the only alternative. In other work, I have argued for a notion of dignity grounded in the care humans are both able to give and receive, not, if you will, in the idea that we are all children of God, but a secular analogue, the idea that we are all "some mother's child".
>
> *(Kittay, 2007: 469)*

Employing Martin Luther King Jr. as an example, Kittay describes what she shares with those of religious faith on issues of social and political importance as an "overlapping consensus" (Ibid: 471) which is possible in a pluralist society. Kittay takes issue with fellow panelist Susan J. Stabile who contends a primary difference between Catholic and secular feminism can be found in the latter's commitment to equality and individualism to the point of denigrating familial care (2007: 435). Stabile references the work of Elizabeth Fox Genovese in *Feminism and the Unraveling of the Social Bond* (2007: 436), a historian who converted to Catholicism and became a leading anti-feminist voice in the United States. Stabile concludes her presentation by delineating commonalities and differences between feminists and religious scholars. Beyond the shared commitment to a better valuation of the work done in the home between secular and religious feminists, Stabile claims,

> The primacy of the traditional family in Catholic thought, combined with an acceptance of immutable differences between men and women, means that

**172** Invitations and Provocations

there will be points along this road where the paths of Catholic and secular feminist will part company.

*(2007: 468)*

Kittay responds by reviewing some of the relational work done in feminist psychology and philosophy. She clarifies that "secular feminists are united in fierce commitment to equality, but not to individualism" (2007: 475). Although Kittay found resonance between the two positions, she could not condone the advocacy of traditional familial structures and theological positions over the relational moral obligations that human dependency generates:

It is hard for this secular feminist to understand why, when religious feminists want to emphasize relationality, the value of caring labor, equal dignity of each individual, the importance of raising children and caring for those who cannot care for themselves, the emphasis is not on the units of dependency relations rather than the family as understood and constituted by patriarchy. So here there is a real divide. Predictably, I would urge the religious feminists to come over to our side, for in my perspective, it is far more consistent with all their other feminist positions and attitudes towards care.

*(Ibid: 484)*

Thus we see that Keller, Noddings, and Kittay criticize certain forms of institutional religions' violent and divisive elements but fall short of the blanket condemnation found, for example, among some in the New Atheism movement. The suggestion in this chapter is not that one committed to care cannot hold religious beliefs or identify as part of organized religion. Instead, a commitment to care should suggest resistance to the divisive and destructive elements of religious morality when it drives a wedge between people and inhibits human flourishing.

## Religious Care: More Than Thoughts and Prayers

Care is a value that permeates religious teachings. Although there is warranted cynicism regarding public officials offering "thoughts and prayers" as a substitute for meaningful action, this cynicism should not discount how much care is central to the theology of major religions and delivered through good works done in the name of religion. Universally condemning or praising the morality of those who identify as religious or as atheists/humanists is another example of binary thinking that is too simplistic for a nuanced understanding of the other required by good care. Religion can be a significant motivator and inspiration for good. In this section, I briefly examine moral theology and religious good works.

It is hard to imagine an organized religion that does not value care as codified in its sacred texts. As religious historian Peter Donovan describes:

> I maintain that every major religion of the world—Buddhism, Christianity, Confucianism, Hinduism, Islam, Jainism, Judaism, Sikhism, Taoism, Zoroastrianism—has similar ideals of love, the same goal of benefiting humanity through spiritual practice, and the same effect of making their followers into better human beings.
>
> *(Donovan, 1986: 367)*

The last phrase in this quote regarding making followers "better human beings" is telling. Donovan stresses that religious morality is not something other-worldly or supernatural but endeavors to spur humans to reach their full potential.

For example, the Roman Catholic Church has a rich tradition of social teaching that is replete with the value of care.[4] The United States Conference of Catholic Bishops names seven themes of Catholic Social teaching: (1) Life and Dignity of the Human Person. (2) Call to Family, Community, and Participation. (3) Rights and Responsibilities. (4) Option for the Poor and Vulnerable. (5) The Dignity of Work and Rights of Workers. (6) Solidarity. (7) Care for God's Creation (United States Conference of Catholic Bishops, n.d.). The themes represented here are admirable, integrating relationality with actions that can respond to the needs of others. The Roman Catholic Church's response to needs is more than words as it supports concrete actions. For example, Catholic Charities USA, which does not receive funding from the institutional Catholic Church, is well over a century old. Catholic Charities reports serving 15 million people in 2020 by distributing 20 million pounds of food and creating emergency housing and affordable housing for almost 200,000 people without homes. The nonprofit also responds to domestic disasters, engages in workforce development, and assists those migrating to the United States (Catholic Charities USA, 2020). These practices represent tangible care in the lives of those who receive assistance, and Catholic Charities USA should be praised for its responsiveness to need. Catholic Charities has a code of ethics for which "care" is prominent, including a paragraph regarding care for employees. After the US government, Catholic Charities USA is the largest social safety net provider.

Religion-identified charitable organizations are as numerous as there are organized religions (actually more so since each belief system has inspired many philanthropic organizations). There are Buddhist, Hindu, Islamic, Jewish, Sikh, and other organizations that are engaging in the good work of care.

It bears repeating that religious affiliation neither precludes nor guarantees the delivery of good care. For example, some have argued that the population of the United States is becoming less charitable because it is becoming less religious (Zinsmeister, 2019). Given the historical rhetorical association between

**174** Invitations and Provocations

Christianity and generosity, such a correlation makes intuitive sense. However, the evidence does not always support this connection. Social scientist Laura R. Saslow et al. conclude from a series of studies, "the prosociality of less religious individuals is driven to a greater extent by levels of compassion than is the prosociality of the more religious" (2013: 31).

Accordingly, those who advocate care theory need not have qualms with the caring capacity of those choosing a religious identity. What is argued in this chapter is that when religious affiliation causes a conflict with a caring response, then the care commitment should take precedence (the categorical commitment to care discussed in Chapter 3).

## Private Beliefs and Public Values

Recall that care theory is a non-ideal theory and a process morality. Assessing the rightness or wrongness of a caring action is not as crucial as endeavoring to improve care through humble inquiry, inclusive connection, and responsive action. The caring work of religious institutions is commendable. Still, that praise must be tempered when theological constraints prevent unassuming knowledge acquisition, foster exclusion and prejudice, or limit meeting the needs of others. Is it possible to relegate some religious tenets as private beliefs while acting to promote the public value of care?

The work of Catholic Charities USA is an example of a great deal of moral good that occasionally falls short of good care. In 2010, the State of Illinois passed legislation requiring adoption agencies to consider same-sex couples as potential foster care and adoptive parents if they want to receive state funding. The United States Bishops condemned the law as infringing on religious freedom. The Illinois Catholic Charities closed its foster care centers rather than comply with the law. The conflict exasperated one center director: "We have 600 children abused and neglected in an area where there are hardly any providers" (Goldstein, 2011). The actions of Illinois Catholic Charities are an example of placing moral theology (in this case, the condemnation of homosexuality) ahead of caring relations. But, of course, the route the Catholic Bishops took is not the only choice. Laurie Goodstein explains:

> Taking a completely different tack was the agency affiliated with the conservative Lutheran Church Missouri Synod, which, like the Catholic Church, does not sanction same-sex relationships. Gene Svebakken, president and chief executive of the agency, Lutheran Child and Family Services of Illinois, visited all seven pastoral conferences in his state and explained that the best option was to compromise and continue caring for the children. "We've been around 140 years, and if we didn't follow the law we'd go out of business," Mr. Svebakken said. "We believe it's Godpleasing to serve these kids, and we know we do a good job".
>
> *(Goodstein, 2011)*

Despite their religious position, Lutheran Child and Family Services chose to continue to do the work of care. They subordinated some of their moral beliefs to the public good of care.

The above conflict, replicated in other areas, is an example of a caring tradition of a religious identity clashing with some other tenet of the religious institution. The practices, in this case finding good foster homes, are justified on religious grounds, such as the aforementioned themes of Catholic social teaching regarding supporting families and option for the vulnerable. However, moral actions are resisted because of another aspect of the Catholic tradition, anti-homosexual bias. The Roman Catholic legacy of viewing homosexuality as sinful can be traced to (and perhaps beyond) Thomas Aquinas's teaching in the *Summa Theologica*.[5] Under these circumstances, it becomes the task of religious leaders to decide the highest values to be honored.

## The Primacy of Care

Associating care with humanism can mitigate barriers between those who do not believe in a deity and the general population. Pointedly, psychologists Ain Simpson and Kimberly Rios conducted several studies to ascertain the nature of anti-atheist prejudice. The study of over 400 participants determined that perception regarding care was crucial for whether atheists were considered moral. When someone perceives an atheist as uncaring, anti-atheist prejudice rises. According to Simpson and Rios, "Atheists' perceived capacity to be kind, caring, and compassionate appears to be the central moral concern implicated in judgments of atheists, rather than perceived atheist concerns for fairness, loyalty, respect for authority, and purity" (2017: 507). This conclusion might have implications for the popular perception of aggressive New Atheism. The researchers mention the work of Richard Dawkins as off-putting in this manner.

Recall that the argument in this chapter is not to advocate for atheism but rather that those committed to care should be open to humanism when religious dictates lack humble inquiry, inclusive connection, and responsive action. This claim applies equally to atheists and those who identify as religious. Can religious institutions engage in good care? Of course, they can. However, that will mean adapting to the various needs of people in the present (humble inquiry), recognizing and empathizing with a diversity of people (inclusive inquiry), and providing for the privations of individuals (responsive action). At times, perhaps not that often, a caring stance will mean subordinating moral traditions to the caring response in the present. Religions already support caring values, so the leap requested here is not without internal resources. However, it does mean rethinking some vociferously held ideas, for example, regarding sexual mores and sexual identities.

A long time ago, I gave a talk titled "Was Jesus a Care Ethicist?" There are many challenges in answering that question because I was addressing someone

**176** Invitations and Provocations

who lived two millennia ago and who not only did not write anything down but whose followers only started writing their recollections of his teaching three decades after his death. Layer on the politicization of Jesus's teachings even as they are presented in the Second Testament, and the understanding is obscured. However, critical biblical scholars endeavor to assess what appears to be the most historically accurate representation.[6] An analysis of their findings indicates Jesus's ethical approach eschewed strict consequentialism and rule-based morality but praised acts of forgiveness and compassion.[7] This cursory analysis would suggest that Jesus appeared to have a message that resonated with feminist care ethics. Of course, I have argued that care theory is anti-authoritarian and requires no validation from a religious figure like Jesus. The point here is that a commitment to care should not be unfamiliar to Christians, as found in their beloved texts.

However, too often, religious institutions and their leaders offer uncaring and divisive claims in the name of superior moral authority. For example, in 1996, the Southern Baptist Convention, the largest Protestant denomination in the United States, published "Resolution on a Christian Response to Homosexuality." The document declares, "Even a desire to engage in a homosexual relationship is always sinful, impure, degrading, shameful, unnatural, indecent, and perverted." Subsequent pronouncements reinforced this position. This exclusionary and moralistic language cannot be found in the Christian Gospels and is a far cry from the moral trajectory of Jesus described above.

The previously mentioned publications of Kristin Kobes Du Mez is instructive for understanding the alienation of evangelical Christianity from its caring values. Her work also ties together several of the provocations offered in this book. Kobes Du Mez finds certain powerful and influential strains of Christianity embracing a toxic mix of aggressive masculinity and neoliberal capitalism, which I have described as hindering a more caring society. She offers a prominent example in the words of James Dobson, best-selling author and media figure who founded Focus on the Family. This organization promotes conservative social views on several fronts. Dobson, who suggests that children are inherently sinful and justifies corporeal punishment, strenuously argues for traditional and heteronormative gender roles in the family. In one of his popular books, Dobson calls for a return to "the traditional masculine role as prescribed in the Good Book" and defensively adds, "If this be macho, sexist, chauvinist, and stereotypical, then I'm guilty as charged" (2020: 83).

Of course, many Baptists do not agree with the presumed official stance described above, as there are Evangelicals who do not agree with Dobson. Such dissidence offers hope for a more inclusive and caring posture. From the standpoint of a commitment to care, a reassessment of moral stances that create further hate, violence, and suffering is what is asked in this provocation and invitation to consider humanistic response when religious ones fall short. One does not have to abandon their religious traditions, but some, like Fanny

Wright, may choose to do so. The priority of care is most significant for transforming society into a more caring one.

## Notes

1 In 2007 78% of US adults identified as religiously affiliated but by 2021 that number dropped to 63% (Smith, 2021).

2 A.C. Grayling points out that everyone is an atheist of one form or another as no one believes in the existence of all the deities that civilization has proffered throughout history. *Against All Gods* (London: Oberon Boos, 2007), 35.

3 Noddings has faced criticism that her philosophy of care is essentialist leading to reinforcing the historical burden of care on women. However, critics often overlook the number of times Noddings has endeavored to clarify her position as distinct from essentialism. For example, in the 2003 second addition of her groundbreaking work, *Caring,* she addressed why she used "feminine" in the title of her 1984 groundbreaking book: "'Feminine' pointed to a mode of experience, not to an essential characteristic of women, and I wanted to make clear that men might also share this experience. I still believe that if we want males to participate fully in caring, a change of experience is required" (2013: xxiv).

4 I use the Catholic Church as an example here not to reinforce a Christian-centric view of the world but because it is the moral theology I am most familiar with Catholicism having spent years of graduate work studying it as well as working with eminent moral theologian Charles Curran. Much of what is claimed here is applicable to other major religions although with different manifestations and nuances.

5 Written in the thirteenth century, the *Summa Theologica* addresses over 500 questions of faith applying Aquinas's natural law approach based on the natural order of all things. That which is not employed for its purported nature is unnatural and sinful. In regard to homosexuality, Aquinas lists it among four unnatural vices: "Thirdly, by copulation with an undue sex, male with male, or female with female, as the Apostle states (Rm. 1:27) and this is called the 'vice of sodomy'" (II-II, 154, 11). The other three named unnatural vices are sex during a woman's menses (unclean), bestiality, and unnatural manners of copulation.

6 Although there are many critical biblical scholars that take strive to look at biblical passages without theological bias and based on the best available scientific evidence, I am referring to the work of the Jesus Seminar (1985–2005), a group of 150 scholars who sought to understand the best historically defensible picture of what Jesus said and did. They rated Gospel passages for their likely historicity (Funk and Hoover, 1993).

7 According to the Jesus Seminar, the highest-rated passages for historical authenticity from the Gospels include Jesus's call to turn the other cheek (Matt 5:39 & Luke 6:29), love of enemies (Luke 6:27), giving to beggars (Matt 5:42 & Luke 6:30) and the parable of the Good Samaritan (Luke 10:30-35).

# 8
# VEGANISM AND POST-HUMAN CARE

### Prologue: Continuities and Discontinuities of Tradition

Margaret Robinson is a self-identified bisexual, two-spirit feminist scholar, public researcher, and activist who has published on the experiences of sexually non-conforming individuals. Methodologically, her work interrogates the effect of intersecting oppressions drawing upon critical, postcolonial, and queer theories, intersectionality, and third-wave feminism (Dalhousie University). Furthermore, Robinson has authored a series of articles on veganism, which is surprising given her identity with the Lennox Island Mi'kmaq First Nation[1] people who traditionally inhabited the eastern coast of North America and strongly identified with the fishing of their land:

> Archaeological evidence and oral traditions indicate the presence of our ancestors on the shores of Malpeque Bay dating back 10,000 years. Our spiritual attachment and connection endures here and this place in the Malpeque Bay has significance to us, which all Canadians can appreciate.

> For thousands of years, our people have been sustained by the sea. While methods have changed and technology has advanced, our connection with the fishery has remained. Lennox Island currently has 32 boats in the commercial and traditional lobster fishery. Our citizens harvest oysters, snow crab, clams and countless other fish resources. The fishery is our largest employer and we remain eternally grateful to the sea for its bounty. It is with respect, dignity and thanks that our people accept these offerings.

> *(Bernard)*

Robinson is keenly aware of the tensions between vegan practices and Mi'Kmaq identity. However, rather than the prevailing narrative that eating meat is a core cultural heritage of indigenous people, Robinson counters that veganism is more faithful to Mi'kmaq beliefs.

In "Veganism and Mi'Kmaq Legends," Robinson elucidates the complexity of cultural traditions and intersectional oppression. Although acknowledging the Mi'Kmaq tradition of living from the sea, she also notes the fundamental respect that the community has for animals. Her analysis reveals that the Mi'Kmaq culture has much in common with vegan morality; it also points out how colonization has intensified the divergence from vegan values. In particular, she names two barriers to aboriginal acceptance of veganism: its association with whiteness and class privilege (Robinson, 2013). Robinson cites numerous examples of native people labeling veganism as another attempt by white colonizers at domination; in this case, replacing traditional indigenous diets with what is portrayed as morally superior. Furthermore, she observes that veganism is viewed as unaffordable to poverty-stricken aboriginals. However, Robinson finds both arguments lacking. She contends that animal consumption binds indigenous people to hegemonic capitalism, including that those who live on resource-poor reservations experience food deserts that force the consumption of highly processed meat products.

Additionally, because indigenous communities are closely tied to the land, they directly experience acute environmental destruction from animal farming. This ecosystem harm is a hidden cost of meat consumption masked by its affordability and availability. Furthermore, land rights treaties with the Federal government often require hunting and fishing to demonstrate that the owners are working the land. She views this as another example of how meat consumption by the Mi'kmaq benefits non-indigenous interests.

Robinson demonstrates that the traditions of the Mi'kmaq, although allowing for the killing of animals, contain a different set of moral values than that of the Western understanding of animals as objects of domination. These ancient stories find animals as equals, as beings with agency. The legends describe animals respectfully and reveal that animals provide consent before dying for human consumption. Frequently there are also expressions of regret by the humans who must kill the animals. As Robinson describes,

> In our stories, the othering of animal life that makes meat-eating psychologically comfortable is replaced by a model of creation in which animals are portrayed as our siblings. Mi'kmaq legends view humanity and animal life as being on a continuum, spiritually and physically.
>
> *(Ibid: 191)*

Robinson employs these stories to suggest that veganism aligns more with indigenous philosophy and spirituality than meat eating.

**180** Invitations and Provocations

Furthermore, Robinson notes that hunting reinforced a patriarchal division of labor in indigenous communities, given that women were the food preparers and vegetable gatherers while men usually killed the animals.[2] She indicates that it is vital for women to reclaim aboriginal oral traditions to resist patriarchal themes regarding separate spheres of work and the primacy of meat consumption. Robinson declares, "There is more to our culture and to our relationship with the land, particularly as women, than hunting and killing animals" (Robinson, 2013: 193). Most importantly, Robinson finds the resistance to indigenous veganism as playing into the hands of white stereotypes of native peoples as fixed in the past rather than living in the present. Like all cultures, there is a dynamism to indigenous cultures that makes them capable of adapting fundamental values to the present context. Accordingly, one such adaptation is

> to embody our traditional values in new rituals. With the adoption of a vegan diet, our meal preparation and consumption can become infused with transcendent significance, as we recall our connection with other animals, our shared connection to the Creator."
>
> *(Ibid: 194)*

Elsewhere, Robinson argues that Mi'kmaq's understanding of the human-animal relationship has a kind of reciprocity characterized by mutual obligation (Robinson, 2014). However, this reciprocity is not a contractual obligation of calculated exchange. Instead, it is care and respect for one another so that both can thrive. Consequently, it is unsurprising that Robinson finds masculine-dominated sport hunting particularly egregious in violating this reciprocity.

Like the other individuals featured in the chapter prologues, Robinson is not a care theorist. However, care permeates her thinking about veganism. For example, when discussing the Mi'kmaq phrase "Msit No'kmaq," which is translated as "all my relations," Robinson associated veganism with relationality:

> The phrase "all my relations" summarizes a view rooted in Mi'kmaw culture that humans aren't a separate, special being, or superior to others. We're part of a network of related creatures. It's a focus on the communal rather than the individual. To have integrity we need to honor those relationships. For me, that means not killing other animals, and avoiding practices that make me complicit in their death. It's not always easy. I don't always know enough to make a good decision. But the effort is always worth making.
>
> *(Robinson, 2020)*

There are many ways to argue for the morality of veganism. Similarly, there are sundry explanations for not becoming vegan. Like other indigenous communities, the Mi'kmaq people have solid reasons to be wary of veganism.

Nevertheless, Robinson argues for veganism by foregrounding caring relationships with animals.

## A Radical Provocation for a Meat Culture

Despite offering invitations and provocations for the progressive ideas of feminism, socialism, and humanism, this chapter on veganism is probably the most challenging for readers based on demographics and national disposition. Only about 3% of Americans identify as vegan, given the large population, this represents over ten million people (Reinhart, 2018). Similar percentages are observed in worldwide polling, with variation by culture and rising numbers among young people (Mathieu and Ritchie, 2022).[3] Nevertheless, veganism is often publicly ridiculed as a fringe position adopted by radicals. For example, Lizzy Rosenberg, an editor at Green Matters, recounts the backlash when the United States restaurant chain Cracker Barrel simply decided to add vegan meat alternatives for some items on the menu:

> "YOU CAN TAKE MY PORK SAUSAGE WHEN YOU PRY IT FROM MY COLD, DEAD HANDS!! DON'T TREAD ON MY PORK!!," one person wrote with exuberance.
>
> "Won't be eating hear any more," another, who seemingly doesn't have spell check, responded.
>
> "Are you kidding me? Who do you think your customer base is? I still order the double meat breakfast and it's not even on the menu anymore," another added.
>
> "I Use to Love your store Now No Way," another who liberally uses caps followed up.
>
> "Go Woke, Go Broke!" one person responded.
>
> "I'm not a rabbit. I love meat!! Lettuce is as far as I'll go," said someone who wants to make hating veganism their personality.
>
> "What is this nasty sausage? Stick to the real deal, country sausage," another added.
>
> "Send them back to Gates," someone else said. "We don't eat in an old country store for woke burgers".
>
> *(Rosenberg, 2022)*

Comments also included praise for the vegan additions, but the negative response attracted national attention. Although the above reactions may be extreme, they align with what philosopher Annie Potts describes as the worldwide phenomenon of meat culture. Accordingly, meat culture "encompasses the representations and discourses, practices and behaviors, diets and tastes that generate shared beliefs about, perspectives on, and experiences of meat" (Potts, 2016: 19–20). Despite regional, cultural, and individual differences, eating

**182** Invitations and Provocations

meat and dairy products is the worldwide norm. World meat consumption doubled in the two decades before 2018, reaching 320 million tons (Stifting, 2021: 12). The per capita meat consumption in the United States exceeds 100 kilograms (220 pounds) annually (Ibid). However, meat culture is not just about gross consumption. Cultures are complex and dynamic reflections of values and meaning. Meat culture is entangled with patriarchy (Adams, 1990, 2010, 2015), capitalism (Painter, 2016), and some institutional religions (Newall, 2021). Acknowledging the interconnection of oppressions, philosopher Deane Curtin states,

> To choose one's diet in a patriarchal culture is one way of politicizing an ethic of care. It marks a daily, bodily commitment to resist ideological pressures to conform to patriarchal standards, and to establishing contexts in which caring for can be nonabusive.
>
> *(Curtin, 1991: 72)*

Carnism is the ideological norm making veganism the "other," the marginalized outsider, just as masculinity, has historically been the assumed norm and women have been considered the other (de Beauvoir, 1949).

I submit that if one is committed to caring, one should consider adopting veganism as a lifestyle choice. The prevalence of meat culture makes this chapter the most provocative the provocation chapters in the book. Veganism entails more than just eating practices. However, since eating is a core human activity, it receives the bulk of the attention in this chapter. Food plays a unique role in the human experience. It is needed for sustenance, but that biology requirement does not begin to address the rich and evocative meaning invested in eating. Sensual pleasure, cultural and familial traditions, habituation, commercialization, and emotion play into our relationship with food. Most of the world's population includes and values animals in their diets. Veganism is an extreme position even among those who embrace the examined life. From anecdotal evidence, I would venture to claim that most ethicists and care ethicists are not vegan. The same claim can be made about people who care deeply about animals, even those who share their homes with companion animals.

Remember that care theory, particularly the revolutionary care advocated in this book, is more than just a normative approach to adjudicating moral decisions. Although care theory can provide an ethical guide, it does not aspire exclusively to moral judgment. Accordingly, stating that those committed to care should consider adopting a vegan lifestyle is not a license to judge those who are not vegan. The reflection here is an expansive one endeavoring to magnify the circle of care, in this case, to animals. Care is not a zero-sum game: caring for animals does not replace or preclude caring for people. The message across all the provocations in this book is that fomenting more and better care is paramount.

Referencing the previous provocations, masculine men can become better at care, as can capitalists and devout religious adherents.

Similarly, animal consumers can and do care. Nevertheless, the moral imagination should be allowed to consider, pursue, and inhabit the caring possibilities of radical propositions such as feminism, socialism, humanism, and veganism. Care theory does not provide an abstract arbiter of moral correctness. Noddings reminds us that people are more important than ethical ideals:

> When I dare to make an ethical judgment of someone else's behavior, when I insist that he should behave as I would in a given situation, I must also offer my support and help. Otherwise, I forfeit myself as one-caring.
>
> *(Noddings, 2013: 185)*

However, *Revolutionary Care* is not asking anyone to judge others ethically. The commitment-centered approach utilized throughout this book respects the individual's moral agency. This chapter proposes that if care is central to one's ethical worldview, one should consider veganism as a possible ancillary commitment that aligns with and affirms the categorical commitment to care.

The moral provocations in this book surely exasperate some readers: *Along with everything else asked of a commitment to care, must a care revolution be vegan too?* Taking a position contrary to prevalent norms and traditions can be daunting. But it is essential to do so; veganism represents a significant and exemplary step in a care revolution. Decisions about consumption are among those where the personal and political entwine. Individual choices to care, such as not eating meat, alter our relationships with animals. Such decisions, along with other caring actions, can accrue and participate in an ethos of care that more fully imbues our existence. Even the simplest of meals can be a ritual of care that sets the tone for other relational practices.

One chapter is inadequate to address the nuances and complexity of veganism. Therefore, I limit the discussion to providing the primary argument to view veganism as a reasonable and compelling option for those who commit to care. In what follows, I briefly explore the term veganism as it is employed in this book and then review care theorists' positions on the morality of a vegan lifestyle. Next, I interrogate the significance of the moral imagination in making inclusive connections of care. I then explore indigenous social imaginaries as lessons for Western thinking. Given that the chiasm between Western colonial thought and indigenous worldviews appears wide, I employ the final section to strike a hopeful tone regarding practices to expand our emotional connection to animals, further bolstering a holistic care ethos.

## Veganism Defined

Vegan, as used in this chapter, refers to a lifestyle that seeks to avoid killing or harming animals. It entails not eating or consuming animal products,

**184** Invitations and Provocations

such as purchasing leather or fur jackets. In this instance, animals are defined broadly to include insects but not plants.[4] Veganism is a social movement that supports a vegan lifestyle. Legal scholar and philosopher Gary L. Francione's describes: "Veganism involves not eating, wearing, or using animals or animal products to the extent practicable with the goal of abolishing all animal use because such use cannot be morally justified" (2020: 125). Francione is an animal abolitionist who seeks to eliminate the construct of animals as the property of humans because he argues that animals will always be exploited if their status is that of a commodity. Francione's position reveals the diversity of vegan philosophy as he differentiates himself from other animal advocates because he favors abolitioning all uses of animals by humans. Definitions of veganism tend to stress the moral value of the stance vis-à-vis being an omnivore. Eating meat is the well-established norm, so the moral benefits of not consuming animals are consistently offered as a crucial differentiating aspect of being vegan.

Those who argue for the moral value of a vegan lifestyle have primarily employed deontological (focus on rights) and utilitarian (focus on consequences) frameworks to the moral status of animals. "Animal rights" has emerged as the banner for protecting animals, although from a philosophical standpoint, a right-based approach is only one pathway to moral status. To further clarify terminology, in public discourse, "animal rights" is considered the more radical position employed to support veganism through the inherent dignity of animals. In contrast, "animal welfare" demarcates an anti-cruelty position that does not alter the property status of animals.

A deontological position on veganism argues that raising animals for food is immoral because animals have certain rights, and we have duties toward them. Kant, a leading historical figure in deontological thinking, did not personally or philosophically advance an argument for veganism. However, he did argue that animals have value. From a Kantian perspective, humans are of the highest importance because they are the only beings who are ends in themselves. Nevertheless, a general duty to animals can be derived from our duty to cultivate feelings conducive to morality.

> violent and cruel treatment of animals is far more intimately opposed to a human being's duty to himself, and he has a duty to refrain from this; for it dulls his shared feeling of their suffering and so weakens and gradually uproots a natural disposition that is very serviceable to morality in one's relations with other men.
>
> *(Kant, 1996: 192–3)*

According to Kant, animals are only conferred indirect duties because animals are excluded from having rights as they are not ends-in-themselves as humans are (Howe, 2019: 138–9).

Philosopher Tom Regan also employs a Kantian position further to argue for veganism by claiming all nonhuman animals have rights as "subjects of a life" (1985). A significant voice in the modern animal rights movement, Regan called for the elimination of all animal testing for medical and scientific testing, commercial agriculture, and sport hunting. He staked out an animal rights position vis-à-vis any other approach. He criticized utilitarian methods for failing to make a case for animals on utilitarian grounds, finding that they often relied on underlying rights-based assumptions (1980). Responding to early care theorists, Regan found an ethic of care to be a choice "between a morally inadequate ethic [based on partiality] or a logically inconsistent one [based on an abstract principle of universal care]." Regan employs examples such as "Do white racists have any moral responsibilities to Asians and Chicanos? Given the present interpretation of the ethic of care, it seems not; after all, they fail to care for them." Regan's analysis indicates he understood care ethics as essentialist and confused care social phenomena with care norms (1995: 179).

Philosopher Christine Korsgaard contends that Kant's philosophy could be the basis for a robust animal ethic given human exceptionalism as rational beings.

> We are the beings who create the order of moral values, the beings who choose to ratify and endorse the natural concern that all animals have for themselves. But what we ratify and endorse is a condition shared by the other animals. So we are not the only beings who matter. We are the only beings who on behalf of all animals can shake our fists at the uncaring universe, and declare that in spite of everything we matter.
>
> *Korsgaard (2004: 109)*

Note that in this configuration, what humans care about matters in constructing any nonhuman morality. Animals are not inherently the source of moral significance in this application of Kantianism.

Utilitarians have a long history of advocating for advancing the moral status of animals. For example, Jeremy Bentham and John Stuart Mill offered the radical notion that animals could suffer and that suffering should be minimized. However, they did not call for the approbation of animal killing. Peter Singer, the most well-known modern utilitarian animal advocate, takes the utilitarian claim further than his predecessors. He views the negative consequences of eating meat for the animals and the Earth as outweighing the positive consequences of their consumption. For Singer, utilitarianism is the driving force, and he treats food consumption like any other topic in weighing the outcomes: "I am a vegetarian because I am a utilitarian" (1980: 325). Note that despite publishing a book titled, *Why Vegan? Eating Ethically*, Singer admits that he is not absolutely vegan.

**186** Invitations and Provocations

I call myself a "flexible vegan." I'm predominantly vegan, but I don't treat veganism like a religion. I judge actions by their consequences, and the consequences that matter are the benefit or harm we cause to sentient beings. Minor departures from vegan eating don't really matter much.

*(2020: x)*

Singer's statement is revealing in the exploration of the nature of commitment. Singer is committed to the ethical system of utilitarianism rather than a commitment to animals per se. I interpret Singer's invocation of religion above as a cautionary warning against absolutist positions, an approach consistent with care theory.

To this point, veganism[5] is to abjure all animal consumption for food or sport to mitigate unnecessary suffering and death. My argument is that individuals who commit to care should be open to seriously considering adopting a vegan lifestyle or moving toward veganism to improve one's care. This connection between a care commitment and veganism is made more strongly here than in the care ethics literature, where the relationship has been inconsistent. The following section explores how care theorists have addressed veganism.

## The Care Ethics Literature on Veganism

Many care theorists have commented on the moral status of animals and what care contributes to the discussion. However, the radical threshold of veganism as an ethical demand amidst a meat culture has resulted in a lack of advocacy for a vegan lifestyle. In *Caring*, Noddings offers a chapter on "Caring for Animals, Plants, Things, and Ideas." She admits that the ethical distinction between animals and humans is artificial and not as sharp as traditionally espoused. Noddings clarifies, "An ethic built on caring must consider the possibility that the ethical domain reaches beyond our relations with human beings to those we may establish with animals" (Noddings, 2013: 48). However, like Kant, Noddings is unwilling to grant animals subjectivity given their inability to offer reciprocity as humans do.

Despite her criticism of Peter Singer's disregard for reciprocity, Noddings employs a consequentialist approach. She indicates that sometimes animals must suffer to prevent human suffering; concerning animal experimentation, Noddings writes: "If animal pain is inescapable in the investigation of ways to relieve human suffering, she [the one caring] must logically accept this" (Ibid: 150). Other care theorists and I have emphasized how central knowledge is to care. The presupposition that animal testing leads to alleviating human suffering is spurious. Approximately 800,000 animals were used in research, testing, experimentation, and teaching in 2019, and this number does not include rats and mice bred for research (USDA, 2021). Such experimentation often results in physical harm or death for the animal subjects. However, the view of Noddings

Veganism and Post-Human Care **187**

and others—that animal testing is a necessary evil for the greater good is a mistaken one. A growing body of evidence demonstrates animals make poor surrogates for human physiology.

Furthermore, misleading results from animal testing can lead to harmful treatments for humans (Akhtar, 2015). Approximately 96% of drugs tested on animals fail to receive FDA approval (Pippin, 2013). There are many reasons for this failure rate, but one factor is that animal physiology does not always translate well to human physiology. Furthermore, alternatives to animal testing exist that can lead to accurate data, including human organs in the lab, human organs on computer chips, and 3D printing of human tissues. Exploring such alternatives can be seen as an element of the humble inquiry needed for good care; the inquiry need not be limited to the particular parties involved in a caring relationship. It must also include the more generalized knowledge or facts that impact that relationship. The notion that animals must suffer for the greater good of human health is too simply stated; deeper investigation shows that the claim is not generalizable.

Noddings appears to turn again to consequentialism when she asks what would happen if everyone became vegetarian (2013: 153). She answers her question by claiming that farm animals would overrun the world, and we would likely have to kill them anyway. Ultimately, Noddings advocates for a caring animal welfare when possible, but the caring cannot be robust for animals with which we have no relationship. For example, she describes caring for cats because she has a relationship with them, but not with rats, about whom she states, "I would not torture it, and I hesitate to use poisons on it for that reason, but I would shoot it cleanly if the opportunity arose" (Ibid: 156).

In 1990, literary scholar Josephine Donovan published an article in *Signs: Journal of Women and Culture in Society* that traces the history of the animal rights philosophy and juxtaposes its rationalist approach against feminist relational thinking on the moral status of animals. She decries the hierarchical thinking of many who apply a binary understanding of the moral status of, for example, mammals versus insects as typical of masculinist ethical frameworks. Donovan concludes her article:

> Out of a women's relational culture of caring and attentive love, therefore, emerges the basis for a feminist ethic for the treatment of animals. We should not kill, eat, torture, and exploit animals because they do not want to be so treated, and we know that. If we listen, we can hear them.
>
> *(1990: 375)*

Donovan seems to be laying the foundation for a care ethical approach toward animals by suggesting veganism. However, in the article's last footnote, Donovan only references Noddings's work when she accuses her of speciesism by pointing to the passage regarding the cat and rat described above.

**188** Invitations and Provocations

Specifically, Donovan is critical of Noddings for not advocating abstinence from meat consumption: Noddings "rejects the main tenets of animal rights theory, including not eating meat" (Ibid: 374).

In 1991, *Signs* printed a reply to Donovan by Noddings. Although Donovan only refers to Noddings in a single footnote, Noddings is "dismayed" to have her work labeled "unexamined speciesism," and takes issue with the claim. However, Noddings reiterates the same position offered in *Caring* that although animal suffering should be avoided, the lack of response and reciprocity makes some animals more deserving of moral responsibility than others. Further, she repeats the claim that agricultural animals would have to be slaughtered if everyone did not consume animal products. On veganism, Noddings states, "I am unwilling to brand farmers, ranchers, and 'tea ladies' unethical because they raise animals for food or eat meat. Many, many of these people truly care for their animals" (Noddings, 1991: 421). She concludes the comment by suggesting that she has demonstrated that her position is not "unexamined speciesism." In the same journal issue, Donovan replies to Noddings that she remains unconvinced that Noddings is not speciesist. However, Donovan also falls short of advocating veganism as she grants the possibility of animals providing eggs and dairy under non-factory farm conditions.

Dan Engster clearly and succinctly explains how care theory is differentiated from traditional approaches to the moral status of animals:

> The reason to oppose animal suffering from the perspective of care ethics is not because we wish to maximize utility or consistently apply our rights theory across species, but because we have relations with animals and care about them.
>
> *(Engster, 2006: 521)*

For Engster, caring for animals is a logical extension of the rationale for caring for other humans rather than an abstract construct of the animal's moral standing. He claims that care theory derives moral obligation from our interdependency as vulnerable beings (Ibid: 525). Although ostensibly, animals don't need humans,there are circumstances when they need our help or have been made more vulnerable through our activity, thus warranting our caring for them if we can. One example is the companion animal we have made dependent upon us, and thus for whom we are committed to care. Like other care theorists, he finds no room for oppressive factory farming in care theory. Engster employs some of the same presuppositions as Noddings; he applies them differently but ultimately comes to a similar advocacy position. Like Noddings, Engster abhors the cruelty that befalls many animals raised for meat production. He also shares Noddings's contention that were it not for meat consumption, such animals would not exist and, therefore, could not enjoy a good life until slaughter. But, unlike Noddings, Engster recognizes that slaughter, even if quick and painless, might preclude a notion of care. After weighing the arguments, Engster concludes that those applying care theory can reasonably disagree on moral vegetarianism or veganism. Accordingly, "Care ethics does not necessarily support moral vegetarianism on philosophical grounds" (Ibid: 533).

Philosopher Grace Clement authored several articles on the relationship of care theory to nonhuman animals. Clement was an early adopter of care theory, publishing her first book on the subject in 1996 when concerns over the distinction between justice and care, as well as gender essentialism, were paramount (1996). In addressing the distinction between our moral relation to wild animals versus companion animals, Clement concludes that justice approaches (like that of Regan) make more sense for wild animals. In comparison, care ethics makes more sense for companion animals, although the categories of wild animals and companion animals are artificial and not necessarily mutually exclusive (2022). Although there is little in her critique of Regan that addresses veganism, she does emphasize the emotions associated with care. She cites analysis that children's sympathies are not to eat the product of a slaughtered animal until they are offered rationale to do so (Ibid). In "'Pets or Meat'? Ethics and Domestic Animals" Clement leverages an anecdote from Michael Moore's classic documentary *Roger and Me*, which chronicles the strife of Flint, Michigan, following the departure of major General Motors car manufacturing (1989). One entrepreneurial woman has a roadside business that offers "Rabbits or Bunnies, Pets or Meat for Sale." This vignette highlights the moral dichotomy between how companion animals are treated and those that do not receive such a designation. Again, Clement applies the justice and care distinction to the dichotomy of pets and meat. She correctly points out that care theorists have been ambivalent about giving up meat eating. Still, those who use justice approaches are better equipped to argue for an injunction against animal consumption (2011). However, Clement takes up no explicit position. In a subsequent article, Clement argues that "animals can participate in our moral development and the development of our moral understanding" (2013: 12).

In 2006, 15 years after her dialogue with Noddings, Donovan appeared to have changed her position and was open to advancing a firmer stance on meat consumption in the name of care theory. Donovan posits a "dialogical care theory" whereby caring for animals is "extended to mean not just 'caring about their welfare' but 'caring about what they are telling us'" (2006: 310). She applies feminist standpoint theory to valorize the perspective of animals. Donovan elaborates on the inclusive connection of effective care. Rather than simply empathizing with animals' plight and context, she reinforces the significance of listening to them to understand their standpoint and agential desires. Employing this approach, Donovan sharpens the care argument for veganism: "If we care to take seriously in our ethical decision-making the communicated

**190** Invitations and Provocations

desires of the animal, it is apparent that no animal would opt for the slaughterhouse" (Ibid). Although the implications are clear, Donovan fails to employ the term "veganism."

If Noddings, Engster, and Donovan are guarded in linking care theory and consuming animals, Carol J. Adams and Nancy M. Williams have embraced the tie. Adams is a prolific feminist author on problematizing the consumption of meat. Her most famous work is *The Sexual Politics of Meat*. This landmark study ties flesh-eating to patriarchal values and an argument consistent with the concerns in Chapter 5 regarding toxic masculinity as a barrier to caring. Adams has also published on care labor but does not specialize in care theory. Although she is wary of some care theorists, Adams applies a care approach to animal morality. For example, she criticizes Noddings for adopting assumptions that veganism will end the existence of species used in agriculture (1994: 115). Adams identifies a false dichotomy between caring for the suffering of humans and animals: "Violence against people and that against animals is interdependent. Caring about both is required" (2007: 22). She argues that animals represent humanity's original form of oppression that continues today as a "war on compassion," which spills over to how we treat one another. Adams is a vociferous advocate of moral veganism, not from a rights-based or consequentialist stance, but out of care and compassion.

Perhaps the most direct connection between care theory and veganism is offered by philosopher Nancy M. Williams. In response to Engster, she acknowledges how compelling his argument and framing are. Still, she disagrees with his conclusion that a care theorist could reasonably not adopt veganism if significant efforts are taken to mitigate the pain and suffering of animals in food production—so-called "humane meat" often associated with the label "free-range." Williams provides evidence to assert, "Common practices in the 'humane' meat industry routinely violate the basic aims of care" (2015: 267). She addresses factory farms, non-intensive farming, and backyard farming, recognizing the differences in cruelty and, thus, the discrepancies in moral weight. However, even under the best scenario, Williams suggests that the care offered to animals used in food production is "a thin account of care" (Ibid: 270). Care is a practice and a disposition: a holistic process that cannot ignore significant parts of the relationship to satisfy a consequentialist-like standard of less suffering. Williams is conclusive about veganism in a manner that most care theorists heretofore have not been: "On philosophical grounds, care ethics supports moral vegetarianism because bringing animals into existence when their ultimate fate is slaughter runs counter to what it means to bestow care in an attentive, responsive, respectful, and trusting manner" (Ibid: 274–5).

In the next section, I briefly describe a commitment to veganism as an extension of a moral imagination rooted in our corporeal reality.

## Care and the Embodied Imaginary

Care theorists generally have not mandated veganism because care theory is not a morality of absolute rules, nor is it strictly engaged with parsing right and wrong. Similarly, *Revolutionary Care* is not aiming to establish the rules for a caring revolution. Offering provocations and invitations is a deliberative approach to morality that suggests the concomitants for a categorical commitment to care. Individuals must decide what a commitment to care includes. Policies and practices can be collective signposts of care standards, but a caring revolution will be advanced through what individuals choose to do in relationships with others. In this section, I extend the arguments offered by care theorists on the moral status of animals by emphasizing the embodied and imaginative aspects of care. To accomplish this, I briefly revisit and apply the three components of effective care: humble inquiry, inclusive connection, and responsive action.

There seems to be little doubt that humans care for animals and that it is morally valuable to do so. The complex question is how this care should manifest, an issue that ultimately arises for all forms of care, which is why the discussion of good care is vital. Beginning with the practice of humble inquiry, what do we know about animals and their needs? The humility called for is not to fall back on tropes such as "animals do not feel pain the way we do" or "medical animal testing is necessary to reduce human suffering and even death." There is substantial evidence that many tropes regarding animals' lives are dubious. For example, animals do feel pain (although its exact nature is unknown) (Langley, 2016), the benefit of vivisection for medical advances is marginal, and consuming animal products is generally unhealthy (WHO, 2021). Our relational choices regarding animals should be based on the best available information rather than tradition or narratives of common sense. Given the politicization of information, it can be challenging to find unbiased data. For example, many corporations and industry groups fund studies that advance their products' cause (Arbetter, 2019). Although acquiring reliable information is vital, how we process the data is perhaps just as crucial. Accordingly, how does the unknowability of animal pain impact our caring for them? Many people experience pain differently, and it does not seem to be a relevant moral factor for assessing violence, for example. The violent act carries moral weight rather than the victim's ability to deal with it. Accordingly, if we administered anesthesia to our murder victims before killing them or injuring them, does that mitigate the morality of the actions? Humble inquiry suggests an openness to the best available information and reflecting on that information's meaning.

Humble inquiry can include both explicit and implicit information. Regarding animals, our shared embodiment offers a vital opportunity for tacit knowledge that, while imperfect, can provide important insight that is rational and non-rational. Approximately 70% of US households have companion animals. The presence of nonhuman animals creates enormous opportunities for tacit learning about animals through tactile interactions (Hamington, 2008). Despite the lack of verbal communication, we learn much about companion animals from touch, movement, bodily position, expression, etc. Although our understanding of our companion animals is incomplete, it is sufficient to cohabitate and foster care: an astounding interspecies feat. However, it is left to the moral imagination to transform such relationships into something more than a parochial and insular experience.

Imaginative considerations are not forays into that which is utterly new and previously unknown. Rather, imagination involves a habit of the mind that radiates from the known to the less familiar. Just as a metaphor helps us leap from the known to something strange, the imagination can help us with those linkages. When the imagination is guided by care, it can be said to be a moral imagination, where the leap to the unknown is intended to explore a sympathetic understanding. As applied to animals, companion animals' familiar, caring relationships allow us to take the imaginative leap to empathize with other animals, thus expanding the circle of care. Despite his utilitarian proclivities, Peter Singer stopped eating meat in 1970 after sharing a meal with someone who helped him realize the pain and suffering that meat represented on his plate (Singer, 2021). He was given information and evidence (inquiry), but his moral imagination allowed him to make a connection to the suffering.

Regarding veganism, making an inclusive connection to animals is crucial as there are powerful forces driving narratives of disconnection. Economic narratives have driven the rhetoric of meat culture that serves to obfuscate the origin of meat and dairy products. Sanitized and packaged, animal sources of consumables are kept at a psychic distance. Carol Adams refers to this phenomenon as the "absent referent": "Once the existence of meat is disconnected from the existence of an animal who was killed to become that 'meat,' meat becomes unanchored by its original referent (the animal), becoming a free-floating image instead" (2010: 13). The moral imagination has the opportunity to reconnect the animals to the steak, leather jacket, and fur coat. Such connections are more complex with non-mammals but not impossible. In some ways, animals represent the ultimate test for inclusive connection. It is challenging enough to connect with someone from another culture who does not speak my language, but at least we share physiology. Animals share less with us, making the work of inclusive connection through imaginative connection difficult. Furthermore, some claim we should not try, as the temptation to anthropomorphize what we imagine for animals is great. However, care theory as a non-ideal process morality does not require a perfect understanding of the animal's plight. Even anthropomorphizing can be praised as a caring effort at finding connection as long as it is not regarded as complete knowledge. The notion of attuned empathy is applicable here. Just as all our imaginative forays need to be checked by inquiry, our empathetic understanding of animals can be fine-tuned by scientific evidence.

Although care theory is not only about emotion, it does maintain a role for emotion. Making a connection to animals, as described above, entails feelings at some level. There are excellent rational arguments for caring. However, an ethical theory that relies on abstract analytic arguments can also be manipulated by what I have described as game-playing with rules and consequences. Although caring is imperfect, a commitment to care entails a disposition that resists exploitation. Philosopher Susanna Picket argues,

> Veganism is, as such, not an analytic truth to be derived from abstract moral principles but rather a moral way of life. Arguably, it is also a moral requirement. Principles such as causal inefficacy and unnecessary harm can be turned against veganism via analytic rationalisations which exploit scepticism and err on the side of narrow human self-interest, rather than an altruistic stance towards animals. Despite difficult technical and analytic considerations, one can experience veganism as an inescapable imperative; as a spiritual necessity; or as a powerful political identity against the oppression of animals.
>
> *(2021: 18)*

This inescapable imperative, spiritual necessity, and political identity aptly describes a care ethos applied to nonhuman animals.

A third aspect of good or effective care is responsive action which I also offered as a sub-commitment of the categorical commitment to care. Veganism is a compelling responsive action to knowing and connecting with animals. There is no evidence that animals desire pain and suffering, and there is plenty to support the contrary (Alvaro, 2017). Avoiding animal consumption is a means of meeting an implicit need for animals to live and to live without harm. I only frame this as an implicit need rather than an explicit need because non-human animals cannot express the need directly. Noddings places a great deal of emphasis on meeting expressed needs (2012), but in the case of animals, the level of attentiveness required to grasp expressed needs must overcome the lack of language. Care theorists almost universally value the role of attentiveness in caring relations. Still, environmental theorist Traci Warkentin describes how interspecies care requires pro-active corporeal listening:

> an ethical praxis of paying attention requires much more than mere politeness or mildly observing ... the kind of attentiveness we are concerned with here involves one's whole bodily comportment and a recognition that embodiment is always in relation to social others, both animal and human.
>
> *(2010: 102)*

Thus, if we are attentive to the needs of animals, veganism seems like an appropriate action to take.[6]

**194** Invitations and Provocations

Estelle Ferrarese reminds us that caring is not always easy in *The Fragility of Concern for Others: Adorno and the Ethics of Care*. She describes political and social mechanisms that conspire to prevent individuals from "perceiving needs or suffering, to hold her back from responding to them or to induce her to respond to them inappropriately" (2021: 3). Ferrarese adopts Theodor Adorno's term "coldness" to interrogate widespread disaffection with the plight of others. The fragility of care for others manifests in concern for animals, who become an afterthought in an anthropocentric meat culture. Although not explicitly addressing the morality of animal consumption, Ferrarese's book contains many references to humanity's failure to care for animals. For Ferrarese, care initiates from the body: "A concern for other is, from the perspective of an ethic of care, a particular relationship between two (or multiple) bodies" (Ibid: 14). This is true of human and animal bodies. Concern for particular animals can, through inquiry, connection, and action, lead to caring regard for all animals:

> Our moral relationship with animals concerns our being engaged in a common world with them and thus is about always-already existing practices. The perspective that seeks to establish our community or our difference with animals on the basis of biological capacities is shown to be not only irrelevant but also unbearable from a moral point of view. All that is admissible is the *sensation* of a moral burden, the repugnance felt at the sight of an injury being inflicted, on a being with whom we share a form of life.
>
> *(Ibid: 21)*

Unfortunately, many humans have become inured to the idea of animal injury. Accordingly, veganism is an act of resistance to forgetting animal bodies and recalling our connection to them.

### Meet the Meat: Introducing the Absent Referent, Esther the Wonder Pig

As referenced above, Adams demonstrates how meat consumption narratives create euphemisms for animals (beef instead of cows, veal instead of baby cows, hamburger instead of cows, bacon instead of pigs). This separation of the animal from the derived commercial product creates a challenge for a moral imagination seeking to understand the pain, suffering, and death of the beings who are consumed:

> Our culture further mystifies the term "meat" with gastronomic language, so we do not conjure dead, butchered animals, but cuisine. Language thus contributes even further to animals' absences. While the cultural meanings of meat and meat eating shift historically, one essential part of meat's meaning is static: One does not eat meat without the death of an animal. Live animals

are thus the absent referents in the concept of meat. The absent referent permits us to forget about the animal as an independent entity; it also enables us to resist efforts to make animals present.

*(2010: 66)*

However, moral imagination can provide moments of epiphany when the connection between a meal and its source is realized.

In 2012, Steve Jenkins and Derek Walter adopted what they were told was a 6-month-old miniature pig weighing less than 4 pounds and about 8 inches long. They named her Esther. In a few months, it became clear that Esther was not a miniature pig but a pig intended for human consumption. Consistent with her breeding, she grew to 600 pounds. Jenkins and Walter had a typical North American diet that included meat and dairy products. However, the presence of Esther changed their thinking, although not immediately. Jenkins describes the transition:

*Of course it's okay to eat meat*, you think. Most people do.

Bringing a pig into the house hadn't been enough to make us want to shun animal meat overnight. …

But realizing Esther had once literally been intended to be someone's dinner removed my ability to compartmentalize eating bacon while having a pig as a family member. Eating bacon now would be like eating one of our dogs. Or *any* dog.

*(2016: 48)*

Jenkins and Walter did not turn to veganism because of a moral rule or a calculation about reducing suffering but because they cared for a being. They became familiar with and thus gained knowledge of Esther, connected with her, and responded with care. Jenkins and Walter went on to purchase a farm they turned into an animal sanctuary. Esther has a Facebook page and a website. Jenkins and Walter help people see the morality of the absent referent of meat. Many people have expressed that they have become vegan after forming virtual connections with Esther. They call this the "Esther Effect" (Ibid: 100). Rhetoric and tradition can be barriers to care, but they are not invincible. Choosing to be vegan can be an isolated act of care, yet it can potentially participate in the broader spirit of care. After living longer than factory farmed pigs normally do, Esther passed away in 2023 at the age of 11.

## Veganism as Participating in a Holistic Ethos of Care

If a person lives to the age of 82 and assuming they take three meals per day, they will eat 90,000 times, not including snacks. Few iterative activities so permeate human existence. Each meal is an opportunity to choose between health, carbon footprint, and animal suffering. Although this chapter has focused on caring for animals, one can argue that veganism radiates care in multiple ways. First, veganism can be construed as care of the self. When manifested as a whole food, plant-based diet, veganism is the healthiest consumption pattern for human beings, with evidence of extending life and diminishing the impact of many diseases. Noncommunicable diseases account for about 74% of all deaths globally (WHO, 2022). In double-blind and randomized studies, many diseases, including heart disease, hypertension, and type 2 diabetes, are controlled or reversed through plant-based diet and lifestyle choices (Gregor, 2015; Campbell and Campbell, 2016). The possibility of less personal suffering comes with the choice to be vegan.

Additionally, a vegan lifestyle reduces human strain on the global environment. Whole foods such as fruits, vegetables, grains, legumes, nuts, and seeds produce lower greenhouse gas emissions than animal agriculture (WHO, 2021). Given the vast land needed to raise animals for slaughter or dairy products, a vegan diet can also help preserve the Earth's biodiversity by slowing deforestation (Tilman et al., 2017: 78–9). There is no more significant existential threat than the climate change we witness in the current geological age of human impact, known as the Anthropocene (Flower and Hamington, 2022). A single response to the crisis, such as adopting a vegan lifestyle, will not end the threat. Still, many scientists argue that it can effectively mitigate the Anthropocene's advance (Poore and Nemeck, 2018). Caring about the environment may not have the same relational affect that caring for a human or nonhuman animal does. However, given the Earth's role in providing us with a home and its need for repair, care is imperative. A growing number of ecofeminist care theorists would agree.

Care that embraces self, both human and nonhuman others, and the environment exemplifies the claim in Chapter 7 that care can balance humanism and nonhumanism. Care theory can accommodate naturalizing moral authority, thus removing it from divine sources while dampening a human-centric hierarchy. As Margaret Robinson demonstrated, this holistic spirit of care resonates with many long-standing indigenous cultural traditions. Unfortunately, it has taken Western theorists a long time to appreciate what aboriginal peoples have known and lived about care.

In viewing the universe, including humans and nonhuman animals, in a more connected fashion, the indigenous moral imagination comes to issues of care differently. Rachelle K. Gould, Māhealani Pai, Barbara Muraca, and Kai M.A. Chan describe how long-standing Hawaiian relational values support and contribute to a growing field of sustainability science. These relational values include "pono (~ righteousness, balance); ho'omana (~ creating spirituality); mālama (~ care); kuleana (~ right, responsibility); aloha (~ love, connection)" (2019: 1213). Unlike the dichotomous Western tradition, the Hawaiian imaginary sees the distinction between human and nonhuman animals as fluid.

Gould, Pai, Muraca, and Chan reference indigenous scholars who support the notion that indigenous worldviews maintain the dignity of animals as worthy of relational considerations on par with humans. For example, Osage scholar Tink Tinker claims,

> For Indian people, relationship never signaled merely human relationships, but has always been inclusive of all "people," from humans to animals, birds, trees, mountains, and even rocks. So when we pray, "For all my relatives" ... we mean to include all of life and not just next of kin within our own species.
>
> *(Tinker, 2015: 216)*

Similarly, Potawatomi philosopher Kyle Whyte contends that indigenous concepts of interdependence mean "there is no privileging of humans as unique in having agency or intelligence, [therefore] one's identity and caretaking responsibility *as a human* includes the philosophy that nonhumans have their own agency, spirituality, knowledge, and intelligence" (2018: 127). Gould, Pai, Muraca, and Chan identify numerous examples of animal presence in the modern daily life of Native Americans. They reference indigenous children often taking the perspective of animals, animal imagery in Native Hawaiian art, and using the term mālama (~care) in road signs regarding animals and the forest (2019: 1216). They identify feminist care theory as best able to capture the inclusive spirit of indigenous worldviews because of care's liminality. Expressly, they point to care theory's character of holding the particular experience and imagining the generalized extension of it:

> embodied acts of care—and the contextual values with which they are intertwined—also impact general or transcendental values. The relational value of care thus takes both transcendental and contextual forms, and these forms may derive force from each other.
>
> *(Ibid: 1218)*

This expanded form of nonhierarchical caring for animals may be possible for the indigenous mind, but is it for the Western mind?

English scholar Jessica Michelle Holmes answers the question in the affirmative. As an avenue of nonhierarchical caring, Holmes suggests the practice of "vegan poetics" "in service of an inclusive liberatory struggle and by way of imaginative translation, transformation and embodiment of animals" (2021: 11). Holmes argues that aesthetic experience, specifically poetry, can help broaden the social imaginary to better connect with animals. This argument resonates strongly with what Ce Rosenow and I asserted in *Care Ethics and Poetry*: "Poetry and care are peak human experiences of imagination," and poetry helps us develop habits of imagination useful for caring (2019: 64 and 65). Holmes claims,

If veganism is to be understood as part of a broader ecofeminist project of cultivating an ethic of care across difference—toward all beings, including nonhuman animals and the natural world—poetry and poetic forms of storytelling constitute a valuable tool.

*(2021: 23)*

Poetry can expand the empathetic imagination and help evoke emotional connection in ways that are challenging to achieve with rational arguments alone (Ibid: 163). Recalling that a caring ethos, the spirit of care, is a mixture of emotional, visceral, and rational elements, aesthetic experience cannot be dismissed as morally irrelevant despite modernist neoliberal proclivities to do so.

How does one commit to veganism? Peter Singer is a (near) vegan because he is a utilitarian. Jessica Michelle Holmes is a vegan because she is a reader. Carol J. Adams is a vegan because she is a feminist. From a care perspective, the path one takes to this practice may be unimportant. However, if care is the categorical moral imperative, and thus being moral is to commit to care, perhaps one can choose to be a vegan because one is a care-er. A holistic ethos of care might find buoyancy in the care for animals that is consistent and reinforces other care practices.

## Notes

1 "Aboriginal" or "indigenous" are umbrella terms that include three populations in Canada: *Inuit*, are made up of 53 communities near the Arctic. Inuit have a common language; *Métis* refers to a collective of cultures and ethnic identities resulting from unions between Aboriginal and European people; and *First Nations* is an umbrella term that includes all other indigenous identities. The Mi'Kmaq fall under the latter category.

2 It is vital to keep in mind that it is not possible to generalize the native cultural experience on subjects like the gendered division of labor given the hundreds of different nations with divergent cultural practices. There are 574 federally recognized native nations in the United States.

3 The rising number of vegans is motivated to take up the lifestyle for different reasons. Research suggests that the three primary motivators for becoming vegan are a concern for animal wellbeing, the environment, and personal health (Braunsberger and Flamm, 2019). One study indicated that anti-speciesism was the most vital driver of affinity and motivation for veganism (Brouwer et al., 2022).

4 The inclusion of insects is not agreed upon by vegans. However, the exclusion of plants as morally relevant in veganism is often employed by those critical of vegans as a moral inconsistency. Sentience is a major factor utilized in discriminating between plants and animals. However, the idea that humans must eat plants to live does not preclude that one can care about plants and have a moral disposition toward them. For example, old growth forests need to be afforded a great deal of respect and care despite the fact that we eat spinach and apples.

5 It should be noted that although on the same moral trajectory, veganism is not the same as vegetarianism. The term "vegetarianism" usually refers to a lifestyle practice that eschews eating meat but includes the consumption of animal products such as milk, eggs, and honey. Although there are differences in agricultural practices,

the production of dairy and other animal foodstuffs entails some degree of spatial limitation, suffering, and death. Factory farming may be the most egregious form of animal oppression, but even backyard agriculture contributes to animal suffering to some degree (Williams, 2015). This chapter does not have the space for a comprehensive referendum on the morality of veganism or vegetarianism but rather suggests that a commitment to care must raise questions about consumption choices.

6 As Margaret Robinson indicated, there are narratives that veganism is elitist and expensive and thus a challenging action to take on behalf of animals. Although any major life change such as a dietary switch can be unfamiliar and thus difficult, studies have shown that vegan diets are not more expensive than omnivorous diets. One study found vegan diets to be less costly in upper-income to high-income countries but more pricey in lower-middle-income to low-income countries. However, when climate and health outcomes are factored in, vegan diets are less expensive at all income levels (Springmann et al., 2021).

# CONCLUSION

## *Disponibilité*, Moral Progress, and Revolution

### Prologue: The Power of Hospitality

Richard McKinney joined the Marines in 1985 for many reasons: to serve his country, to straighten out his life after a troubled and drug-fueled youth, and to earn the respect of his psychologically distant father, a former Marine. McKinney was discharged from active duty in 2006 because of injuries after tours in Operation Desert Storm and wars in Afghanistan, Bosnia, and Somalia. Because he was so uncomfortable with civilian life, McKinney joined the Army for six years after leaving the Marines (Roddel and McKinney, 2018). Like many ex-military, he returned to his home in Muncie, Indiana, deeply affected by his battle experience. McKinney found the challenges of transitioning to civilian life immense. In particular, his involvement with so much death, both the lives he took in combat and the loss of his military brethren, left him feeling like a changed person. He claims to have stopped counting how many enemy combatants he killed at 26, each marked with a teardrop tattoo on his arm. McKinney reflects on the disaffection that comes with battle:

> One time, I had a discussion with a higher-ranking person about coping. Looked at me straight in the eye, says, "Mac, you're on the range, you're shooting at a paper target. As long as you can look at them as anything but human, you won't have any problems." … And that's what I did.
>
> *(Seftel, 2022)*

Upon returning home, alcohol helped him deal with the emotional and physical scars. During this time of personal struggle, he developed hostility toward

DOI: 10.4324/9781003368625-12

Muslims. Muncie has a small but vibrant Muslim community, and seeing Muslims became a source of rage for McKinney. He admits to incivility towards Muslims in public without provocation. His family was aware of his baseless vitriol. Dana, McKinney's wife at the time, recounts: "We would go to Walmart, and you walk down the aisle, and I would see a woman in hijab and would intentionally divert our path" (Ibid). Interviews reveal that McKinney had difficulty pinpointing the origin of his prejudice, yet the hate was strong.

> *Roddel:* So I know you spent a lot of time in combat—some with Marines, some with the Army. What impact do you think that your time in combat had on your feelings toward Islam?
> *McKinney:* I think it would be very naive of me to say that it did not impact it in some way. I can't honestly outward answer that it did, because I don't really know that it did. There wasn't any one incident that happened that made me hate Muslims, or hate Islam, or, you know. As I put it, seeing it [Islam] as a cancer in the world that needed to be surgically removed. I really don't—it just turned one day.
>
> *(Roddel and McKinney, 2018)*

McKinney's hostility and general angst coalesced into a secret plan to destroy the Islamic Center of Muncie. He had enough military knowledge to create an IED (improvised explosive device). McKinney was meticulous in his scheming. He took two years to plot the details, including acquiring combustible materials, bomb placement, timing, and detonation location to maximize the harm to the Muslim community (Seftel, 2022). McKinney kept the whole plan secret from everyone, including his family. They only discovered his nefarious goal when FBI agents searched for the incendiary material three months after he aborted the scheme. At that point, the FBI did not find any explosives and deemed McKinney not a credible threat (Ibid). Nevertheless, McKinney intended to commit mass murder in a horrendous act of domestic terrorism. Unfortunately, there are approximately 30 mass killings yearly (defined as 4 or more fatalities), and most are perpetrated with firearms. Marginalized communities and churches are often targeted (Fox and Levin, 2022).

In 2009, when McKinney was ready to operationalize his destructive plan, his adopted seven-year-old stepdaughter, Emily, nudged him out of his hate-filled revery. He and his daughter are very close. One day, McKinney became inappropriately upset about one of her daughter's Muslim friends at school. She looked at him in a manner that caused him to pause and reflect on his actions. Although subtle, the exchange was palpable to McKinney, who loved his daughter very much and did not want to lose her approval. He had convinced himself that Muslims were evil killers, so he became determined to gather proof that his anger was justified. McKinney wanted to show his daughter that he was right to target them.

So McKinney surreptitiously went to the Islamic Center on a reconnaissance mission seeking evidence to legitimate his antagonistic stance as, in fact, a rational moral choice. However, members of the Center greeted him with a disarming communal spirit that he had not anticipated. First, someone met him with the simple question, "Can I help you?" Then they had a lengthy discussion regarding the tenets of Islam. McKinney listened but remained skeptical and insecure as the only non-Muslim in the building. After the conversation, McKinney sat on a couch in the Center, and Afghani refugee Dr. Saber Bahrami, a family physician and founding leader of the Islamic Center, further welcomed him. Bahrami greeted McKinney with a hug and became emotional in his compassionate conversation while seated at McKinney's feet and hugging his leg. Despite being somewhat frightened by McKinney's demeanor, Bahrami's wife, Bibi, invited McKinney to their house for dinner.

Saber and Bibi are the real heroes of this story. They had helped create a caring Islamic community through hospitality, and McKinney was treated no differently than other community members. Their compassion not only prompted McKinney to abandon his destructive plan, but he kept returning to the Center to learn more about Islam and engage the community's ethos of care, peace, and happiness. McKinney remarks, "The more time I spent around them, the more I started to change" (Seftel, 2022). Furthermore, he claims he would have never planned the destruction had he known the community. They "showed me what true humanity is about" (Ibid). In what seems like a romantic Hollywood ending, McKinney converted to Islam eight weeks after first walking into the Islamic Center. Subsequently, McKinney became a leader of the Islamic Center.

McKinney's conversion is extraordinary. Care is revolutionary. Unbeknown to them, the Bahramis' care saved many lives in a situation that could have turned out tragically. Care can transform an individual, and that change can have a social and communal impact. The welcoming nature of the Bahramis in McKinney's story is inspiring and can provide a glimpse of what a care ethos might engender in a revolution. This story is not about Islamic ideology-inspired insight but rather how responsive, caring practices, which indeed were consistent with many Islamic teachings, helped someone overcome his fear of what he did not know. This anecdote shows how powerful care can be in sparking epiphany and change.

### *Disponibilité* to Life's Provocations

In this book, I have argued that given the enormous significance of care, we should morally commit to it as a categorical ethical imperative. Such a commitment ought to entail a desire to deliver the best care possible in any situation. Thus, we should also dedicate ourselves to improving our care through humble inquiry, inclusive connection, and responsive action. Iterations of these practices enhance our care but, more importantly, can transform our society, thus leading to systemic change that both participates in and contributes to the renewal of a care ethos. Such an ethos adds momentum and spirit to caring political practices, including legal and social achievements that help sustain and spread them.

The nimbleness and improvisation of good care requires our openness to others and their context. Given the emergent normativity that I have suggested participates in the contextual nature of care—the moral ideal that must be adapted to each situation—it is worth reviewing the concept of *disponibilité*.

Often translated from the French as "availability" or "openness," philosopher Gabriel Marcel framed *disponibilité* as an idea with significant moral content. For Marcel, a disponible person makes themselves available to others in more than superficial ways. This disponibilité represents an inner state whereby one feels connected and interconnected with others. Marcel describes, "The person who is disponible does not demure from saying that she truly does desire the best for the other person and that she truly desires to share something of herself with the other" (1964: 154). Thus, applying *disponibilité* to care means one is responsive to the context of the other to provide appropriate care (Hamington and Rosenow, 2019: 89–91). Actor and drama teacher Jacques Lecoq framed *disponibilité* as a central feature of acting integrity in body and mind. Lecoq viewed *disponibilité* as an assertive curiosity that made performance deeply authentic (Hamington, 2020a: 21–35). What is true for stage performance is also true for our everyday encounters.

Philosopher Melvin Chen claims *disponibilité* is a position of one who comports themselves as making their resources (defined broadly) available to others. Specifically, he describes the disponible person as lending a "listening ear" to the narrative of the cared for. Chen applies this to the origins of care theory in Carol Gilligan's work:

> Gilligan managed to pick out the voice of care within the narrative not simply by virtue of her literary training, but also by virtue of her *disponibilité* and willingness to extend a listening ear to this voice. Unlike Kohlberg and his fellow developmental psychologists, Gilligan was willing to listen to the voice of care and to invest her resources in the narrative.
>
> *(2015: 788)*

Note how Chen's approach reinforces the notion of care theory as a process morality where habits and methods participate just as much as normative considerations. The disposition of *disponibilité* creates the imaginative space for us to be open to life's provocations and the possibility of connection to lives outside of our direct experience.

Section 2 of this book offered a series of provocations and invitations to rethink what it means to care through feminism, socialism, humanism, and veganism. Each of these was an attempt to cross boundaries and extend the

**204** Conclusion

circle of care despite barriers established by certain forms of masculinity, aspects of market capitalism, strict ideological religion, or traditions of animal oppression. These four chapters are just examples from a few significant arenas of social life that call for greater care. Life is so beautifully complex that we could name many more provocations challenging us to care. We confront those provocative opportunities in small and sometimes profound moments of contact that can lead to relational epiphanies. In the following brief section, I name a few more marginalized or challenging social stances that a commitment to care might cause us to consider, including pacifism, environmentalism, and antiracism. None of these areas is mutually exclusive of the others. They represent controversial or unsettled matters in the social imaginary. A care revolution includes openness to these ideas with the potential for ownership and commitment. When a spirit of care becomes a part of our identity, a willingness to listen and align with unfamiliar positions becomes possible.

### Pacifism

Many in society have become so inured to violence that systemic acts of brutality can go virtually unnoticed. Mass incarceration, homelessness, police brutality, and war are a backdrop to modern society. Such casual violence is antithetical to a care ethos; thus, an openness to pacifism is appropriate. Like all the provocations previously addressed, a commitment to pacifism from a care perspective does not reflect an unobtainable, absolutist perfection of nonviolence. Instead, it seeks to make us more sensitive to destructive behavior that damages human relationships and flourishing. Caring can sometimes entail being assertive, disruptive, and angry when required to support self-defense. For example, Leonard Harris (2002) and Lee McBride (2021) have effectively argued for insurrectionist ethics, which posits that acts levied against an oppressor, even violent acts, are justified, although they violate moral norms. In other words, circumstances matter. Pacifism can be advocated by those who benefit from the subjugation of others as a political weapon to maintain the status quo of oppressive systems. Care should not silence the oppressed but motivate allies to join the cause. Sometimes, as in self-defense, violence is warranted. Nevertheless, people should not undertake violence without carefully considering the lives it impacts. A care ethos ultimately desires peace because the conditions of tranquility and harmony are conducive to a caring society. However, this peace cannot be simply an absence of war or a peace that suppresses and maintains the violence of oppression.

Being open to pacifism, although appearing to be a condition of serenity, still entails considering some radical and revolutionary ideas, particularly in a rather violent society. According to the Centers for Disease Control and Prevention, 41% of women and 26% of men have experienced intimate partner violence (IPV), defined as physical violence, sexual violence, stalking, and psychological aggression (CDC, 2022). The CDC's recommendation for mitigating IPV includes measures that focus on caring relationships, including teaching healthy relationship skills to young people and couples, engaging men and boys as allies in prevention, providing parenting and family relationship skills, and improving social and economic environments for families (Ibid). In other words, it is crucial to infuse local institutions with the values and spirit of care, and a holistic approach to caring for people is vital. Care's personal, communal, social, and political cultures are interrelated.

The proliferation of guns in the United States exacerbates the IPV problem. Every 16 hours, a woman in the United States is fatally shot by her current or former intimate partner. According to reporter Jennifer Gollan, "Guns are the No 1 weapon in domestic violence killings in the U.S. – just owning a firearm makes an abuser five times more likely to take a partner's life" (2021). Furthermore, there is no evidence that owning a gun is a way to care for one's family. Statistics indicate that there are more guns per person in the United States than in any other country, and gun homicides and suicides are extraordinarily high. The BBC reports that there are 1.2 firearms per resident in the United States. The following highest ratio is in Yemen, with .53 guns per resident (BBC, 2023). The CDC notes that in 2020, 45,222 people died from gun-related injuries in the United States. This number is increasing. It is also probably underreported because it depends on police statistics (Gramlich, 2022). As Cass Crifasi, the Director of the Johns Hopkins Center for Gun Violence Solutions, indicated, "If firearms everywhere made us safer … we would be the safest place in the world" (2022).[1] Without dictating any particular approach, a commitment to care points to reasonable gun control and safety procedures.

A care-based analysis includes the hard work of examining the complexity of social problems. Single-variable answers like gun control will not solve modern violence concerns. The pacificism required for the care revolution also suggests reconsidering sacrosanct social institutions. For example, in the United States, for the years 2017 to 2022, the number of people shot to death by the police averaged more than 1,000 per year, an average trending upward. Compared to population demographics, this statistic evidences a disproportionate number of deaths among people of color (Statista, 2023). The calls to "abolish" or "defund" the police may sound like a slippery slope to anarchy for some. Still, the spirit of openness and humble inquiry should lead the person committed to care to try to understand the motivation to rethink policing.

For example, activist, educator, and organizer Mariame Kaba has written and spoken extensively about abolishing the prison industrial complex (PIC) and defunding the police. The words "defund" and "abolish" may marginalize Kaba's message in popular discourse, but investigating her arguments reveals a common sense approach rooted in care. When she calls for the defunding of the police, she is asking to redirect the budget to social programs that can ameliorate the circumstances leading to violence (consistent with what the

**206** Conclusion

CDC advocates for IPV) and fund non-incendiary responses to conflicts in the community. One such de-escalatory program is Critical Assistance Helping Out on the Streets (CAHOOTS) in Eugene, Oregon, which can be described as participating in a caring interventionist infrastructure (Hamington and Flower, 2021: 295–296). Kaba supports "transformative justice," which seeks to radically reimagine justice as a practice of understanding the circumstances of injustice and why they happened, so we can learn how to transform unjust situations rather than focusing on retributive punishment. She views the abolition movement as involving entangled imagination and action: "Being intentionally in relation to one another as part of a collective, helps to not only imagine new worlds, but also to imagine ourselves differently" (2021: 4). Kaba's language is imbued with relational concern. Like the founders of the Black Lives Matter movement, Kaba's vision is not narrowly focused on a particular community's injustice, even as it arises from race-based oppression. Kaba seeks the transformation of individual hearts and minds while striving for social and political change. Her abolition movement is compatible with a care revolution.

### Environmentalism

Given the climate crisis and the Anthropocene (an unofficial name given to the current geological era characterized by human activity causing species and environmental decline), care theorists have made a growing effort to address the idea of caring for the environment (Johns-Putra, 2013; Groves, 2014; Gottlieb, 2022; Flower and Hamington, 2022). The term "ecofeminist care" has received increasing attention (Serafini, 2021; Brazal, 2021). For example, feminist environmentalist Mary Phillips writes, "An ecofeminist notion of embodied care is developed as a social and political as well as individual practice necessary to bring about radical changes in our relationships in a more-than-human world" (2016: 471). Even when Tronto and Fischer formulated their now often-repeated definition of care in 1990, they specifically articulated a concern for the environment. They stated that care includes "everything that we do to maintain, continue, and repair our 'world' so that we can live in it as well as possible" (1990: 40). Chapter 8 of this book suggested an openness to veganism, a form of nonhuman care, as an invitation and provocation resulting from a commitment to care. Animals provide us an analog to human care as living embodied creatures. Although we physically live on the earth, the environment remains a complex abstraction that includes "nonliving" matter, making it more challenging to care about than individual beings. Political philosopher Thomas Randall offers an example of environmental analysis from a care framework that might help us rise to the occasion. He finds care for the environment rooted in our ability to engage our imaginations in caring beyond human others. Randall employs the term "imaginal" to avoid confusion with fictional concerns (2019).

Care's relational and humanistic concerns are not mutually exclusive of its post-humanistic considerations.

Furthermore, consider reciprocity (Sander-Staudt, 2010). Although often understood as inherent to care, it must take on a new form when the environment is part of the caring relation. Such reciprocity might be a more diffuse understanding rooted in empirical data regarding the health of an environment, given that the environment sustains our existence. Nevertheless, whether or not direct reciprocity is present, a commitment to care with a disposition toward openness to caring opportunities and need suggests that identifying with environmentalism should be a live consideration.

### Antiracism

African American Studies scholar Ibram X. Kendi frames opposition to racism as an active commitment rather than a passive one: "There is no neutrality in the racial struggle. The opposite of 'racist' isn't 'not racist.' It is 'antiracist.'" (2019: 9). Accordingly, a commitment to care should provoke an openness to antiracism instead of simply striving to be nonracist. Matching the process approach of good care, Kendi views antiracism as a journey of betterment rather than a destination of perfection. He defines antiracism as espousing racial equality and actively supporting policies that lead to racial equity or justice (2019). Note how quickly the definition moves from the individual to the social. Being antiracist is not an individual virtue that people can develop apart from recognizing and responding to society's ills. Specifically, Kendi names racism as structural, institutional, and systemic, so an antiracist position acknowledges society has historically been organized to facilitate identity oppression.

Such recognition of extant white supremacy is difficult for those in power or who fear losing real or imagined dominance. In *The Sum of Us: What Racism Costs Everyone and How We Can Prosper Together*, economic and social theorist Heather C. McGhee resists the presupposition of racism and white apathy as a zero-sum game (2021: xxi). She argues that a subtext of racist systems, a view that at least partly accounts for the lack of political will behind antiracist efforts, is the notion that white privilege and power will suffer and wane if people of color obtain greater parity in jobs, wealth, and infrastructure. In other words, one group must lose for the other to gain. These zero-sum renderings of competition for resources are a by-product of capitalist and neoliberal narratives, according to McGhee. As a particular instance, she chronicles the lessening of infrastructure spending as rising out of the fear of loss. For example, the notion that Medicaid or healthcare expansion results in groups of people (most often understood as people of color) "freeloading" off of the taxes paid by hard-working Americans (often imagined as white) is a common misconception (Ibid: 59). By contrast, McGhee proposes a new vision of mutual support that can result in what she describes as the "solidarity dividend." When diverse groups

**208** Conclusion

with varied identities work together for mutual support, the economic, psychic, social, and moral benefits can be tremendous. McGhee supports her claim by citing numerous examples of immigrants treated with hospitality and integrated into a community that resulted in thriving municipalities (Ibid: 255–70). Much like the care revolution, McGhee views the solidarity dividend coming through a change of practice and a change of heart as zero-sum mindsets are vanquished.

A commitment to care requires serious consideration to a commitment to antiracism in the active sense, which can be uncomfortable in a society with so much racism embedded in its structure and history. Note that the previous sentence also defines critical race theory; it recognizes that racism is more than a few "bad apples." It does not suggest that all people are racist, but much of today's social privilege derives from identity-based oppression. Someone who participates in racist activities can also act in caring ways to many people, a parallel claim to the other provocations in Section 2. However, the level of commitment needed for the care revolution means a willingness to engage in self-reflection and change such that caring is more consistent and inclusive. Care cannot be just a private matter for friends and family if society is to fulfill its potential.

A caring ethos suggests an ongoing openness to people and their plights, as witnessed in Marcel's description of the open spirit, *disponibilité*. Although she uses the term disposable rather than disponible, Nel Noddings identified the centrality of Marcel's characterization of the caring attitude in her pivotal work, *Caring*: "One who is disposable recognizes that she has a self to invest, to give. She does not identify with her objects and possessions. She is present to the cared-for" (1984: 19). This willingness to invest oneself in others through a commitment to care is the basis for moral progress. Rather than a static moral horizon prefixed by normative frameworks, the person committed to care is open to change and moral progress toward new moral horizons of care.

### Care as Moral Progress

> While the nature and sources of moral progress consistently thwart many theoretical hopes, the idea of moral progress is a plausible, critically important, and morally constructive principle of historical interpretation.
> —Michelle Moody-Adams (2017: 153)

The ideas of good care, revolution, and moral progress are tied together. In Chapter 1, I offered a heuristic of good care. Generally, progress is defined metaphorically through directional movement: we advance toward a goal connoting improvement as we head for something better. The notion of progress has applications to different spheres of the human experience: technological, economic, environmental, etc. In 2019, Brown University sponsored a public debate between Nobel Prize-winning economist Paul Krugman and the prolific author and psychologist Steven Pinker in the Janus Forum Lecture Series on "Is Humanity Progressing?" The subjects of the discussion included life expectancy, prosperity, literacy, I.Q. scores, education rate, and climate change (Kimball, 2019). "Moral" progress was absent from the debate.

Accordingly, "moral progress" is not the most common instance of social advancement in the popular imagination. Furthermore, it is helpful to distinguish between the progress of moral ideals (thought) from the improvement of ethical behavior (actions). Philosopher Michelle Moody-Adams describes this distinction between belief and practice: "Moral progress in belief involves deepening our grasp of existing moral concepts, while moral progress in practices involves realizing deepened moral understandings in behavior or social institutions" (1999: 168). When someone questions if society is making moral progress, they are likely responding to social phenomena provoked by narratives and observations. The assumption is that one's ethical values manifest through moral behavior—or its lack: murders, wars, criminal behavior, and the like. Although skewed by the partiality of anecdotal evidence and news media's bias, these actions manifest an underlying social morality (or its absence). In a sense, there are operant moral values and aspirational moral values.

However, applying social morality is not the same as the moral ideal. For example, there was a time in the Western world when the racist brutalization of people of color and indigenous people was quite acceptable. There was little thought that such behavior violated a social moral ideal. Today, the violence and victimization of BIPOC individuals and communities continue, albeit in different forms. However, the moral ideal has progressed to the point of public outcry with every case of what appears to be racially motivated police abuse, even if the political will to change systems of oppression has not caught up to the ideal. Of course, it would be highly preferable if social behavior (the "is") matched the moral ideal (the "ought"), but this seldom occurs. Nevertheless, the moral ideal is a pull to continue the movement metaphor on social behavior.

Moody-Adams makes several observations regarding moral progress consistent with the processual revolution advocated in this book and fleshed out later in this chapter. First, moral progress occurs "once a newly deepened moral understanding is concretely realized in individual behavior or social institutions." This claim recognizes the tension between vision and practice and emphasizes the incremental and process nature of moral transformation. Moody-Adams' use of the term "newly deepened moral understanding" (1999: 169) is intentional, given that the moral progress of belief is always rooted in the familiar but with new understanding, appreciation, and valuation. Accordingly, care is nothing new. If humans are relational beings, care has been present from the beginning; however, that does not mean it has always been valorized. Moody-Adams suggests that one sign of moral progress is if practices (such as greater caring, for our purposes) are adopted with minimum violence and coercion. However, she points out that the lack of opposing forces is not a sufficient

**210** Conclusion

condition for moral change. No one overtly opposes care, but the social transformation sought here means a higher degree of commitment to care. Moral progress, such as in greater and more profound social care, occurs when our ethical ideals and standards have advanced to where our expectations regarding caring responses are higher. Accordingly, often, a discourse that laments "political correctness" or "wokeness" appears to represent resistance to advancing moral standards.

At this point, it is helpful to turn to *Care Ethics and Poetry* (Palgrave Macmillan, 2019), where Ce Rosenow and I suggest that good caring skills are the basis for moral progress and that engagement with the arts, including poetry, is a means for exercising and habituating those skills. We reflected on personal moral progress of caring as "Growth in the practices of the heart (sympathetic understanding) and mind (inquiry into particular and generalized knowledge) reflected in respect, understanding, and action in response to the need of others" (110). We focused on individual moral progress through aesthetic exercising of the moral imagination, particularly by engaging poetry. Although personal experience cannot be neatly differentiated from social experience, I am more concerned with social progress and transformation as part of a care revolution. Simply stated, the goal is more and better care wherever possible. As addressed earlier, this is a paradoxical, non-ideal theory. Care is indeed the overarching ideal, but the practices are local and varied depending on circumstance and need and not dictated by a singular outcome. Likewise, moral progress in society does not include perfection or utopian care. Still, it seeks betterment and improvement so that more people are cared for in improving ways. The arts can spur moral progress through aesthetic experience.

Philosophers Allen Buchanan and Rachell (formerly Russell) Powell, in *The Evolution of Moral Progress: A Biocultural Theory*, offer a comprehensive and convincing inquiry into contemporary notions of moral progress. The richness of their analysis cannot be fully appreciated here, yet I draw from their work. They begin by tracing the history of moral progress theory, including its fall from favor in recent theoretical scholarship. In opposition to that fall, Buchanan and Powell argue that ideas of moral progress are necessary to provide a means for actually making practical advancement. Such theories can provide consolation in dark times, hope for the future, and motivate change (2018: 20). Buchanan and Powell offer the characteristics of a theory of moral progress rather than a simple definition. They contend that moral progress should be non-ideal, naturalistic, pluralistic, and inclusive, with an open-ended understanding of normativity. On the latter point:

> Our basic understanding of moral progress should reflect our fallibility and should acknowledge our capacity for open-ended normativity, which enables us to detect errors in our thinking about moral progress and to correct them accordingly. This in turn suggests that a sound conception of moral progress

will understand its own characterization of moral progress as only provisional—as the best we can do for now.

*(Ibid: 93–4)*

The contours of moral progress offered by Buchanan and Powell should seem familiar as they resonate strongly with this book's framing of good care. However, the purpose of my project is not to claim that care theory is a theory of moral progress but rather to suggest that good care is a crucial component of moral progress. It is possible to move from merely caring for familiar others to "better" levels of care, as evidenced by widening the circle of care or providing improved responses to the needs of others, is possible. To do so, as suggested in this book, means reflectively engaging in cycles or iterations of learning (humble inquiry), connecting with others (making empathetic leaps), and responding to the needs of others.

There are many compelling critiques of the language of progress. One criticism is the implied homogeneity of progress, a "one size fits all" future. However, extending standpoint theory to the social and political realm, we can be described as living in a pluriverse or multiverse where a plurality of worldviews organize social systems. Accordingly, competing visions of moral progress can and do conflict with one another. The provocation of humanism in Section 2 exemplifies such a clash. One concept of moral progress might include a return to specific religious values clarified in sacred texts and delineated by well-defined rules. Such a vision diverges from a care-ethical moral ideal that is responsive, imaginative, and thus not bound by specific ethical rules. So, does a caring picture of moral progress stymie diversity of thought and practice? The answer is what one might expect from a postmodern theory of human morality: yes and no. A position of care should conflict with alternative visions of moral progress that do not prioritize care for others. For example, if a moral ideal diminishes care for people because of their chosen identity, that vision of progress should result in scrutiny and resistance from a care perspective. However, the skills/habits/heuristic of good care should support local, culturally valued, and spiritual differences in specific practices and, therefore, not suppress other visions of moral progress. To the latter point, philosopher Maggie Fitzgerald argues that care theory is particularly well suited for operating in a pluriverse, "a multiplicity of worlds that are deeply connected, but also differently situated, within relations of power" (2022: 16). For Fitzgerald, care theory's commitment to interrogating relations of power and prioritizing vulnerability means that it can and should traverse worlds. Accordingly, care's methodology is essential: "An approach to morality built on the ethics of care, therefore, pays close attention how our moral judgements themselves (re)produce and are co-constitutive of worlds, and therefore may be culpable in the (re)production of certain harms" (Ibid: 17). The moral progress envisioned here is not intended to be parochial and must account for different worlds.

**212** Conclusion

The notion of "good care" suggests amelioration even if the standards for that improvement are not formulaic or necessarily quantifiable. We make moral progress if we become better at caring, and those skills lead us to care for more people in better ways. Being disponible to unfamiliar others can be the first step in caring for more unfamiliar others. Similarly, society makes moral progress if more people are cared for with improved quality of care. Revolutions reflect a desire for change with an aim for something better. Although the rhetoric of revolutions usually reflects material changes—rights for women, economic conditions, and wealth distribution, moral ideals inform those changes.

Care as an impetus for moral progress is rooted in the power and potential of the moral imagination. All notions of moral progress rely on an imaginative projection toward conditions of improved ethical understanding. As Moody-Adams describes, "deepening moral understanding [necessary for moral progress] requires the successful exercise of creative imagination" (2017: 155). To foment moral imagination, Moody-Adams suggests that people need "perceptual space" that stimulates the mind. Such perceptual space corresponds to the *disponibilité* to provocations discussed in this book. For Moody-Adams, expanding perceptual space entails "dislodging prejudices and habits of belief that limit our ability to take a novel view of the world, our place in it, and our relationships to others, as might be required by new moral interpretations" (Ibid: 163). In a sense, the commitment to care is an openness to epiphanies, whether they be gradual or sudden, to free or minds to make imaginative, empathetic connections.

Good caring is imbued with imaginative activity. Grounded in the knowledge work of humble inquiry, the forays of the imagination allow us to traverse alterity to find relational connections to other people. Although the language of care often overlooks the receiver of care, imaginative outreach is a reciprocal process. Good care is enhanced if the one cared for is also imaginatively empathizing with the caregiver and helping them to understand the context of need. The imaginative process is fallible for both the caregiver and the care receiver. Thus iterations of inquiry are necessary to assess whether one's imagination is on a serviceable trajectory. Nevertheless, imagination is crucial for understanding the other and their situation and formulating responsive action, as the latter must originate in the mind before enaction. Although imagination is essential for good care, it is also the basis for moral progress. Reflecting on local action and experience can coalesce into improved caring patterns on one's overall moral outlook. For example, reflecting on one's relationship with animals by imaginatively understanding their pain and terror in dying for one's meal and checking that understanding through humble inquiry might improve one's caring to include more beings in enhanced ways. Veganism requires critical imagination, as animals will never be able to organize and protest their treatment. A commitment to care is a commitment to being open to moral progress.

Conclusion **213**

Generalizing moral progress thus contributes to and participates in a care ethos that advances a care revolution.

## A Care Movement

I use the term care revolution to describe the deep-seated personal, social, and political valorization of care I envision. However, as discussed at the end of Chapter 4, the revolution I call for also represents a movement. Sociologist James DeFronzo defines a social movement as "a persistent, organized effort by a relatively large number of people either to bring about social change or to resist it" (2022: 9). By comparison, he characterizes a revolutionary movement as "a social movement in which participants strive to drastically alter or totally replace existing social, economic, or political institutions" (Ibid: 10). Accordingly, a revolution is a particular form of a social movement.[2] Both the terms "revolution" and "movement" are appropriate in the case of care. Invoking "revolution" signals the systemic institutional change needed, while the label "movement" names the widespread effort toward improvement.

Care scholars have addressed the need for a movement for many years. In 2010, political theorist Deborah Stone wrote, "We have the Bill of Rights, and we have civil rights. Now we need a Right to Care, and it's going to take a movement to get it" (2000: 13). Her primary concern was caregiving in society. Stone suggested a three-fold movement composed of those receiving care, families who care for their members, and those who engage in care labor as a profession. Stone eloquently connects the needed political change to personal change:

> Caring is the essential democratic act, the prerequisite to voting, joining associations, attending meetings, holding office and all the other ways we sustain democracy. Care, the noun, requires families and workers who care, the verb. Caring, the activity, breeds caring, the attitude, and caring, the attitude, seeds caring, the politics. That is why we need a care movement.
>
> *(Ibid)*

Stone's observation regarding care's fundamental role in democracy is reminiscent of Joan Tronto's arguments for a political understanding of care. She views care and democracy as ideally nested in a reciprocal relationship whereby caring practices are "carried out in a democratic way and that caring become a central value for democracies" (2013: 29). Tronto expands on Stone's call for a movement by criticizing the gender divide in the care policies and practices of American democracy. Accordingly, men do not acknowledge how they are the recipients of care. For Tronto, a care movement is necessary to "redefine care as a concern that is neither feminine nor masculine but human" and "to overcome the indifference of a political system that benefits the well-to-do, who currently benefit from the availability of inexpensive care assistance at

**214** Conclusion

their beck and call" (2005: 142). Tronto's work sheds light on the inequality of care responsibilities in the United States and what it will take to overcome the disparities.

Dan Engster fills out the call for a care movement by offering specific strategies for its enactment. He recognizes the challenge of overcoming the egocentric individualistic ethos in the United States. Engster proposes a valuable and practical approach to realizing progress in a care movement. On the one hand, he correctly acknowledges that the psychosocial resistance to valuing care in our political structures makes the notion of a care movement daunting. However, on the other hand, Engster's recommendations are common sense and manageable, making the goal appear quite logical and achievable. Engster provides the following elements for achieving a care movement:

(1) linking particular care constituencies and initiatives to a larger care movement.
(2) supporting universal over means-tested programs.
(3) working with market mechanisms and business interests.
(4) finding ways to garner greater public support among the American people for care policies (2010).

While Engster's approach is eminently practical, others offer a metanarrative of change.

In her later publications, Carol Gilligan introduces another concept into the discussion of social transformation: resistance. In *Joining the Resistance*, Gilligan revisits her pivotal publication, *In a Different Voice*, from two decades later. Toward the end of the book, she begins to see in the words of young girls not only the different voice of morality, but the different voice of personal empowerment. She finds young girls dissatisfied with the dissociative responses to modern challenges. Gilligan describes her studies as finding "an ethic of care, grounded in voice and relationship as an ethic of resistance both to injustice and to self-silencing" (2011: 175). Although feminists vary in attachment to care theory, Gilligan aligns the feminist movement closely with care ethics. Gilligan and David A. J. Richards describe, "Feminism with its ethic of care then becomes the key to liberation, because as the movement to free democracy from patriarchy it acts both to prevent the moral injury inflicted by patriarchy and to release us from moral slavery" (2018: 12). Gilligan and Richards explicitly name the Movement for Black Lives and the #MeToo movement as social resistance undergirded by an ethic of care (Ibid: 124).

Narratives of a care movement described above are an essential development in recentering care in our personal, social, and political lives. We can only bring something into being if we imagine it and discuss it first. Expanding and deepening care in our relational lives means changing social norms and practices. However, we want a sustainable transformation. One way to achieve

Conclusion **215**

sustainability is to view the revolution needed as not necessarily the ends of an ideal but a never-ceasing process of moral progress.

## Care: the Processual Revolution

Caring for the Revolution equals making it.

—Eva von Redecker (2021: x)

Despite the richness of today's political theories of care, revolution is not a subject that receives much attention. Estelle Ferrarese observes, "Caring coincides with the perpetual mending of the ordinary world, care theories do not take up the task of conceiving this world's destruction, nor even its radical transformation" (2021: 29). Generally speaking, Ferrarese is correct. However, the reticence toward describing a care revolution may be changing. The publication of the previously discussed, *The Care Manifesto: The Politics of Interdependence* by The Care Collective (2020), Andreas Chatzidakis, Jamie Hakim, Jo Littler, Catherine Rottenberg, and Lynne Segal (henceforth, The Care Collective), signals that demand for social transformation is growing and receiving articulation. Manifestos don't necessarily accompany revolutions, but they can help.

Manifestos are public declarations with political implications. Not every manifesto blatantly has the word "manifesto" in its title, but employing the term indicates a demand for change contained within. The most famous and influential is *The Communist Manifesto*, in which Karl Marx and Friedrich Engels describe history as a class struggle. After describing the grievances of communists against capitalists, Marx and Engels conclude, "the Communists everywhere support every revolutionary movement against the existing social and political order of things. ... They openly declare that their ends can be attained only by the forcible overthrow of all existing social conditions" (2012: 102). This document influenced several communist revolutions. Although sharing a public and political declaration for change, *The Care Manifesto* strikes a different tone than *The Communist Manifesto*.

The Care Collective explains that their manifesto responds to the crisis of care prompted by the Covid-19 pandemic and the resulting challenges, but, as other authors have argued, the problem of systemic social care failures existed long before the pandemic (2020: 4). The Care Collective recognizes that despite the crisis, there exists a rich tradition of "care-in-practice" to draw upon and valorize. The manifesto aims to "offer a progressive vision of a world that takes the idea of care as its organising principle seriously, an idea that has been repudiated and disavowed for too long" (Ibid: 19). The small book has drawn some significant praise. Feminist economist Nancy Folbre is exuberant in her support for the general trajectory of *The Care Manifesto*:

This book is superb. In often electrifying language, it condemns the growing carelessness of global neoliberalism and its efforts to appropriate the rhetoric

**216** Conclusion

of care. ... I love the book's enthusiasm for the solidarity economy—the many decentralized efforts to develop more cooperative and egalitarian economic institutions.

*(2021: 849)*

Folbre has some reservations that *The Care Manifesto* focuses singularly on resisting neoliberalism as resolving all the care deficits, but that does not diminish her support for the effort.

Similarly, geographer and care theorist Parvati Raghuram finds *The Care Manifesto* a welcome call for change: *The Care Manifesto* is a stark reminder that to be in the world requires caring relationships" (2021: 865). However, she points out that *The Care Manifesto* is more of a comprehensive vision statement than a blueprint for action. Given the worldwide nature of the social change called for by The Care Collective, Raghuram suggests that multiple care manifestos from various social contexts are needed beyond a singular manifesto written by scholars from a particular cultural background (Ibid: 871). Accordingly, in 2021, a concise *Care Manifesto* was created by organizations representing women in Latin America, Asia, and Sub-Saharan Africa (Femnet, 2021). Nevertheless, *The Care Manifesto* effectively offers a "queer-feminist-anti-racist-eco-socialist political vision of 'universal care,'" but does not employ the language of revolution. The Care Collective calls for social change and thus participates in the nascent yet growing desire for relational solutions to the world's many needs. Even if *The Care Manifesto* is not the definitive call for a care revolution, it marks an essential step in precipitating a care movement.

On the surface, it appears audacious to claim that a care revolution is possible, particularly given the prevalent imagery of revolutions. Sociologist Jack A. Goldstone describes revolutions in the following manner:

We can therefore best define revolution in terms of *both* observed mass mobilization and institutional change, *and* a driving ideology carrying a vision of social justice. *Revolution* is the forcible overthrow of a government through mass mobilization (whether military or civilian or both) in the name of social justice, to create new political institutions.

*(2013: 4)*

This definition is reasonably common and matches the popular conception of revolution.

However, for the analysis of revolution offered in this book, I shift the framing to resonate with the scholarship of German philosopher Eva von Redecker. Goldstone's definition has two sentences that can be described as reflecting elements that are not mutually dependent. The first sentence matches the vision of care revolution I am arguing for: mass mobilization (broadly construed)[3] and institutional changes motivated by a shift in social ideology to greater care. The second sentence mirrors the tangible experience of revolutions as events, most often characterized by violent change. The latter represents the newsy historical images that we associate with revolutions such as the American Revolution, the Communist Revolutions in China in 1949 and Cuba in 1953, or the uprisings that resulted in the Arab Spring in 2010 and the Iranian Revolution in 1979. Events of bloodshed and destruction of structures that symbolize the current oppressive order of society are the common conception of revolution. On the other hand, von Redecker persuasively argues that powerful revolutions can occur without noteworthy specific events that illustrate their existence. Such events may be the anchors for social narratives, but social transformation, even radical social change, can occur without visible moments of physical upheaval.[4]

As noted in the Introduction, the care revolution will not be televised, but perhaps not for the same reasons that Gil Scott-Heron thought when he wrote the poem that became a song. Scott-Heron was an activist artist who abhorred the violence in political protest but was committed to social change. He spent much of his life participating in political actions while writing books, poetry, and songs. Upon watching demonstrations on television, he was struck by the contrast between his experience on the streets and the sanitized version aired that came with commercial breaks. Accordingly, he wrote the poem. However, given von Redecker's analysis, a revolution can occur with nothing to televise. That does not mean a care revolution won't have conflict, mass mobilization, or even violence. Still, the care revolution will not arrive through tearing down a symbolic wall or overthrowing a government. The care revolution will come as a process, perhaps without a significant definable moment. Maybe it has already begun.

In *Praxis and Revolution: A Theory of Social Transformation*, von Redecker distinguishes reform from revolution by claiming that while reforms impact various sectors of society, revolution is experienced by the whole as a radical and profound transformation. She further clarifies that although political revolutions focus on the relationship between the people and their government, social changes address oppressive relations between people: "Social revolutions can challenge not just how we are ruled, but who we are, who owns what, how we relate to one another, and how we reproduce our material life" (2021: vii). Much of von Redecker's description of social transformation echoes care theory. If we take care as a process morality seriously, our commitment to care can challenge who we are, how we come to knowledge, and how we relate to one another. Care is fundamentally a relational concept. Accordingly, a care revolution seeks to transform our relations. A commitment to care and all that such a commitment entails is a reexamination of our relational identity with materialist implications. The provocations in the second part of this book suggest opportunities to participate in the care revolution through a *disponibilité* toward identification with feminism, socialism, humanism, and veganism. Each

**218** Conclusion

has relational and material significance for self-in-relation that can participate in advancing the care revolution with the goal of a more caring society.

Von Redecker rereads the history of revolutions to challenge the prevalent event-driven legacy and imagery. She reframes revolutions as processual and more diffuse in origin than is currently conceived. Rather than sweeping moments of radical change, von Redecker finds lengthy processes of transformation that draw from socially ostracized themes in the present and brings them to fruition. Akin to the cultural "slow movement," which has advocated for slowing the pace of life, von Redecker argues that revolutions are much more deliberate than customarily imagined. Revolutions transform what was once unthinkable into reality, but "for this process, rehearsing the future and repurposing the present are more vital than uprisings and rupture" (Ibid: 1). There is continuity and discontinuity to such a progression. The radical change of a revolution witnesses a marginalized idea brought to the center, but it is not an entirely new idea nor an overnight success. Indeed, care is not a foreign idea. The term "care" is quite ubiquitous. However, it is not consistently valued or discussed. Furthermore, the deep quality of care addressed in this project, marked by humble inquiry, inclusive connection, and responsive action, is marginalized by certain powerful narratives of masculinity, capitalism, and religious ideology. A care revolution brings care from the margins of social value to the center through the iterative actions of individuals, groups, communities, and governments.

Although not a care theorist, von Redecker repeatedly invokes care as an essential element of revolutions. For example, in addition to the quote that opens this section, she claims, "No longer detached from the reproduction of everyday life, radical politics can be seen as arising from the labor of care and from the concrete concern for freedom and survival in oppressed communities" (Ibid: x). The emotion and connection inherent in caring, amplified by a commitment to care, is the ethotic engine of social transformation—Redecker's "concrete concern." The ethos can be motivated by both positive and negative emotions.[5]

Von Redecker brings a rich political theory vocabulary to her interrogation of revolutions. Two significant terms for her are "interstices" and "metalepsis." She describes revolutions as interstitial because they are not as linear, sequential, or eventual as one might suppose. Instead, they emerge from diffuse in-between spaces of society in a dynamic fluidity that makes them difficult to predict. The process of valorizing marginalized ideas participates in von Redecker's understanding of revolution. Still, she emphatically claims that such a movement is not definitive or stable (2021: 28). The relational ontology that undergirds care theory presupposes working in liminal spaces because caring is always between people (and/or nonhuman animals or objects, etc.). Thus a care revolution methodologically matches von Redecker's revolution mechanics.

Metalepsis refers to questions of what socially changes to what von Redecker juxtaposes metalepsis with dialectic thinking that argues conflict and

Conclusion **219**

contradiction can lead to resolution. Metalepsis is much more chaotic than a dialectic:

> How do we get from this total mess to a place where things make sense? How indeed, if the mess won't even fit into the mold of one supercharged contradiction? Metalepsis, as a figure of speech, is on the surface utterly absurd and unintelligible.
>
> *(Ibid: viii)*

Care theory has a postmodern character because of the messiness of the relational human condition, which defies neat categorical frameworks. The more and better caring that the revolution portends will not make life easier or simpler yet will ameliorate need and suffering. The metaplectic and interstitial nature of revolutions, and by implication, a care revolution, is a descriptive analysis for real-world social change rather than a blueprint for achieving transformation. However, understanding how a processual revolution manifests does not make the goal of a more caring society any less worthwhile. It does, nevertheless, make it seem possible. As von Redecker claims, the metaleptic and interstitial understanding "liberates revolutions from the hyperbolic notion of a single, central contradiction. Changes in constellation can take place not only gradually but also in kaleidoscopic manner, the regrouping of diverse points of intersection" (Ibid: 220).

The care revolution does not require saints or perfection but represents a challenge for us to change. All moral systems ask for difficult considerations. This care revolution calls for personal, communal, social, and political change. As sociologist Ruha Benjamin claims, "It isn't possible to change a social structure without changing its culture, and we can't change culture without changing ourselves" (2022: 58). Many of today's revolutionaries see a connection between personal and political transformation. For example, historian Robin D. G. Kelley, in discussing black radicalism, states, "Making a revolution is not a series of clever maneuvers and tactics but a process that can and must transform us" (2002: xii).

The care revolution is a type of "norm evolution." The life cycle of social norms consists of emergence, cascade, and internalization (Romaniuk and Grice, 2018). Describing care as an emergent norm seems odd because care has always been present. However, the confinement, control, and marginalization of care often render it invisible. Once released from its oppressors (patriarchy, neoliberalism, religious ideology, anthropocentrism, etc.), care can cascade as people value and commit to care and spread its practices through a spirit of care. Subsequently, as that care norm becomes internalized, personal, social, and political decisions can be filtered through a care lens. We can co-create this norm evolution.

Activist James Boggs and activist philosopher Grace Lee Boggs poignantly connect evolution and revolution. They viewed any revolution as tied to

**220** Conclusion

an evolution of humanity, a vision that includes "new man/woman" and "new concepts of the relations between people" (2008: 205). Care can be just such a revolution.

## Join the Revolution

> Achieving the kinds of changes needed to create a society that values caring will require transforming the ways we think about ourselves, our relationships with others, the family, civil society, the state, and the political economy.
>
> —Evelyn Nakano Glenn (2000: 93)

Allison Gornik, Matthew Stevenson, Moshe Ash, and Derek Black; the people of Gander and the airline passengers who landed there on September 11, 2001; Alicia Garza and the founders of the Black Lives Matter movement; Yuri Kochiyama and her many communities of oppression resisters; the students and founders of the Umoja program in New York schools; Aaron Jackson and Takoda; Fanny Wright and the Nashoba community; the women participating in the Karma Kutir program in India; Margaret Robinson, and the people of the Lennox Island First Nation; and Saber and Bibi Bahrami as well as Richard McKinney—all for better or worse participate in extraordinary stories of giving and receiving care. As we all do from time to time. Care can be a subtle pleasantry, a terrible chore, a moment of deep affection, a messy challenge, or a moral epiphany. A care revolution does not change the range of care experiences, but it calls for and enacts better and more care from all of us, our institutions, and our communities.

As I indicated earlier, the care revolution may have already begun. The beauty of this revolution is that everyone can contribute by drawing from our embodied capacities, reflecting on our lives, and honing our relational skills. As James and Grace Lee Boggs describe, "A revolutionary must have a profound belief in the capacity of humankind" (2008: 246). There are certainly signs from various sectors, academia among them, that reconceptualizing social values around care is an attractive and necessary idea. We can find beautiful examples of an ethos of care in pockets of society if we look carefully. Given the forces creating pervasive precarity and a crisis of care, the success of this revolution is far from guaranteed. Nevertheless, regardless of political, religious, or cultural identity, everyone can commit to care. Who doesn't want more caring—in the best sense of the word—in their lives? Caring is how we actualize our relational embodied selves. This revolution does not require perfection, and there is no utopian end to a revolution with no singular conclusion. It is a process revolution for a process morality of continually growing and changing humans. A commitment to care means striving to improve at caring for others and ourselves, knowing that we will fail

Conclusion **221**

and often fall short. Sacrifices are required, but we make sacrifices for those we care for.

Care matters. It is powerful in our lives.
Care is revolutionary.

## Notes

1 A study of the relationship between gun ownership and homicides in the United States for the three decades prior to 2010 found, "Gun ownership was a significant predictor of firearm homicide rates (incidence rate ratio=1.009; 95% confidence interval=1.004, 1.014). This model indicated that for each percentage point increase in gun ownership, the firearm homicide rate increased by 0.9%" (Siegel, Ross, and King, 2013). Gun ownership rates after the study have accelerated.
2 DeFronzo points out that most revolutions include violence to be successful. Although Care Revolution argued for here must shed masculinist notions of violent overthrow as in a coop, that does not mean it will be entirely nonviolent. Care is commitment to peace but without a purity test for perfection.
3 Given current social ethical values, mass mobilization on behalf of care in a collective and visible sense appears unlikely except on targeted care concerns. However, many mobilizations entail a demand for greater care on specific issues such as labor actions, Black Lives Matter protests, and environmental demonstrations. For example, a union strike can be viewed as a cry for greater care on behalf of workers. A general march for care is doubtful but if the moral norms of society shift, perhaps it can occur, if we indeed catch the spirit of care.
4 The claim that a care revolution will not necessarily entail a destructive or belligerent event is not intended as a pacifist value judgment. There are times when oppressed people must resist violence as in the aforementioned work of the Black Panthers to provide self-defense against a racist onslaught of attacks. Violent resistance may be necessary but it is not sufficient for social change. A widespread transformation of disposition and practice is needed for lasting and sustained collective moral progress.
5 One of the many lessons of Myisha Cherry's analysis of rage is how it participates in social justice work such as anti-racism. In particular, she describes how Lordean Rage (based on Audre Lorde's reflections on anger) is a justified response to injustice that does not seek to hurt someone but rather fuels resistance. For Cherry, and Lorde, rage only works in a context of care for self and others. In other words, do we care about the victims if we are not enraged by injustice and oppression? Are we human? (Cherry, 2021).

For nothing is fixed, forever and forever and forever, it is not fixed; the earth is always shifting, the light is always changing, the sea does not cease to grind down rock. Generations do not cease to be born, and we are responsible to them because we are the only witnesses they have.

The sea rises, the light fails, lovers cling to each other, and children cling to us. The moment we cease to hold each other, the moment we break faith with one another, the sea engulfs us and the light goes out.

—James Baldwin (1964: 12)

# BIBLIOGRAPHY

Adams, C.J. (1990 [2010, 2015]) *The Sexual Politics of Meat: A Feminist-Vegetarian Critical Theory*. New York: Continuum.

Adams, C.J. (1994) *Neither Man Nor Beast: Feminism and the Defense of Animals*. New York: Continuum.

Adams, C.J. (2007a) "The War on Compassion." In Donovan, J. and Adams, C.J., eds. *The Feminist Care Tradition in Animal Ethics: A Reader*. New York: Columbia University Press, pp. 21–36.

Addams, J. (2007b [1895]) "The Settlement As Factor in the Labor Movement." In Residents of Hull-House, eds. *Hull-House Maps and Papers: A Presentation of Nationalities and Wages in a Congested District of Chicago, Together with Comments and Essays on Problems Growing out of the Social Conditions*. Champaign: University of Illinois Press, pp. 138–150.

Adichie, C.N. (2012) *We Should All Be Feminists*. New York: Anchor Books.

Ahmed, F. (2010) "Welcoming Courtyards: Hospitality, Spirituality and Gender." In Hamington, M., ed. *Feminist Hospitality: Gender in the Host/Guest Relationship*. Lanham: Lexington Books, pp. 109–124.

Ahmed, S. (2006) *Queer Phenomenology: Orientations, Objects, Others*. Durham: Duke University Press.

Ahmed, S. (2017a) Interviewed by Mehra, N.J. "Sara Ahmed; Notes from a Feminist Killjoy." *Guernica*, p. 17. https://www.guernicamag.com/sara-ahmed-the-personal-is-institutional/. Accessed 10/20/2021.

Ahmed, S. (2017b) *Living a Feminist Life*. Durham: Duke University Press.

Akhtar, A. (2015) "The Flaws and Human Harms of Animal Experimentation." *Cambridge Quarterly of Healthcare Ethics* 24 (4), pp. 407–419.

Alcoff, L.M. (2006) *Visible Identities: Race, Gender, and the Self*. New York: Oxford University Press.

Alcorn, M.W. (1994) "Self-Structure as a Rhetorical Device: Modern Ethos and the Divisiveness of the Self." In Baumlin, J.S. and French Baumlin, T., eds. *Ethos: New*

*Essays in Rhetorical and Critical Theory.* Dallas: Southern Methodist University Press, pp. 29–62.

Alvaro, C. (2017) "Ethical Veganism, Virtue, and Greatness of the Soul." *Journal of Agricultural and Environmental Ethics* 30, pp. 765–781.

Americans for Tax Reform (n.d.) "About Grover Norquist." www.atr.org/about-grover. Accessed 1/14/2022.

Antle, A. (2018) "Gander's Ripple Effect: How a Newfoundland town's kindness made it to Broadway."CBC News, 18 August 2018. https://www.cbc.ca/news/canada/newfoundland-labrador/broadway-gander-9-11-new-york-musical-theatre-documentary-1.4777839. Accessed 8/4/ 2021.

Anderson, E.S. (2007) "If God Is Dead, Is Everything Permitted?" In Antony, L.M., ed. *Philosophers Without Gods: Meditations on Atheism and the Secular Life.* Oxford: Oxford University Press, pp. 215–230.

Anzaldúa, G. (2000a) *Interviews/Entrevistas*, Keeting, A., ed. New York: Routledge.

Anzaldúa, G. (2000b) "Toward a Mestiza Rhetoric: Gloria Anzaldúa on Composition, Postcoloniality, and the Spiritual. An Interview with Lunsford, A." In Keating, A. and Anzaldúa, G.E., eds. *Interviews/Entrevistas.* New York: Routledge, pp. 1–27.

Anzaldúa, G. (2001) "Foreword." In Moraga, C. and Anzaldúa, G.E., eds. *This Bridge Called My Back: Writings by Radical Women of Color.* Berkeley: Third Woman Press, pp. xxxiv–xix.

Anzaldúa, G. (2007) *Borderlands, La Frontera: The New* Mestiza, 3rd edition. San Francisco: Aunt Lute.

Aquinas, T. (1266–1273) *Summa Theologiae.*

Arbetter, L. (2019) "Meat Wars Heat Up: Lobbyists Have It in for Plant-Based Meat Alternatives." *The Beet* (December 6). https://thebeet.com/the-meat-wars-heat-up-lobbyists-launch-campaign-against-plant-based-alternatives/. Accessed 10/17/2022.

Associated Press (2021) "About 333,000 Children Were Abused within France's Catholic Church, a Report Finds." *NPR* (October 5). https://www.npr.org/2021/10/05/1043302348/france-catholic-church-sexual-abuse-report-children. Accessed 6/27/2022.

Baier, A.C. (1982) "Caring about Caring: A Reply to Frankfurt." *Synthese* 53 (2), pp. 273–290.

Baier, A.C. (1989) "Hume, the Women's Moral Theorist." In Kittay, E.F. and Meyers, D.T., eds. *Women and Moral Theory.* Lanham: Rowman and Littlefield, pp. 37–55.

Baker, P.R. (1963) "Introduction." In Wright, F., ed. *Views of Society and Manners in America.* Cambridge: Belknap Press, pp. ix–xxiii.

Baldwin, J. (1964) In Avedon, R., ed. *Nothing Personal.* Lucerne: C.H. Bucher. Reprinted (2008) *Contributions in Black Studies: A Journal of African ad Afro-American Studies* 6 (5), pp. 1–12.

Barad, K. (2003) "Posthumanist Performativity: Toward an Understanding of How Matter Comes to Matter." *Signs: Journal of Women in Culture and Society* 28 (3), pp. 801–31.

Barad, K. (2007) *Meeting the Universe Halfway: Quantum Physics and The Entanglement of Matter and Meaning.* Durham: Duke University Press.

Barad, K. (2012) Interviewed by Kleinman, A."Intra-Actions." *Mousse* 34, pp. 76–81.

Baram, M. (2014) "Why Gil Scott-Heron Wrote 'The Revolution Will Not Be Televised'." *Cuepoint* (November 11). https://medium.com/cuepoint/why-gil

**226** Bibliography

-scott-heron-wrote-the-revolution-will-not-be-televised-6e298f9d4e2. Accessed 2/10/2022.

Basu, M. (2017) "Seeing the New India through the Eyes of An Invisible Woman." *CNN* (October). https://www.cnn.com/interactive/2017/10/world/i-on-india-income-gap/. Accessed 12/13/2021.

Baumlin, J.S. (1994) "Introduction: Positioning *Ethos* in Historical and Contemporary Theory." In Baumlin, J.S. and Baumlin, T.F., eds. *Ethos: New Essays in Rhetorical and Critical Theory.* Dallas: Southern Methodist University Press, pp. 82–91.

Baumlin, J.S. and Meyer, C.A. (2018) "Positioning Ethos in/for the Twenty-First Century: An Introduction to *Histories of Ethos.*" *Humanities* 7 (3), pp. 1–26. https://www.mdpi.com/2076-0787/7/3/78/htm. Accessed 9/23/2020.

BBC: British Broadcasting Company (2023) "Gun Violence in US and What the Statistics Tell Us." (January 24) https://www.bbc.com/news/world-us-canada-41488081. Accessed 2/10/2023.

Beams, N. (2020) "Modern Monetary Theory and the Crisis of Capitalism: Part 1 and 2." *World Socialist Web Site* (October 23 and 25). https://www.wsws.org/en/articles/2020/10/24/kel1-o24.html. Accessed 5/19/2021.

Beaumont, M. (2016) "Imagining the End Times: Ideology, the Contemporary Disaster Movie, *Contagion.*" In Flisfeder, M and Willis, L.P., eds. *Zizek and Media Studies.* New York: Palgrave Macmillan, pp. 79–89.

Beirich, H. (2014) "White Homicide Worldwide." *Southern Poverty Law Center Intelligence Report*, pp. 1–7. https://www.splcenter.org/sites/default/files/d6_legacy_files/downloads/publication/white-homicide-worldwide.pdf. Accessed 6/23/2021.

Benhabib, S. (1987) "The Generalized and the Concrete Other: The Kohlberg-Gilligan Controversy and Moral Theory." In Kittay, E.V. and Meyers, D.T., eds. *Women and Moral Theory.* Lanham: Rowman and Littlefield Publishers, pp. 154–177.

Benhabib, S. (1992) *Situating the Self: Gender, Community and Postmodernism in Contemporary Ethics.* New York: Routledge, pp. 148–177.

Benjamin, R. (2022) *Viral Justice: How We Grow the World We Want.* Princeton: Princeton University Press.

Bentham, J. (1992) quoted in Morris, C. *Fanny Wright: Rebel in America.* Urbana: University of Illinois Press.

Berman, M. (2003) "The Hyper-Dialectic in Merleau-Ponty's Ontology of The Flesh." *Philosophy Today* 47 (4), pp. 404–420.

Bernard, D. (n.d.) "A Welcome From The Chief." *Lennox Island First Nation.* https://lennoxisland.com. Accessed 7/31/2022.

Bhandary, A. (2017) "The Arrow of Care Map: Abstract Care in Ideal Theory." *Feminist Philosophy Quarterly* 3 (4), pp. 1–26. https://ir.lib.uwo.ca/fpq/vol3/iss4/5. Accessed 4/4/2022.

Bhandary, A. (2020) *Freedom to Care: Liberalism, Dependency Care and Culture.* New York: Routledge.

Bhandary, A. (2022) "Précis: *Freedom to Care.*" *Critical Review of International Social and Political Philosophy* 25 (6), pp. 816–819.

Black Lives Matter (n.d.) "About." [Website]. https://blacklivesmatter.com/about/. Accessed 6/10/2022.

Black, D. (2016) "Why I Left White Nationalism." *New York Times* (November 27). https://www.nytimes.com/2016/11/26/opinion/sunday/why-i-left-white-nationalism.html. Accessed 6/24/2021.

# Bibliography 227

Black, D. quoted in Dickson, C. (2013) "Renounced Racist Derek Black Speaks Out." *Daily Beast* (July 29). https://www.thedailybeast.com/renounced-racist-derek-black-speaks-out. Accessed 6/25/2021.

Blackburn, S. (1994) "Norm." In *The Oxford Dictionary of Philosophy.* New York: Oxford University Press , p. 265.

Blustein, J. (1991) *Care and Commitment: Taking the Personal Point of View.* New York: Oxford University Press.

Boff, L. (1999) *Essential Care: An Ethics of Human Nature*, Guilherme, A., trans. Waco: Baylor University Press.

Boggs, J. and Boggs, G.L. (2008) *Revolution and Evolution In the Twentieth Century.* New York: Monthly Review Press.

Bourgault, S. (2016) "Attentive Listening and Care in a Neoliberal Era: Weilian Insights for Hurried Times." *Ethics & Politics* 18 (3), pp. 311–337.

Bourgault, S. (2020) "Democratic Practice and 'Caring to Deliberate': A Gadamerian Account of Conversation and Listening." In Petr Urban, P. and Ward, L., eds. *Care Ethics, Democratic Citizenship and the State.* Cham: Palgrave Macmillan, pp. 31–51.

Bourgault, S. and Pulcini, E. (2018) "Introduction." In Bourgault, S. and Pulcini, E., eds. *Emotions and Care: Interdisciplinary Perspectives.* Leuven: Peeters, pp. 1–14.

Bowden, P. (1997) *Caring: Gender-Sensitive Ethics.* London: Routledge.

Bozalek, V., Zembylas, M., and Tronto, J.C., eds. (2021) *Posthuman and Political Care Ethics for Reconfiguring Higher Education Pedagogies.* New York: Routledge.

Braidotti, R. (1994) *Nomadic Subjects: Embodiment and Sexual Identity in Contemporary Feminist Theory.* New York: Columbia University Press.

Braunsberger, K. and Flamm, R.O. (2019) "The Case Of The Ethical Vegan: Motivations Matter When Researching Dietary And Lifestyle Choices." *Journal of Managerial Issues* 31 (3), pp. 228–245.

Brazal, A.M. (2021) "Ethics of Care In Laudato Si': A Postcolonial Ecofeminist Critique." *Feminist Theology* 29 (3), pp. 220–233.

Brock, G. and Miller, D. (2019) "Needs in Moral and Political Philosophy." In Zalta, E.N., ed. *Stanford Encyclopedia of Philosophy.* https://plato.stanford.edu/archives/sum2019/entries/needs/. Accessed 7/3/2021.

Brouwer, A.R., D'Souza, C. Singaraju, S., and Arango-Soler, L.A. (2022) "Value Attitude Behaviour and Social Stigma in the Adoption of Veganism: An Integrated Model." *Food Quality and Preference* 97, n.p.

Brown, M. (1997) "Kantian Ethics and Claims of Detachment." In Schott, R.A., ed. *Feminist Interpretations of Immanuel Kant.* University Park: The Pennsylvania State University Press, pp. 145–172.

Brugère, F. (2020) "Feminism and Liberalism: At the Margins of the Enlightenment." In Bourgault, S. and Vosman, F., eds. *Care Ethics in Yet a Different Voice: Francophone Contributions.* Leuven: Peeters, pp. 271–294.

Brugère, F. (2021) *L'Éthique du « care »* Paris: Presses Universitaires de France.

Buchanan, A. and Powell, R. (2018) *The Evolution of Moral Progress: A Biocultural Theory.* New York: Oxford University Press.

Bui, Q. (2015) "50 Years of Shrinking Union Membership, in One Map." (April 23). https://www.npr.org/sections/money/2015/02/23/385843576/50-years-of-shrinking-union-membership-in-one-map. Accessed 2/3/2022.

Bunting, M. (2020) *Labours of Love: The Crisis of Care.* London: Granta Books.

Bureau of Labor Statistics (2022) "Union Members Summary." (January 20). https://www.bls.gov/news.release/union2.nr0.htm. Accessed 2/3/2022.

**228** Bibliography

Burley, S. (2021) *Why We Fight: Essays on Fascism, Resistance and Surviving the Apocalypse*. Oakland: AK Press.

Butler, J. (1999) *Gender Trouble: Feminism and the Subversion of Identity*, 2nd edition. New York: Routledge.

Calhoun, C. (2009) "What Good Is Commitment?" *Ethics* 119 (4), pp. 613–641.

Campbell, M. (2007) "We Need to Return to the Principles of Wahkotowin." *Eagle Feather News* (November 5). https://www.eaglefeathernews.com/quadrant/media//pastIssues/November_2007.pdf. Accessed 10/4/2021.

Campbell, T.C. and Campbell II, T.M. (2016) *The China Study: The Most Comprehensive Study of Nutrition Ever Conducted and the Startling Implications for Diet, Weight Loss and Long-term Health*, Rev. edition. Dallas: BenBella Books.

Canales, K. (2020) "Amazon is Using Union-Busting Pinkerton Spies to Track Warehouse Workers and Labor Movements at the Company, According to a New Report." *The Business Insider* (November 23). https://www.businessinsider.com/amazon-pinkerton-spies-worker-labor-unions-2020-11. Accessed 2/3/2022.

Cardinal, H. (2009) "Reconciliation, Repatriation and Reconnection: A Framework for Building Resilience in Canadian Indigenous Families." [Ph.D. thesis]. University of Alberta, Edmonton.

Carnevale, A.P., Sablan, J.R., Gulish, A., Quinn, M.C., and Cinquegrani, G. (2020) *The Dollars and Sense of Free College*. Georgetown Center on Education and the Workforce. https://1gyhoq479ufd3yna29x7ubjn-wpengine.netdna-ssl.com/wp-content/uploads/CEW-The-Cost-of-Free-College-FR.pdf. Accessed 1/14/2022.

Catholic Charities USA (2020) "2020 Annual Report." https://www.catholiccharitiesusa.org/wp-content/uploads/2021/08/2020-Annual-Report-1.pdf. Accessed 7/12/2022.

CDC: Center for Disease Control and Prevention (2022) "Fast Facts: Preventing Intimate Partner Violence." (October 11). https://www.cdc.gov/violenceprevention/intimatepartnerviolence/fastfact.html. Accessed 2/9/2023.

Chatzidakis, A.H., Littler, J., Rottenberg, C., and Segal, L. (2020) *The Care Manifesto: The Politics of Interdependence*. London: Verso.

Chen, M. (2015) "Care, Narrativity, and the Nature of *Disponibilité*." *Hypatia* 30 (4), pp. 778–793.

Cherry, M. (2021) *The Case for Rage: Why Anger is Essential to Anti-Racist Struggle*. New York: Oxford University Press.

Chisale, S.S. (2018) "*Ubuntu* As Care: Deconstructing The Gendered *Ubuntu*." *Verbum et Ecclesia* 39 (1), pp. 1–8.

Christ, C.P. (2006) "Ecofeminism and Process Philosophy." *Feminist Theology* 14 (3), pp. 289–310.

Chung, I. quoted in Workman, T. (n.d.) "Leadership in Action at AMS." *Defining US* [Website]. https://definingus.org/leadership-in-action-at-ams/. Accessed 8/24/2021.

Clark, C.J., Liu, B.S., Winegard, B.M., and Ditto, P.H. (2019) "Tribalism Is Human Nature." *Current Directions in Psychological Science* 28 (6), pp. 587–592.

Clem, S. (2023) "Christian Ethics, Religious Ethics, and Secular Ethics: A Contemporary Reappraisal." *Journal of Religious Ethics* 51 (1), pp. 11–31.

Clement, G. (1996) *Care, Autonomy, and Justice: Feminism and the Ethic of Care*. New York: Routledge.

Clement, G. (2003) "The Ethic of Care and the Problem of Wild Animals." *Between the Species* 3 (2). https://digitalcommons.calpoly.edu/bts/vol13/iss3/2/. Accessed 10/15/2022.

Clement, G. (2011) "'Pets or Meat'? Ethics and Domestic Animals." *Journal of Animal Ethics* 1 (1), pp. 46–57.

Clement, G. (2013) "Animals and Moral Agency: The Recent Debate and Its Implications." *Journal of Animal Ethics* 3 (1), pp. 1–14.

Cobb, J.B. and Ray, D. (1953) *Reality As Social Process: Studies in Metaphysics and Religion*. Glencoe: Free Press.

Cobb, J.B. and Ray, D. (1976) *Process Theology: An Introductory Exposition*. Philadelphia: Westminster Press.

Code, L. (2015) "Care, Concern, and Advocacy: Is There a Place for Epistemic Responsibility?" *Feminist Philosophical Quarterly* 1 (1), n.p.

Collins, S. (2015) *The Core of Care Ethics*. London: Palgrave Macmillan.

Connell, R.W. (1987) *Gender and Power*. Palo Alto: Stanford University Press.

Connell, R.W. (2019) quoted in Salter, M. "The Problem with a Fight Against Toxic Masculinity." *The Atlantic* (February 17). https://www.theatlantic.com/health/archive/2019/02/toxic-masculinity-history/583411/. Accessed 10/27/2021.

Countryman, L.W. (1988) *Dirt, Greed, and Sex: Sexual Ethics in the New Testament and Their Implications for Today*. Philadelphia: Fortress Press.

Crawley, S.L., Foley, L.J., and Shehan, C.L. (2007) *Gendering Bodies*. Lanham: Rowman & Littlefield Publishers.

Crifasi, C. (2022) quoted in Smith Rogers, L. "Debunking Myths About Gun Violence." *Johns Hopkins Bloomberg School of Public Health* (May 26). https://publichealth.jhu.edu/2022/debunking-myths-about-gun-violence. Accessed 2/10/2022.

Curtin, D. (1991) "Toward An Ecological Ethic of Care." *Hypatia* 6, pp. 60–74.

Dalmiya, V. (2002) "Why Should a Knower Care?." *Hypatia* 17 (1), pp. 34–52.

Dalmiya, V. (2016) *Caring to Know: Comparative Care Ethics, Feminist Epistemology, and the Mahābhārata*. New Delhi: Oxford University Press.

Daly, A. (2016) *Merleau-Ponty and the Ethics of Intersubjectivity*. London: Palgrave Macmillan.

Davenport, J. (2007) *Will As Commitment and Resolve: An Existential Account of Creativity, Love, Virtue, and Happiness*. New York: Fordham University Press.

Davis, A. (2000) "Forward." In Wing, A.K., ed. *Global Critical Race Feminism: An International Reader*. New York: New York University Press, pp. xi–xiii.

Davis, F.E. (2019) *The Little Book of Race and Restorative Justice*. New York: Good Books.

de Beauvoir, S. (1949) *Le deuxième sexe*. Paris: Gallimard.

de Jong, J.L. (2012) *Empowerment and Interconnectivity: Toward a Feminist History of Utilitarian Philosophy*. University Park: Penn State University Press.

Defede, J. (2021) *The Day the World Came to Gander: 9/11 in Gander, Newfoundland*. New York: William Morrow.

DeFronzo, J. (2022) *Revolutions and Revolutionary Movements*, 6th edition. New York: Routledge.

Department of Sociology and Social Anthropology (n.d.) "Margaret Robinson." *Dalhousie University* [Website]. https://www.dal.ca/faculty/arts/sociology-social-anthropology/faculty-staff/our-faculty/margaret-robinson.html. Accessed 11/5/2022.

Depierri, K.P. (1968) "One Way of Unearthing the Past." *The American Journal of Nursing* 68 (3), pp. 521–524.

Derrida, J. (1999) *Adieu to Emmanuel Levinas*, Brault, P.-A. and Naas, M., trans. Stanford: Stanford University Press.

**230** Bibliography

Derrida, J. and Dufourmantelle, A. (2000) *Of Hospitality: Anne Dufourmantelle Invites Jacques Derrida to Respond*, Bowby, R., trans. Palo Alto: Stanford University Press.

Desai, R.M. and Joshi, S. (2013) "Collective Action and Community Development: Evidence from Self-Help Groups in Rural India." World Bank Policy Research Working Paper No. 6547. (July 1) https://papers.ssrn.com/sol3/papers.cfm?abstract _id=2303103. Accessed 12/16/2021.

Dewey, J. (1983 [1922]) "Human Nature and Conduct." In Boydston, J.A., ed. *The Middle Works, 1899–1924 Vol. 14: 1922*. Carbondale: Southern Illinois University Press, pp. 1–234.

Dewey, J. (1988 [1938]) "Logic: The Theory of Inquiry." In Boydston, J.A., ed. *The Later Works, 1925–1953*. Carbondale: Southern Illinois University Press, pp. 1–527.

Di Paolo, E., Rohde, M., and De Jaegher, H. (2010) "Horizons for the Enactive Mind: Values, Social Interaction, and Play." In Stewart, J., Gapenne, O., and Di Paolo, E.A., eds. *Enaction: Towards a New Paradigm for Cognitive Science*. Cambridge: MIT Press, pp. 33–87.

DiAngelo, R. (2018) *White Fragility: Why It's So Hard for White People to Talk About Racism*. Boston: Beacon Press.

Dickler, J. (2018) "Why Credit Card Debt Can Be Bad For Your Health." *CNBC* (February 13). https://www.cnbc.com/2018/02/13/credit-card-debt-can-be-bad-for -your-health.html. Accessed 5/2/2022.

Dickson, C. (2013a) "Derek Black, the Reluctant Racist, and His Exit from White Nationalism." *Daily Beast* (July 29). https://www.thedailybeast.com/derek-black-the -reluctant-racist-and-his-exit-from-white-nationalism. Accessed 6/25/2021.

Dickson, C. (2013b) "Renounced Racist Derek Black Speaks Out." *Daily Beast* (July 29). https://www.thedailybeast.com/renounced-racist-derek-black-speaks-out. Accessed 6/24/2021.

Dobson, J. (2020) quoted in Du Mez, K.K. *Jesus and John Wayne: How White Evangelicals Corrupted a Faith and Fractured a Nation*. New York: Liveright Publishing Corporation.

Donovan, J. (2006) "Feminism and the Treatment of Animals: From Care to Dialogue." *Signs: Journal of Women in Culture and Society* 31 (2), pp. 305–329.

Donovan, J. (2016) *The Aesthetics of Care*. London: Bloomsbury.

Donovan, P. (1986) "Do Different Religions Share Moral Common Ground?" *Religious Studies* 22, pp. 367–375.

Dowden, B. (2022) "Fallacies." *Internet Encyclopedia of Philosophy*. https://iep.utm.edu /fallacy/#AppealtoAuthority. Accessed 7/11/ 2022.

Dowling, E. (2021) *The Crisis of Care: What Caused It and How Can We End It?* London: Verso.

Driver, J. (2005) "Consequentialism and Feminist Ethics." *Hypatia* 20 (4), pp. 183–199.

Du Mez, K.K. (2020) *Jesus and John Wayne: How White Evangelicals Corrupted a Faith and Fractured a Nation*. New York: W.W. Norton & Company.

Duyndam, J. (2017) "Humanism As A Positive Outcome Of Secularism." In Shook, J.R. and Zuckerman, P., eds. *The Oxford Handbook of Secularism*. New York: Oxford University Press, pp. 706–720.

Dworkin, G. (1971) "Paternalism." In Wasserstrom, R., ed. *Morality and the Law*. Belmont: Wadsworth Publishing.

## Bibliography 231

Dworkin, G. (2020) "Paternalism." In Zalta, E.N., ed. *The Stanford Encyclopedia of Philosophy* (Fall 2020 Edition). https://plato.stanford.edu/archives/fall2020/entries/paternalism/. Accessed 7/28/2021.

Eales, L. and Peers, D. (2021) "Care Haunts, Hurts, Heals: The Promiscuous Poetics of Queer Crip Mad Care." *Journal of Lesbian Studies* 25 (3), pp. 163–181.

Easterlin, R. (2013) "Happiness, Growth, and Public Policy." WEAI 2012 Presidential Address. *Economic Inquiry* 51 (1), pp. 1–15.

Eggebroten, A., ed. (1994) *Abortion: My Choice, God's Grace.* Pasadena: New Paragon Books.

Eggebroten, A. (1994) "The Bible and Choice." In Eggebroten, A., ed., *Abortion: My Choice, God's Grace.* Pasadena: New Paragon Books, pp. 209–233.

Eldredge, J. (2001) *Wild at Heart: Discovering the Secret of a Man's Soul.* Nashville: Thomas.

Elliott, K. (2016) "Caring Masculinities: Theorizing an Emerging Concept." *Men and Masculinities* 19 (3), pp. 240–259.

Elliott, L. (2016) "Austerity Policies Do More Harm Than Good, IMF Study Concludes." *The Guardian* (May 27). https://www.theguardian.com/business/2016/may/27/austerity-policies-do-more-harm-than-good-imf-study-concludes. Accessed 5/19/2021.

Engster, D. (2006) "Care Ethics and Animal Welfare." *Journal of Social Philosophy* 37 (4), pp. 521–536.

Engster, D. (2007) *The Heart of Justice: Care Ethics and Political Philosophy.* New York: Oxford University Press.

Engster, D. (2010) "Strategies for Building and Sustaining a New Care Movement." *Journal of Women, Politics and Policy* 31 (4), pp. 289–312.

Engster, D. (2015) "Care In The State of Nature: The Biological and Evolutionary Roots of the Disposition to Care." In Engster, D. and Hamington, M., eds. *Care Ethics and Political Theory.* New York: Oxford University Press, pp. 227–251.

Femnet: the African Women's Development and Communication Network (2021) "The Care Manifesto." https://femnet.org/wp-content/uploads/2021/06/EJR-AC_CSO_Care-Manifesto.pdf. Accessed 1/2/2023.

Ferrarese, E. (2022) *The Fragility of Concern for Others: Adorno and the Ethics of Care*, Corcoran, S., trans. Edinburgh: Edinburgh University Press.

Fieser, J. (2019) "Ethics." *Internet Encyclopedia of Philosophy.* http://www.iep.utm.edu/ethics/#H2. Accessed 9/21/2015.

Fisher, B. and Tronto, J. (1990) "Toward A Feminist Theory of Caring." In Abel, E.K. and Nelson, M., eds. *Circles of Care.* Albany: SUNY Press.

FitzGerald, M. (2022) *Care and the Pluriverse: Rethinking Global Ethics.* Bristol: Bristol University Press.

Flaminio, A.L. (2013) "Gladue Through wahkotowin: Social History Through Cree Kinship Lens In Corrections and Parole." [Thesis]. University of Saskatchewan, Saskatoon.

Flannery, M.E. (2018) "How Higher Education Helped Derek Black Renounce White Supremacy." *NEA Today* (September 19). https://www.nea.org/advocating-for-change/new-from-nea/how-higher-education-helped-derek-black-renounce-white-supremacy. Accessed 6/24/2021.

Flower, M. and Hamington, M. (2022) "Care Ethics, Bruno Latour, and the Anthropocene." *Philosophies* 7 (31), pp. 1–17.

## 232 Bibliography

Folbre, N. (1993) "Socialism, Feminist and Scientific." In Ferber, M. and Nelson, J.A., eds. *Beyond Economic Man: Feminist Theory and Economics*. Chicago: University of Chicago Press, pp. 94–110.

Folbre, N. (2014) *Who Cares? A Feminist Critique of the Care Economy* [Study]. New York: Rosa Luxemburg Stiftung.

Folbre, N. (2020) *The Rise and Fall of Patriarchal Systems: An Intersectional Political Economy*. London: Verso.

Folbre, N. (2021) "Thoughts on *The Care Manifesto.*" *Social Politics: International Studies in Gender, State and Society* 28 (4), pp. 849–853.

Foster, S.L. (2008) "Movement's Contagion: The Kinesthetic Impact of Performance." In Davis, T.C., ed. *The Cambridge Companion to Performance Studies*. Cambridge: Cambridge University Press, pp. 46–59.

Fox, J.A. and Levin, J. (2022) "Mass Murder in America: Trends, Characteristics, Explanations, and Policy Response." *Homicide Studies* 26 (1), pp. 27–46.

Francione, G.L. (2020) *Why Veganism Matters: The Moral Value of Animals*. New York: Columbia University Press.

Frank, R.H. (2017) *Success and Luck: Good Fortune and the Myth of Meritocracy*. Princeton: Princeton University Press.

Frankfurt, H. (1982) "The Importance of What We Care About." *Synthese* 53 (2), pp. 257–272.

Fraser, N. (2016) "Contradictions of Capital and Care." *New Left Review* 100 (July/August), pp. 99–117.

Friere, P. (2005) *Pedagogy of the Oppressed, 30th Anniversary Edition*, Ramos, M.B., trans. New York: Continuum.

Fujino, D.C. (2005) *Yuri Kochiyama: Heartbeat of Struggle*. Minneapolis: University of Minnesota Press.

Fujino, D.C. (2009) "Grassroots Leadership and Afro-Asian Solidarities: Yuri Kochiyma's Humanizing Radicalism." In Theoharis, J., Woodard, K., and Gore, D.F., eds. *Want to Start a Revolution? Radical Women in the Black Freedom Struggle*. New York: NYU Press, pp. 294–316.

Funk, R.W. and Hoover, R.W. (1993) *The Five Gospels: The Search for the Authentic Words of Jesus*. New York: Macmillan.

Gallagher, S. (2017) *Enactivist Interventions: Rethinking the Mind*. New York: Oxford University Press.

Gardiner, J.K. (2004) "Men, Masculinities and Feminist Theory." In Kimmel, M.S., Hearn, J.R., and Connell, R.W., eds. *Handbook of Studies on Men and Masculinities*. Thousand Oaks: SAGE Publications, pp. 35–50.

Gardiner, J.K. (2013) "Masculinity's Interior: Men, Transmen, and Theories of Masculinity." *Journal of Men's Studies* 21 (2), pp. 112–126.

Garza, A. (2020) *The Purpose of Power: How to Build Movements for the 21st Century*. New York: Penguin.

Garza, A. and Hayes, C. (2019) "Remembering Why Black Lives Matter with Alicia Garza." *Think: Opinions, Analysis, Essays* [Podcast Transcript] (June 11) https://www.nbcnews.com/think/opinion/remembering-why-black-lives-matter-alicia-garza-podcast-transcript-ncna1013901. Accessed 6/9/2022.

Ghatak, M. (2021) "India's Inequality Problem." *The India Forum* (July 2). https://www.theindiaforum.in/article/does-india-have-inequality-problem. Accessed 12/10/2021.

# Bibliography   233

Gheaus, A. (2009) "The Challenge of Care to Idealizing Theories of Distributive Justice." In Tessman, L., ed. *Feminist Ethics and Social and Political Philosophy, Theorizing the Non-Ideal.* New York, Springer, pp. 105–119.

Giddens, A. (1989) *Sociology.* Cambridge: Polity Press.

Gilbert, M. (2014) *Joint Commitment: How We Make the Social World.* New York: Oxford University Press.

Gilbert, M. (2015) "Joint Commitment: What It Is and Why It Matters." *Phenomenology and Mind* 9, pp. 18–26.

Gilligan, C. (1982) *In A Different Voice: Psychological Theory and Women's Development.* Cambridge: Harvard University Press.

Gilligan, C. (2011) *Joining the Resistance.* Cambridge: Cambridge University Press.

Gilligan, C. and Richards, D.A.J. (2018) *Darkness Now Visible: Patriarchy's Resurgence and Feminist Resistance.* Cambridge: Cambridge University Press.

Ginzberg, L. (1994) "'The Hearts of Your Readers Will Shudder': Fanny Wright, Infidelity, and American Freethought." *American Quarterly* 46 (2), pp. 195–226.

Glenn, E.N. (2000) "Creating a Caring Society." *Contemporary Sociology* 29 (1), pp. 84–94.

Goldman, A.I. (1979) "What Is Justified Belief?" In Pappas, G.S., ed. *Justification and Knowledge: New Studies in Epistemology.* Dordrecht: Reidel, pp. 1–25.

Goldstein, L. (2011) "Bishops Say Rules on Gay Parents Limit Freedom of Religion." *New York Times* (December 11). https://www.nytimes.com/2011/12/29/us/for-bishops-a-battle-over-whose-rights-prevail.html. Accessed 7/17/2022.

Goldstone, J.A. (2013) *Revolutions: A Very Short Introduction.* New York: Oxford Academic.

Gollan, J. (2021) "How The US Fails to Take Away Guns from Domestic Abusers: 'These Deaths Are Preventable'." *The Guardian* (October 26). https://www.theguardian.com/us-news/2021/oct/26/domestic-abuse-gun-violence-reveal. Accessed 2/9/2023.

Gottlieb, R. (2022) *Care-Centered Politics: From the Home to the Planet.* Cambridge: The MIT Press.

Gould, R.K., Pai, M., Muraca, B., and Chan, K.M.A. (2019) "He 'ike 'ana aa a ka pono (It Is a Recognizing of the Right Thing): How One Indigenous Worldview Informs Relational Values and Social Values." *Sustainability Science* 14, pp. 1213–1232.

Gouws, A. and van Zyl, M. (2016) "Towards a Feminist Ethics of *Ubuntu*: Bridging Rights and *Ubuntu*." In Engster, D. and Hamington, M., eds. *Care Ethics and Political Theory.* New York: Oxford University Press, pp. 164–186.

Govier, T. (2006) "Kindness." in Irvine, A.D. and Russell, J.S., eds., *In the Agora: The Public Face of Canadian Philosophy.* Toronto: University of Toronto Press.

Gramlich, J. (2022) "What the Data Says about Gun Deaths in the U.S." *Pew Research Center.* (February 3). https://www.pewresearch.org/fact-tank/2022/02/03/what-the-data-says-about-gun-deaths-in-the-u-s/. Accessed 2/10/2023.

Grayling, A.C. (2007) *Against All Gods.* London: Oberon.

Greene, J. (2003) "From Neural 'Is' to Moral 'Ought': What Are the Moral Implications of Neuroscientific Moral Psychology." *Nature* 4, pp. 847–850.

Greene, J. (2013) *Moral Tribes: Emotion, Reason and the Gap Between Us and Them.* New York: The Penguin Press.

Gregor, M. (2015) *How Not to Die.* New York: Flatiron Books.

**234** Bibliography

Groenhout, R.E. (2003) "I Can't Say No: Self-Sacrifice and an Ethics of Care." In Groenhout, R.E. and Bower, M., eds. *Philosophy, Feminism, and Faith*. Bloomington: Indiana University Press.

Groves, C. (2014) *Care, Uncertainty And Intergenerational Ethics*. Basingstoke: Palgrave Macmillan.

Hamington, M. (2002) "A Father's Touch: Caring Embodiment and a Moral Revolution." In Tuana, N., Cowling, W., Hamington, M., Johnson, G., and MacMullan, T., eds. *Revealing Male Bodies*. Bloomington: Indiana University Press, pp. 269–286.

Hamington, M. (2004) *Embodied Care: Jane Addams, Maurice Merleau-Ponty, and Feminist Ethics*. Urbana: University of Illinois Press.

Hamington, M. (2008) "Learning Ethics from Our Relationships with Animals: Moral Imagination." *International Journal of Applied Philosophy* 22 (2), pp. 177–188.

Hamington, M. (2009a) "Business Is Not a Game: The Metaphoric Fallacy." *Journal of Business Ethics* 86 (4), pp. 473–484.

Hamington, M. (2009b) *The Social Philosophy of Jane Addams*. Champaign: University of Illinois Press.

Hamington, M., ed. (2010) *Feminism and Hospitality: Gender in the Host/Guest Relationship*. Lanham: Lexington Books.

Hamington, M. (2012) "Care Ethics and Corporeal Inquiry in Patient Relations." *International Journal of Feminist Approaches to Bioethics* 5 (1), pp. 52–69.

Hamington, M. (2014) "Loyalty to Care: Royce and a Political Approach to Feminist Care Ethics." *Pragmatism Today* 5 (1), pp. 8–17.

Hamington, M. (2015) "Politics Is Not a Game: The Radical Potential of Care." In Engster, D. and Hamington, M., eds. *Care and Political Theory*. Oxford: Oxford University Press, pp. 272–292.

Hamington, M. (2017) "Empathy and Care Ethics." In Maibom, H., ed. *Routledge Handbook of Philosophy of Empathy*. New York: Routledge, pp. 264–272.

Hamington, M. (2018) "Care, Competency, and Knowledge." In Visse, M. and Abma, T., eds. *Evaluation for a Caring Society*. Charlotte: Information Age Publishing, pp. 27–50.

Hamington, M. (2020a) "Care Ethics and Improvisation: Can Performance Care?" In Stuart Fisher, A. and Thompson, J., eds. *Performing Care*. Manchester: Manchester University Press, pp. 21–35.

Hamington, M. (2020b) "Confronting Neoliberal Precarity: The Hyperdialectic of Care." In Vosman, F. and Nortvedt, P., eds. *Care Ethics and Phenomenology: A Contested Kinship*. Louvain: Peeters Publishers, pp. 107–132.

Hamington, M. (2023) "Labor Unions as a Factor in a Caring Democracy." In Shields, P.M., Hamington, M, and Soeters, J., eds. *The Oxford Handbook of Jane Addams*. New York: Oxford University Press, pp. 111–128.

Hamington, M. and Flower, M., eds. (2021) *Care in the Age of Precarity*. Minneapolis: University of Minnesota Press.

Hamington, M. and Rosenow, C. (2019) *Care Ethics and Poetry*. Cham: Palgrave Macmillan.

Hanlon, N. (2012) *Masculinities, Care and Equality: Identity and Nurture in Men's Lives*. Basingstoke: Palgrave Macmillan.

Harper, R. (2021) "New Frontiers: Wild at Heart and Post-Promise Keeper Evangelical Manhood." *Journal of Religion and Popular Culture* 24 (1) (2012), pp. 97–112.

Harrington, C. (2021) "What Is 'Toxic Masculinity.' and Why Does It Matter?." *Men and Masculinities* 24 (2), pp. 345–352.

Harris, L. (2002) "Insurrectionist Ethics: Advocacy, Moral Psychology, and Pragmatism." In Howie, J., ed. *Ethical Issues for a New Millenium*. Carbondale: Southern Illinois University Press, pp. 175–188.

Hatzisavvidou, S. (2016) *Appearances of Ethos in Political Thought: The Dimension of Practical Reason*. Lanham: Rowman & Littlefield.

Hayakawa, S. (2016) "The Virtue of Receptivity and Practical Rationality." In Mi, C., Slote, M., and Sosa, M., eds. *Moral and Intellectual Virtues in Western and Chinese Philosophy: The Turn toward Virtue*. New York: Routledge, pp. 235–252.

Hayakawa, S. (2021) "Illness Narratives and Epistemic Injustice: Toward Extended Empathic knowledge." In Lai, K.L., ed. *Knowers and Knowledge in East-West Philosophy*. Cham: Palgrave Macmillan, pp. 111–138.

Held, V. (1990) "Feminist Transformations of Moral Theory." *Philosophy and Phenomenological Research* 50 (Supplement), pp. 321–344.

Held, V. (2006) *The Ethics of Care: Personal, Political, and Global*. New York: Oxford University Press.

Held, V. (2015) "Gender, Care And Global Values." In Moellendorf, D. and Widdows, H., eds. *The Routledge Handbook of Global Ethics*. New York: Routledge, pp. 49–60.

Held, V. (2018) "Taking Responsibility for Global Poverty." *Journal of Social Philosophy* 49 (3), pp. 393–414.

Hennighausen, T. and Heinemann, F. (2014) "Don't Tax Me? Determinants of Individual Attitudes Toward Progressive Taxation." *German Economic Review* 16 (3), pp. 255–289.

Herring, J. (2019) "Ethics of Care and the Public Good of Abortion." *University of Oxford Human Rights Hub Journal* 1, pp. 1–18. https://ohrh.law.ox.ac.uk/wp-content/uploads/2020/11/OxHRH-JOURNAL-2019.pdf. Accessed 6/27/2022.

Herring, J. (2021) "The Case for the Decriminalisation of Abortion." *National Law School Of India Review* 33, pp. 92–106.

Hickman, L. (1998) "Dewey's Theory of Inquiry." In Hickman, L., ed. *Reading Dewey: Interpretations for a Postmodern Generation*. Bloomington: Indiana University Press, pp. 206–230.

Hinton, E. (2021) *America on Fire: The Untold History of Police Violence and Black Rebellion Since the 1960s*. New York: Liveright Publishing Corporation.

Holmes, J.M. (2021) *An Applied Vegan Poetics* [Dissertation]. Seattle: University of Washington.

hooks, b. (2000) *Feminist Theory: From Margin to Center*, 2nd edition. Cambridge: South End Press.

hooks, b. (2004) *The Will to Change: Men, Masculinity, and Love*. New York: Atria Books.

hooks, b. (2015) *Feminism Is for Everyone: Passionate Politics*, 2nd edition. New York: Routledge.

Houseworth, L.E. (2021) "The Radical History of Self-Care." *Teen Vogue* (January 14). https://www.teenvogue.com/story/the-radical-history-of-self-care. Accessed 1/20/2023.

Howe, A. (2019) "Why Kant Animals Have Rights." *Journal of Animal Ethics* 9 (2), pp. 137–142.

## Bibliography

Howell, N.B. (1988) "The Promise of a Process Feminist Theory of Relations." *Process Studies* 17 (2), pp. 78–87. https://www.dal.ca/faculty/arts/sociology-social-anthropology/faculty-staff/our-faculty/margaret-robinson.html. Accessed 7/31/2022.

Iacoviello, V., Valsecchi, G., Berent, J., Borinca, I., and Falomir-Pichastor, J.M. (2021) "Is Traditional Masculinity Still Valued? Men's Perceptions of How Different Reference Groups Value Traditional Masculinity Norms." *The Journal of Men's Studies* 30 (1), pp. 7–27.

Jackson, A.J. (2021) *Worlds of Care: The Emotional Lives of Fathers Caring for Children with Disabilities*. Berkeley: University of California Press.

Jackson, I., Sealey-Ruiz, Y., and Watson, W. (2014) "Reciprocal Love: Mentoring Black and Latino Males Through an Ethos of Care." *Urban Education* 49 (4), pp. 394–417.

Jacobs, M.C. (2019) *The Secular Enlightenment*. Princeton: Princeton University Press.

Jacqui, A.M. (2006) *Pedagogies of Crossing: Meditations on Feminism, Sexual Politics, Memory, and the Sacred*. Durham: Duke University Press.

Jaffe, S. (2015) "Socialist in Seattle." *Cities Rising* 6 (13) (July), pp. 21–25.

Jaffe, S. (2016) *Necessary Trouble: Americans in Revolt*. New York: Nation Books.

Jameson, F. (2003) "Future City." *New Left Review* 21 (May/June). https://newleftreview.org/issues/ii21/articles/fredric-jameson-future-city. Accessed 4/9/2022.

Jarrett, S. (n.d.) "Frances 'Fannie.' Wright and her Turkish Trousers." *Maggie May Clothing* [Website]. https://maggiemayfashions.com/calicoball/vignettes/frances-fannie-wright-and-her-turkish-trousers/. Accessed 6/6/22.

Jenkins, S., Walter, D., and Crane, C. (2016) *Esther the Wonder Pig: Changing the World One Heart at a Time*. New York: Grand Central Publishing.

Johns-Putra, A. (2013) "Environmental Care Ethics: Notes Toward a New Materialist Critique." *Symploke* 21 (1–2), pp. 125–135.

Johnson, E.M. (2019) *The Struggle for Coexistence: Peter Kropotkin and the Social Ecology of Science in Russia, Europe, and England, 1859–1922* [Dissertation]. Vancouver: The University of British Columbia.

Johnson, R. and Cureton, A. (2022) "Kant's Moral Philosophy." In Zalta, E.N., ed. *The Stanford Encyclopedia of Philosophy* (Spring 2022 edition). https://plato.stanford.edu/archives/spr2022/entries/kant-moral/. Accessed 2/11/2022.

Jones, J.M. (2020) "Public Opinion Review: Americans' Reactions to the Word 'Socialism'." *Gallup* (March 6). https://news.gallup.com/opinion/polling-matters/287459/public-opinion-review-americans-word-socialism.aspx?version=print. Accessed 12/14/2021.

Jones, R.K. (2020) "People of All Religions Use Birth Control and Have Abortions." *Guttmacher Institute* (October). https://www.guttmacher.org/article/2020/10/people-all-religions-use-birth-control-and-have-abortions. Accessed 5/25/2022.

Kaba, M. (2021) *We Do This 'Til We Free Us: Abolitionist Organizing and Transforming Justice*. Chicago: Haymarket Books.

Kai, D., Du Tait, L., and Lauw, D. (2013) "Feminist Ethics of Care and Ubuntu." *Obstetrics and Gynaecology Review* 23 (1), pp. 29–33.

Kamb, L. (2013) "Growing Wealth Gap Spurs On Socialist In Seattle Council Race." *Seattle Times* (August 11). https://www.seattletimes.com/seattle-news/growing-wealth-gap-spurs-on-socialist-in-seattle-council-race/. Accessed 12/13/2021.

## Bibliography

Kant, I. (1996) *The Metaphysics of Morals*, Gregor, M., ed. Cambridge: Cambridge University Press.

Karma Kutir (n.d.) "Success Stories." http://www.karmakutir.in/success.html. Accessed 12/13/2021.

Kearney, R. (2010) *Anatheism: Returning to God After God.* New York: Columbia University Press.

Keller, C. (1986) *From a Broken Web: Separation, Sexism and Self.* Boston: Beacon Press.

Kelley, R.D.G. (2002) *Freedom Dreams: The Black Radical Imagination.* Boston: Beacon Press.

Kelton, S. (2021) *The Deficit Myth: Modern Monetary Theory and the Birth of the People's Economy.* New York: Public Affairs.

Kendi, I.X. (2019) *How to be An Antiracist.* New York: One World.

Khader, S. (2019) *Toward a Decolonial Feminist Universalism.* New York: Oxford University Press.

Kimball, J. (2019) "Is Humanity Progressing? Pinker, Krugman Debate the Question." *Brown University* (April 3). https://www.brown.edu/news/2019-04-02/pinker -krugman. Accessed 1/30/2023.

Kimura, A.H. (2012) "Feminist Heuristics: Transforming the Foundation of Food Quality and Safety Assurance Systems." *Rural Sociology* 77 (2), pp. 203–224.

King, M.L. (1967) "Beyond Vietnam: A Time to Break Silence." *New York: Riverside Church* [Speech] (April 4). https://www.commondreams.org/views/2018/01/15/beyond-vietnam-time-break-silence. Accessed 2/12/2022.

King, M.L. (2010) *Where Do We Go From Here? Chaos or Community.* Boston: Beacon Press.

Kirsch, Z. (2020) "When Siblings Become Teachers: It's Not Just Parents Who Find Themselves Thrust Into the Demanding Role of At-Home Educators." *The Urban Assembly* (April 10). https://urbanassembly.org/news-press/when-siblings-become -teachers-its-not-just-parents-who-find-themselves-thrust-into-the-demanding-role -of-at-home-educators. Accessed 8/25/2021.

Kittay, E.F. (1999) *Love's Labor: Essays on Women, Equality, and Dependency.* New York: Routledge.

Kittay, E.F. (2007) "Searching for an Overlapping Consensus: A Secular Care Ethics Feminist Responds to Religious Feminists." *University of St. Thomas Law Journal* 4 (3), pp. 468–488.

Kittay, E.F. (2019a) "Caring About Care." *Philosophy East & West* 69 (3), pp. 856–863.

Kittay, E.F. (2019b) *Learning from My Daughter: The Value and Care of Disabled Minds.* New York: Oxford University Press.

Klaver, K. and Baart, A. (2011) "Attentiveness in Care: Towards a Theoretical Framework." *Nursing Ethics* 18 (5), pp. 686–693.

Kochiyama, Y.K. (2004) *Passing it On—A Memoir.* Los Angeles: UCLA Asian American Studies Center Press.

Kochiyama-Ladson, A. (1994) "An Activist Life: 15 Minutes with Yuri Kochiyama." *A Magazine* (December 1), p. 33.

Kornacki, S. (2018) *The Red and the Blue: The 1990s and the Birth of Political Tribalism.* New York: HarperCollins.

Korsgaard, C. (2004) "Fellow Creatures: Kantian Ethics and Our Duties to Animals." *Tanner Lectures on Human Values* 24, pp. 77–110.

## 238 Bibliography

Kraut, R. (2020) "Altruism." In Zalta, E.N., ed. *The Stanford Encyclopedia of Philosophy*. https://plato.stanford.edu/archives/fall2020/entries/altruism/. Accessed 7/21/2021.

Kristeva, J. (2009) *This Incredible Need to Believe*. New York: Columbia University Press.

Kropotkin, P. (1902) *Mutual Aid: A Factor in Evolution*. New York: McClure, Philips, and Company.

Krznaric, R. (2014) *Empathy: Why It Matters, and How to Get It*. New York: Perigee.

LaBoucane-Benson, P. (2009) "Reconciliation, Repatriation and Reconnection: A Framework for Building Resilience In Canadian Indigenous Families." [Ph.D. thesis]. Edmonton: University of Alberta.

Langley, L. (2016) "The Surprisingly Humanlike Ways Animals Feel Pain." *National Geographic* (December 3). https://www.nationalgeographic.com/animals/article/animals-science-medical-pain#:~:text=Mammals%20share%20the%20same%20nervous,they%20don't%20experience%20it. Accessed 10/17/2022.

Larue, G. (1983) *Sex and the Bible*. Buffalo: Prometheus Books.

Latour, B. (2013) *An Inquiry Into Modes of Existence: An Anthropology of the Moderns*, Porter, C., trans. Cambridge: Harvard University Press.

Laugier, S. (2020) "The Ethics of Care as A Politics of the Ordinary." In Bourgault, S. and Vosman, F., eds. *Care Ethics in Yet a Different Voice: Francophone Contributions*. Leuven: Peeters, pp. 29–58.

Leffers, M.R. (1993) "Jane Addams and John Dewey Inform the Ethic of Care." *Hypatia* 8 (2), pp. 64–77.

Lerner, G. (1993) *The Creation of Feminist Consciousness: From the Middle Ages to Eighteen-seventy*. New York: Oxford University Press.

Leroy, C. (2021) *Phenomenology of Dance*. Paris: Hermann. DeepL translation.

Lewis, S. (2022) *Abolish the Family, a Manifesto for Care and Liberation*. London: Verso.

LIFE Magazine Staff Writers (1965) "The Violent End of Malcolm X." *LIFE* 58 (9) (March 5), pp. 26–31.

Llanera, T. (2019) "Disavowing Hate: Group Egotism From Westboro To The Klan." *Journal of Philosophical Research* 44, pp. 13–31.

Løgstrup, K.E. (1997) *The Ethical Demand*. Notre Dame: University of Notre Dame Press.

Loomis, E. (2018) *A History of America in Ten Strikes*. New York: The New Press.

Lorde, A. (2017) *A Burst of Light: And Other Essays*. Mineola: Ixia Press.

Lugones, M.C. (1978) *Morality and Personal Relationships* [Dissertation]. Madison: University of Wisconsin.

Madhok, B. (2019) "The Theory-Practice Nexus of Care Ethics and Global Development: A Case Study From India." *Journal of Global Ethics* 15 (1), pp. 21–31.

Mahadevan, K. (2014) *Between Femininity and Feminism: Colonial and Postcolonial Perspectives on Care*. New Delhi: Indian Council of Philosophical Research.

Malatino, H. (2019) "Tough Breaks: Trans Rage and the Cultivation of Resilience." *Hypatia* 34 (1), pp. 121–140.

Malatino, H. (2020a) "Incomplete, Visionary, Non-Utopian." *The New Inquiry* (August 31). https://thenewinquiry.com/incomplete-visionary-nonutopian/. Accessed 11/8/2021.

Malatino, H. (2020b) *Trans Care*. Minneapolis: University of Minnesota Press.

# Bibliography 239

Malatino, H. (2021) "The Promise of Repair: Trans Rage and the Limits of Feminist Coalition." *Signs: Journal of Women in Culture and Society* 46, pp. 827–851.

Mama, A. (2001) Interviewed by Salo, E. "Talking about Feminism in Africa." *Agenda: Empowering Women for Gender Equity* 50, pp. 58–63.

Mama, A. (2017) "The Power of Feminist Pan-African Intellect." *Feminist Africa* 22, pp. 1–15.

Mann, B. (2014) *Sovereign Masculinity: Gender Lessons from the War on Terror*. New York: Oxford University Press.

Mann, B., Mckenna, E., Russell, C., and Zambrana, R. (2019) "The Promise of Feminist Philosophy." *Hypatia* 34 (3), pp. 394–400.

Mann, H.S. (2012) "Ancient Virtues, Contemporary Practices: An Aristotelian Approach to Embodied Care." *Political Theory* 40 (2), pp. 194–221.

Manne, K. (2017) *Down Girl: The Logic of Misogyny*. London: Oxford University Press.

Manne, K. (2020) *Entitled: How Male Privilege Hurts Women*. New York: Crown.

Marcel, G. (1964) *Creative Fidelity*, Rosthal, R., trans. New York: Farrar, Strauss and Company.

Marx, K. and Engels, F. (2012 [1848]) *The Communist Manifesto*, Isaac, J.C., ed. New Haven: Yale University Press.

Marx, W. (1992) *Towards a Phenomenological Ethics: Ethos and the Life-World*. New York: The State University of New York Press.

Mason, M. (2016) *The Subtle Art of Not Giving a F\*CK*. New York: Harper.

Mathieu, E. and Ritchie, H. (2022) "What Share of People Say They are Vegetarian, Vegan, or Flexitarian." *Our World in Data* (May 13). https://ourworldindata.org/vegetarian-vegan. Accessed 7/11/2022.

Mayeroff, M. (1971) *On Caring*. New York: Harper and Row.

McBride III, L.A. (2021) *Ethics and Insurrection: A Pragmatism for the Oppressed*. London: Bloomsbury.

McGhee, H.C. (2021) *The Sum of Us: What Racism Costs Everyone and How We Can Prosper Together*. New York: One World.

McKnight, J. (1995) *The Careless Society: Community and Its Counterfeits*. New York: Basic Books.

McNeill, W. (2006) *The Time of Life: Heidegger and Ethos*. New York: SUNY Press.

Mehrabian, A. and Ferris, S.R. (1967) "Inference of Attitudes from Nonverbal Communication in Two Channels." *Journal of Consulting Psychology* 31 (3), pp. 248–252.

Melgar, K.Y. (2020) "Umoja: A Brotherhood to Empower Young Men of Color." [Ph.D. Dissertation]. New Brunswick: The Graduate School of Education, Rutgers, The State University of New Jersey.

Merleau-Ponty, M. (1994) *The Visible and the Invisible. Followed by Working Notes*, Lefort, C., ed. and Lingis, A., trans. Evanston: Northwestern University Press.

Miller, S.C. (2012) *The Ethics of Need: Agency, Dignity, and Obligation*. New York: Routledge.

Mills, C. (2005) "'Ideal Theory.' as Ideology." *Hypatia* 20 (3), pp. 165–184.

Mohanty, C.T. (1988) "Under Western Eyes: Feminist Scholarship and Colonial Discourses." *Feminist Review* 30, pp. 61–88.

Mohanty, C.T. (2003a) "'Under Western Eyes.' Revisited: Feminist Solidarity through Anticapitalist Struggles." *Signs* 28 (2), pp. 499–535.

**240** Bibliography

Mohanty, C.T. (2003b) *Feminism Without Borders: Decolonizing Theory, Practicing Solidarity.* Durham: Duke University Press.

Mohanty, C.T. (2013) Interviewed by Alcoff, L.M. "Feminists We Love: Chandra Talpade Mohanty." *The Feminist Wire* 4 (October). https://www.thefeministwire.com/2013/10/feminists-we-love-chandra-mohanty/. Accessed 10/20/2021.

Monbiot, G. (2017) *Out of the Wreckage: A New Politics for an Age of Crisis.* London: Verso.

Monk, M. (2020) "The History of Catholic Teaching on Abortion Isn't As Clear Cut As You Think." *The Outline* (January 16). https://theoutline.com/post/8536/catholic-history-abortion-brigid. Accessed 7/5/2022.

Moody-Adams, M.M. (1999) "The Idea of Moral Progress." *Metaphilosophy* 30 (3), pp. 168–185.

Moody-Adams, M.M. (2017) "Moral Progress and Human Agency." *Ethical Theory and Moral Practice* 20, pp. 153 168.

Moore, M. (1989) *Roger and Me* Flint: Dog Eat Dog Films.

Morales, E. (2015) "Machismo(s): A Cultural History, 1928–1984." [Dissertation]. Ann Arbor: The University of Michigan.

Morris, C. (1984) *Fanny Wright: Rebel in America.* Urbana: University of Illinois Press.

Mortari, L. (2021) "Care: The Primacy of Being." In Hamington, M. and Flower, M., eds. *Care in the Age of Precarity.* Minneapolis: University of Minnesota Press.

Mortari, L. (2022a) "Spiritual Care: The Spiritual Side of a Culture of Care." In Nistelrooij, I.V., Sander-Staudt, M., and Hamington, M., eds. *Care Ethics, Religion, and Spiritual Traditions.* Leuven: Peeters, pp. 121–158.

Mortari, L. (2022b) *The Philosophy of Care.* Cham: Springer.

Motel, S. (2015) "5 Facts On How Americans View Taxes." *Pew Research Center* (April 10). https://www.pewresearch.org/fact-tank/2015/04/10/5-facts-on-how-americans-view-taxes/. Accessed 1/18/2022.

Mungai, C. (2019) "Pundits Who Decry 'Tribalism.' Know Nothing About Real Tribes." *The Washington Post* (January 30). https://www.washingtonpost.com/outlook/pundits-who-decry-tribalism-know-nothing-about-real-tribes/2019/01/29/8d14eb44-232f-11e9-90cd-dedb0c92dc17_story.html. Accessed 5/9/2022.

Myers, E. (2014) *Worldly Ethics: Democratic Politics and Care for the World.* Durham: Duke University Press.

Nagarajan, S. (2021) "Starbucks Accused of Using 'Overwhelming Psychological Force.' Against Workers at a Buffalo Store Who Considered Trying to Unionize." *Business Insider* (December 18). https://www.businessinsider.com/starbucks-union-accused-overwhelming-psychological-force-managers-workers-buffalo-store-2021-12. Accessed 2/3/2022.

Nakamura, D. and Parker, A. (2018) "'It Totally Belittled The Moment': Many Look Back in Dismay at Trump's Tossing of Paper Towels in Puerto Rico." *Washington Post* (September 13). https://www.washingtonpost.com/politics/it-totally-belittled-the-moment-many-look-back-in-anger-at-trumps-tossing-of-paper-towels-in-puerto-rico/2018/09/13/8a3647d2-b77e-11e8-a2c5-3187f427e253_story.html. Accessed 8/4/2021.

Narayan, U. (1995) "Colonialism and Its Others: Considerations on Rights and Care Discourses." *Hypatia* 10 (2), pp. 133–140.

National War Tax Resistance Coordinating Committee. www.nwtrcc.org. Accessed 1/14/2022.

New York Daily Times (1852) "Fanny Wright Obituary." (December 18).

Newall, M. (2021) "Biblical Veganism: An Examination of 1 Timothy 4:1-8." *Journal of Animal Ethics* 11 (1), pp. 11–35.

Nguyen, C.T. (2020) "Echo Chambers and Epistemic Bubbles." *Episteme* 17 (2), pp. 141–161.

Nguyen, C.T. (2021) "The Seductions of Clarity." *Royal Institute of Philosophy Supplement* 89, pp. 227–255.

Nistlerooij, I.V. (2014) "Self-Sacrifice and Self-Affirmation Within Care-Giving." *Medical Health Care and Philosophy* 17, pp. 519–528.

Nistlerooij, I.V., Sander-Staudt, M., and Hamington, M., eds. (2022) *Care Ethics, Religion, and Spiritual Traditions.* Leuven: Peeters.

Nistlerooij, I.V. and Visse, M. (2019) "*Me?* The Invisible Call of Responsibility and Its Promise for Care Ethics: A Phenomenological View." *Medicine, Health Care and Philosophy* 22, pp. 275–285.

Noddings, N. (1984) *Caring: A Feminine Approach to Ethics & Moral Education.* Berkeley: University of California Press.

Noddings, N. (1989) *Women and Evil.* Berkeley: University of California Press.

Noddings, N. (1991) "Comment on Donovan's Animal Rights and Feminist Theory." *Signs: Journal of Women and Culture in Society* 16 (2), pp. 418–422.

Noddings, N. (1993) *Educating for Intelligent Belief or Unbelief.* New York: Teachers College Press.

Noddings, N. (2002a) *Starting at Home.* Berkeley: University of California Press.

Noddings, N. (2002b) *Educating Moral People: A Caring Alternative to Character Education.* New York: Teachers College Press.

Noddings, N. (2003a) "Why Should We Listen?." *Philosophy of Education* 59, pp. 19–21.

Noddings, N. (2003b) "A Skeptical Spirituality." In Groenhout, R.E. and Bower, M., eds. *Philosophy, Feminism and Faith.* Bloomington: Indiana University Press, pp. 213–227.

Noddings, N. (2003c) *Happiness and Education.* Cambridge: Cambridge University Press.

Noddings, N. (2005) *The Challenge to Care in Schools: An Alternative Approach to Education.* New York: The Teachers Press.

Noddings, N. (2010) *The Maternal Factor: Two Paths to Morality.* Berkeley: University of California Press.

Noddings, N. (2012) "The Language of Care." *Knowledge Quest* 40 (4), pp. 52–56.

Noddings, N. (2013) *Caring: A Relational Approach to Ethics and Moral Education,* 2nd edition updated. Berkeley: University of California Press.

Noriega, S. (2021) quoted in Burley, S. *Why We Fight: Essays on Fascism, Resistance and Surviving the Apocalypse.* Oakland: AK Press.

Obama, B. (2007) [Radio Broadcast] Excerpt, Pesca, M. "Does America Have an 'Empathy Deficit'?" *National Public Radio* (March 7). https://www.npr.org/templates/story/story.php?storyId=7755013. Accessed 7/21/2021.

Obama, B. (2021) Interviewed by Shahani, A. "Art of Power." [Radio Podcast] WBUR (aired May 21).

Painter, C. (2016) "Non-Human Animals Within Contemporary Capitalism: A Marxist Account of Non-Human Animal Liberation." *Capital & Class* 40 (2), pp. 327–345.

**242** Bibliography

Paul II, J. (1995) *Evangelium Vitae* [Papal Encyclical] (March 25). https://www.vatican.va/content/john-paul-ii/en/encyclicals/documents/hf_jp-ii_enc_25031995_evangelium-vitae.html. Accessed 7/5/2022.

Peter G. Peterson Foundation (2021a) "Budget Basics: National Defense." https://www.pgpf.org/budget-basics/budget-explainer-national-defense. Accessed 1/14/2022.

Peter G. Peterson Foundation (2021b) "What Is Free College and How Much Would It Cost?" https://www.pgpf.org/blog/2021/07/what-is-free-college-and-how-much-would-it-cost. Accessed 1/14/2022.

Pettersen, T. (2008) *Comprehending Care: Problems and Possibilities in The Ethics of Care.* Lanham: Lexington Books.

Pettersen, T. (2011) "The Ethics of Care: Normative Structures and Empirical Implications." *Health Care Analysis* 19, pp. 51–64.

Phillips, M. (2016) "Embodied Care and Planet Earth: Ecofeminism, Maternalism and Postmaternalism." *Australian Feminist Studies* 31 (90), pp. 468–485.

Phillips, M. and Willatt, A. (2019) "Embodiment, Care and Practice in a Community Kitchen." *Gender, Work, and Organization* 27, pp. 198–217.

Pichi, A. (2015) "Union: Walmart Shut 5 Stores Over Labor Activism." *CBS News* (April 20). https://www.cbsnews.com/news/union-walmart-shut-5-stores-over-labor-activism/. Accessed 2/3/2022.

Pickett, S. (2021) "Veganism, Moral Motivation and False Consciousness." *Journal of Agricultural and Environmental Ethics* 34 (15), pp. 1–15.

Pigden, C. (1988) "Anscombe on 'Ought'." *Philosophical Quarterly* 38, pp. 20–41.

Piketty, T. (2020) *Capital and Ideology*, Goldhammer, A., trans. Cambridge: Belknap.

Piketty, T. (2021) *Time for Socialism: Dispatches from a World on Fire, 2016–2021.* New Haven: Yale University Press.

Pippin, J.P. (2013) "Animal Research in Medical Sciences: Seeking a Convergence of Science, Medicine, and Animal Law." *South Texas Law Review* 54, pp. 469–511.

Pitts, A.J. (2021) *Nos/Otras: Gloria E. Anzaldúa, Multiplicitous Agency, and Resistance.* New York: SUNY Press.

Plato (~399–395 BCE) *Euthyphro.*

Plotica, L.P. (2012) "Deliberation or Conversation: Michael Oakeshott on the Ethos and Conduct of Democracy." *Polity* 44 (2), pp. 286–307.

Poore, J. and Nemecek, T. (2018) "Reducing Food's Environmental Impacts Through Producers and Consumers." *Science* 360, pp. 987–992.

Potts, A. (2016) "What Is Meat Culture?" In Potts, A., ed. *Meat Culture.* Leiden: Brill, pp. 19–20.

Press Trust of India (2021) "WEF's Gender Gap Index: India Slips 28 Places, Ranks 140 Among 156 Nations." *Business Standard* (April 1). https://www.business-standard.com/article/current-affairs/wef-s-gender-gap-index-india-slips-28-places-ranks-140-among-156-nations-121040100015_1.html. Accessed 12/10/2021.

Puig de la Bellacasa, M. (2011) "Matters of Care in Technoscience: Assembling Neglected Things." *Social Studies of Science* 41 (1), pp. 85–106.

Puig de la Bellacasa, M. (2017) *Matters of Care: Speculative Ethics in More Than Human Worlds.* Minneapolis: University of Minnesota Press.

Pulcini, E. (2009) *Care of the World: Fear, Responsibility and Justice in the Global Age.* Dordrecht: Springer.

Raghuram, P. (2021) "Caring for the Manifesto—Steps toward Making It an Achievable Dream." *Social Politics: International Studies in Gender, State and Society* 28 (4), pp. 865–873.

Randall, T. (2019) "Care Ethics and Obligations to Future Generations." *Hypatia* 34 (3), pp. 527–544.

Raworth, K. (2017) *Donut Economics: 7 Ways to Think Like a 21st Century Economist.* White River Junction: Chelsea Green.

Redecker, E.V. (2021) *Praxis and Revolution: A Theory of Social Transformation,* Duggan, L., trans. New York: University of Columbia Press.

Regan, T. (1980) "Utilitarianism, Vegetarianism, and Animal Rights." *Philosophy & Public Affairs* 9 (4), pp. 305–324.

Regan, T. (1985) "The Case for Animal Rights." In Singer, P., ed. *In Defense of Animals.* New York: Basil Blackwell, pp. 13–26.

Regan, T. (1995) "Obligations to Animals Are Based on Rights." *Journal of Agricultural and Environmental Ethics* 8 (2), pp. 171–180.

Reich, R.R. (2018) *The Common Good.* New York: Alfred A. Knopf.

Reinhart, R.J. (2018) "Snapshot: Few Americans Vegetarian or Vegan." *Gallup* (August 1). https://news.gallup.com/poll/238328/snapshot-few-americans-vegetarian-vegan .aspx. Accessed 7/11/2021.

Rescher, N. (2000) *Process Philosophy: A Survey of Basic Issues.* Pittsburgh: University of Pittsburgh Press.

Rifkin, J. (2009) *The Empathic Civilization: The Race to Global Consciousness in A World in Crisis.* New York: Jeremy P. Tarcher.

Robinson, D. and Robinson, M. (2020) "Decolonizing Veganism: An Interview with Dr. Margaret Robinson." *Animal People Forum* (September 23). https:// animalpeopleforum.org/2020/09/23/decolonizing-veganism-an-interview-with-dr -margaret-robinson/. Accessed 10/1/2021.

Robinson, F. (1999) *Globalizing Care: Ethics, Feminist Theory, and International Relations.* Boulder: Westview Press.

Robinson, F. (2011) *The Ethics of Care: A Feminist Approach to Human Security.* Philadelphia: Temple University Press.

Robinson, M. (2013) "Veganism and Mi'Kmaq Legends." *The Canadian Journal of Native Studies* 33 (1), pp. 189–196.

Robinson, M. (2014) "Animal Personhood in Mi'kmaq Perspective." *Societies* 4, pp. 672–688.

Roddel, R. and McKinney, R. (2018) "Muslims in Muncie." *Ball State University* [Interview] (March 1 and 29). https://dmr.bsu.edu/digital/collection/MuslimsMuncie /id/0/rec/18. Accessed 2/9/2023.

Romaniuk, S.N. and Grice, F. (2018) "Norm Evolution Theory and World Politics." *E-International Relations* (November 15). https://www.e-ir.info/2018/11/15/norm -evolution-theory-and-world-politics/. Accessed 2/14/2023.

Roosevelt, F.D. (1944) "State of the Union Message to Congress." (January 11). http:// www.fdrlibrary.marist.edu/archives/pdfs/state_union.pdf. Accessed 5/5/2022.

Rosenberg, L. (2022) "Cracker Barrel's Vegan Sausage Controversy Is Inciting Hilarious Outrage Among Meat-Eaters." *Green Matters* [Website] (August 5). https://www .greenmatters.com/food/cracker-barrel-plant-based-sausage-controversy. Accessed 7/5/2022.

Royce, J. (1936) *The Philosophy of Loyalty.* New York: Macmillan.

**244** Bibliography

Salter, M. (2019) "The Problem with a Fight Against Toxic Masculinity." *The Atlantic* (February 17) https://www.theatlantic.com/health/archive/2019/02/toxic-masculinity-history/583411/. Accessed 10/27/2021.

Sandel, M.J. (2020) *The Tyranny of Merit: What's Become of the Common Good?* New York: Farrar, Straus and Giroux.

Sander-Staudt, M. (2010) "Su Casa es Mi Casa? Hospitality, Feminist Care Ethics, and Reciprocity." In Hamington, M., ed. *Feminist Hospitality: Gender in the Host/Guest Relationship*. Lanham: Lexington Books, pp. 19–38.

Sander-Staudt, M. (n.d.) "Caring Reciprocity as a Political Ideal." In *Why Writing Works: Disciplinary Approaches to Composing Texts*. Marshall: Southwest Minnesota State University. http://otb.smsu.edu/annotated-works1/phil-scholarly-annotated-Caring%20Reciprocity%20as%20a%20Political%20Ideal.html. Accessed 7/30/2022.

Sarachild, K. (1978) "Consciousness-Raising: A Radical Weapon." In Sarachild, K., ed. *Feminist Revolution*. New York: Random House, pp. 144–150.

Saslow, E. (2018) *Rising Out of Hatred: The Awakening of a Former White Nationalist*. New York: Anchor Books.

Saslow, L.R., Willer, R., Feinberg, M., Piff, P.K., Clark, K., Keltner, D., and Saturn, S.R. (2013) "My Brother's Keeper?: Compassion Predicts Generosity More Among Less Religious Individuals." *Social Psychological and Personality Science* 4 (1), pp. 31–38.

Sawant, K. (2009) "Elderly Labor Supply in a Rural, Less Developed Economy: An Empirical Study." [Dissertation]. Raleigh: North Carolina State University.

Sawant, K. (2015) quoted in Jaffe, S. "Socialist in Seattle." *Cities Rising* 6 (13) (July), pp. 21–5.

Sawant, K. (2023) "Why I'm Not Running Again for City Council: I'm Launching a National Movement Called Workers Strike Back." *The Stranger* (January 19). https://www.thestranger.com/guest-editorial/2023/01/19/78821484/why-im-not-running-again-for-city-council. Accessed 5/17/2023.

Schlafly, P. (2012) "The Stupidity of Feminism." *Self-Educated American* [Web Post]. https://www.phyllisschlafly.com/?s=stupidity+of+feminists. Accessed 10/18/2021.

Schmertz, J. "Constructing Essences: Ethos and the Postmodern Subject of Feminism." *Rhetoric Review* 18 (1), pp. 82–91.

Schroeder, P. (2022) "U.S. Bank Profits Jump in 2021 As Firms Shed Credit Loss Reserves, FDIC Says." *Reuters* (March 1). https://www.reuters.com/business/finance/us-bank-profits-jump-2021-firms-shed-credit-loss-reserves-fdic-says-2022-03-01/. Accesses 4/9/2022.

Scott-Heron, G. (1971) *The Revolution Will Not Be Televised* [Song]. New York: RCA Records.

Sculos, B.W. (2017) "Who's Afraid of 'Toxic Masculinity'?" *Class, Race and Corporate Power* 5 (3). https://digitalcommons.fiu.edu/classracecorporatepower/vol5/iss3/6/. Accessed 10/25/2021.

Seftel, J. (2022) "Director, Stranger at the Gate." *The New Yorker* [Documentary]. https://www.youtube.com/watch?v=GPbbl1S6foM. Accessed 2/10/2023.

Seibt, J. (2022) "Process Philosophy." In Zalta, E.N., ed. *The Stanford Encyclopedia of Philosophy*. https://plato.stanford.edu/archives/sum2022/entries/process-philosophy/. Accessed 8/22/2022.

Bibliography **245**

Serafini, P. (2021) "A Decolonial, Ecofeminist Ethic of Care." *Social Anthropology* 29 (1), pp. 222–224.

Sevenhuijsen, S. (1998) *Citizenship and the Ethics of Care: Feminist Considerations on Justice, Morality and Politics*. New York: Routledge.

Shotwell, A. (2011) *Knowing Otherwise: Race, Gender, and Implicit Understanding*. University Park: Pennsylvania State University Press.

Shotwell, A. (2012) "Open Normativities: Gender, Disability, and Collective Political Change." *Signs* 37 (4), pp. 989–1016.

Shpall, S. (2014) "Moral and Rational Commitment." *Philosophy and Phenomenological Research* 88 (1), pp. 146–172.

Shutte, A., (2001) *Ubuntu: An Ethic for a New South Africa*. Pietermaritzburg: Cluster Publications.

Siegel, M. Ross, C.S., and King III, C. (2013) "The Relationship Between Gun Ownership and Firearm Homicide Rates in the United States, 1981–2010." *American Journal of Public Health* 103 (11), pp. 2098–2105.

Silverman, M. (2012) *Virtue Ethics, Care Ethics, and "The Good Life of Teaching"*. New York: Montclair State University Digital Commons. https://digitalcommons .montclair.edu/cali-facpubs/23. Accessed 1/20/2023.

Simpson, A. and Rios, K. (2017) "The Moral Contents of Anti-Atheist Prejudice (and Why Atheists Should Care About It)." *European Journal of Social Psychology* 47, pp. 501–508.

Singer, P. (1980) "Utilitarianism and Vegetarianism." *Philosophy & Public Affairs* 9 (4), pp. 325–337.

Singer, P. (2020) *Why Vegan? Eating Ethically*. New York: Norton.

Singer, P. (2021) "Give Up The Meat—I've Been Doing It for 50 Years." *The Sydney Morning Herald* (January 31). https://www.smh.com.au/national/give-up-the-meat-i -ve-been-doing-it-for-50-years-20210131-p56y57.html. Accessed 10/18/2022.

Singh, G. (2001) "National Culture and Union Density." *The Journal of Industrial Relations* 43 (3), pp. 330–339.

Skærbæk, E. (2011) "Navigating in the Landscape of Care: A Critical Reflection on Theory and Practise of Care and Ethics." *Health Care Anal* 19, pp. 41–50.

Slote, M. (2007) *The Ethics of Care and Empathy*. New York: Routledge.

Slote, M. (2010) *Moral Sentimentalism*. New York: Oxford University Press.

Smiley, M. (2020) "Re-thinking 'Paternalism.' for a Democratic Theory of Care." In Urban, P. and Ward, L., eds. *Care Ethics, Democratic Citizenship and the State*. Cham: Palgrave Macmillan, pp. 93–115.

Smith, A. (1759) Edinburgh. *The Theory of Moral Sentiments*.

Smith, G.A. (2021) "About Three-in-Ten U.S. Adults are Now Religiously Unaffiliated." *Pew Research Center* (December 14). https://www.pewresearch.org/religion/2021 /12/14/about-three-in-ten-u-s-adults-are-now-religiously-unaffiliated/. Accessed 6/22/2022.

Sosa-Provencio, M.A. (2016) "Seeking a Mexicana/Mestiza Critical Feminist Ethic of Care: Diana's *Revolución* of Body and Being." *Journal of Latinos and Education* 15 (4), pp. 303–319.

Sosa-Provencio, M.A. (2017) "Seeking a Mexicana/Mestiza Ethic of Care: Rosa's *Revolución* of Carrying Alongside." *Race Ethnicity and Education* 20 (5), pp. 650–665.

Southern Poverty Law Center. "Stormfront." https://www.splcenter.org/fighting-hate/ extremist-files/group/stormfront. Accessed 6/23/2021.

## 246   Bibliography

Spade, D. (2020) *Mutual Aid*. London: Verso.

Springmann, M., Clark, M.A., Rayner, M., Scarborough, P., and Webb, P. (2021) "The Global and Regional Costs of Healthy and Sustainable Dietary Patterns: A Modelling Study." *The Lancet* 5 (11) https://www.thelancet.com/journals/lanplh/article/PIIS2542-5196(21)00251-5/fulltext. Accessed 10/18/2022.

Stabile, S.J. (2007) "Can Secular Feminists and Catholic Feminists Work Together to Ease the Conflict Between Work and Family?." *University of St. Thomas Law Journal* 4 (3), pp. 432–467.

Stainton, R.S. and Papoulias, D.B. (1985) "Heuristics—The Relational Approach." *European Journal of Operational Research* 17, pp. 16–20.

Stake, R. and Visse, M. (2021) *A Paradigm of Care*. Charlotte: Information Age Publishing.

Statista (2023) "Number of People Shot to Death by the Police in the United States from 2017 to 2023, by Race." (January) https://www.statista.com/statistics/585152/people-shot-to-death-by-us-police-by-race/. Accessed 2/9/2023.

Stifting, H.B. (2021) *The Meat Atlas*. Berlin: Bund für Umwelt und Naturschutz.

Stone, D. (2000) "Why We Need a Care Movement." *The Nation* 270 (10) (March 13). https://www.thenation.com/article/archive/why-we-need-care-movement/. Accessed 8/8/2022.

Su-Yeung, A. (2017) "Umoja." *The Home Room: Stories About New York City Schools* (March 21). https://medium.com/@angelauyeung. Accessed 8/25/2021.

Sumpter, S. (2020) "Organizing from and for a Radical Ethics of Care." [Blog]. https://samsumpter.com/2020/05/14/organizing-from-for-a-radical-ethics-of-care/. Accessed 2/2/2022.

Sur Ray, P. (2017) "Chapter 3: Phulrenu Guha." In *A Study of Five Women as Social Workers/Activists in Bengal* [Dissertation]. Kolkata: University of Calcutta, pp. 176–239.

Sussman, A.B., and White, S.M. (2018) "Negative Responses to Taxes: Causes and Mitigation." *Policy Insights from the Behavioral and Brain Sciences* 5 (2), pp. 224–231.

Tamir, C., Connaughton, A., and Salazar, A.M. (2020) "The Global God Divide." *Pew Research Center*. https://www.pewresearch.org/global/2020/07/20/the-global-god-divide/. Accessed 6/23/2022.

Taylor, J.E. (2022) "The New Atheists." *Internet Encyclopedia of Philosophy*. https://iep.utm.edu/n-atheis/. Accessed 6/28/2022.

Tcherneva, P.R. (2018) *The Job Guarantee: Design, Jobs, and Implementation*. Levy Economics Institute of Bard College. https://www.levyinstitute.org/pubs/wp_902.pdf. Accessed 5/19/2021.

The Ascent Staff (2019) "Study: The Psychological Cost of Debt." *The Ascent* (May 17). https://www.fool.com/the-ascent/research/study-psychological-cost-debt/. Accessed 5/2/2022.

The Care Collective, Chatzidakis, A., Hakim, J., Littler, J., Rottenberg, C., and Segal, L. (2020) *The Care Manifesto: The Politics of Interdependence*. London: Verso.

The MenEngage Alliance. https://menengage.org/about/. Accessed 9/22/2022.

The Movement for Black Lives [Website]. https://m4bl.org. Accessed 6/10/2022.

Thompson, J. (2020) "Towards An Aesthetic of Care." In Fischer, A.S. and Thompson, J., eds. *Performing Care: New Perspectives on Socially Engaged Performance*. Manchester: Manchester University Press, pp. 36–48.

# Bibliography 247

Thompson, J. (2023) *Care Aesthetics: For Artful Care and Careful Art*. London: Routledge.

Tilman, D., Clark, M., Williams, D.R., Kimmel, K., Polasky, A., and Packer, S. (2017) "Future Threats to Biodiversity and Pathways to Their Prevention." *Nature* 546, pp. 73–81.

Tinker, T. (2015) "The Irrelevance of Euro-Christian Dichotomies for Indigenous Peoples Beyond Nonviolence to a Vision of Cosmic Balance." In Omar, I.A. and Duffey, M.K., eds. *Peacemaking and the Challenge of Violence in World Religions*. Malden: Wiley Blackwell, pp. 206–225.

Tittle, P. (2000) "Needs & Wants." *Philosophy Today* 28 (August/September). https://philosophynow.org/issues/28/Needs_and_Wants. Accessed 7/23/2021.

Torres, E.P. (2021) "Godless Grifters: How the New Atheists Merged with the Far Right." *Salon*. https://www.salon.com/2021/06/05/how-the-new-atheists-merged-with-the-far-right-a-story-of-intellectual-grift-and-abject-surrender/. Accessed 6/28/2022.

Tronto, J.C. (1993) *Moral Boundaries: A Political Argument for an Ethic of Care*. New York: Routledge.

Tronto, J.C. (2005) "Care as the Work of Citizens: A Modest Proposal." In Friedman, M., ed. *Women and Citizenship*. Oxford: Oxford University Press, pp. 1–21.

Tronto, J.C. (2013) *Caring Democracy: Markets, Equality, And Justice*. New York: New York University Press.

Tronto, J.C. (2015) *Who Cares? How to Reshape a Democratic Politics*. New York: Cornell Selects.

Tronto, J.C. (2017) "There Is An Alternative: *Homines Curans* and the Limits of Neoliberalism." *International Journal of Care and Caring* 1 (1), pp. 27–43.

Tronto, J.C. (2020) "Caring Democracy: How Should Concepts Travel?" In Urban, P. and Ward, L., eds. *Care Ethics, Democratic Citizenship and the State*. Cham: Palgrave Macmillan, pp. 181–197.

Trzebiatowska, M. (2019) "'Atheism Is Not the Problem: The Problem Is Being a Woman": Atheist Women and Reasonable Feminism." *Journal of Gender Studies* 28 (4), pp. 475–487.

Tuerff, K. (2018) *Channel of Peace: Stranded in Gander on 9/11*. Toronto: Anansi Press.

Tutu, D. (1999) *No Future Without Forgiveness*. New York: Image.

United States Conference of Catholic Bishops (n.d.) *Seven Themes of Catholic Social Teaching*. United States Conference of Catholic Bishops. https://www.usccb.org/beliefs-and-teachings/what-we-believe/catholic-social-teaching/seven-themes-of-catholic-social-teaching. Accessed 7/5/2022.

Urban, P. (2015) "Enactivism and Care Ethics: Merging Perspectives." *Filozofia* 70 (2), pp. 119–129.

USDA (2021) "Research Facility Annual Usage Summary & Archive Reports." (April 30). https://www.aphis.usda.gov/aphis/ourfocus/animalwelfare/sa_obtain_research_facility_annual_report/ct_research_facility_annual_summary_reports. Accessed 6/22/2022.

Vallelly, N. (2021) *Futilitarianism: Neoliberalism and the Production of Uselessness*. London: Goldsmiths.

Varela, F.J., Thompson, E., and Rosch, E. (1991) *The Embodied Mind*. Cambridge: MIT Press.

Vosloo, R. (2003) "Public Morality and the Need for an Ethos of Hospitality." *Scriptura* 82, pp. 63–71.

**248** Bibliography

Waghid, Y. and Smeyers, P. (2012) "Reconsidering Ubuntu: On the Educational Potential of a Particular Ethic of Care." *Educational Philosophy and Theory* 44 (S2), pp. 6–20.

Waling, A. (2019) "Problematising 'Toxic.' and 'Healthy.' Masculinity for Addressing Gender Inequalities." *Australian Feminist Studies* 34 (101), pp. 362–375.

Walsh, J.P. (2018) "Care, Commitment, and Moral Distress." *Ethical Theory and Moral Practice* 21 (3), pp. 615–628.

Warin, J. (2017) "Creating a Whole-School Ethos of Care." *Emotional and Behavioural Difficulties* 22 (3), pp. 188–199.

Warkentin, T. (2010) "Interspecies Etiquette: An Ethics of Paying Attention to Animals." *Ethics and the Environment* 15 (1), pp. 101–121.

Watson, W., Sealey-Ruiz, Y., and Jackson, I. (2016) "Daring to Care: The Role of Culturally Relevant Care in Mentoring Black and Latino Male High School Students." *Race Ethnicity and Education* 19 (5), pp. 980–1002.

Weil, S. (2002) *The Need for Roots*. London: Routledge.

Welch, S. (2012) *A Theory of Freedom: Feminism and the Social Contract*. New York: Palgrave Macmillan.

Welch, S. (2013) "Radical-cum-Relation: Bridging Feminist Ethics and Native Individual Autonomy." *Philosophical Topics* 41 (2), pp. 203–222.

Welizarowicz, G. (2018) "Junipero Serra's Canonization or Eurocentric Heteronomy." *Studia Anglica Posnaniensia: International Review of English Studies* 53 (1), pp. 267–294.

Western, D. (2013) *Gender-Based Violence and Depression in Women: A Feminist Group Work Response*. New York: Springer.

White, S.K. (2009) *The Ethos of a Late-Modern Citizen*. Cambridge: Harvard University Press.

Whyte, K. (2018) "Settler Colonialism, Ecology, and Environmental Injustice." *Environment and Society* 9 (1), pp. 125–144.

Wildcat, M. (2018) "Wahkohtowin in Action." *Constitutional Forum Constitutionnel* 27 (1), pp. 13–24.

Williams, B. (1981) *Moral Luck*. Cambridge: Cambridge University Press.

Williams, B. (1985) *Ethics and the Limits of Philosophy*. Cambridge: Harvard University Press.

Williams, N.M. (2015) "The Ethics of Care and Humane Meat: Why Care Is Not Ambiguous About 'Humane'." *Meat Journal of Social Philosophy* 46 (2), pp. 264–279.

Wing, A.K. (2000) "Global Critical Race Feminism for the Twenty-First Century." In Wing, A.K., ed., *Global Critical Race Feminism: An International Reader*. New York: New York University Press, pp. 1–23.

Woodly, D.R. (2022) *Reckoning: Black Lives Matter and the Democratic Necessity of Social Movements*. New York: Oxford University Press.

World Health Organization (2021) "Plant-Based Diets and Their Impact on Health, Sustainability, and the Environment: A Review of the Evidence." https://apps.who .int/iris/bitstream/handle/10665/349086/WHO-EURO-2021-4007-43766-61591-eng .pdf?sequence=1&isAllowed=y. Accessed 10/17/2022.

World Health Organization (2022) "Noncommunicable Diseases." https://www .who.int/news-room/fact-sheets/detail/noncommunicable-diseases#:~:text =Noncommunicable%20diseases%20(NCDs)%20kill%2041,%2D%20and%20 middle%2Dincome%20countries. Accessed 10/19/2022.

Wright, F. (1821) *Views of Society and Manners in America*. Longman: Longman, Hurst, Rees, Orme, and Brown.

Wright, F. (1829) *Course of Popular Lectures*. New York: Office of the Free Enquirer.

Wright, F. (1977) quoted in O'Donnell, M.M. *Reflections On A Free Enquirer: An Analysis of the Ideas of Frances Wright* [Dissertation]. Bowling Green: Bowling Green State University.

Wright, F. (n.d.) quoted by "Humanist Heritage." [Website]. https://heritage.humanists.uk/frances-wright/. Accessed 7/12/2022.

Yoos, G.E. (1979) "A Revision of the Concept of Ethical Appeal." *Philosophy & Rhetoric* 12 (1), pp. 41–58.

Zager, S. (2022) "The Pain of Imagining Others: Caring for the Abstract and the Particular in Jewish Thought." In Nistelrooij, I.V., Sander-Staudt, M., and Hamington, M., eds. *Care Ethics, Religion, and Spiritual Traditions* Leuven: Peeters, pp. 49–88.

Zaki, J. (2019) *The War for Kindness: Building Empathy in A Fractured World*. New York: Broadway Books.

Zambrana, R. (2021) *Colonial Debts: The Case of Puerto Rico*. Durham: Duke University Press.

Zinsmeister, K. (2019) "Philanthropy Roundtable." *Less God, Less Giving? Religion and Generosity Feed Each Other in Fascinating Ways* (Winter). https://www.philanthropyroundtable.org/magazine/less-god-less-giving/. Accessed 7/12/2022.

Zuckerman, P. and Shook, J.R. (2017) "Introduction: The Study of Secularism." In Shook, J.R. and Zuckerman, P., eds. *The Oxford Handbook of Secularism*. New York: Oxford University Press, pp. 1–20.

Zygadło, G. (2017) "Nos/Otras Living in Nepantla: Gloria Anzaldúa's Concepts of Borderland Identity in Contemporary World." *Roczniki Humanistyczne* 65 (11), pp. 207–219.

# INDEX

Adams, C. J. 182, 190, 194, 198
Adams, M. M. 208–9, 211–12
Addams, J. 85, 151
Adichie, C. N. 117, 130
Adorno, T. 194
agential realism 95
agnosticism 162
Ahmed, S. 102, 117–18, 120
Alcoff, L. 114–15
altruism 60–2, 141
analytic philosophy 29, 107
Anderson, E. S. 165–6
animal rights 184–5, 187–8; animal
    welfare 184, 187; testing 185–7
anthropocentrism 165, 219
antiracism 207–8
Anzaldúa, G. 29, 83, 91, 104–6, 117–18
atheism 163
attentiveness 14, 33, 55, 193

Baart, A. 14, 35
Baier, A. 29, 80
Barad, K. 84, 94–5
Baumlin, J. S. 90, 93
Benjamin, R. 106, 219
Bentham, J. 158–9, 195
Bhandary, A. 6, 30, 130
Black, D. 1–5, 14, 17, 20–1, 41, 220
Black Lives Matter 45–7, 51, 206, 220–1
Boggs, G. L. 12, 219–20
Boggs, J. 12, 219–20

Bourgault, S. 33, 96
Brugère, F. 43, 96
Bunting, M. 11, 18–19

capitalism 18, 79, 124, 127, 135–8, 140–2,
    146, 153, 176, 179, 182
care aesthetics 30–1, 48; care ethics
    29–31, 37, 39; care revolution 38; care
    theory 32, 33, 37, 40, 41, 43, 48; and
    colonialism 48, 57–8; commitment
    to care 57; and competence 31; crisis
    of 17–19, 69, 103–4, 139, 215, 220;
    and democracy 37, 41, 71, 141–2, 156,
    213–14; duty to 56–7, 69–70; and
    embodiment 31, 40, 63, 103, 115, 119,
    206; and ethos of 87–110; good care
    61, 63–4; as improvisation 31, 42–3,
    78, 92, 111, 203; as moral progress
    17, 19, 112, 208–13; need as impetus
    for 56–7; and normativity 45–65; and
    paternalism 57–60; primacy of 175–7;
    as pursuit of the good 53–5; as radical
    4–5, 10–11, 63, 151; of the self 60–3; as
    social movement 213–15; *see also* care
    economy
care economy 140; debt and 152–3;
    infrastructure and 140, 144–7; taxation
    16, 136, 138, 146–50, 155; unionization
    16, 136, 146, 150–2, 155–6, 166, 221
care ethics as anti-authoritarian 162, 166,
    176; definition of 8–9, 29–31, 42–3;

history of 29; as non-binary 12–13, 15, 20, 61, 82, 128; as process morality 7–8, 10–12, 54–6, 64–5, 111–12; and veganism 186–90
*The Care Manifesto* 19, 79, 215–16
care revolution 12, 15–16, 19, 63, 85, 106, 108, 112, 183, 204–8, 213–21
care theory defined 7–9; as non-ideal 7, 9–10, 15, 21, 32, 134, 192, 210; as postmodern 21, 52, 77, 82–3, 93, 105, 211, 219; and religion 168–72
Catholic Church California missions 58, 65; condemnation of homosexuality 174–7; Illinois Catholic Charities case 174; prohibition of abortion 166–8; social tradition 166, 173
Chisale, S. S. 98–9
Christianity 162–3, 165, 168–9, 173–7; *see also* Wright, F.
Code, L. 81
Collins, S. 29–30
colonialism 48, 58, 99, 119
commitment constitutive 154, 156; definition of 10; joint 73; necessity of 20; *see also* commitment to care
commitment to care as categorical moral imperative 77–86; concomitants of care *see* commitment; and embodiment 30; as improving care 68; meaning of 74–6; and mutual vulnerability 36; as necessary 20, 28, 39; and norms 51; rationale for 68–71; and self-reflexivity 37; as taking action 62, 68, 71–4
the commons 138, 140, 143, 145–6, 148–9, 156
companion animals 182, 188–9, 191–2
concomitants of care inclusive sympathetic understanding 82–3; learning and truth 80–2; moral action 84–5
Connell, R. 124, 126
*conocimiento* 29, 91, 103–6
consequentialism 6, 32, 48–9, 53, 91, 176, 187; *see also* utilitarianism
Covid-19 pandemic 19, 60, 215

Dalmiya, V. 37, 81–2, 86
Davis, A. 120–1
Davis, F. E. 98
debt *see* care economy
DeFronzo, J. 213, 221
deontological ethics 53, 69, 170, 184

Derrida, J. 102–3
Dewey, J. 8, 29, 34–5, 169
*disponibilité* 17, 202–3, 208, 212, 217
Donovan, J. 187–90
Du Mez, K. K. 124, 167, 176
Dworkin, G. 58

echo chamber 4–5, 40
economic growth 128, 142
effective care *see* good care
emotion and the body 43; capacities 38, 81; and care ethos 16, 90–1, 95–7, 108; in care theory 13–14, 107, 189, 193; in commitment 80–3; and connection 40, 55, 183, 218; and empathy 39–40; and family 36; and food 182; and infrastructure 147; labor 39, 89; and masculinity 122, 124; and morality 140; and motivation 20; and poetry 198
empathy attuned 10, 36–41, 192; deficit 17; embodied capacity for 20; and emotion 55, 83, 95; in the hyper-dialectic 94; as kinaesthetic 97; masculine subordination of 113; necessary but insufficient condition for care 14, 44; as normative in care 50; and sympathy 82
enactivism 84–5
Engster, D. 39, 43–4, 70–1, 106, 149, 188–90, 214
Enlightenment Era 101, 162
environmentalism 206–7
epistemic humility 33
Esther the Wonder Pig 194–5
ethos of care 90–1; as a co-created moral identity 93–5; holistic understanding of 195–8; as hospitality 102–3; as an indefinite moral commitment 91–5; as an integration of emotional, visceral, and rational commitments 95–8; significance of 106–9; as spirituality 103–6; and veganism 195–8
expressed need 57, 193

factory farming 188, 199
family broad definition of 36, 67, 85, 108, 160–1, 172, 195; care labor of 17–19; as commitment to care 6, 36, 169; as creating care nostalgia 18, 141; and gun ownership 205; as heteronormative 114, 125, 129, 171, 176; as "natural" caring 37, 40; as oppressive 36

**252** Index

feminine-coded goods 123
feminism and consciousness raising
  127–9; dark side of 117–22; defined
  117–22; missionary 119
feminist consciousness 10, 127–8
Ferrarese, E. 42, 54, 57, 194, 215
FitzGerald, M. 43, 55, 211
Flower, M. 19, 44, 64, 106, 145, 147,
  196, 206
Folbre, N. 136–7, 141, 215–16
Francione, G. L. 184
Frankfurt, H. 74
Fraser, N. 17–18
Fujino, D. C. 66–7

Gander, Canada 25–8, 43, 65, 220
Gardiner, J. K. 122, 124
Garza, A. 45–7, 51, 54, 63–4, 220
Giddens, A. 137
Gilligan, C. 20, 29, 43, 50, 60–2, 106,
  108, 119, 122–3, 203, 214
god and morality 165–6
good care defined 9–10, 25–44; heuristic
  of 42–3, 49, 208, 211 and humble
  inquiry 33–6; and inclusive connection
  36–41; norms of 63–4; and responsive
  action 41–2
Grayling, A. C. 162, 164, 177
gun violence 205

Hayakawa, S. 51, 108
Held, V. 28, 43, 49, 71–2
heteronormativity 36–7, 42, 65, 114, 116,
  125, 129, 158, 176
hooks, b. 11, 114–15, 118–21, 126
hospitality 27, 67, 91, 99, 102–3, 163,
  202, 208
humanism 163–5
humble inquiry *see* good care
Hume, D. 29
hyper-dialectic 94

imagination: aesthetic 210; and care
  82, 97, 169, 212; and connecting
  with others 39, 101; economic 16,
  143–4, 149, 154, 156; embodied
  191–4; empathic 5, 15, 62; errors of
  40; indigenous 196; moral 20, 38, 75,
  183; and poetry 197–8; posthuman
  206; social 25, 107, 109, 140, 162, 170,
  191–4, 209
inclusive connection *see* good care
incommensurability 101

indigenous moral traditions 29, 91, 98;
  *ubuntu see wâhkôhtowin*
infrastructure 16, 60, 135–6, 140,
  144–50, 155–6, 206–7
interstices 218; *see also* Redecker, E. V.
intimate partner violence 133, 204–5
intra-activity 94–5

Jackson, A. 113–16, 121, 130, 220
Jesus 167, 170, 175–7

Kaba, M. 205–6
Kamar Kutir 134–5, 139, 220
Kant, I. 13, 15, 21, 48, 56, 69, 77, 94,
  184–6
Kelton, S. 144–6
Khader, S. 119–20
King Jr., M. L. 11, 67, 171
Kittay, E. 39, 43, 58, 75–6, 116, 171–2
knowledge generalized 33, 35, 187, 210;
  contextualized 33; implicit 34–5, 91;
  particular 33–6; propositional 34–5,
  80, 85
Kochiyama, Y. 66–8, 85–6, 220
Kropotkin, P. 139
Krznaric, R. 38, 44

Laugier, S. 90
Leroy, C. 30, 97
liberalism 47, 130
listening 33, 44, 46, 59, 61, 80, 128, 189,
  193, 203
Løgstrup, K. E. 77–8
Lorde, A. 63, 221
Lugones, M. 29, 120

Malatino, H. 13, 36–7, 41–2, 85–6, 92,
  107, 120
Manne, K. 123, 127, 131
Marcel, G. 203, 208
Marx, K. 127, 138, 141, 146, 215
masculine-coded goods 123
masculinity caring 129–31; defined
  122–4; toxic 124–5
Mayeroff, M. 33, 62
McKinney, R. 200–2, 220
meat culture 181–3
Merleau-Ponty, M. 31, 94–5
metalepsis 218–19
metaphoric fallacy 144
Mi'Kmaq 178–80
Miller, S. C. 56–7, 59, 69–71
Mills, C. 9

Index **253**

misogyny 10, 116, 120, 123, 125, 127, 131, 156
modern monetary theory (MMT) 144
Mohanty, C. T. 118–20
Moody-Adams, M. M. 208–9, 212
moral commitment 68–71
moral goods 6, 31, 34, 53, 76, 89
moral norms 48–50
moral progress 77, 156, 161–2, 221; *see also* care as moral progress
moral responsibility 9, 64, 72, 95, 188; *see also* Tronto, J.
moral theology 174, 177
Mortari, L. 43, 53, 104
mutual aid 139–41

neoliberalism 11, 21, 63, 78, 80, 82, 103, 108–9, 136–47, 152–6, 198, 207, 215–16
Nguyen, C. T. 4, 5, 43
Nistelrooij, I. V. 48, 61–2, 64, 104, 168
Noddings, N.: on care as a moral ideal 53, 75, 183; on caring for animals 186–90, 193; and commitment 78; on empathy 39–40, 43; and essentialism 119, 177; on natural versus ethical caring 37, 169; and origins of care ethics 29; on religion and spirituality 104, 106, 169–70, 172; on the responsiveness of care 20–1, 33, 50, 52, 56–7, 59, 208
non-ideal theory 9; *see also* care theory as non-ideal
normativity definition of 48–50; as emergent 15, 31, 50–3, 69, 94, 166, 203
*nos/otras* 29, 83, 105–6

Obama, B. 1, 17, 129
othering 40–1, 105, 169

pacifism 204–6
paternalism 48, 57–60, 125
patriarchy 13, 60–1, 114, 116, 119–31, 172, 182, 214, 219
Pettersen, T. 43, 61–2, 64
Piketty, T. 134, 137–8, 142–3
Pitts, A. 29, 83, 105–6
posthumanism 94, 164–5
postmodern theory *see* care theory as postmodern
pragmatist philosophy 8, 47, 49
privileged irresponsibility 62, 108
process morality *see* care ethics as process morality

processual revolution 17, 209, 220; *see also* Redecker, E. V.
Puig de la Bellacasa, M. 43, 91–3, 165

racism 3, 11, 88, 103, 117–18, 156; *see also* anti-racism
radical and conscientisation 128; demand of morality 77–8; implications of care 60, 71, 126, 129, 151, 181–6, 204–6; nature of care 92; of self-care 63; and transformation of society 215–19; *see also* Wright, F.
Raghuram, P. 216
Randall, T. 206
Raworth, K. 142–3, 156
reasonable care standard 60
Redecker, E. V. 12, 215–19
relational ontology 9, 29, 31, 39, 62, 68, 82–3, 94–5, 99, 102, 170–1, 218
relativism 13, 49, 64, 81, 119
reliabilism 81–2
Religion 7, 161–6, 182, 186, 204; *see also* Care theory and religion; Catholic Church; Wright, F.
responsiveness 41, 49, 55–7, 76, 86; *see also* good care
revolution 5, 11–12, 17, 37–8, 64, 213–15, 220–1; *see also* processual revolution; Redecker, E. V.
rights 19, 70, 76–7, 92, 98, 103, 117, 213; *see also* animal rights; Second Bill of Rights
Robinson, F. 43, 94, 147, 154
Robinson, M. 178–81, 196, 199, 220
Roosevelt, F. D. 145, 154–5
Rosenow, C. 197, 203, 210
Royce, J. 75, 86

Sawant, K. 134–5, 156
Scott-Heron, G. 21, 217
Sealey-Ruiz, Y. 87–9
Second Bill of Rights 154–5
secularism 162
self-care *see* care of the self
self-sacrifice 57; *see also* Nistelrooij, I. V.
September 11th Terrorist Attacks 25
sexism 11, 110, 118, 125, 134; *see also* Manne K.
Shotwell, A. 34–5, 65
Singer, P. 185–6, 192, 198
Slote, M. 39, 43, 50, 156
Smith, A. 142, 156–7
socialism 136–8

**254** Index

Social/ist Darwinism 139
Stone, D. 106, 213
supererogatory actions 21, 28, 73
sympathy 82–3, 96, 159–60, 164; *see also*
empathy

taking responsibility 71–4; *see also* moral
commitment
Thompson, J. 30–1, 43, 62
trans community *see* Malatino H.
tribalism 40, 83
Tronto, J.: on capitalism 141; on care
contextuality 76; on care movement
106, 213; and care responsibilities
70–1, 156, 214; definition of care
7–8, 42–3, 50, 206; on democracy
and care 37, 41, 71, 213; on *homines
curans* 140–1, 143; on intentions 58;
on moral and political boundaries
154; on patriarchy 123; phases of
care ethics 31–2; *see also* privileged
irresponsbility

Tutu, D. 99–100

*ubuntu* 95–100
umoja 87–90, 109
Urban, P. 84–5
utilitarianism 40, 53, 159, 185–6; *see also*
consequentialism

veganism 183–6; *see also* care ethics and
veganism
veganism defined: and the care ethics
literature 186–90; and Mi'kmaq
beliefs 179; as participating in a195–8
virtue ethics 29, 170
Visse, M. 43, 48, 64, 107

*wâhkôhtowin* 100–2
Welch, S. 73–4, 101–2
Woodly, D. R. 5, 47, 97
Wright, F. 157–62, 177, 220

Zambrana, R. 117, 152–3

Printed and bound by CPI Group (UK) Ltd, Croydon, CR0 4YY
22/09/2024
01036663-0006